THE COMPLETE **IDIOT'S** GUIDE® TO

D1220617

Learning Italian

Fourth Edition

by Gabrielle Euvino

ALPHA

A member of Penguin Group (USA) Inc.

ALPHA BOOKS

Published by Penguin Group (USA) Inc.

Penguin Group (USA) Inc., 375 Hudson Street, New York, New York 10014, USA • Penguin Group (Canada), 90 Eglinton Avenue East, Suite 700, Toronto, Ontario M4P 2Y3, Canada (a division of Pearson Penguin Canada Inc.) • Penguin Books Ltd., 80 Strand, London WC2R 0RL, England • Penguin Ireland, 25 St. Stephen's Green, Dublin 2, Ireland (a division of Penguin Books Ltd.) • Penguin Group (Australia), 250 Camberwell Road, Camberwell, Victoria 3124, Australia (a division of Pearson Australia Group Pty. Ltd.) • Penguin Books India Pvt. Ltd., 11 Community Centre, Panchsheel Park, New Delhi—110 017, India • Penguin Group (NZ), 67 Apollo Drive, Rosedale, North Shore, Auckland 1311, New Zealand (a division of Pearson New Zealand Ltd.) • Penguin Books (South Africa) (Pty.) Ltd., 24 Sturdee Avenue, Rosebank, Johannesburg 2196, South Africa • Penguin Books Ltd., Registered Offices: 80 Strand, London WC2R 0RL, England

Publisher: *Mike Sanders*

Executive Managing Editor: *Billy Fields*

Acquisitions Editor: *Brook Farling*

Senior Development Editor: *Christy Wagner*

Senior Production Editor: *Janette Lynn*

Copy Editor: *Cate Schwenk*

Cover Designer: *William Thomas*

Book Designers: *William Thomas, Rebecca Batchelor*

Indexer: *Julie Bess*

Layout: *Ayanna Lacey*

Proofreader: *John Etchison*

Audio production: *Robert Euvino*

Italian voice talent: *Michele Mariotti*

Contents

Foreword

The Complete Idiot's Guide to Learning Italian, Fourth Edition, will teach, inspire, illuminate, and educate you in a user-friendly manner that's also downright fun.

I have been a language teacher for nearly 50 years, and since 1981 until it closed, I was director of the Language Immersion Institute (LII) at the State University of New York at New Paltz. Ms. Euvino, a graduate from SUNY New Paltz, comes from the new generation of language teachers who instruct using immersion. Her mentor, the late Dr. Gianni Azzi, was a good friend of mine and one of the most dynamic teachers I've ever known.

Anyone who has ever taken one of Ms. Euvino's classes will invariably be affected by her infectious enthusiasm and love of the Italian language, both of which make her classes so successful. That's why I'd have to say that the next best thing to taking one of Gabrielle's courses is to read this book.

Ms. Euvino's book is perfect for the traveler getting ready for a *viaggio* to Italy. Newlyweds will find all the language they need to make it from the airport to their hotel suite and then a little more. Wine connoisseurs and epicureans will light up when they discover the ample food-related vocabulary that fills the book like delicate *antipasti*. Sports enthusiasts, hikers, people on the go, literary types, sedentary, young or old, Italian or not—no matter who you are, you'll be amazed by how much you can learn in such a short amount of time.

Ms. Euvino's book immerses you in the language, culture, and food of Italy while explaining the grammar in clear, concise terms that makes learning Italian easy. Her practical, down-to-earth style takes you to the streets of Italy, walks you through Rome's alleys, guides you to the canals of Venice, waltzes you to the sound of Puccini, and accompanies you to the doctor (if need be). Finally, but no less important, you will hear Ms. Euvino's voice as she continually praises the reader for their determination and *intelligenza*. After all, you deserve to be commended for trying to learn a new language.

In today's rapidly shrinking world, communication skills are vital. Drawing from her vast teaching experience, Ms. Euvino has created a book that makes studying Italian a rewarding and inspiring experience.

Dr. Henry Urbanski
Distinguished Service Professor, Founder and Director, Language Immersion Institute, State University of New York at New Paltz

Introduction

The great Italian filmmaker Federico Fellini said it perfectly: "A different language is a different vision of life." Whatever your motives, by studying Italian, you'll find yourself entering a new world.

Anyone can learn Italian, no matter how "language deficient" they believe themselves to be. By following the outline of the Italian language I've provided for you in this book, you'll acquire more Italian—and with less pain and frustration—than you ever imagined *possibile* (possible). All you have to do is wrap your mouth around the different vowels and have fun rolling your *R*s.

The operative word here is *acquire*. You don't need to memorize an entire dictionary or obsess over *la grammatica* (grammar). Build on what you already know (and you know a lot more than you realize!). Look for connections between words that share etymological roots.

From toddlers to octogenarians, I've taught people from all walks of life—brigadier generals and astronauts, celebrities, doctors, lawyers, teachers, landscapers, musicians, artists, actors, film-makers, home-makers, home-wreckers, accountants, business people, entrepreneurs, college students, mechanics, builders, writers—the list goes on. Every single one has their own special reasons for wanting to learn Italian.

The more you're able to integrate *la bella lingua* of Italian into your daily life, the better your chances of *successo*. If you love to eat *la cucina italiana*, find a cookbook that's been translated into Italian and try to follow the directions. Buy an Italian *calendario*, and you'll learn the days of the week and months in no time. Or subscribe to an Italian-language bulletin. Visit a music library and listen to *Rigoletto* sung by five different artists. Start a collection of children's books. Read the Italian fashion magazines. Gather the menus of your favorite Italian *ristoranti*. Many museums, such as the Metropolitan Museum of New York, offer guided tours on tape in a number of languages, including Italian. If you're a film buff, rent Italian movies.

This updated fourth edition offers something brand new: an audio CD, with me, Gabrielle Euvino, coaxing you through the process. (More on that in a bit.)

How to Use This Book

This book has been organized to maximize your understanding of key Italian concepts and terms. It is my solemn *promessa* that by following the lessons, you can develop your Italian language skills and construct a solid foundation for future studies.

Keep in mind that the vocabulary lists provided in each chapter are just that: word lists. There's no order in which you need to develop your vocabulary. The best thing to do is find a topic you feel passionately about and build a lexicon that's relevant to *your* interests.

This book also offers the most important aspects of grammar and verbs supported by practical, contemporary *vocabolario* related to a number of real-life situations. If you feel like you could use a little extra help in the grammar department, read the book from the beginning—you'll find the answers to many of your questions in language that is clear and to the point. If you're already familiar with the basic grammatical terms and lessons offered, by all means, don't linger on what you already know—skip ahead!

Regardless of your level, learning Italian requires *pazienza* (patience) and *ripetizione, ripetizione, ripetizione* (repetition, repetition, repetition). And to help you with your practice, in each chapter I've included a few exercises so you can test what you've learned.

Make use of the appendixes—they contain helpful verb tables and other linguistic and grammatical aids. (If you're a novice just starting out, many of the tables will contain information that makes absolutely no sense to you. Bear in mind that this will change as you metabolize the information presented.)

How This Book Is Organized

This book is organized into four parts, followed by a series of appendixes that supplement your learning experience.

Part 1, *Essenziali*: The Basics, is sort of like elementary school for language learners. To start, you're given essential Italian phrases. You're introduced to key grammatical terms and parts of speech and offered a refresher of English grammar. You discover how much you already know using cognates, words that look, sound, and mean the same thing between languages. You also learn your ABCs, 1,2,3s, days of the week, and how to spell your name. There's even a little primer on three of Italy's most important poets: Dante, Boccaccio, and Petrarca.

Consider **Part 2, Building Blocks: Verbs with Verve,** the "boot camp" of your Italian language learning experience. First, I give you the low-down on regular verb conjugations in the present tense. Then I focus on how to conjugate several of the most essential irregular verbs, including *avere* (to have) *essere* (to be), *fare* (to do/make), and *stare* (to be/stay), and others. The fun doesn't end there. I give you the modal verbs and show you how to use the reflexive verbs. I also explain how to create the present progressive tense. Learn how to make suggestions, ask questions, talk about the time, and discuss the weather.

Part 3, The Nitty Gritty, takes you to a new level and introduces the imperative—the "command" form of a verb—like when your *nonna* tells you *Mangia!* (Eat!) Indicate your preferences with the verb *piacere*. Talk about the past using the present perfect and imperfect tenses. Enjoy everything you love about Italy with the extensive vocabulary lists related to food, music, film, the arts, sports, shopping, and holidays.

You're in the big league when you get to **Part 4, Minutiae.** Learn how to form the future tense, the conditional, the subjunctive mood, and the *passato remoto* (past absolute), a tense used to talk about the good old days. Develop practical letter writing skills, learn how to text, make a *telefonata*, and survive the *ufficio postale*. In the business section, you develop the lingo necessary to talk shop with your colleagues. To sum things up, I give you a few tricks on how to translate text, and as a parting gesture, I've included a poem written by the beloved St. Francis of Assisi.

Appendix A, Word Lists, supports your Italian studies and offers hundreds of helpful vocabulary words and exclamations used by the Italians. This word list should not substitute for a good Italian/English dictionary, however.

Appendix B, Verb Tables, summarizes more verb tenses than you probably care to memorize.

Appendix C, Idiomatic Expressions, reviews many commonly used Italian idiomatic expressions and gives you a chance to apply your Italian skills.

Appendix D, Italian *Grammatica* at a Glance, offers you concise tables outlining the essentials of Italian grammar.

Bonus Audio CD

Accompanying this edition is an audio CD. Look for the CD icon as you read through the book. When you plug in the CD, you'll hear me talking to you, just as if I were standing in front of you in a classroom or, better yet, at a table somewhere in Italy with lots of good things to eat and drink.

The object of listening to the audio is to engage your senses and give you a chance to work on your pronunciation skills. For this reason, most (but not all) of the CD icons you'll see are in the earlier chapters. My goal was to produce an audio track that would be both engaging and practical. It's not a substitute for a live, up-close class or audio language program. (Pimsleur and Rosetta Stone are my favorites.)

Throughout the audio, you're prompted to repeat what you hear. Although the two work together, there will be times when the audio does not completely reflect word for word what's in the book. Keep in mind that the audio serves as back-up to the text in the book, but it can also stand on its own. If all you manage to do is listen to the audio on your iPod or in your car, you're still making progress!

You'll also enjoy the voice of my colleague, the talented Michele Mariotti, a native of Italy and a professional whose widely recognized voice is the official MGM voice used in Italian movie trailers and who can often be heard on radio programs and ads.

Production of the audio was a family affair. Working beside me was my brother Robert Euvino, whose sound engineering skills plus a terrific sense of humor brought the audio to life. The little voice you hear chime in is Sabine, my daughter, who at the time of printing is 7 years old.

As a special treat, I've also included several Italian tongue twisters. Once you're able to repeat them three times without making a mistake, you're on your way to fluency. It might take a while, but there's no rush.

The most important things to remember: speak bravely, and repeat, repeat, repeat!

Bite-Size Extras

As an extra perk, I've scattered extra bits of information throughout the book. Here's what to look for

AS A *REGOLA*

These sidebars highlight or expand on aspects of Italian grammar.

ATTENZIONE!

Be sure to read these sidebars that highlight elements of the Italian language that merit special attention.

BUON'IDEA

For useful suggestions, study techniques, and helpful resources, check out these sidebars.

LA BELLA LINGUA

These sidebars are notes on dialect, idioms, and helpful vocabulary, which may or may not pertain directly to the lesson.

WHAT'S WHAT

These sidebars reveal idiot-proof definitions of terms.

But Wait! There's More!

Have you logged on to idiotsguides.com lately? If you haven't, go there now! As a bonus to the book, we've included bonus chapters that provide you a scaled-down Italian thesaurus and an expanded resources section devoted to further your study of Italian. Point your browser to idiotsguides.com/learningitalian, and enjoy!

Acknowledgments

I am very grateful to the publisher Marie Butler-Knight and the people at Alpha Books for the opportunity to continuously expand and improve this book throughout its many editions. Special thanks go to the Senior Acquisitions Editor Brook Farling for his foresight and recognizing the importance of supplementing the book with an audio component. I appreciate the efforts of Senior Production Editor Janette Lynn for her *pazienza*, excellent production abilities, and management skills. If it weren't for the holistic approach taken by Senior Development Editor Christy Wagner, the book would not have the consistency and flow that it currently does. It was a relief knowing I had the careful eyes of Cate Schwenk for her meticulous copy editing … no easy task with a book of this magnitude! Special thanks as well go to Silvia Dupont, the technical reviewer, who was also amazing. Not only did she catch typos; she also offered sound, practical ways to further improve the book. It's wonderful to have the opportunity to work with such talent!

I'm also grateful to my "little" brother Robert Euvino and his sound engineering studio Night Owl Productions Inc. for his part in the creation of the audio CD. Rob's direction combined with his attention to detail were the perfect blend to bring out the best of me and this book. To learn more about Robert, check out nightowlproductionsinc.com.

A big welcome is extended to the talented Michele Mariotti for the sublime job he did as the male voice in the audio. To learn more about Michele, visit michelemariotti.it.

I want to thank my students, whose infectious curiosity and undying commitment make them heroes in my book. I love the expression "When the pupil is ready, the teacher will appear" because you are all my teachers, and I continually learn and expand my awareness as a result of the synergy we create together. A good teacher learns just as much as she teaches from her students. My job is to facilitate; that's all. You do the work. It's an honor to join you in the search for knowledge.

And finally, thanks go to artist, teacher, and friend Cristina Melotti for her insights. Gratitude and lots of love to Amy Albert ("Nanette"), Arthur Anderson, Laura Anson, the Davis family, Laurie DiBenedetto, Frank and Gail Duncan, Kilian Ganly, Nina Jecker-Byrne, Adriana Kaufman-Bhamla, Paul McMahon, Jessica Mezyk, Richard "F-Stop" Minissali, Jeff Moran, the Salamone family, and Agnes and Richard West, for their love, time, and support during the writing of this book.

Special Thanks to the Technical Reviewer

The Complete Idiot's Guide to Learning Italian, Fourth Edition, was reviewed by a team of experts who double-checked the accuracy of what you'll learn here, to help us ensure that this book gives you everything you need to know about the Italian language. Special thanks are extended to Silvia Dupont

A native of Florence, Italy, Silvia Dupont works as an independent translator, editor, and language instructor. Formerly assistant director of the Italian language program at the University of Notre Dame, she has also been a lecturer at Indiana University and the University of Virginia. She is currently teaching with Speak! Language Center in Charlottesville, Virginia, offering small-group courses and private tutoring to adult learners while completing a second-level Master's degree in the teaching and promotion of Italian language and culture to foreigners through Università Ca' Foscari in Venice.

Trademarks

All terms mentioned in this book that are known to be or are suspected of being trademarks or service marks have been appropriately capitalized. Alpha Books and Penguin Group (USA) Inc. cannot attest to the accuracy of this information. Use of a term in this book should not be regarded as affecting the validity of any trademark or service mark.

Essenziali: The Basics

Part 1 lays the foundation of your Italian learning experience, bringing you in-depth definitions and explanations of key grammatical forms, verbs, and parts of speech.

In the following chapters, you become familiar with the great Italian poets Dante, Boccaccio, and Petrarca and their influence on the Italian language. You study *parole simili* (cognates)—what I like to call linguistic cousins—and begin to see the relationship between the English and Italian languages. You learn how to spell your name in Italian and how to properly pronounce words like *gnocchi* (*nyoh-kee*) and *famiglia* (*fah-meel-yah*) without making a fool of yourself. You learn how to talk about *i giorni della settimana* (the days of the week), *i mesi* (months), and *i numeri* (numbers). Finally, welcome to the vast world of nouns and articles, where you learn how to determine the gender of a noun just by following a few basic guidelines. Adjectives are just as simple.

Anyone Can Learn
la Bella Lingua

In This Chapter

- Setting goals and developing a learning strategy
- Immersing yourself in everything Italian
- Finding Italian language resources
- Common greetings and salutations
- Basic communications

Benvenuti! (Welcome!) You've taken one of the most important steps in your linguistic *viaggio* (journey) … the first one. As cliché as it may be, this is the beginning of a long and endlessly rewarding road that will take you to new places, open your horizons, and give you something you hadn't planned on: a newfound confidence in your cognitive prowess.

All this from studying Italian? You can count on it. The way we think affects the way we act. *L'informazione* is power. Having access to the Italian language is like having a hall pass to Latin. Latin may be considered a "dead" language because it's no longer spoken, but it remains the root language used in just about everything that matters—*l'arte, la scienza, la psicologia, la storia, la letteratura, la legge, la musica ….* (art, science, psychology, history, literature, law, music …). And because of its close relationship to Latin, Italian rocks.

Aside from the fact that studying Italian will make you *smarter* because it encourages your synapses to spark, and *happier* because you're giving yourself the gift of knowledge, you have your own personal reasons for learning Italian. Perhaps you've always wanted to speak a foreign language and Italian is at the top of your list. Maybe your Italian *famiglia* is planning a reunion, and you're taking the whole gang over for the event. Maybe you've been listening to the language since you were a child but probably never learned the grammar or how to read and write in the language as you'd like.

You could be one of the lucky students planning on spending a semester abroad (or maybe your children are!). You're retired and can finally find the time. You're an opera buff. You're doing business in Italy. You're interested in fashion, film, or design. You're in love with *la cucina italiana* (Italian cooking), or maybe you're in love with an Italian.

What Are Your Goals?

Like any relationship, beginning to learn Italian is exciting! Everything is new, and the possibilities seem endless. Then comes the hard work part. (It's really not that hard, but the more you learn about something, the more you realize there is to discover.) And sometimes, it gets a little complicated. The same applies to learning Italian.

LA BELLA LINGUA

Outside Italy, Italian is the fourth most popular language spoken at home in the United States. Italy is one of the top five tourist destinations in the world.

Determine your needs and set some goals now, as you start. How much Italian do you want to know? Enough to get by on a trip to Italy? Do you want to be fluent and understand every word? Your end goal determines how you approach your studies.

Most people, because they're living ridiculously busy, full lives, believe that they don't have the time to properly study Italian. As a result (and I hear this all the time), they quit, promising that "Once my schedule frees up, I'll get back to it."

Take the advice I got from an editor once (*grazie* Amy Zavatto!): you do the best you can in the time you've got. If you shift your goal slightly, and approach learning Italian like you would if it were a hobby, you'll never make yourself feel guilty again. Make it fun and you'll make it far.

I'll help you. If I weren't able to continually refresh myself with it, I'd have died of boredom long ago. So take a leap of faith, keep an open mind, and follow the script I've given you. It's a *promessa* (promise): you will learn Italian using my methods.

Immersione Is the Answer

The word *disciplina* (discipline) generally makes people stiffen up and think of rigid taskmasters waiting to flog them at the first mistake. There is another definition— one that won't make you cringe. Discipline also can mean simply being a good student, as in *disciple*. Rewire yourself to see discipline as commitment. When you do, you'll find that keeping true to your goal of learning Italian isn't as hard as you first thought.

By creating opportunities to integrate Italian into your daily life, you'll discover that you *do* have the time. Five *minuti* here and there—while waiting in line at the *ufficio postale*, at the *banca*, or when stuck in *traffico*, for example—can add up to more than you imagine.

It's easy to squeeze in some Italian practice into your day if you think about it. Listen to CDs, podcasts, Italian music, and good old-fashioned audio tapes while you're driving or doing chores, even if you're only remotely paying *attenzione* (attention). Local librarians are usually thrilled to help you track down something within your library system. Schools often have media available as well.

Think efficiently as you practice your new language. For example, rather than trying to say "Would you happen to know where I can find a bank?" keep things simple by asking "Where is a bank?" (*Dov'è una banca?*) It's a lot easier to hop from English to Italian if the English is concise. I can't emphasize this point enough!

When grocery shopping, go to the Italian food section and notice the *ingredienti* listed on the back of the package. Compare the English to the Italian.

Sponsor a weekly Italian salon with others interested in developing their language skills. Pick a topic, find a table, add some nibbles, and sip a glass of *vino* or a cup of tea (depending on what time of day it is). Focus on a particular poet, decipher an Italian recipe, or try to translate a news article. You can't learn Italian in a vacuum, after all.

BUON'IDEA

Use Post-Its to label the things around you. You'll soon acquire a practical *vocabolario* you can begin using immediately. To get you started, try these helpful terms, each given with the appropriate article: the book (*il libro*), the table (*il tavolo*), the chair (*la sedia*), the door (*la porta*), the window (*la finestra*), the cat (*il gatto*). (The cat, however, probably won't appreciate having a Post-It stuck on its nose.)

Inspiration often comes from the unexpected. Go to your bookstore and leaf through several books in the Italian language section. Check out library fairs for used Italian textbooks. Children's books are another fun way of building *vocabolario*.

If you're in Italy, or know someone who is, there's nothing like the local *libreria* (bookstore)—pick up a few books to immerse yourself in. Or the next time a friend takes a trip to Italy, ask him or her to bring back the in-flight magazine. The Italian airline company Alitalia produces a wonderful publication that has the Italian and the English side by side.

Pick up a box of flashcards at any bookstore or make your own. That unused box of business cards from your old job or leftover pages from your last address book are *perfetti*. Punch holes in them and put 10 or 20 on a key ring so you can put them in your pocket or bag for "study quickies."

Expect to be completely confused at times. *La confusione* (confusion) is a beautiful thing: it's the merging together of new ideas. Trust the *processo* (process). It takes time. Similar to developing the skills you now take for granted (walking, talking, swimming, riding a bicycle, driving, and so on), you'll go through a *fase* (phase) when you'll probably experience frustration. You *will* move past it. Don't let it throw you off course. It's like getting a flat tire. Your whole vehicle isn't broken, so just fix the flat and you're on your way again.

Keep high hopes, but have low expectations, and you can't fail. You've already made a great start by picking up this *libro* (book). I'm genuinely pleased to have the honor of assisting you!

Get Help!

The best way to learn how to speak Italian is to spend time listening to it. Listen to the audio CD provided with this book, for example. But don't stop there.

Also check out other language CDs. If you're computer savvy, invest in an Italian-English *dizionario* or educational translation. Some even pronounce the words for you. Visit your local *biblioteca* (library) or *libreria* (bookstore) to see what they have on hand to help you develop your listening skills. You might want to see if your local *università* has a language lab you can use.

Many online dictionary sites like WordReference.com (a personal favorite) offer definitions, usage examples, verb conjugations, and audio samples. Switch your home page to an Italian-related site. If you have one, change your Facebook page to Italian.

Search out Italian media. Listen to Italian operas. Check out Italian rock bands. Find an Italian radio station. Familiarize yourself with Pandora radio online and design your own Italian music channel. Watch Italian YouTube videos. For a good laugh, check out Monty Python's Italian lesson!

Find out what station carries Italian news. RAI, the Public Italian television and radio network, airs programs every day. Sure, it'll sound like they're speaking a million miles a *minuto*, but by exposing your ears to the *lingua*, you'll eventually begin to understand it.

Do you live by your smartphone? If so, download an Italian app. There are a million out there. Subscribe to a daily Italian word, or find an Italian-English dictionary app you can keep at your fingertips.

> **BUON'IDEA**
>
> Find birds of a feather. You can't learn to speak a language if you don't have someone to practice with. Study the *lingua* with a friend. Take a course. Can't find one? Invest in a private tutor to meet with you every couple weeks. Create a potluck once a week to celebrate the things you love most about Italy. Use food to enhance your vocabulary skills, and eat your way to fluency!

What better source to learn Italian than from native speakers? Italians are among the most warm, hospitable, easy-going, open-minded people you'll ever meet. Your attempt to speak Italian, even in the most basic of ways, will elicit nothing less than enthusiasm and delight. Say *buongiorno* (good day) every time you walk into an establishment, and watch the response. They'll be listening to what you're trying to express, not what mistakes you might have made.

Okay, enough with the pep talk. Let's get to work.

First Steps: Practical Phrases You Should Know

If you want to learn how to swim, you're going to have to get wet. So let's "get wet" with Italian by learning some basic words and expressions.

2

English	*Italiano*	Pronunciation
Yes	*Sì*	*see*
No	*No*	*no*
Please	*Per favore*	*per fah-__voh__-reh*
	Per piacere	*per pee-ah-__cheh__-reh*
Thank you	*Grazie*	__grah__*-tsee-yeh*
You're welcome	*Prego*	__pray__*-goh*
I'm sorry	*Mi dispiace*	*mee dees-pee-__ah__-cheh*
Excuse me	*Mi scusi* (formal)	*mee __skoo__-zee*
	Scusami (informal)	__skoo__*-zah mee*
Forgive me	*Mi perdoni* (formal)	*mee per-__doh__-nee*
	Perdonami (informal)	*per-__doh__-nah-mee*
Help!	*Aiuto!*	*ah-__yoo__-toh*
I love you!	*Ti amo!*	*tee __ah__-moh*

LA BELLA LINGUA

There's more than one way to say thank you, including *mille grazie* (thanks a million) and *tante grazie* (thanks so much). *Di niente* (it's nothing) is another way to say "you're welcome."

Greetings and Salutations

Before you go throwing kisses and blurting out *Ciao* to everyone you meet, keep in mind these pointers. For strangers, VIPs, and people you encounter on a regular basis (such as your local vendor or a neighbor), you're best off using the polite forms of greetings and salutations. When dealing with friends, colleagues, family, and children, it's appropriate to use the less formal, more familiar terms.

Come Sta? (How Are You?): Formal Greetings

You almost always want to begin a *conversazione* with a stranger in the polite form of address, using the formal *Lei* (you) form of a verb. It gives you a chance to warm up to someone and then switch into the informal *tu* (you) after a relationship has been established. It's like calling someone by their last name until you've been invited to call them by their first name.

As you read aloud, try to sound *naturale*. To help you with the pronunciation, the stress has been indicated in bold. Stress all words ending with an accent on the last syllable. Emphasize doubled consonants when you see them. Raise your voice at the end of a sentence to make a question. And animate your speech. After all, this is Italian! The last thing you want to sound like is a drone.

Straniero in a Strange Land

3

Let's start by reading aloud some greetings you might use when meeting someone new.

Formal Salutations and Expressions

English	*Italiano*	Pronunciation
Good morning/day/afternoon/ Hello (use until early afternoon).	*Buongiorno.*	*bwon **jor**-noh*
Good evening. (Begin using after 3 P.M.)	*Buona sera.*	***bwoh**-nah **seh**-rah*
Good night.	*Buona notte.*	***bwoh**-nah **noht**-teh*
Mr./Sir	*Signore*	*see-**nyoh**-reh*
Mrs./Ms.	*Signora*	*see-**nyoh**-rah*
Miss	*Signorina*	*see-nyoh-**ree**-nah*
How are you?	*Come sta?*	***koh**-meh stah?*
I am well, and you?	*Sto bene, e Lei?*	*stoh **beh**-neh, eh lay?*
Very well.	*Molto bene.*	***mol**-toh beh-neh*
Not bad.	*Non c'è male.*	*nohn cheh **mah**-leh*
Pretty well.	*Abbastanza bene.*	*ah-bah-**stahn**-zah **beh**-neh*
It's a pleasure.	*Piacere.*	*pee-ah-**cheh**-reh*
I'm very pleased to meet you.	*Sono molto lieto(a) di fare la sua conoscenza.*	***soh**-noh **mol**-toh lee-**yeh**-toh(ah) dee **fah**-reh lah **soo**-ah koh-noh-**shen**-zah*
Until next time.	*ArrivederLa.**	*ahr-ree-veh-**der**-lah*

*The capital L *is used in written Italian but does not change the pronunciation.*

    WHAT'S WHAT

Ciao is an informal way of saying "hi" and "bye." *Ci vediamo* is used often to express "catch you later." *Arrivederci* means to re-see one another. The word is also commonly used to say good-bye to friends or colleagues. Friends and family usually kiss hello and good-bye. Give a quick peck on the right cheek, and move to the left. *ArrivederLa* is used under more formal circumstances.

Ciao! Informal Greetings and Salutations

4

If you're talking to peers, friends, or younger people, use the informal greetings and phrases outlined in the following table.

Informal Salutations

English	*Italiano*	Pronunciation
Hi!/Bye!	*Ciao!*	*chow*
Greetings!	*Saluti!*	*sah-**loo**-tee*
Hey!	*Salve!*	***sahl**-veh*
How are you?	*Come stai?*	***koh**-meh sty?*
How's it going?	*Come va?*	***koh**-meh vah?*
It's going well.	*Va bene.*	*vah **beh**-neh*
It's going great.	*Va benissimo.*	*vah beh-**nees**-see-moh*
Not bad.	*Non c'è male.*	*nohn cheh **mah**-leh*
Okay.	*Okay.*	*oh-**kay***
So-so.	*Così così.*	*koh-**zee** koh-**zee***
Catch you later.	*Ci vediamo.*	*chee veh-dee-**ah**-moh*
Until later.	*A più tardi.*	*ah pyoo **tar**-dee*
See you tomorrow.	*A domani.*	*ah doh-**mah**-nee*
See you soon.	*A presto.*	*ah **pres**-toh*
	Arrivederci.	*ar-ree-veh-**der**-chee*

Le Comunicazioni (Communications)

5

Use your hands, study facial expressions, and speak bravely! Italians understand that to get along, you've got to be able to communicate. You'll want to explain that you're not quite fluent yet. The questions are offered using both the polite as well as the familiar conjugations of the verbs. You'll want to err on the side of too polite rather than too informal.

Communications

English	*Italiano*	Pronunciation
Do you understand?	*Capisce?* (formal)	*kah-**pee**-shay?*
	Capisci? (informal)	*kah-**pee**-shee?*
I understand.	*Capisco.*	*kah-**pee**-skoh*
I don't understand.	*Non capisco.*	*non kah-**pee**-skoh*

English	*Italiano*	Pronunciation
I get it.	*Ho capito.* (I have understood.)	*oh kah-**pee**-toh*
Do you speak English?	*Parla inglese?* (formal)	***par**-lah een-**gleh**-zeh?*
	Parli inglese? (informal)	***par**-lee een-**gleh**-zeh?*
I don't speak Italian.	*Non parlo **italiano**.*	*non **par**-loh ee-tah-lee-**ah**-noh*
I am studying Italian.	*Studio **italiano**.*	***stoo**-dee-oh ee-tah-lee-**ah**-noh*
Please speak slowly.	*Parli lentamente per favore.* (formal)	***par**-lee len-tah-**men**-the per vah-**voh**-reh*
	Parla lentamente per favore. (informal)	***par**-lah len-tah-**men**-the per vah-**voh**-reh*
Please repeat that.	*Lo ripeta per favore.* (formal)	*loh ree-**peh**-tah per fah-**voh**-reh*
	Ripetilo per favore. (informal)	
What does it mean?	*Che cosa significa?*	*keh koh-zah seeg-**nee**-fee-kah?*
How do you spell it?	*Come si scrive?*	***koh**-meh see **skree**-veh?*
I don't know.	*Non lo so.*	*non loh soh*
What is your name?	*Come si chiama?* (formal)	***koh**-meh see kee-**ah**-mah*
	Come ti chiami? (informal)	***koh**-meh tee kee-**ah**-mee*
My name is …	*Mi chiamo …* (I call myself …)	*mee kee-**ah**-moh*

Chi, Quando, Dove (Who, When, Where)

6

In English, question words are often called the wh- words. Who's on first? What's on second? You may not understand the answer, but at least you can ask basic questions using these Italian interrogatives.

Question Words

English	*Italiano*	Pronunciation
Who?	*Chi?*	*kee?*
What?	*Che cosa?*	*keh **koh**-zah?*
Where?	*Dove?*	***doh**-vay?*
Where is …?	*Dov'è …?*	*doh-**vay** …?*
When?	*Quando?*	***kwahn**-doh?*
Why?	*Perché?*	*per-**kay**?*
How?	*Come?*	***koh**-meh?*
How much (does it cost)?	*Quanto (costa)?*	***kwahn**-toh?*
Is there?	*C'è?*	*ch-**ay**?*
Are there?	*Ci sono?*	*chee **soh**-noh?*

Compliments

7

This is unbelievably simple to do and will open doors for you. Say nice things, especially complimentary ones that praise your hosts, and the world will be your oyster, to use an idiom.

English	*Italiano*
Best of luck!	*Buona fortuna!*
Break a leg!	*In bocca al lupo! (Literally:* "In the mouth of the wolf!")*
Compliments!	*Complimenti!*
Congratulations!	*Auguri!*
How beautiful! (when speaking to a woman)	*Che bella!*
How handsome! (when speaking to a man)	*Che bello!*
You are very kind.	*Lei è molto gentile.*

**Whenever this expression is used, Italians respond with* Crepi il lupo!*

Expressing Your Honest Opinion

8

You can sound like a veritable Italian with just a few exclamations. The first group is used to express your appreciation and marvel.

Exclamations Expressing Appreciation

English	*Italiano*	Pronunciation
Excellent!	*Eccellente!*	*eh-chel-**len**-teh*
Fantastic!	*Fantastico!*	*fan-**tas**-tee-koh*
Fabulous!	*Favoloso!*	*fah-voh-**loh**-zoh*
Magnificent!	*Magnifico!*	*mag-**nee**-fee-koh*
Marvelous!	*Meraviglioso!*	*meh-rah-vee-**lyoh**-zoh*
Stupendous!	*Stupendo!*	*stoo-**pen**-doh*

Italians don't mince words. The second group expresses when things don't quite live up to our expectations or hopes. (In general, double consonants will be indicated where possible).

Exclamations Expressing Dismay

English	*Italiano*	Pronunciation
Horrible!	*Orribile!*	or-**ree**-bee-leh
Terrible!	*Terribile!*	ter-**ree**-bee-leh
How ugly!	*Che brutto!*	keh **broot**-toh
Ridiculous!	*Ridicolo!*	ree-**dee**-koh-loh
What a disaster!	*Che disastro!*	keh dee-**sas**-troh
What a ruckus!	*Che chiasso!*	keh kee-**ahs**-soh

You're No Idiot

You're not an idiot, or you wouldn't be reading this book. Did you know the word *idiot* comes from the Greek root *idios* and means "of a particular person, private, own"? In Latin, an *idiota* simply refers to a private person. You see this root in the words *idiom* and *idiosyncrasy*.

Lame and suffering from a speech impediment, Claudius (10 B.C.–54 A.D.) is remembered as a scholar and a competent administrator during the time he reigned. Against all odds, this "idiot" rose up to become Roman Emperor, making a fool of everyone. Claudius' secret? He didn't give up. He kept at things. He didn't let anyone or anything outside himself dictate what he did with his mind.

On the other hand, it would be idiocy to *not* learn Italian when it's all right here, right now. What are you waiting for? Join the party: more than 60 million people speak Italian worldwide—and any one of them will be happy to speak with you, especially if you ask nicely.

The Least You Need to Know

- If you can learn to speak one language (English), you can learn to speak another (Italian). Remember that you can communicate even if your pronunciation and grammar are less than perfect.
- Approach learning Italian like a hobby. Find your pace, and stick with it.
- Finding ways to integrate Italian into your everyday activities makes the language more familiar to you.
- Create a study group by finding others to celebrate everything Italian with you!
- Look for interesting Italian websites and language cassettes to support your language studies.

Getting Your *Bocca* Around the ABCs

In This Chapter

- Making friends with your dictionary
- Mastering Italian pronunciation
- The Italian *alfabeto*
- To stress or not to stress?
- Spelling your *nome* in *italiano*

Languages can be compared to musical instruments. Italian is sort of like a piano. Even if you've never played a note, you can hit the key and hear a lovely sound. Some languages, like French, are more like the violin, and require a great deal more practice so that what is produced doesn't sound like someone scratching a blackboard!

Learning a new language can be daunting. Enjoy the fact that Italian is so accessible. Without much study, you'll find the rules of pronunciation very simple, and you'll be able to get your *bocca* (mouth) around the basics quickly. In this chapter, I give you the nuts and bolts of Italian pronunciation and help you learn your ABCs.

There's no substitution for hearing the real thing. Listen to the examples offered on the CD, and accustom your ear to the different letter combinations and their pronunciation.

Your *Dizionario* (Dictionary) Is Your Best Friend

Having a good bilingual Italian-English *dizionario* (dictionary) is essential to learning the Italian alphabet, getting a grasp of Italian spelling, understanding pronunciation, and so much more. Make sure to buy a dictionary that provides stress accentuation for the Italian words (many dictionaries indicate irregularly stressed syllables) and parts of speech, and keep it within easy reach, using it as a map as you navigate your new Italian experience.

Most good Italian-English dictionaries indicate what type of word an entry is—noun, adjective, pronoun, etc.—often listing this information as an abbreviation to save space. Taking time to understand the significance of the abbreviations used in the definitions helps your overall goal of learning Italian. The following table lists a few abbreviations you should know.

Dictionary Abbreviations

English Abbreviation	Italian Abbreviation	Meaning
adj.	*agg.*	Adjective
adv.	*avv.*	Adverb
fam.	*fam.*	Familiar/colloquial
n.	*f.*	Feminine noun
n.	*m.*	Masculine noun
pl.	*pl.*	Plural
prep.	*prep.*	Preposition
pron.	*pron.*	Pronoun
v.i.	*v.i.*	Intransitive verb
—	*v.rifl.*	Reflexive verb
v.t.	*v.t.*	Transitive verb

> **BUON'IDEA**
>
> Cross-referencing is the best way to ensure you have the desired translation. For example, the word *inside* can be translated in Italian with several words: *dentro, in, all'interno, entro,* etc. To be sure your selection is the correct translation, find the same word in your Italian-English dictionary. Take the word *dentro.* Does it correspond with your intended meaning? If you're looking to sit *inside, dentro* would make sense. What about *entro*? No. Why? Because *entro (un'ora)* would be referring to *inside (an hour)*.

Idiomatically Speaking

Idioms are important for a complete and correct understanding of a language. They are the spice that makes language interesting. If verbs and grammar are the brain of a language, idioms are the *personalità*. They express the various idiosyncrasies of the speaker's *tradizioni*, customs, values, and social mores.

Some idioms translate between languages. In Italian, you can ask *Posso dare una mano?* (Can I give you a hand?) However, in Italian, you wouldn't be able to say it's "raining cats and dogs" without "raising an eyebrow" (another idiom).

Italian Pronunciation

Almost all Italian words end in a *vocale* and are often pronounced as if joined together. As a phonetic language, in Italian, what you see is what you say … at least most of the time. Occasionally, you'll see a word that has had its last letter cut, such as with the expressions *man mano* ("hand hand") and *pian piano* ("slow slow") both of which mean gradually, slowly. Some infinitive verbs are also used (especially in songs) without the final -*e*.

9

To ask someone (like your teacher or a bilingual friend) how to say something in Italian, use this expression:

> How do you say …?
> *Come si dice …?*
> (**koh**-*meh see* **dee**-*cheh*)

To ask someone how something should be pronounced in Italian, use this expression:

> How do you pronounce …?
> *Come si pronuncia …?*
> (**koh**-*meh see proh*-**noon**-*chah*)

To ask someone how to spell something in Italian, say:

> How do you write it?
> *Come si scrive?*
> (**koh**-*meh see* **skree**-*veh*)

One way to understand the basic differences between the English and Italian rules of pronunciation is to take a cognate like the word *cinema*. In Italian, it's pronounced **chee**-*neh-mah*. (The bold tells you the first syllable is stressed.) The same letter combination *ci* is used in the greeting *Ciao*. To remember that *ch* in Italian is pronounced like a *k* sound, think of the words *zucchini* and the Italian wine-region *Chianti*.

BUON'IDEA

Context is key. Absorb the significance of a *parola* (word) by looking at the words surrounding it. When you learn how to decode the Italian language, you'll begin to see patterns emerge. From there, it's just a matter of time before the words begin pouring out of you! It doesn't hurt to learn words in pairs. It's like getting two for the price of one!

Italian requires clean diction. Enunciate vowels. Double consonants in words such as *anno* (***ahn***-*noh*; year), *birra* (***beer***-*rah*; beer), and *gatto* (***gaht***-*toh*; cat) should be emphasized. Avoid sounding overly nasal or guttural.

Unless otherwise indicated, the first syllable is slightly more stressed in two-syllable words such as *cento* (***chen***-*toh*).

Learning Your Italian ABCs

The Italian language uses the Latin alphabet. Unlike English, however, the Italian alphabet contains only 21 letters, borrowing the letters *j, k, w, x,* and *y* for words of foreign origin.

As you read, you'll discover that the spelling of Italian words follows a logical pattern.

The Italian Alphabet

10

A practical way of remembering the alphabet is to learn how to spell your name in Italian. In the following table, the Italian equivalent is given beside the English letter. The stressed syllable is in bold. Examples of foreign letters are given with commonly used nouns. As part of the Latin alphabet, the letter *V* is pronounced *voo* and sometimes *vee*, depending on the region.

If you're extramotivated, use the Italian alphabet as a way to learn more about Italian geography. Why not look for these Italian locations on a map?

Here, the CD can be particularly helpful.

LA BELLA LINGUA

When spelling out words, in English, we often use proper names to clarify letters: *T* as in Tom, for example. In Italian, names of Italian cities are used instead: *A come Ancona, I come Imola,* and *T come Torino* (*A* as in *Ancona, I* as in *Imola, T* as in *Torino*). Italians don't always agree about which cities to use, and you can feel free to change your example to a different city. Instead of *C* for *Cagliari,* you could subsitute *C* for *Como,* for example.

L'Alfabeto Italiano

Letter	Italian Name of Letter	Pronunciation	Example	Pronunciation
A	*a*	*a*	*Ancona*	*ahn-**koh**-nah*
B	*bi*	*bee*	*Bologna*	*boh-**loh**-nyah*
C	*ci*	*chee*	*Cagliari*	***kahl**-yah-ree*
D	*di*	*dee*	*Domodossola*	*doh-moh-**dohs**-soh-lah*
E	*e*	*eh*	*Empoli*	***em**-poh-lee*
F	*effe*	***ehf**-fay*	*Firenze*	*fee-**ren**-zay*
G	*gi*	*jee*	*Genova*	***jeh**-noh-vah*
H	*acca*	***ahk**-kah*	*hotel*	***oh**-tel*
I	*i*	*ee*	*Imola*	***ee**-moh-lah*
J*	*i lunga*	*ee **loon**-gah*	*jolly*	***jol**-lee*
K*	*cappa*	***kahp**-pah*	*kaiser*	***ky**-zer*
L	*elle*	***ehl**-lay*	*Livorno*	*lee-**vor**-noh*
M	*emme*	***ehm**-may*	*Milano*	*mee-**lah**-noh*
N	*enne*	***ehn**-nay*	*Napoli*	***nah**-poh-lee*
O	*o*	*oh*	*Otranto*	*oh-**tran**-toh*
P	*pi*	*pee*	*Palermo*	*pah-**ler**-moh*
Q	*cu*	*koo*	*quaderno* (notebook)	*kwah-**der**-noh*
R	*erre*	***ehr**-ray*	*Roma*	***roh**-mah*
S	*esse*	***ehs**-say*	*Sassari*	***sahs**-sah-ree*
T	*ti*	*tee*	*Torino*	*toh-**ree**-noh*
U	*u*	*oo*	*Udine*	***oo**-dee-neh*
V	*vu/vi*	*voo/vee*	*Venezia*	*veh-**neh**-zee-ah*
W*	*doppia vu*	***dohp**-pee-yah voo*	*Washington*	***wash**-eeng-ton*
X*	*ics*	*eeks*	*xenofobo* (xenophobe)	*kzeh-**noh**-foh-boh*
Y*	*ipsilon* also *i greca*	***eep**-see-lohn* also *ee **greh**-kah*	*York*	*york*
Z	*zeta*	***zeh**-tah*	*Zara*	***zah**-rah*

These letters have been borrowed from other languages.

Getting the *Accento* (Accent)

Italian uses the grave accent (`; pronounced *grave*) on words where the stress falls on the final syllable: *caffè, città, università.*

Italian also makes use of the acute accent (´; pronounced *acuto*), particularly with the words *benché* (although), *perché* (because/why) and *affinché* (so that).

The written accent is also used to distinguish several Italian words from others that have the same spelling but a different meaning. Note that the word for *is* in Italian is *è*, while the word for *and* is *e*, without an accent. The accented *è* should utilize a more open sound, like in the word *bell*. The simple *e* is pronounced with a more closed sound like in the word *gourmet*. If at first you don't get the subtle differences, no sweat.

Let's look at some more examples:

è	is	*e*	and
sì	yes	*si*	oneself
dà	gives	*da*	from
sè	himself	*se*	if
là	there	*la*	the
lì	there	*li*	them
né	nor	*ne*	some

ATTENZIONE!

Some Italian letter combinations are seldom found in English. These sounds include the *gl* combination in words such as *figlio* (son; pronounced **feel**-*yoh*); the word *gli* (the; pronounced *ylee*, like the *ll* in *million*); and the *gn* combination, seen in words such as *gnocchi* (potato dumplings; pronounced **nyohk**-*kee*), and *bagno* (bathroom; pronounced **bahn**-*yoh*, like the *ny* sound in *canyon* or the *ni* sound in *onion*).

Italian sounds so beautiful because everything connects in a smooth, melodic manner. Italian uses an apostrophe when an article or preposition precedes a noun starting with a vowel. Study the examples:

l'animale instead of *lo animale* (the animal)

d'Italia instead of *di Italia* (of Italy)

dov'è instead of *dove è* (where is)

Don't Get Stressed Out!

11

There are exceptions to every rule, but let's review the basics on where to stress an Italian word.

Stress the last syllable when you see an accent mark at the end of a word, such as *città* (city; *chee-**tah***), *università* (university; *oo-nee-ver-see-**ta***), and *virtù* (virtue; *veer-**too***). Accented words do not change in the plural.

As a rule, most Italian words that are four or more syllables tend to be stressed on the next-to-last syllable, called the penultimate syllable: *signorina* (miss; *see-nyoh-**ree**-nah*), *minestrone* (*mee-neh-**stroh**-neh*).

Some words are stressed on the third-to-last syllable: *automobile* (*ow-toh-**moh**-bee-leh*), *dialogo* (dialogue; *dee-**ah**-loh-goh*).

Many verb forms are stressed on the fourth-to-last syllable, such as *studiano* (they study; ***stoo**-dee-ah-noh*; third-person plural) and *telefonano* (they telephone; *teh-**leh**-foh-nah-noh*).

Consult a good dictionary when you're unclear about which syllable to emphasize. Generally, you'll see either an accent placed above or a dot placed below the stressed vowel. Eventually, you'll get the hang of things. Don't let yourself get flustered if you're not speaking fluently by the end of the week.

Fool's Rules

12

Even when you've learned all the rules of pronunciation and where to put the stress, you'll still find exceptions. Some words are spelled the same, but depending on the way they're stressed, they can mean completely different things. Listen to the audio to hear some examples of these tricksters.

English	*Italiano*	*Pronunciation*
again	*ancora*	*ahn-**koh**-rah*
anchor	*ancora*	***ahn**-koh-rah*
captain	*capitano*	*kah-pee-**tah**-noh*
they happen	*capitano*	***kah**-pee-tah-noh*
washed	*lavati*	*lah-**vah**-tee*
Wash yourself!	*lavati*	***lah**-vah-tee*
royal	*regia*	***reh**-jah*
direction (film)	*regia*	*reh-**jeeh**-ah*

Rolling Your *R*s

13

A few sounds in Italian aren't found in English, the most obvious being the rolled *R*. If you're having trouble trilling your *R*s, try placing the tip of your tongue so it's touching the roof of your mouth just behind your front teeth. Now curl the tip of your tongue and exhale. You should get the beginning trill of a rolled *R*. Listen to the audio to hear these examples of the trilled *R:*

fear	love	romantic	yesterday
paura	*amore*	*romantico*	*ieri*

You can let out your inner Italian and go to town with these double RR:

butter	iron	war	produce
burro	*ferro*	*guerra*	*produrre*

Easy does it! In linguistic parlance, the term *rhotacism* is defined as, among other things, the incorrect use or overuse of Rs in pronunciation. Note the differences between these examples. The addition of one little *R* completely changes the meaning.

caro/carro   *sera/serra*
dear; expensive/cart   evening/greenhouse

AS A *REGOLA*

The pronunciation in this book is designed to be read phonetically. Say what you see. Always remember to enunciate vowels. Double *RR*s should be held and emphasized when trilled. Double consonants should always be emphasized— but never as separate sounds. They should be joined and slide into one another, as in the word *pizza* (**peet**-*tsah*).

The Long and the Short of It: Vowels

14

The Italian word for vowel (*vocale*) is almost the same as the English word *vocal* (and related to the word *voice*) and serves as a good reminder that Italian vowels should always be pronounced clearly. If you can master the vowels, you're already halfway to the point of sounding Italian.

Repeat these words aloud to practice. See how well you can guess their meaning. Listen to the CD to hear them pronounced.

Pronouncing Vowels Properly

Vowel	Sound	Example	Pronunciation
a	*ah*	*artista*	*ar-**tee**-stah*
e	*eh*	*elefante*	*eh-leh-**fahn**-teh*
i	*ee*	*isola*	***ee**-zoh-lah*
o	*oh*	*opera*	***oh**-peh-rah*
u	*oo*	*uno*	***oo**-noh*

Practice your vowels the next time you sing "Old McDonald Had a Farm"! *AH-EH-EE-OH-OO!*

Answers: artist, elephant, island, opera, a/an, or *one*

> **LA BELLA LINGUA**
>
> Remember how a particular letter combination should be pronounced by recalling a word you already know. *Ad esempio* (for example), the word *ciao* is pronounced with the soft *c*, as in the word *chow*. Other words with the *c + i* combination include *cinema* (**chee**-neh-mah; cinema), *bacio* (**bah**-choh; kiss), and *amici* (ah-**mee**-chee; friends). The word *Chianti* is pronounced with a hard *c,* as in *kee-**ahn**-tee*. When you come across other words (such as *chi* [who] and *perché* [why]) with this *combinazione* (combination), you'll know just how they're pronounced.

A Special Note About *E* and *O*

15

The two Italian vowels *e* and *o* both possess an open and a closed sound that varies depending on the region.

The open *e* (*eh*) is pronounced like the English words *bet, set,* and *hen*. Italian examples include the words *vento* (wind), *bella* (beautiful), and the simple verb conjugation *è* (is). The grave accent mark ` is used to indicate stress on open vowels.

The closed *e* (*ay*) is pronounced like the English words *hay, main, fade,* and *say*. Italian examples include the words *me* (me), *per* (for), and *e* (without the accent, meaning "and"). The acute accent mark ´ is used to indicate stress on closed vowels.

The open *o* (*aw* or *ah*) is pronounced like the English words *spot*, *dog*, and *got*. Italian examples include the words *olio* (oil), *moda* (fashion), and *brodo* (broth).

The closed *o* (*oh*) is pronounced like the words *toe*, *soul*, *row*, and *ghost*. Italian examples include *sole* (sun), *mondo* (world), and *nome* (name).

Regional differences and dialects also affect the way these vowels are pronounced. If you don't get the subtle differences at first, you'll still make yourself understood!

Vocalizing

16

Italian vowels should sound pure and clean. Pronounce them using the following examples as your guide. Listen to the audio, paying special attention to the relationship vowels have with the other letters in a word.

A: Say *ah:*

madre	*canto*	*casa*	*strada*
mah-dreh	**kahn**-toh	**kah**-zah	**strah**-dah
mother	song	home	street

E: Say *eh:*

padre	*sera*	*bene*	*festa*
pah-dreh	**sah**-rah	**beh**-neh	**feh**-stah
father	evening	well	party

I: Say *ee:*

idiota	*piccolo*	*pulire*	*idea*
ee-dee-**aw**-tah	**peek**-koh-loh	poo-**lee**-reh	ee-**deh**-ah
idiot	small	to clean	idea

O: Say *oh:*

bello	*cosa*	*uomo*	*donna*
behl-loh	**koh**-zah	**woh**-moh	**dohn**-nah
beautiful	thing	man	woman

U: Say *oo:*

luna	*una*	*tuo*	*lupo*
loo-*nah*	**oo**-*nah*	**too**-*oh*	**loo**-*poh*
moon	a	your	wolf

Give Me the Combo

17

It's time to put it all together. The following examples illustrate many letter combinations you'll find in Italian.

C Is for "Casa"

Check out all you can do with the letter *c*.

Letter Combination	Sound	Pronunciation Guide	
c + e, i	*ch*	Say *cheese*	
accento	*cena*	*città*	*bacio*
*ah-**chen**-toh*	***cheh**-nah*	*chee-**tah***	***bah**-choh*
accent	dinner	city	kiss
c + *a, h, o, u*	*k*	Say *camp*	
casa	*caro*	*cubo*	*Chianti*
***kah**-zah*	***kah**-roh*	***koo**-boh*	*kee-**ahn**-tee*
house	dear	cube	Chianti

G Is for "Gamba"

Practice getting your *g* sounds right.

The letter combination *gh* is also pronounced like the *g* in *go*, as in *funghi* (***foon**-ghee;* mushrooms).

Letter Combination	Sound	Pronunciation Guide	
g + e, i	*j*	Say *Gianni*	
gelato	*giovane*	*giacca*	*viaggio*
*jeh-**lah**-toh*	***joh**-vah-neh*	***jahk**-kah*	*vee-**ahj**-joh*
ice cream	young	jacket	voyage
g + n	*ny*	Say *onion*	
lavagna	*signore*	*legno*	*gnocchi*
*lah-**vah**-nyah*	*see-**nyoh**-reh*	***lehn**-yoh*	***nyohk**-kee*
blackboard	sir, Mr.	wood	potato dumplings
g + a, h, o, u	*g*	Say *Gabrielle* (and I'll come running!)	
gamba	*ghetto*	*prego*	*gufo*
***gahm**-bah*	***geht**-toh*	***preh**-goh*	***goo**-foh*
leg	ghetto	you're welcome	owl

S Is for "Scandalo"

The letter *s* in Italian is quite slippery. Emphasize the double *ss* when you see words like *passera* (***pahs**-seh-rah*; sparrow), *cassa* (***kahs**-sah*; cashier), and *sasso* (***sahs**-soh*; stone, rock).

Letter Combination	Sound	Pronunciation Guide	
sc + a, h, o, u	*sk*	Say *skin*	
sconto	*scusa*	*scandalo*	*pesca*
***skohn**-toh*	***skoo**-zah*	***skahn**-dah-loh*	***pess**-kah*
discount	excuse	scandal	peach
sc + e, i	*sh*	Say *sheet*	
pesce	*scena*	*sciroppo*	*sci*
***peh**-sheh*	***sheh**-nah*	*she-**rohp**-poh*	*shee*
fish	scene	syrup	skiing

When there's an *s* after a vowel within a word, it's more like a *z* sound.

peso	*Luisa*	*frase*	*casa*
peh-*zoh*	*loo*-**ee**-*zah*	**frah**-*zeh*	**kah**-*zah*
weight	Luisa	phrase	house/home

Did you notice the similarity between the words you just read and their English counterparts?

Diphthongs

18

No, a diphthong is not a teeny-weeny bikini. The term *diphthong* (*dittongo* in Italian) refers to any pair of vowels that begins with one vowel sound and ends with a different vowel sound within the same syllable. The term, originally from Greek, literally means "two voices" (*di* = two; *thong* = tongue/voice).

Italian utilizes many diphthongs such as *Italia* (*ee*-**tahl**-*yah*; Italy), *ciao* (*chow*; hi), *olio* (**ohl**-*yoh*; oil), *quanto* (**kwahn**-*toh*; how much), and *pausa* (**pow**-*zah*; pause).

Two vowels do not *necessarily* produce a diphthong. The word *zia* (**zee**-*ah*; aunt) maintains two distinct, separate sounds and consequently does not produce a diphthong. The name Maria (*mah*-**ree**-*ah*) is also a good example of this.

Double Consonants

19

Any time you see a double consonant in a word, it's important to emphasize that consonant or else you may be misunderstood. Let's take a look at a few words whose meanings change when there's a double consonant. As you will see, in some cases you *definitely* want to emphasize those double consonants!

ano (**ah**-*noh*; anus)	*anno* (**ahn**-*noh*; year)
casa (**kah**-*zah*; house)	*cassa* (**kahs**-*sah*; cash register)
pena (**peh**-*nah*; pity)	*penna* (**pehn**-*nah*; pen)
pene (**peh**-*neh*; penis)	*penne* (**pen**-*neh*; pens)
sete (**seh**-*teh*; thirsty)	*sette* (**set**-*teh*; seven)
sono (**soh**-*noh*; I am)	*sonno* (**sohn**-*noh*; sleepy)

Practice pronouncing the following words, remembering to slide the syllables together:

mamma	*sorella*	*cappello*	*atto*
mahm-*mah*	soh-**rel**-*lah*	kahp-**pel**-*loh*	**aht**-*toh*
mom	sister	hat	act

AS A *REGOLA*

Unless beginning a word, a single *s* is pronounced like *z*, as in the name *Gaza,* or *s*, as in *busy* and the Italian word *casa* (house). A double *ss* is pronounced like the *s* in the English word *tassel* and the Italian word *passo* (pass). A single *z* is pronounced like the *z* in the word *zebra*. A double *zz* is pronounced like the *ts* in the English word *cats* and the Italian word *piazza* (plaza).

The Least You Need to Know

- Dictionaries aren't just for geeks. Invest in a good Italian-English dictionary that shows the stressed syllables for the Italian words you're trying to learn. Many dictionaries are slanted toward one or the other language (rarely both).
- Idioms are essential to any language and are often difficult to translate between languages.
- The Italian alphabet has 21 letters.
- Let your tongue do the talking. Tickle a single *R,* but *rrrrrrr*oll your double *RR*s. Rev them like an engine, purr like a cat, or growl like a bear.
- Enunciate your vowels, yet keep your Italian from sounding forced and unnatural.
- Pay special attention to double consonants!
- Fluidity is key. Slide syllables together!

You Have *Amici:* Cognates

In This Chapter

- Bridging the gap between languages by using cognates
- You know a lot more Italian than you think
- Naming nouns and other words
- Why you should beware of false friends (in the Italian language, that is!)

What if I told you you were already halfway to speaking Italian? Remember that English, although a Germanic language, contains many words of Latin origin. The list of Italian words you already know is longer than you probably think. Some are virtually the same, whereas most are easily identified by their similarity to English. *Telefono* (telephone), *attenzione* (attention), *università* (university), *automobile* (automobile), *studente* (student)—the list goes on and on.

So What's Your *Storia?*

L'etimologia (etymology) is a fancy term used to describe the study of words, but you don't need to be a linguist to appreciate the *origine* (origin) of a word. By using your powers of deduction, it's often *possibile* (possible) to figure out a word's *significato* (significance) simply by looking at its root.

Take the word *pomodoro*, for example, which means "tomato" in Italian. Coming from the Latin words *pomum* (apple or fruit) and *oro* (gold), the word derives from the Latin *aurum* (connected to the word *aurora*, meaning "dawn" or "redness"). Thus, the word *pomodoro* breaks down to mean literally "golden fruit."

The English words *Vermont* and *verdant* both share a common root: *vert* (coming from Latin *viridis* and meaning "green"). In Italian, the word for the season spring is *primavera*, meaning "first green." The words *carnivore, carnal, charnel,* and *carnival* all derive from the Latin stem *carn,* meaning "flesh." Are you a verbose person? Think *verb,* or in Latin, *verbum,* meaning "word."

> **LA BELLA LINGUA**
>
> Do you remember the periodic table of elements from science class? Ever wonder why AG stood for silver, PB for lead, and FE for iron? Look at the Italian words for these elements: silver is *argento,* lead is *piombo,* and iron is *ferro.* Isn't that cool?

Cognates: A Bridge Between Languages

Cognates—or in Italian, *parole simili* (similar words)—are words in different languages that derive from the same root and are similar in both spelling and meaning, such as with the words *familiar* and *familiare, possible* and *possibile,* and so on. By learning how to dissect a word, searching for clues that will help reveal the mystery of its meaning, you'll discover how much you already know.

Breaking Words Down to Decipher Their Meaning

Study the following words, isolating the common denominator that connects them all: *cotto.*

- *Bis**cotto***
- *Mani**cotti***
- *Ri**cotta***
- *Panna **cotta***
- *Terra **cotta***

I've always thought someone should use a *biscotto* as a weapon in a mystery novel; they're hard enough to put an eye out! And what makes those delicious little biscuits so hard? If you've ever made them, you know that they're cooked (*cotto*) once, cooled, and cooked again. The *bi-* refers to "two," as you can infer from the words *bicicletta* (bicycle), *binario* (binary; track), and *bifocale* (bifocal).

Next, using your taste buds as memory enhancers, look at the word *ricotta* (recooked). This soft cow's milk cheese is stuffed into *manicotti,* hand-cooked pasta sleeves. The word for hands is *mani;* other related Italian cognates include *manuale* (manual), *manoscritto* (manuscript), and *manico* (handle).

Let's look at *panna cotta.* The word *panna* refers to "cream." Add *cotta* and you've got "cooked cream." Yummy.

Now, study the word *terra cotta.* You know that *cotta* means "cooked." Can you deduce the significance of the word *terra?* If you intuited "earth," you were right! *Congratulazioni!* Additional words related to *terra* include *terreno* (terrain), *terrazza* (terrace), and *territorio* (territory).

Trucchi (Tricks) of the Trade

Many English words can be made into Italian simply by changing the endings. Look what happens with the examples in the following table.

It's All About the Ending

English to Italian Endings	English to Italian Examples
-ble → *-ibile*	possible → *possibile*
-ence → *-enza*	essence → *essenza*
-ent → *-ente*	president → *presidente*
-ism → *-ismo*	socialism → *socialismo*
-ous → *-oso*	famous → *famoso*
-tion → *-zione*	action → *azione*
-ty → *-tà*	identity → *identità*

Why memorize a hundred words when you can study a handful of endings? The *possibilità* are endless! Although exceptions exist, it's amazing how many English words can be easily converted into Italian by substituting a little letter, as shown in the following table.

Finding Common Threads

English	*Italiano*	Examples
al	*o*	practical → *pratico*
c	*z*	force → *forza*
k, ck	*c, cc*	sack → *sacco*
ph	*f*	telephone → *telefono*
th	*t*	theater → *teatro*
x	*s, ss*	taxi → *tassi*
xt	*st*	extreme → *estremo*
y	*i*	style → *stile*

ATTENZIONE!

Watch out for false cognates, as they can easily mislead you. In Italian, the word *parenti* means "relatives," not "parents," as you might think. *Ape* refers to bees, and *cane* is a dog. (More on false cognates later in the chapter.)

If It Looks Like a Duck ...

The Italian language has only a few perfect cognates, such as the words *banana, opera, panorama, pizza, via,* and *zebra.* Although the endings and pronunciations may be slightly *differente*, near cognates are essentially the same.

Let's start with cognates of place and time. Study the places and the times and dates in the following sections to get *un'idea* of how many *parole simili* exist between Italian and English. Nine out of ten times, your initial gut response will be correct—trust it!

Going Places

Where to begin? Wherever you are. Look at the cognates in the following table. Each Italian noun is given with the appropriate definite article to get you started understanding the concept of gender.

Develop your vocabulary by using this phrase in conjunction with the following places:

> Where is ...?
> Dov'è ...?

AS A *REGOLA*

English has only one definite article: the. Italian has several definite articles, all of which indicate gender (masculine or feminine) and number (singular or plural). All Italian nouns are marked by a definite article. Although the gender of nouns is easily identifiable in Italian, it's best to learn the noun with its appropriate definite article. It might seem confusing at first. For now, keep in mind the following rules: *il* is used for most masculine singular nouns; *lo* is used for masculine singular nouns beginning with s + consonant, or z; *l'* is used for any singular noun that begins with a vowel; and *la* is used for all other feminine singular nouns.

Luoghi (Places)

English	Italiano	English	Italiano
the agency	*l'agenzia*	the mountain	*la montagna*
the airport	*l'aeroporto*	the museum	*il museo*
the apartment	*l'appartamento*	the ocean	*l'oceano*
the bank	*la banca*	the office	*l'ufficio*
the bar	*il bar*	the paradise	*il paradiso*
the café	*il caffè*	the pharmacy	*la farmacia*
the castle	*il castello*	the plaza	*la piazza*
the cathedral	*la cattedrale*	the post office	*l'ufficio postale*
the center, downtown	*il centro*	the restaurant	*il ristorante*
the cinema	*il cinema*	the stadium	*lo stadio*
the circus	*il circo*	the station	*la stazione*
the city	*la città*	the studio/office	*lo studio*
the course, track	*la corsa*	the supermarket	*il supermercato*
the discothèque	*la discoteca*	the terrace	*la terrazza*
the garden	*il giardino*	the theater	*il teatro*
the hospital	*l'ospedale*	the village	*il villaggio*
the market	*il mercato*		

It's About Time

You don't know what time it is? Sure you do! The following table lists some cognates related to time.

Time and Dates

English	Italiano	English	Italiano
the anniversary	*l'anniversario*	the minute	*il minuto*
annual	*annuale*	the night	*la notte*
biannual	*biennale*	the hour	*l'ora*
the date	*la data*	the second	*il secondo*
the holiday (as in "festive")	*la festa*	the time (also, weather)	*il tempo*
the millennium	*il millennio*		

How *Intelligente* You Are!

Convert the following words into Italian by changing the endings accordingly.

1. position   *posizione*
2. incredible   _____
3. nation   _____
4. presence   _____
5. identity   _____

6. pessimism   _____
7. prudent   _____
8. continent   _____
9. religious   _____
10. difference   _____

Answers: 2. incredibile 3. nazione 4. presenza 5. identità 6. pessimismo 7. prudente 8. continente 9. religioso 10. differenza

Adjectives: How *Grande!*

Thinking about everything you've learned so far in this chapter on cognates, cover the English translation columns in the following table with a piece of paper, and try to guess the meanings of these adjective cognates. Italian adjectives must agree in gender and number with the nouns they modify. The following are all listed in the masculine.

Cognate Adjectives

English	*Italiano*	English	*Italiano*
ambitious	*ambizioso*	frequent	*frequente*
blond	*biondo*	generous	*generoso*
brunette	*bruno*	gentle, kind	*gentile*
calm	*calmo*	grand, big	*grande*
courteous	*cortese*	honest	*onesto*
curious	*curioso*	ignorant	*ignorante*
delicious	*delizioso*	important	*importante*
different	*differente*	impossible	*impossibile*
divorced	*divorziato*	incredible	*incredibile*
elegant	*elegante*	intelligent	*intelligente*
energetic	*energico*	interesting	*interessante*
excellent	*eccellente*	jealous	*geloso*
false	*falso*	last, ultimate	*ultimo*
famous	*famoso*	long	*lungo*
fortunate	*fortunato*	magnificent	*magnifico*

English	*Italiano*	English	*Italiano*
married (think spouse)	*sposato*	sage, wise	*saggio*
modern	*moderno*	secure, sure	*sicuro*
natural	*naturale*	serious	*serio*
necessary	*necessario*	sincere	*sincero*
nervous	*nervoso*	splendid	*splendido*
normal	*normale*	strange	*strano*
numerous	*numeroso*	strong	*forte*
organized	*organizzato*	stupendous	*stupendo*
poor	*povero*	stupid	*stupido*
popular	*popolare*	tall	*alto*
possible	*possibile*	terrible	*terribile*
practical	*pratico*	tropical	*tropicale*
rapid	*rapido*	violent	*violento*
rich	*ricco*	virtuous	*virtuoso*
romantic	*romantico*		

Names of Things: Nouns

In the following sections, I've listed the Italian nouns (called *nomi* or *sostantivi*) according to their gender. Your job is simply to write down what they mean in English.

Masculine Nouns

Study the different articles used in front of these masculine nouns. Do you see a pattern beginning to emerge?

Masculine Nouns

Italian Masculine Noun	English Translation	Italian Masculine Noun	English Translation
l'aeroplano	_____	*il motore*	_____
l'anniversario	_____	*il museo*	_____
l'arco	_____	*il naso*	_____
l'attore	_____	*l'odore*	_____
l'autobus	_____	*il paradiso*	_____
il caffè	_____	*il presidente*	_____

continues

Italian Masculine Noun	English Translation	Italian Masculine Noun	English Translation
il colore	_____	*il profumo*	_____
il comunismo	_____	*il programma*	_____
il continente	_____	*il rispetto*	_____
il cotone	_____	*il salario*	_____
il direttore	_____	*il servizio*	_____
il dizionario	_____	*il socialismo*	_____

Feminine Nouns

Try the same thing with the feminine nouns in the following table.

Feminine Nouns

Italian Feminine Noun	English Translation	Italian Feminine Noun	English Translation
l'arte	_____	*l'identità*	_____
la bicicletta	_____	*l'inflazione*	_____
la carota	_____	*l'insalata*	_____
la chitarra	_____	*la lampada*	_____
la classe	_____	*la lettera*	_____
la condizione	_____	*la lista*	_____
la conversazione	_____	*la medicina*	_____
la cultura	_____	*la musica*	_____
la curiosità	_____	*la nazione*	_____
la depressione	_____	*la persona*	_____
la dieta	_____	*la possibilità*	_____
la differenza	_____	*la probabilità*	_____
la discussione	_____	*la professione*	_____
l'emozione	_____	*la regione*	_____
l'esperienza	_____	*la religione*	_____
l'espressione	_____	*la rosa*	_____

English Words Used in *Italiano*

Many English nouns have been incorporated into Italian. In Italian, these words are given a gender and, with a few exceptions, are pronounced similarly. Check out the following list of words. Each is shown with the appropriate Italian definite article.

l'antenna	*il cinema*	*l'idea*	*lo shopping*
l'area	*il cocktail*	*il jazz*	*lo snob*
l'autobus	*il computer*	*i jeans*	*lo sport*
il bar	*il film*	*la radio*	*lo studio*
il blues	*l'hamburger*	*lo shampoo*	*il weekend*
il camping	*l'hotel*	*lo shock*	*lo zoo*

Trojan Horses—*Falsi Amici* (False Friends)

As touched on earlier in the chapter, a *false cognate* is a word in Italian that sounds like an English word but means something different. Fortunately, in Italian there aren't many *falsi amici*. Your *dizionario* will also provide useful information regarding false friends. Look for examples such as this one:

mansione f. office, function, capacity; *(compito)* task, job.

ATTENZIONE: **mansione** ≠ mansion.

How do you know when you're correctly using a cognate? Test out your new skills and see how far you can go. Most of the time, your first guess is right. Trust your *istinti* (instincts), but don't kick yourself in the *stinco* (shin) if it takes a little while. Test yourself with the following table of false cognates that are good to know.

Falsi Amici (False Friends)

Italiano	Meaning	*Italiano*	Meaning
ape	bee (≠ ape)	*firma*	signature (≠ firm)
argomento	issue (≠ argument)	*grosso*	large (≠ gross)
camera	room (≠ camera)	*libreria*	bookstore (≠ library)
come	how (≠ come)	*lunatico*	moody (≠ lunatic)
commozione	emotion (≠ commotion)	*magazzino*	department store (≠ magazine)
con	with (≠ convict)	*marrone*	brown (≠ maroon)
fabbrica	factory (≠ fabric)	*morbido*	soft (≠ morbid)
fattoria	farm (≠ factory)	*pesante*	heavy (≠ peasant)

continues

Italiano	Meaning	Italiano	Meaning
rumore	noise (≠ rumor)	*stampa*	press (≠ stamp)
sano	healthy (≠ sane)	*stinco*	shin (≠ stink)
sensibile	sensitive (≠ sensible)	*testa*	head (≠ test)

How Much Do You Understand Already?

20

Read the following sentences, and try to determine their meaning. Listen to the accompanying CD, and pay particular attention to the *c*s and *g*s. Translate the sentences. On the audio, after each example, you'll hear a timer before the answer is given. Think quick: see if you can figure out the meaning before time runs out!

1. *La città è bella.*
2. *La pasta è deliziosa.*
3. *La giacca è grande.*
4. *Gianni è onesto.*
5. *Il servizio è buono.*
6. *La montagna è alta.*

Answers: 1. The city is beautiful. 2. The pasta is delicious. 3. The jacket is big. 4. Gianni is honest. 5. The service is good. 6. The mountain is high.

Your Turn

Now try to fake it 'til you make it by translating these sentences into Italian. Look back at your cognate list to be sure you're using the appropriate article. You can do a lot with one little letter, *è* (is). Again, time is limited.

1. The doctor is elegant.
2. The president is famous.
3. The actor is blond.
4. Violence is stupid.
5. The discussion is important.
6. Art is interesting.

Answers: 1. Il dottore è elegante. 2. Il presidente è famoso. 3. L'attore è biondo. 4. La violenza è stupida. 5. La discussione è importante. 6. L'arte è interessante.

Verbi (Verbs)

Verbs are the action words in a sentence. Italian verbs seem tricky because they have so many forms, or tenses—present, past, future, conditional, and so on. Many

Italian verbs, especially irregular ones, change significantly after they're conjugated. So when you look up a verb in a dictionary, it's important to be able to identify its infinitive form—that's the "to" form of the verb, such as *parlare* (to speak).

The infinitive of a verb is simply a verb in its unconjugated form, as in *to eat* (in Italian, *mangiare*), *to read* (in Italian, *leggere*), or *to finish* (in Italian, *finire*). With few exceptions, there are three kinds of verb endings (also known as verb families) in Italian: *-are*, *-ere*, and *-ire*.

This isn't *difficile* after you understand the basic rules of verbs. Think of it as a mystery and you must get to the *root* of the *problema*. In linguistic terms, the root of a verb tells you everything. I'll show you what I mean.

Study the following words, and identify their roots. Give your best shot at guessing their meaning.

> *studi**are**   to _____
>
> *assist**ere**   to _____
>
> *dorm**ire**   to _____

Answers: to study; to assist; to sleep

Put It All Together

It's time for you to test yourself and see where you stand. How much have you learned so far? Test the *acqua* with the following exercises.

Translation, Please

21

You shouldn't have too much of a *problema* deciphering the meaning of these cognate-rich sentences:

1. *L'Italia fa parte del continente europeo.*

2. *Lo studente studia la matematica e la scienza.*

3. *L'attore è molto famoso nel cinema.*

4. *Il meccanico ripara l'automobile.*

5. *Il cuoco prepara un'insalata e un antipasto.*

6. *Il dottore conversa con il paziente.*

7. *La famiglia desidera un appartamento moderno e grande.*

8. *La turista americana visita il museo e la cattedrale.*

9. *Il presidente presenta il programma.*

10. *Roberto preferisce la musica classica.*

AS A *REGOLA*

The letter *e* is actually a word, meaning "and." The accented letter *è* is also a word, meaning "is."

Answers: 1. Italy is part of the European continent. 2. The student is studying mathematics and science. 3. The actor is very famous in the cinema. 4. The mechanic repairs the automobile. 5. The cook (chef) prepares a salad and an appetizer. 6. The doctor converses with the patient. 7. The family desires a modern and large apartment. 8. The American tourist visits the museum and the cathedral. 9. The president is presenting the program. 10. Robert prefers classical music.

What's Your Take?

Imagine that you've just arrived in Italy, and you want to express your opinions to a fellow traveler. Use what you've learned in this chapter and try to express the following:

1. The pasta is delicious.

2. The restaurant is magnificent.

3. The city is splendid.

4. The perfume is elegant.

5. The conversation is interesting.

6. The doctor is sincere.

7. The student is intelligent.

8. The museum is important.

9. The cathedral is high.

10. The train is fast.

Answers: 1. La pasta è deliziosa. 2. Il ristorante è magnifico. 3. La città è splendida. 4. Il profumo è elegante. 5. La conversazione è interessante. 6. Il dottore è sincero. 7. Lo studente è intelligente. 8. Il museo è importante. 9. La cattedrale è alta. 10. Il treno è rapido.

A Latin Primer

Italian derives from classical Latin, the literary language of ancient *Roma* and the language used principally by the upper classes, the educated, and later, the clergy. From Latin came the Romance languages French, Spanish, Portuguese, Romansch, and Rumanian. Rome (called *Roma* by Italians) resides in the province called *Lazio* (*Lathium* in English), named as such because it was originally inhabited by the *Latini.*

Within the Italian peninsula lived the Estruscans (giving Tuscany its name), Faliscans, Oscans, Umbrians, and a slew of other tribes. The Italic languages of the tribes all contributed to the eventual development of the language we now recognize as Italian. It's not clear when Italian became a distinct language from Latin, because no Italian text has been recorded before the tenth century; however, we do know that by the fourth century, St. Jerome had translated the Bible from Latin into the language spoken by the common people.

As a result, the Italians have developed a flexible and adaptable attitude when it comes to communication. All those hand gestures stereotypical to native Italian speakers probably developed in part because of the Italian character, but ultimately, the art of gesticulation developed out of necessity.

LA BELLA LINGUA

The poet Dante Alighieri (1265–1321) is to the Italian language what Shakespeare is to English. It was his poetry that legitimized the Italian language as we know it today because all his predecessors wrote exclusively in Latin. His most famous work, *La Divina Commedia* (*The Divine Comedy*), is an epic poem depicting an imaginary journey through hell, purgatory, and paradise. That work was actually influenced by another of the world's greatest poets, the Latin poet Virgilio (Publius Vergilius Maro, 70–19 B.C.E.), who served as Dante's guide both literally, as a writer (he was, after all, the author of the great epic adventure story the *Aeneid*), and figuratively, in the story itself.

Il Dialetto: Dialect

Due to Italy's varied terrain and mountain ranges (the Alps and the Appenini), many different dialects developed. A dialect is a variation of a language, usually particular to a region and often quite different from the standard spoken vernacular. Due to its shape and long history of outside influences, Italy has hundreds of different dialects, many of which are still used today. Each dialect has its own colloquialisms and idiomatic expressions.

Other dialects are like different languages. For example, up north in Lombardia, you'll hear a specifically German accent and a softening of the *R*s, a result of the district's rule by Austria at one time. In the Piemonte region, you can hear the French influence. Down south near Napoli, you can hear Spanish and French, whereas in Calabria, certain expressions are quite clearly Greek (*kalimera* means "good day" in modern Greek and is also used in Calabria to say "hello") or Albanian in nature.

Many Italian *immigranti* (immigrants) brought their dialects to the Americas, including the United States, where they were further influenced by factors such as culture, English, and other dialects. This partly explains why the Italian spoken by many immigrants often differs greatly from the Italian presented in this book—and why you may still have difficulty communicating with your *nonna* (grandmother) after having mastered the basics. Italian is spoken around the world today, in such places as Switzerland and many parts of South America such as Venezuela, Argentina, and Brazil, and as far away as Australia.

Tuscan Italian

In modern Italy, the standard language taught in schools and spoken on television is Tuscan Italian, primarily because this was the regional dialect used by the great medieval writers Dante, Petrarca, and Boccaccio, all of whom used what was then only a spoken language. Modern Italian is often quite different from the Italian used during the Middle Ages, but, as when you compare modern English to Old English, there are also striking similarities.

Translating from one language into another is a veritable art form, but translating poetry, with all its symbolism and metaphors, is especially challenging. It's almost impossible to translate word for word. Particularly challenging with Italian is the fact that there was no standard, codified language used back in the middle ages when Dante was writing.

22

Let's check out an excerpt from the first Canto of Dante's *Inferno.* Pay attention to the last word of each line:

> *Nel mezzo del cammin di nostra **vita***
> *mi ritrovai per una selva **oscura**,*
> *che la diritta via era **smarrita**.*
>
> *Ahi quanto a dir qual era è cosa **dura***
> *esta selva selvaggia e aspra e **forte***
> *che nel pensier rinova la **paura**!*

Note the translation:

> In the middle of the journey of our life
> I found myself within a dark wood,
> for the straight way was lost.
>
> Ah how hard a thing it is to say
> What was this forest savage, rough, and rigid,
> the very thought of which renews my fear.

The Italian has a wonderful rhyme quality—the word *vita* working with the word *smarrita*.

LA BELLA LINGUA

If you're a poetry lover, you'll adore the works of Francesco Petrarca (1304–1374). As an early humanist, Petrarca's ideas focused on love and other earthly concerns, making him very popular during the Renaissance. His major works, *I Trionfi* and *Il Canzoniere,* were both written in the vernacular, or in everyday (as opposed to formal) speech. Another of Italy's great poets is Giovanni Boccaccio (1313–1375). A contemporary of Petrarca, he is most known for *Il Decamerone,* a collection of 100 novellas as told through the eyes of 10 young people squatting in an abandoned villa outside Florence. Surprisingly contemporary with a lot of sizzle, Boccaccio's works were banned by the church due to their bawdy content.

The Least You Need to Know

- Italian and English share many common roots.
- Italian and English have many cognates.
- Beware of false friends. You may think you're saying one thing when you're actually saying another.
- Dissecting a word and finding the root can help you decipher its meaning.
- The Italian language derives from Latin and has many dialects reflecting regional and geographical differences.
- Dante, Petrarch, and Boccaccio are three of Italy's most important poets.

Person, Place, or *Cosa:* Nouns and Articles

In This Chapter

* Determining gender
* Working with definite and indefinite articles
* Taking a closer look at nouns
* Producing plurals

In this chapter, we talk about sex. Before you get too excited, keep in mind that we're talking about *gender* as it relates to nouns, adjectives, and articles. You also learn a few handy exclamations you can use all over Italy for any number of circumstances.

The Gender of Nouns

We learned some things about nouns in earlier chapters. Now let's really dig in and examine the building blocks of the Italian language.

Is It a Boy or a Girl?

Unlike in English, all Italian *sostantivi* (nouns), are either *maschile* (masculine) or *femminile* (feminine). The reason why a particular noun is masculine or feminine is not always obvious. Sometimes it's because the noun comes from a foreign language. Many times it's due to a word's etymology. Irregularities often stem from Greek origin as well.

A noun's gender has nothing to do with its user. For example, although mostly worn by men, *la cravatta* (the tie) is a feminine noun while *il vestito* (the dress) is a masculine noun.

Determining a noun's gender is quite easy in Italian. The clue is in the endings. Remember these basic rules of thumb:

- Nouns ending in -*o* such as *il libro* (the book), *il ragazzo* (the boy), and *il gatto* (the cat) are generally masculine.
- Nouns ending in -*a* such as *la casa* (the house), *la scuola* (the school), and *la pizza* (the pizza) are feminine.
- Nouns ending in -*e* can be either masculine or feminine. Examples include the masculine noun *il fiore* (the flower) and the feminine noun *la stazione* (the station).
- The article preceding the noun often indicates its gender.
- Words of foreign origin tend to be masculine.

AS A *REGOLA*

If a noun ends in -*a,* it's generally feminine. If it ends in -*o*, it's masculine. Some words ending in -*e* simply require memorization. Use tricks to help you remember. For example, *la notte* (the night), like *la luna* (the moon), belongs to the feminine ... while *il sole* (the sun), along with *il giorno* (the day) belong to the masculine. Check out the article, too. It always reflects gender. In cases where the gender isn't obvious, such as *l'animale* (the animal), you can also look to the adjective. Study the following example: *La giraffe è un'animale alto.* (The giraffe is a tall animal.) *Alto* describes the noun *animale* (and *not* the word *giraffa;* from this we know the word is masculine. It'll all start to gel soon.

Everyone Must Agree

A noun's gender affects its relationship with other words in a *frase* (phrase), including adjectives (words that describe nouns). If you learn the definite articles along with the nouns, it'll be easier for you to form sentences correctly later.

The key word here is *agreement.* Everyone and everything has to get along. Nouns and adjectives must always agree. For example, if you want to say "the small cat" (*il gatto piccolo*), the adjective small (*piccolo*) must agree in gender with the word *cat* (*il gatto*). We get to adjectives more later. For now, just keep in mind that they follow the same rules.

Understanding Articles

Almost all Italian nouns are preceded by a noun marker. The term *noun marker* refers to an article or adjective that tells you whether a noun is masculine or feminine, singular or plural.

Noun markers expressing "a," "an," or "one" are called indefinite articles, or *articoli indefiniti* or *articoli indeterminativi: uno, una, un'* (the equivalent of "a" or "an" in English). Noun markers indicating "the" are called definite articles, or *articoli determinativi: il, lo, l', la, i, gli, le* (the equivalent of "the" in English).

LA BELLA LINGUA

Italian also uses the definite article in front of a day to describe something habitually done:

We go to church on Sundays.
*Andiamo in chiesa **la** domenica.*

I do yoga on Wednesdays.
*Faccio yoga **il** mercoledì.*

An Indefinite Article

Indefinite articles are simple to use. They're used only before *singular* nouns.

Indefinite Articles

English	Masculine	Feminine
a, an, one	*un, uno*	*una, un'*
	a book	a house
	un libro	*una casa*
	a study	an aspirin
	uno studio	*un'aspirina*

Un is used before singular masculine nouns beginning with either a consonant or a vowel, such as *un palazzo* (a building), *un signore* (a gentleman), and *un animale* (an animal). This does not include those nouns beginning with a *z* or an *s* followed by a consonant.

Uno is used just like the definite article *lo* before singular masculine nouns beginning with *s* followed by a consonant or *z*, such as *uno stadio* (a stadium) and *uno zio* (an uncle). *Uno* is also used with masculine nouns beginning with *gn, ps, pn, x,* and *y.*

Una is used before any feminine noun beginning with a consonant, such as *una farfalla* (a butterfly), *una storia* (a story), and *una strada* (a street).

Un' is the equivalent of *an* in English and is used before all feminine nouns beginning with a vowel, such as *un'italiana* (an Italian woman), *un'amica* (a friend), and *un'opera* (an opera).

The Definite Article

Now for the definite article, *the*. The following table outlines the singular and plural definite articles.

The Definite Article

Gender	Singular	Plural	When It's Used	Examples
Masculine	*il*	*i*	With most masculine nouns	*il nonno → i nonni*
	lo	*gli*	With masculine nouns beginning with *z* and *s* + consonant*	*lo zio → gli zii* *lo studente → gli studenti*
	l'	*gli*	With masculine nouns beginning with a vowel	*l'amico → gli amici*
Feminine	*la*	*le*	With most feminine nouns beginning with a consonant	*la sorella → le sorelle*
	l'	*le*	With feminine nouns beginning with a vowel	*l'amica → le amiche*

This rule also applies to masculine nouns beginning with gn, ps, pn, x, *and* y.

Masculine Definite Articles

Keep in mind the following rules when using masculine definite articles:

Il/i are used in front of masculine nouns beginning with a consonant such as *il ragazzo/i ragazzi* (the boy/the boys) and *il libro/i libri* (the book/the books).

Lo/gli are used in front of masculine nouns that begin with an *s* followed by a consonant such as *lo studente/gli studenti* (the student/the students) or any masculine noun that begins with *z* such as *lo zio/gli zii* (the uncle/the uncles).

L'/gli are used in front of masculine nouns that begin with a vowel such as *l'animale/ gli animali* (the man/the men) and *l'amico/gli amici* (the friend/the friends).

Feminine Definite Articles

Watch how the feminine definite articles work:

La/le are used in front of feminine nouns beginning with a consonant such as *la ragazza/le ragazze* (the girl/the girls) and *la casa/le case* (the house/the houses).

L'/le are used in front of feminine nouns that begin with a vowel such as *l'edicola/le edicole* (the kiosk/the kiosks) and *l'acqua/le acque* (the water/the waters).

Singular Nouns

Some nouns in Italian are easy to mark because they obviously refer to masculine or feminine people.

LA BELLA LINGUA

Ragazzo can mean "boy" or "boyfriend." *Ragazza* can mean "girl" or "girlfriend." *Fidanzato* refers to your fiancé, and *fidanzata* refers to fiancée, and both are also used to describe your special someone.

Note if you were referring to members of your immediate family, you don't have to use an article in front of them. *Questa è mia sorella.* (This is my sister.)

Hermaphrodite Nouns

A few nouns, such as *artista, dentista,* and *musicista,* can be either masculine or feminine. All you have to do is change the identifier—without altering the spelling—to refer to either gender.

The gender of nouns beginning with a vowel, such as *artista,* is difficult to determine (except in context), because the noun marker *l'* is always used. However, if an adjective is being used, it will change to reflect the gender of the subject. Study the following sentences to see how this works:

masculine:	*Il musicista suona.* The musician plays.		either gender:	*L'artista è famoso/a.* The artist is famous.
feminine:	*La musicista suona.* The musician plays.			

Either-Gender Nouns

The following table shows several examples of either-gender nouns. Note the patterns. Most either-gender nouns follow regular rules in the plural. The Italian nouns are given with the corresponding definite article.

Either-Gender Nouns

English	Singular	Plural
artist	*l'artista*	*gli artisti/le artiste*
athlete	*l'atleta*	*gli atleti/le atlete*
dentist	*il/la dentista*	*i dentisti/le dentiste*
director/executive	*il/la dirigente*	*i/le dirigenti*
heir	*l'erede*	*gli/le eredi*
idiot	*l'idiota*	*gli idioti/le idiote*
nomad	*il/la nomade*	*i/le nomadi*
pilot	*il/la pilota*	*i piloti*
relative	*il/la parente*	*i/le parenti*
singer	*il/la cantante*	*i/le cantanti*
tourist	*il/la turista*	*i turisti/le turiste*
youth	*il/la giovane*	*i/le giovani*

Study these, but don't try to memorize them for now. Remember, for every rule there is an exception.

Exceptional Masculine Nouns

As mentioned earlier, some nouns ending in *-e* or *-i* may be masculine or feminine and therefore require you to memorize their gender. See the following table for common masculine nouns ending in *-e*.

One trick is to remember that nouns such as *valore* (value) that end in *-ore* are masculine.

Masculine Nouns Ending in *-e*

English	*Italiano*	English	*Italiano*
animal	*l'animale*	fish	*il pesce*
color	*il colore*	honor	*l'onore*
dog	*il cane*	name/noun	*il nome*

English	*Italiano*	English	*Italiano*
pain	*il dolore*	sun	*il sole*
sea	*il mare*	value	*il valore*
snake	*il serpente*		

Exceptional Feminine Nouns

Although many of the following nouns are considered irregular, it is still possible to see the patterns. Nouns such as *stazione* (station) that end in *-zione* are feminine. Most singular nouns ending in *-i* are also generally feminine. Irregular plurals are indicated.

Feminine Nouns Ending in *-e*

English	*Italiano*	English	*Italiano*
automobile	*l'automobile*	oasis	*l'oasi/le oasi*
conversation	*la conversazione*	ship	*la nave*
crisis	*la crisi/le crisi*	station	*la stazione*
flea	*la pulce*	television	*la televisione*
hare	*la lepre*	thesis	*la tesi/le tesi*
night	*la notte*	translation	*la traduzione*

AS A *REGOLA*

Italian words ending in *-azione* are often the equivalent of English words ending in *-tion,* such as *occupazione* (occupation). These words are always feminine. Most words of foreign origin ending in a consonant are masculine, such as *l'autobus, il bar, il computer, il film,* and *lo sport.*

Rules Are Made to Be Broken

Remember that rules are man-made, designed by linguists to make sense of an otherwise chaotic *universo* (universe). Yet all languages, including Italian, are dynamic. They evolve, expand, and contract over time in accordance with trends, other cultural influences, and values.

Just to drive you *pazzo* (crazy), let's look at a few exceptions to some of the rules you've already learned.

Gender Benders

Sometimes the ending of a noun completely changes that word's significance. The only way to remember these gender benders is to memorize them. In any event, fear not: even if you get the gender wrong, 99 percent of the time the person to you're speaking with will understand what you're saying.

The following table provides a list of words whose meanings change according to the ending.

Disconcerting Genders

Masculine	Feminine	Masculine	Feminine
il ballo (dance)	*la balla* (bundle, bale)	*il muro* (interior wall)	*le mura* (city walls)
il collo (neck)	*la colla* (glue)	*il partito* (political party)	*la partita* (sports match)
il colpo (blow)	*la colpa* (fault, guilt)	*il porto* (port)	*la porta* (door)
il costo (cost)	*la costa* (coast)	*il posto* (place)	*la posta* (mail)
il filo (thread)	*la fila* (line)	*il punto* (detail, dot)	*la punta* (tip)
il foglio (sheet of paper)	*la foglia* (leaf)	*il radio* (radius)	*la radio* (radio, short for *radiografia*)
il legno (wood)	*la legna* (firewood)	*lo scopo* (aim, end)	*la scopa* (broom)
il manico (handle)	*la manica* (sleeve)	*il torto* (mistake)	*la torta* (cake)
il mento (chin)	*la menta* (mint)	*il velo* (veil)	*la vela* (sail, sailing)

Misbehaving Males

Quite a few Italian nouns that end in *-a* are masculine, and many of them derive from Greek. Look at the following table for a few of these misbehaving masculine nouns. Note the prevalence of cognates ending in *-ma*, such as *emblema* (emblem), *poema* (poem), and *problema* (problem). Note the plural forms, too.

Masculine Nouns That End in *-a*

English	Italiano
cinema	*il cinema* (short for *cinematografo*)/*i cinema*
climate	*il clima/i climi*
crossword (puzzle)	*il cruciverba/i cruciverba*
drama	*il dramma/i drammi*
emblem	*l'emblema/gli emblemi*

English	*Italiano*
evangelist	*l'evangelista/gli evangelisti*
gorilla	*il gorilla/i gorilla*
pirate	*il pirata/i pirati*
planet	*il pianeta/i pianeti*
poem	*il poema/i poemi*
pope	*il papa/i papi*
problem	*il problema/i problemi*
program	*il programma/i programmi*

Those Rebellious Females

Feminine nouns can be troublemakers, too. Many of these are also invariable, meaning they don't change in the plural, only the article does. The following table mentions some of them.

Feminine Nouns That End in *-o*

English	*Italiano*
hand	*la mano/le mani*
libido	*la libido/le libido*
motorcycle	*la moto* (short for *motocicletta*)/*le moto*
photo	*la foto* (short for *fotografia*)/*le foto*
radio	*la radio/le radio*
torpedo	*la torpedo/le torpedo*

Sex Changers

Certain words can be made feminine by changing the ending to *-a*, *-essa*, or *-ice*, depending on the gender of the person performing the action.

English	Masculine/Feminine
actor/actress	*l'attore/l'attrice*
boss	*il padrone/la padrona*
director/manager	*il direttore/la direttrice*
doctor	*il dottore/la dottoressa*
lawyer	*l'avvocato/l'avvocatessa*
painter	*il pittore/la pittrice*

continues

English	Masculine/Feminine
poet	*il poeta/la poetessa*
president	*il presidente/la presidentessa*
professor	*il professore/la professoressa*
student	*lo studente/la studentessa*
teacher	*il maestro/la maestra*
waiter/waitress	*il cameriere/la cameriera**

**la cameriera *also refers to a maid.*

In modern usage, the feminine endings of professionals such as actors, doctors, professors, and lawyers are used with less frequency than they used to be.

The *Mela* Doesn't Fall Far …

Fruit is almost always referred to in the feminine as *la frutta*, but a piece of fruit is referred to as *un frutto*. When a specific fruit is made masculine, it becomes the fruit tree. (There's a certain poetry to this, in my opinion.)

> *l'arancia* (the orange) → *l'arancio* (the orange tree)
>
> *la ciliegia* (the cherry) → *il ciliegio* (the cherry tree)
>
> *la mela* (the apple) → *il melo* (the apple tree)
>
> *la pera* (the pear) → *il pero* (the pear tree)

Practice Makes *Perfetto*

Determine the gender of the following by placing the appropriate definite article in front of them. You might have to consult a dictionary for a couple. Don't forget to look at the endings!

1. ___ *casa* (house)
2. ___ *cane* (dog)
3. ___ *albero* (tree)
4. ___ *piatto* (plate)
5. ___ *lezione* (lesson)
6. ___ *estate* (summer)
7. ___ *chiesa* (church)
8. ___ *straniero* (foreigner)
9. ___ *cattedrale* (cathedral)
10. ___ *pianeta* (planet)

Answers: 1. la 2. il 3. l' 4. il 5. la 6. l' 7. la 8. lo 9. la 10. il

More Is More: Compound Nouns

Compound nouns are comprised of two or more words. Even though the majority of Italian compound nouns are masculine, they're often made up of both masculine and feminine nouns. These new combinations take on new meaning. For example, the word *il girasole* (the sunflower) is comprised of two words: *gira* (turn) + *sole* (sun). If you've ever been to Tuscany when the sunflowers are at the height of their splendor, it's amazing to see thousands of flowers staring at the sun. In Italian, the flower *la belladonna* (deadly nightshade) breaks down to *bella* (beautiful) + *donna* (woman). (Interesting undertone, wouldn't you agree?)

Masculine Compound Nouns

The following table offers some of the more frequently used masculine compound nouns.

Masculine Compound Nouns

English	*Italiano*
ashtray	*il portacenere* (literally, carry ash)
bouncer	*il buttafuori* (literally, throw out)
capital	*il capoluogo*
closet/wardrobe	*il guardaroba* (literally, watch stuff)
colander	*lo scolapasta* (literally, strain pasta)
consent	*il benestare*
crossword	*il cruciverba*
evergreen	*il sempreverde*
gentleman	*il gentiluomo*
masterpiece	*il capolavoro*
new year	*il capodanno*
passport	*il passaporto*
skyscraper	*il grattacielo*
snowdrop	*il bucaneve*
stamp	*il francobollo*
subway	*il sottopassaggio* (literally, under passage)
sunflower	*il girasole* (literally, turn sun)
swordfish	*il pescespada*
towel	*l'asciugamano* (literally, dry hand)

Feminine Compound Nouns

The following table shows feminine compound nouns.

Feminine Compound Nouns

English	Italiano
banknote	*la banconota*
deadly nightshade	*la belladonna* (literally, beautiful woman)
earthenwear	*la terracotta* (literally, cooked earth)
etching	*l'acquaforte* (literally, strong water)
mainland	*la terraferma* (literally, firm earth)
mother of pearl	*la madreperla*
parchment	*la cartapecora* (literally, sheep paper)
railway	*la ferrovia* (literally, iron way)
safe	*la cassaforte*

Making Plurals

In English, it's relatively easy to talk about more than one thing. Usually, you just add an *-s* to the word, although there are many plurals that confuse people learning English as a second language. How many "childs" do you have, or rather, children?

Fortunately, forming plural nouns in Italian is as easy as floating in a gondola. The following table illustrates how the ending should change in the plural. The ending must always reflect the gender of a word.

Plural Endings

Singular	Plural	Singular	Plural
-o	*-i*	*ragazzo*	*ragazzi*
-a	*-e*	*donna*	*donne*
-ca	*-che*	*amica*	*amiche*
-e	*-i*	*cane*	*cani*

AS A REGOLA

Family names do not change endings in the plural. Use the article to indicate plurality. For example, if you were talking about the Leonardo family, you would say *i Leonardo* (the Leonardos). Nouns ending in a consonant (such as many words of foreign origin) or accented on the last vowel do not change form in the plural. Only the article changes. For example, *l'autobus* → *gli autobus, il caffè* → *i caffè, la città* → *le città*, and *l'università* → *le università*.

Exceptional Plurals

In certain cases, the plurals of certain nouns and adjectives follow different rules.

Singular feminine nouns and adjectives ending in *-ca* or *-ga* form the plural by changing the endings to *-che* or *-ghe:*

> *amica* → *amiche*
>
> *bianca* → *bianche*
>
> *diga* → *dighe*

Singular feminine nouns ending in *-cia* and *-gia* form the plural with …

> *cie/gie* (if a vowel precedes the singular ending):
>
>> *camicia* → *camicie*
>>
>> *valigia* → *valigie*
>
> *ce/ge* (if a consonant precedes the singular ending):
>
>> *arancia* → *arance*
>>
>> *pioggia* → *piogge*

Most singular masculine nouns and adjectives ending in *-co* and *-go* form the plural by replacing the singular endings with *-chi* and *-ghi:*

> *pacco* → *pacchi*
>
> *bianco* → *bianchi*
>
> *lago* → *laghi*
>
> *largo* → *larghi*

Exceptional Plural Spellings

Look at what happens to these nouns when they're made plural.

Exceptional Singular and Plural Nouns

English	Italiano
the enemy/the enemies	*il nemico/i nemici*
the friend/the friends	*l'amico/gli amici m.*
the friend/the friends	*l'amica/le amiche f.*
the needle/the needles	*l'ago/gli aghi*
the nun/the nuns	*la monaca/le monache*
the place/the places	*il luogo/i luoghi*

You already know one plural—*spaghetti!* Because you could never eat one *spaghetto* (which isn't a real word), you must always use it in the plural. Let's try a sentence: *In Italia, mangiano gli spaghetti al pomodoro.*

La Pratica

Try making the following nouns plural using the rules you just learned. I've done the first one for you.

1. *il libro* (the book) ___*i libri*___ (the books)

2. *il gatto* (the cat) _____ (the cats)

3. *la ragazza* (the girl) _____ (the girls)

4. *la stazione* (the station) _____ (the stations)

5. *l'amico* (the friend, *m.*) _____ (the friends)

6. *l'amica* (the friend, *f.*) _____ (the friends)

Answers: 2. i gatti 3. le ragazze 4. le stazioni 5. gli amici 6. le amiche

Irregular Plural Nouns

Some masculine nouns become feminine when pluralized. As you can see in the following table, many parts of the body are included, again stemming from the fact that many are of Greek origin.

Irregular Plural Nouns

English	*Italiano*	English	*Italiano*
arm/arms	*il braccio/le braccia*	knee/knees	*il ginocchio/le ginocchia*
bone/bones	*l'osso/le ossa/gli ossi**	lash/lashes	*il ciglio/le ciglia*
egg/eggs	*l'uovo/le uova*	lip/lips	*il labbro/le labbra*
finger/fingers	*il dito/le dita*	mile/miles	*il miglio/le miglia*
hand/hands	*la mano/le mani*	pair/pairs	*il paio/le paia*

*Le ossa *refers to human bones;* gli ossi *refers to animal bones, including the ones you throw to the dog.*

Defective Nouns

Here, I'm not talking about someone who defects from their native country. *Defective nouns* (called *i nomi difettivi*) refer to certain Italian nouns that are used in either the singular, like air, or the plural, such as the word *pants*, but never both.

Things that can't be counted, concepts, days of the week, months, elements, and nouns related to sustenance all fall into the always singular category. For example, you either have courage or you don't. There's no plural. Words like *blood (il sangue)* are always used in the singular.

Always Singular, Never Married

Some nouns, like people, are best off in the singular. Let's look at some additional defective nouns:

abstract nouns:	*il coraggio* (courage), *l'intelligenza* (intelligence), *l'orgolio* (pride), *la pietà* (compassion), etc.
diseases:	*il colera* (cholera), *l'influenza* (flu), *il morbillo* (measles)
elements:	*l'argento* (silver), *l'aria* (air), *il bronzo* (bronze), *il ferro* (iron), *l'oro* (gold), etc.
nourishment:	*la fame* (hunger), *il grano* (grain), *il latte* (milk), *il miele* (honey), *il pane* (bread), *il sale* (salt), *la sete* (thirst), etc.

Invariable Nouns

Invariable nouns (*i nomi invariabili*) have one form for both the singular and the plural. This group includes words of foreign origin, monosyllabic nouns, words that end with an accent, and nouns that end in *–i*. To indicate the plural, just change the noun marker, as shown in the following table.

Italian Invariable Nouns

English	Italiano	English	Italiano
the age/the ages	*l'età/le età*	the gorilla/the gorillas	*il gorilla/i gorilla*
the analysis/the analyses	*l'analisi/le analisi*	the king/the kings	*il re/i re*
the city/the cities	*la città/le città*	the ski/the skiis	*lo sci/gli sci*
the coffee/the coffees	*il caffé/i caffé*	the sport/the sports	*lo sport/gli sport*
the crisis/the crises	*la crisi/le crisi*	the university/the universities	*l'università/le università*

Always Plural, Never Alone

Some defective nouns are only used in the plural, such as the pair words *scissors*, *pants*, and *eyeglasses*.

Nouns That Are Always Plural

English	Italiano	English	Italiano
the asparagus	*gli asparagi*	the scissors	*le forbici*
the eyeglasses	*gli occhiali*	the stockings	*i calzini*
the hair (on your head)	*i capelli*	the tweezers	*le pinzette*
the pants	*i pantaloni*	the underwear	*le mutande*
the reins	*le redini*		

Practice Those Plurals

Make the following nouns plural using the appropriate articles:

1. *la cartolina* (postcard)
2. *la rivista* (magazine)
3. *l'animale* (animal)
4. *il libro* (book)
5. *il cane* (dog)
6. *lo studente* (the student)

Answers: 1. le cartoline 2. le riviste 3. gli animali 4. i libri 5. i cani 6. gli studenti

The Least You Need to Know

- Certain endings are almost always masculine (*-o, -i,* consonants) or feminine (*-a, -e*).
- Some nouns can be changed from masculine to feminine by adding an appropriate ending.
- Always look at the article to determine the gender and plurality of a noun.
- Invariable nouns never change form, whether they are used in the singular or the plural. Only the noun marker changes.
- Defective nouns are used in either the singular, or the plural, but never both.
- Plural nouns end in either *-i* or *-e*.

Che Bella Famiglia: Adjectives and Adverbs

In This Chapter

- Describing things: adjectives
- Expressing possession using *di*
- Using possessive adjectives
- Using the demonstratives this/these, that/those
- Forming and using adverbs
- Introducing your *famiglia*

You've learned the nouns and their noun markers, and now you're ready to add some *colore*. In this chapter, you learn all about adjectives, adverbs, and how to express possession using your family members as practice.

Alto, Bruno e Bello: Adjectives

What a bland world it would be without descriptive adjectives. Everything would be all *azione* (action) and no *illustrazione* (illustration). If *i verbi* (verbs) are the skeleton of a language and nouns are the flesh, adjectives are the details of color and nuances of light. They're *bianco* (white) and *rosso* (as in *vino*), or *bello* (beautiful) or *brutto* (ugly), *grande* (big) or *piccolo* (small), and everything in between.

Using Adjectives

The endings used for adjectives are similar to noun endings. Keep in mind the following rules regarding adjectives:

- If describing a masculine noun, simply leave the adjective as is. (Adjectives default to the masculine—it goes way back before women's lib.)

- Similar to Spanish and French, Italian adjectives must reflect the gender and number of the noun they describe.
- Many adjectives that end in -*e*, such as *intelligente, giovane, grande, verde, triste,* and *cortese,* are used to describe both masculine and feminine nouns. The plural endings of these adjectives follow the same rules as nouns ending in -*e* and change to -*i.*
- Colors reflect the gender and number of the noun they describe, *except* when using invariables (words that don't change). Examples include *marrone* (brown), *rosa* (pink), and *viola* (purple).

Placement of Adjectives

The placement of an adjective changes depending on the situation and the adjective's relationship to other words in a sentence. Very often, the adjective's placement has to do with emphasis.

Most Italian adjectives are generally placed *after* the noun:

> *Il **pesce grosso** mangia il piccolo.*
> *Literally:* The **fish big** eats the small one.

> *Laura è una **ragazza generosa**.*
> *Literally:* Laura is a **girl generous**.

Certain Italian adjectives can be placed *before* the noun. Some of these include:

bello (beautiful)	*grande* (large; great)
bravo (good, able)	*lungo* (long)
brutto (ugly)	*nuovo* (new)
buono (good)	*piccolo* (small, little)
caro (dear)	*stesso* (same)
cattivo (bad)	*vecchio* (old)
giovane (young)	*vero* (true)

> *È un **lungo viaggio**.*
> It's a **long trip**.

> *Tu sei una **cara amica**.*
> You are a **dear friend**.

> *Gail è una **bella donna**.*
> Gail is a **beautiful woman**.

Adjectives always follow the noun when modified by an adverb such as *molto* (very):

> *Gail è una donna **molto bella**.*
> *Literally:* Gail is a woman **very beautiful**.

Note that in some cases, the placement of an adjective can change the meaning:

> *un **povero** uomo* (a poor man—refers to a man who evokes sympathy)

> *un uomo **povero*** (a man poor—refers to a man without money)

> *un **vecchio** amico* (an old friend—refers to someone you've known for a long time)

> *un amico **vecchio*** (a friend old—refers to a friend who is old, emphasis on "old")

> **LA BELLA LINGUA**
>
> To indicate that you're in a good or bad mood, use the expressions *Sono di buon umore* (I am in a good mood) and *Sono di cattivo umore* (I am in a bad mood).

Modifying Those Adjective Endings

You've already seen how many Italian adjectives are cognates to English. Look at the endings in the following table, and compare them to the noun endings you just learned.

Adjective Endings

Ending	Example
-o → -i	*famoso → famosi*
-a → -e	*curiosa → curiose*
-ca → -che	*magnifica → magnifiche*
-e → -i	*intelligente → intelligenti*

Character Analysis

Using the adjectives you just learned, try describing the people around you. (You'll find a comprehensive list of family members at the end of this chapter.)

> *Example: Il mio fidanzato è generoso, intelligente, sincero e ricco.*
> *Answer:* My fiancé is generous, intelligent, sincere, and rich.

1. Your significant other (or your fiancé) _____.

2. Your mother _____.

3. Your brother, sister, or cousin _____.

4. Your cat, dog, or other domestic companion _____.

5. Your best friend _____.

6. Your boss _____.

Take the *Brutto* with the *Bello*

You want to describe your special someone, whether your BFF, your wonderful spouse, your children, your new squeeze, your ex, your future ex, your neighbor, or your cat. Are they kind or cruel, good or bad, generous or stingy? The list of adjectives and their antonyms in the following table will add to your array of options.

At the end of the adjectives provided, you will see */a* to remind you that the word must reflect the gender of the subject. The pronunciation provided does not show this difference.

Emotions and Characteristics

English	*Italiano*	Pronunciation	English	*Italiano*	Pronunciation
ambitious	*ambizioso/a*	*ahm-bee-zee-**oh**-zoh*	lazy	*pigro/a*	**pee**-*groh*
beautiful	*bello/a*	**behl**-*loh*	ugly	*brutto/a*	**broot**-*toh*
blond	*biondo/a*	*bee-**ohn**-doh*	brunette	*bruno/a*	**broo**-*noh*
calm	*calmo/a*	**kahl**-*moh*	nervous	*nervoso/a*	*ner-**voh**-zoh*
clever/sly	*furbo/a*	**foor**-*boh*	slow/dull	*lento/a*	**len**-*toh*
courageous	*coraggioso/a*	*koh-rahj-**joh**-zoh*	coward	*codardo/a*	*koh-**dahr**-doh*
courteous	*cortese*	*kor-**teh**-zeh*	discourteous	*scortese*	*skor-**teh**-zeh*
cute/pretty	*carino/a*	*kah-**ree**-noh*	unattractive	*bruttino/a*	*broot-**tee**-noh*

English	*Italiano*	Pronunciation	English	*Italiano*	Pronunciation
fat	*grasso/a*	**grahs**-soh	skinny	*magro/a*	**mah**-groh
funny	*buffo/a*	**boof**-foh	boring	*noioso/a*	noy-**oh**-zoh
generous	*generoso/a*	jeh-neh-**roh**-zoh	stingy	*tirchio/a*	**teer**-kee-yoh
good	*bravo/a*	**brah**-voh	evil	*cattivo/a*	kaht-**tee**-voh
happy	*allegro/a*	ahl-**leh**-groh	sad	*triste*	**trees**-teh
healthy	*sano/a*	**sah**-noh	sick	*malato/a*	mah-**lah**-toh
honest	*onesto/a*	oh-**nes**-toh	dishonest	*disonesto/a*	dee-soh-**nes**-toh
intelligent	*intelligente*	een-tel-lee-**jen**-teh	stupid	*stupido/a*	**stoo**-pee-doh
kind/polite	*gentile*	jen-**tee**-leh	impolite	*scortese*	skor-**teh**-zeh
loyal	*fedele*	feh-**deh**-leh	unfaithful	*infedele*	een-feh-**deh**-leh
lucky	*fortunato/a*	for-too-**nah**-toh	unlucky	*sfortunato/a*	sfor-too-**nah**-toh
married	*sposato/a*	spoh-**zah**-toh	divorced	*divorziato/a*	dee-vor-zee-**ah**-toh
nice	*simpatico/a*	seem-**pah**-tee-koh	disagreeab le	*antipatico/a*	ahn-tee-**pah**-tee-koh
organized	*organizzato/a*	or-gah-neez-**tsah**-toh	unorganized	*disorganizzato/a*	dee-sor-gah-nee-**zah**-toh
perfect	*perfetto/a*	per-**feht**-toh	imperfect	*imperfetto/a*	eem-per-**feht**-toh
proud	*fiero/a*	fee-**yeh**-roh	to be ashamed	*vergognoso/a*	ver-goh-**nyoh**-zoh
romantic	*romantico/a*	roh-**mahn**-tee-koh	practical	*pratico/a*	**prah**-tee-koh
sensitive	*sensibile*	sen-**see**-bee-leh	insensitive	*insensibile*	een-sen-**see**-bee-leh
sincere	*sincero/a*	seen-**cheh**-roh	insincere	*bugiardo/a*	boo-**jar**-doh
strong	*forte*	**for**-teh	weak	*debole*	**deh**-boh-leh
tall	*alto/a*	**ahl**-toh	short	*basso/a*	**bahs**-soh
young	*giovane*	**jyoh**-vah-neh	old	*vecchio/a*	**veh**-kee-yoh
wise	*saggio/a*	**sahj**-joh	uncultured	*incolto/a*	een-**kol**-toh

Antonimi (Antonyms)

Learning things in batches helps your brain retain more information. Use the following list of adjectives and their opposites to help you develop the basic vocabulary you'll need to talk about anything. It's all right here!

Adjectives and Their Antonyms

Adjective	*Italiano*	Pronunciation	Antonym	*Italiano*	Pronunciation
big	*grande*	**gran**-deh	small	*piccolo/a*	**pee**-koh-loh
clean	*pulito/a*	poo-**lee**-toh	dirty	*sporco/a*	**spor**-koh
complete	*completo/a*	kom-**pleh**-toh	incomplete	*incompleto/a*	een-kohm-**pleh**-toh
expensive	*caro/a*	**kah**-roh	inexpensive	*economico/a*	eh-koh-**noh**-mee-koh
first	*primo/a*	**pree**-moh	last	*ultimo/a*	**ool**-tee-moh
full	*pieno/a*	pee-**yeh**-noh	empty	*vuoto/a*	**vwoh**-toh
good	*buono/a*	**bwoh**-noh	bad	*cattivo/a*	kaht-**tee**-voh
hard	*duro/a*	**doo**-roh	soft	*morbido/a*	**mor**-bee-doh
heavy	*pesante*	peh-**zahn**-tay	light	*leggero/a*	lehj-**jeh**-roh
hot	*caldo/a*	**kahl**-doh	cold	*freddo/a*	**fred**-doh
long	*lungo/a*	**loon**-goh	short	corto/a	**kor**-toh
new	*nuovo/a*	**nwoh**-voh	used	*usato/a*	oo-**zah**-toh
next	*prossimo/a*	**prohs**-see-moh	last	*ultimo/a*	**ool**-tee-moh
normal	*normale*	nor-**mah**-leh	strange	*strano/a*	**strah**-noh
open	*aperto/a*	ah-**per**-toh	closed	*chiuso/a*	kee-yoo-**soh**
perfect	*perfetto/a*	per-**feht**-toh	imperfect	*imperfetto/a*	eem-per-**feh**-toh
pleasing	*piacevole*	pee-ah-**chay**-voh-leh	displeasing	*spiacevole*	spee-ah-**chay**-voh-leh
real	*vero/a*	**veh**-roh	fake	*finto/a*	**feen**-toh
safe/sure	*sicuro/a*	see-**koo**-roh	dangerous	*pericoloso/a*	peh-ree-koh-**loh**-zoh
strong	*forte*	**for**-teh	weak	*debole*	**deh**-boh-leh
true	*vero/a*	**veh**-roh	false	*falso/a*	**fahl**-zoh

Buono Is Good

Similar to the rules followed by the indefinite articles, the adjective *buono* (good) changes form in the singular when preceding a noun. (However, when following the verb *essere* or the noun it modifies, it uses the regular forms *buono* and *buona* in the singular.) The plural form of this adjective is regular.

Consult the following table for the different forms. Notice how—in this case—*buono* usually comes before the noun, like in English.

Buono

Gender	Singular	Plural	When It Is Used
Masculine	*il buono studente*	*i buoni studenti*	Before masculine nouns beginning with *s* + consonant or *z*
	il buon libro	*i buoni libri*	Before all other masculine nouns (both consonants and vowels)
	il buon amico	*i buoni amici*	
Feminine	*la buona ragazza*	*le buone ragazze*	Before feminine nouns beginning with a consonant
	la buon'amica	*le buone amiche*	Before feminine nouns beginning with a vowel

Colors (*I Colori*)

23

Remember the first line of the song "*Volare*": "Nel blu, dipinto di blu"? Now you can begin to decipher its meaning with the following colors. Remember that colors are adjectives and must agree with the nouns they describe, whether masculine or feminine, singular or plural—that is, unless they're invariable, such as *blu*, *rosa*, and *viola*. In these cases, they don't change, regardless of the noun.

Colori

English	*Italiano*	Pronunciation
beige	*beige*	*behj*
black	*nero*	**neh**-*roh*
blue	*blu*	*bloo*
brown	*marrone*	*mar*-**roh**-*neh*
gold	*oro*	**or**-*oh*
gray	*grigio*	**gree**-*joh*
green	*verde*	**ver**-*deh*
orange	*arancione*	*ah-ran*-**choh**-*neh*
pink	*rosa*	**roh**-*zah*
purple	*viola*	*vee*-**oh**-*lah*
red	*rosso*	**rohs**-*soh*
silver	*argento*	*ar*-**jen**-*toh*
white	*bianco*	*bee*-**ahn**-*koh*
yellow	*giallo*	**jahl**-*loh*

The black shoes are practical.
Le scarpe nere sono pratiche.

The pink shoes are pretty.
Le scarpe rosa sono carine.

LA BELLA LINGUA

To describe any color as light, simply add the adjective *chiaro* to the color to form a compound adjective, as in *rosso chiaro* (light red). To describe any color as dark, add the word *scuro,* as in *rosso scuro* (dark red).

One Yellow Banana, Please

Fill in the blank with the adjective modified by the subject and then translate the sentences.

> *Example: La banana è _____. (yellow)*
> *Answer: La banana è gialla.*

1. *La casa _____ (white) è _____ (clean).*

2. *Il Colosseo è molto _____ (old).*

3. *Le montagne in Svizzera sono _____ (high).*

4. *Il negozio è _____ (closed) la domenica.*

5. *Quest'albergo è _____ (inexpensive).*

6. *La lingua _____ (Italian) non è _____ (easy).*

Answers: 1. bianca; pulita/The white house is clean. 2. vecchio/The Colosseum is very old. 3. alte/The mountains in Switzerland are high. 4. chiuso/The store is closed on Sundays. 5. economico/This hotel is inexpensive. 6. italiana; facile/The Italian language is not easy.

Making Alterations

Everyone has a birthname, and some people also have a nickname, usually an adaptation of the birthname. In lieu of adjectives, Italian utilizes special suffixes called alterations (called *alterazioni* in Italian) that allow the speaker to attach subtle meaning to a word. This is especially useful when trying to distinguish family members who have the same name—a common event in Italy, where you can easily find three Francos, two Marias, and a couple of Paolos at any major function.

By simply adding a suffix, it's easy to alter a noun to offer a different hue to the Italian word. *Michele* (Michael) becomes *Michelino* (Mikey), or *Michelone* (Big Mike), *Concetta* becomes *Concettina,* and so on.

These name-changers can be broken down into categories:

- Diminutives (*diminutivi*) are used to devalue, diminish something, make smaller.

- Augmentatives (*accrescitivi*) are used to increase, augment the value of something, or make bigger.

- Pejoratives (*dispregiativi*) are used to put down someone or to demean something.

- Terms of endearment (*vezzeggiativi*) are used to form pet names and sweet talk.

Usage depends on linguistic preferences. Watch how the suffix attached to the word *libro* (book) changes the meaning. You can hear how the *sound* of the word infers meaning:

the little book	the big book	the naughty book
il libretto	*il librone*	*il libraccio*

Remember that—like an adjective—the gender and number of the suffix must agree with the noun or adjective it modfies.

There are far more alterations than listed in the following table, but these ought to get you started. When possible, I've used the same noun to show how its meaning changes depending on the ending.

Diminutivi		
-ello/a	*il bambino* (the child)	*il bambinello* (the little child)
-etto/a	*il bacio* (the kiss)	*il bacietto* (the little kiss)
-ino/a	*il ragazzo* (the boy)	*il ragazzino* (the little boy)
Accrescitivi		
-accione	*l'uomo* (the man)	*l'omaccione* (the big guy)
-one	*la minestra* (the soup)	*la minestrona* (the big soup)
Dispregiativi		
-accio/a	*la roba* (the stuff)	*la robaccia* (the rubbish)
-astro/a	*la sorella* (the sister)	*la sorellastra* (the step-sister)
-ucolo/a	*l'uomo* (the man)	*l'omucolo* (the irrelevant man)
Vezzeggiativi		
-acchiotto/a	*l'orso* (the bear)	*l'orsacchiotto* (the stuffed bear)
-olo/a	*il figlio* (the son)	*il figliolo* (the special son)
-otto/a	*il cucciolo* (the puppy)	*il cucciolotto* (the puppy-wuppy)
-uccio/a	*il cavallo* (the horse)	*il cavalluccio* (the horsey)

At this stage, you don't need to memorize them, but it's good to know how they affect the language, given most alterations won't show up in a dictionary.

Are You Possessed?

You will always be somebody's somebody: your mother's child, your brother's sister, your wife's husband, your dog's owner. In English, we use *'s* or *s'* to show possession. In Italian, there are two ways of showing possession.

You can show possession by using the preposition *di* (of/from):

> Silvia is the daughter of Peppe.
> *Silvia è la figlia di Peppe.*

Or you can show possession by using a possessive adjective, as in the following familiar *espressioni:*

> My God!   Mother of mine!
> *Dio mio!*   *Mamma mia!*

Possessives

Italian possessive adjectives convey the idea of my, your, his, her, and so on. Italian has both possessive adjectives and possessive pronouns. The difference is that in Italian, possessive adjectives are ... well, *adjectives*, so like the rest of the descriptives, they must always agree in gender and number with the referenced noun.

ATTENZIONE!

Compare the English possessives to their Italian counterparts in these examples. Contrary to English usage, Italian forms do not distinguish between *his* and *her*. Pay special attention to how *suo* and *sua* are used:

Gino loves **his** mother and **his** father.   Beatrice loves **her** mother and **her**
*Gino ama **sua** madre e **suo** padre.*   father.
                                                  *Beatrice ama **sua** madre e **suo** padre.*

To indicate "mine" just use the possessive adjective without the article, as in *Il cane è mio* (The dog is mine).

Italian makes use of several possessive adjectives. Remember that the Italian possessive adjective is almost always preceded by the definite article. Listen to Michele on the CD to hear how these should be pronounced.

Possessive Adjectives

Possessive	Singular Masculine	Feminine	Plural Masculine	Feminine
my	*il mio*	*la mia*	*i miei*	*le mie*
your	*il tuo*	*la tua*	*i tuoi*	*le tue*
his/her/its (Your)*	*il suo (il Suo)*	*la sua (la Sua)*	*i suoi (i Suoi)*	*le sue (le Sue)*
our	*il nostro*	*la nostra*	*i nostri*	*le nostre*
your	*il vostro*	*la vostra*	*i vostri*	*le vostre*
their	*il loro*	*la loro*	*i loro*	*le loro*

*To distinguish the polite "your" from his/her/its, Italian capitalizes the possessive pronoun. Naturally, you cannot hear this in speech.

A Sense of Belonging

Determine the appropriate possessive adjective using the previous list for the following nouns.

> *Example:* her house
> *Answer: la sua casa*

1. his house _____

2. my school _____

3. her books _____

4. his books _____

5. your (familiar) friend Mario _____

6. their house _____

Answers: 1. la sua casa 2. la mia scuola 3. i suoi libri 4. i suoi libri 5. il tuo amico Mario 6. la loro casa

AS A *REGOLA*

Mamma mia! Another rule?! When speaking of immediate family members, no article is required before the possessive adjective: *Mio fratello abita a Roma.* (My brother lives in Rome.)

Using *Di* to Show Possession

The simplest way to express possession is to use the preposition *di* (of). Look at the following example to see how this works:

This is the house of Mario.   Sabine is the daughter of Gabriella.
Questa è la casa di Mario   *Sabine è la figlia di Gabriella.*

> **AS A REGOLA**
>
> The terms *il signore, la signora,* and *la signorina* are often used in place of the *l'uomo* (the man), *la donna* (the woman), and *la ragazza* (the girl/young woman).

Forming Contractions with *Di*

Notice how the endings of the contractions correspond to the articles, and pay attention to how *di* changes when forming a contraction. All the following examples correspond in translation to *of the.*

Contractions with *Di*

Singular	Plural
di + il = del	*di + i = dei*
di + lo = dello	*di + gli = degli*
di + l' = dell'	*di + le = delle*
di + la = della	

Frasi using contractions with *di* include …

Here [are] the car keys. (Here are the keys of the car.)
*Ecco [sono] le chiavi **della** macchina.*

That is the president's son. (That is the son of the president.)
*Quello è il figlio **del** presidente.*

If you can't remember your possessive adjectives yet, try simply using *di* followed by the name of the possessor to indicate the subject:

The book of Rosetta.   The car of Antonio.
*Il libro **di** Rosetta.*   *La macchina **di** Antonio.*

Making Introductions Using Demonstratives

If you want to say, "I want a little of *this* and a little of *that*," you'll have to use a demonstrative. In Italian, these are referred to as demonstrative adjectives and must change according to the noun being described.

The Demonstratives This and These

Gender	This	These
Masculine	*questo libro* (this book)	*questi libri* (these books)
	quest'anno* (this year)	*questi anni* (these years)
Feminine	*questa penna* (this pen)	*queste penne* (these pens)
	quest'idea* (this idea)	*queste idee* (these ideas)

*All singular nouns beginning with a vowel take quest'.

Questo Is My Brother ...

In most cases, you must include the article before the noun when using a possessive. Even if a friend may feel just like family, she should be introduced using the article. For *example:*

> This is my friend Anna.
> **Questa** *è* **la mia** *amica Anna.*

The exception exists when referring to singular nouns denoting family members (*madre, padre, sorella, fratello* ..., and not *mamma, babbo,* ...), where there's no need to put an article in front of the person being possessed.

> This is my mother.   This is my brother.
> **Questa** *è* **mia** *madre.*   **Questo** *è* **mio** *fratello.*

AS A *REGOLA*

Remember, in both nouns and adjectives, the singular ending *-e* turns to *-i* in the plural: *lo studente intelligente* (the intelligent student) becomes *gli studenti intelligenti* (the intelligent students).

Bello and *Quello*

The adjectives *bello* (beautiful, handsome, nice, good, fine) and *quello* (that/those) follow the same rules, as you can see in the following table. Both have forms similar to those of the definite article.

Bello and *Quello*

Gender	Singular	Plural	When It Is Used
Masculine	*bello/quello*	*begli/quegli*	Before *s* + consonant or *z*
	bell'/quell'	*begli/quegli*	Before vowels
	bel/quel	*bei/quei*	Before consonants
Feminine	*bella/quella*	*belle/quelle*	Before all consonants
	bell'/quell'	*belle/quelle*	Before vowels

Generally speaking, *bello* and *quello* come before the noun, like in English. *Bello* is used to describe anything wonderful: a good meal, a sunset, a beautiful person. If you want to sound like an Italian, use this *espressione* the next time you are moved by something you find extraordinary:

How beautiful!   What beautiful children!
Che bello!   *Che **bei** bambini!*

Those beautiful women are also nice.
***Quelle belle** donne sono anche simpatiche.*

When the adjective *bello* follows the verb *essere*, it retains its full form. (However, it must still reflect the gender and number of the noun it describes.)

That hotel is beautiful.   That girl is beautiful.
*Quell'albergo è **bello**.*   *Quella ragazza è **bella**.*

Make the Connection

Fill in the appropriate forms of the definite article and its corresponding forms of *quello*, and translate.

Definite Article	Quello
1. _____ *libro*	_____ *libro*
2. _____ *libri*	_____ *libri*
3. _____ *penna*	_____ *penna*

Definite Article	Quello
4. _____ *penne*	_____ *penne*
5. _____ *articolo*	_____ *articolo*
6. _____ *articoli*	_____ *articoli*
7. _____ *studente*	_____ *studente*
8. _____ *studenti*	_____ *studenti*

Answers: 1. il/quel 2. i/quei 3. la/quella 4. le/quelle 5. l'/quell' 6. gli/quegli 7. lo/quello 8. gli/ quegli

How Are You? Adverbs

How are you? I hope you're *well* and everything is *fine*.

Well and *fine*, as used here, are adverbs. Adverbs describe verbs or adjectives and indicate *how* you do something, such as, "She plays the piano *beautifully*," or "You are *sincerely* the *most* beautiful person I've ever met." In addition to irregular adverbs, which are covered next and need to be memorized, you can also create an adverb from an adjective.

> **LA BELLA LINGUA**
>
> Every time you use the word *non* in a sentence, you are using an adverb. I'll bet you never (also an adverb) knew the words *no* and *sì* (yes) are both adverbs. Other commonly used irregular adverbs include better (*meglio*), by no means (*nemmeno*), certainly (*certamente*), exactly (*appunto*), maybe (*forse*), never (*mai*), not even (*neanche*), and really (*davvero*).

Forming Adverbs from Adjectives

Many English adverbs end in -*ly*. In Italian, you can form several adverbs by adding -*mente* to the end of the feminine form of the adjective:

seria → *seria***mente**
serious → serious**ly**

profonda → *profonda***mente**
profound → profound**ly**

chiara → *chiara***mente**
clear → clear**ly**

Adjectives ending in *-le* or *-re* drop the final *-e* before adding *-mente:*

> *facile* (easy) → *facilmente* (easily)
>
> *maggiore* (most) → *maggiormente* (mainly)

Take Your Place

A couple points about the placement of adverbs will help you easily incorporate them into your growing *vocabolario.*

Adverbs are generally placed after the verb:

> *Puoi imparare **facilmente** l'italiano.*
> You can **easily** learn Italian.
>
> *Siete **gentilmente** pregati di lasciare un messaggio.*
> You are **kindly** asked to leave a message.
>
> *Ti parlo **seriamente.***
> I'm speaking to you **seriously.**

Some adverbs may come *before* the verb or adjective:

> ***Probabilmente** vado domani.*
> I'm **probably** going tomorrow.
>
> *Firenze è **sempre** bella.*
> Florence is **always** beautiful.

Molti Adverbs

When talking about *quantità,* you might want *meno* (less) or *più* (more), depending on your mood. The following table gives you some of these.

Irregular Adverbs of Quantity

English	*Italiano*	English	*Italiano*
enough	*abbastanza*	quite a lot of	*parecchio*
hardly, scarcely	*appena*	rather, somewhat	*piuttosto*
less	*meno*	too	*troppo**

English	*Italiano*	English	*Italiano*
not very	*poco*	very, much, a lot	*molto**
not any more, no more	*non più*		

*The words troppo *and* molto *can both be used as adjectives and/or adverbs.*

AS A *REGOLA*

It's possible to use the preposition *con* and a noun in lieu of an adverb:

Guidate con attenzione.
Drive attentively. (Drive with attention.)

Parla con sincerità.
He speaks sincerely. (He speaks with sincerity.)

Adverbs of Place

It's good to know your place. The adverbs in the following table will help.

Adverbs of Place

English	*Italiano*	English	*Italiano*
above	*sopra*	in back of	*dietro*
anywhere	*dovunque*	in front of	*davanti*
behind	*indietro; dietro**	inside	*dentro*
beneath	*sotto*	near	*vicino*
down	*giù*	on	*sopra*
down there	*laggiù*	on top of	*su*
elsewhere	*altrove*	outside	*fuori*
everywhere	*dappertutto*	there	*ci, là, lì*
far	*lontano*	up	*su*
here	*qui, qua*		

*Italian uses dietro *if followed by a noun (behind the door).*

The More Things Change

Make the following adjectives into adverbs. Some of these adjectives require that you make them feminine before converting them to adverbs. If the adjective ends in *-e*, just add *-mente.* If it ends in *-o*, change the ending to *-a* and add *-mente.* Don't forget to drop the *-e* when necessary.

> *Example: breve* (brief)
> *Answer:* brevemente (briefly)

1. *dolce* (sweet) _____

2. *sincero* (sincere) _____

3. *intelligente* (intelligent) _____

4. *necessario* (necessary) _____

5. *veloce* (fast/quick) _____

6. *regolare* (regular) _____

7. *difficile* (difficult) _____

8. *probabile* (probable) _____

9. *solo* (only) _____

10. *gentile* (kind) _____

Answers: 1. dolcemente 2. sinceramente 3. intelligentemente 4. necessariamente 5. velocemente 6. regolarmente 7. difficilmente 8. probabilmente 9. solamente 10. gentilmente

One of the Family (*Famiglia*)

24

In Italy, one of the first things people want to know about is your family (*famiglia*). Do you have brothers (*fratelli*) or sisters (*sorelle*)? Listen to the CD to hear how the following terms related to family members should be pronounced. Pay attention to the articles and their impact on how the word sounds when it's pronounced.

Family Members

Feminine	*Femminile*	Pronunciation	Masculine	*Maschile*	Pronunciation
mother	*la madre*	*lah **mah**-dreh*	father	*il padre*	*eel **pah**-dreh*
wife	*la moglie*	*lah **moh**-lyeh*	husband	*il marito*	*eel mah-**ree**-toh*
grandmother	*la nonna*	*lah **nohn**-nah*	grandfather	*il nonno*	*eel **nohn**-noh*
daughter	*la figlia*	*lah **feel**-yah*	son	*il figlio*	*eel **feel**-yoh*
infant	*la bambina*	*lah bahm-**bee**-nah*	infant	*il bambino*	*eel bahm-**bee**-noh*
sister	*la sorella*	*lah soh-**rehl**-lah*	brother	*il fratello*	*eel frah-**tehl**-loh*
cousin	*la cugina*	*lah koo-**gee**-nah*	cousin	*il cugino*	*eel koo-**gee**-noh*
aunt	*la zia*	*lah **tsee**-ah*	uncle	*lo zio*	*loh **tsee**-oh*

Feminine	*Femminile*	Pronunciation	Masculine	*Maschile*	Pronunciation
granddaughter	*la nipote*	*lah nee-**poh**-teh*	grandson	*il nipote*	*eel nee-**poh**-teh*
niece	*la nipote*	*lah nee-**poh**-teh*	nephew	*il nipote*	*eel nee-**poh**-teh*
mother-in-law	*la suocera*	*lah **swoh**-cheh-rah*	father-in-law	*il suocero*	*eel **swoh**-cheh-roh*
daughter-in-law	*la nuora*	*lah **nwoh**-rah*	son-in-law	*il genero*	*eel **jen**-eh-roh*
sister-in-law	*la cognata*	*lah koh-**nyah**-tah*	brother-in-law	*il cognato*	*eel koh-**nyah**-toh*
stepmother	*la matrigna*	*lah mah-**tree**-nyah*	stepfather	*il patrigno*	*eel pah-**tree**-nyoh*
stepsister	*la sorellastra*	*lah soh-reh-**lah**-strah*	stepbrother	*il fratellastro*	*eel frah-teh-**lah**-stroh*
godmother	*la madrina*	*lah mah-**dree**-nah*	godfather	*il padrino*	*eel pah-**dree**-noh*
girlfriend	*la ragazza*	*lah rah-**gahz**-tsah*	boyfriend	*il ragazzo*	*eel rah-**gahz**-tsoh*
fiancée	*la fidanzata*	*lah fee-dahn-**tsah**-tah*	fiancé	*il fidanzato*	*eel fee-dahn-**tsah**-toh*
widow	*la vedova*	*lah **veh**-doh-vah*	widower	*il vedovo*	*eel **veh**-doh-voh*

AS A *REGOLA*

When discussing the collective children, Italian reverts to the masculine plural: *i figli*. The same goes for friends: *gli amici*. One's *genitori* (parents) can be simply referred to as *i miei*. The word *nipote* is used to describe niece or nephew and granddaughter or grandson, and shares the same root as *nepotismo* (nepotism).

25

Use the following expressions to make introductions. Practice using some of the terms you just learned related to the family. Substitute the terms offered with your own.

Helpful Introductory Expressions

English	*Italiano*
I'd like to present ….	*Vorrei presentare ….*
Do You know …? (polite)	*Conosce …?*
Do you know …? (informal)	*Conosci …?*
It's a pleasure to make your acquaintance. (polite)	*È un piacere fare la Sua conoscenza.*
It's a pleasure to make your acquaintance. (informal)	*È un piacere fare la tua conoscenza.*
The pleasure is mine.	*Il piacere è mio.*
This is my brother.	*Questo è mio fratello.*
This is my sister.	*Questa è mia sorella.*
These are my friends. (mixed gender)	*Questi sono i miei amici.*
These are my girlfriends.	*Queste sono le mie amiche.*

True or False

I play this game with my *studenti* all the time. We call it *Vero o Falso?* (True or False?) and it's a fun way to practice using your Italian, no matter your level.

Here's how it works: each person writes down five simple sentences on separate pieces of paper using the adjectives covered in this chapter. Do not write down the English translation, or you'll give away too much information! Fold and throw the pieces of paper into a hat or basket. Pass the hat around until everyone has five new pieces of paper. (Even if you get one of your own, it's okay.) Each person takes a turn and reads one of the picked sentences. The others have to determine whether the statement is *vero* (true) or *falso* (false).

The game helps you develop your ability to comprehend Italian sentences while giving you a chance to apply your newly acquired pronunciation skills. In the meantime, you'll also grab a few choice vocabulary words. Be creative!

Use the word *è* for "is." Modify the adjective as necessary. For example:

> *Mia madre è bionda. Vero o falso?*
> My mother is blond. True or false?

> *La vita bella. Vero o falso?*
> Life is beautiful. True or false?

> *George Clooney è un bell'uomo. Vero o falso?*
> George Clooney is a good-looking man. True or false?

Ask the group to raise their hands when they agree with the statement. Whoever is right gets a point. (The reader doesn't get a point for that round.) When you have finished going through all the pieces of paper, you're done. The one with the most points wins.

Use your best poker face. Swap in additional vocabulary as you see fit. Consult the word list in back of the book. This game can evolve with you as your language studies progress. *Buon divertimento!* Have fun!

The Least You Need to Know

- To show possession in Italian, use the possessive adjectives or the preposition *di*.
- Italian adjectives must agree in gender and number with the nouns they modify.
- Italian possessive adjectives act just like any adjective and must agree in gender and number with the thing being possessed.
- The adjective *buono* follows a pattern similar to the indefinite article.
- Adverbs are formed by adding *-mente* to many feminine adjectives. Many adverbs of time and place are irregular and must be memorized.
- Play the *Vero o Falso* game to practice using your Italian.

Building Blocks: Verbs with Verve

I've reworked and consolidated Part 2 to help you focus your energies where they're most effective. Verbs are the spine of any language, helping shape and form our world. Part 2 heavily focuses on developing present-tense verb skills for both regular and irregular verbs.

Here you learn how to recognize an infinitive verb and conjugate it in the present tense. You'll be able to distinguish between a regular and an irregular verb.

I've also created separate chapters for the irregular but extremely helpful verbs like *avere* (to have), *essere* (to be), *stare* (to be; to stay), and *fare* (to do; to make), all of which follow their own rules.

Additional practical verbiage includes the modal verbs *dovere* (to have to), *potere* (to be able to), and *volere* (to want).

You also learn how to form the progressive tense as well as develop the skills to talk about time and weather, ask questions, and make suggestions.

Avventura Italiana: Regular Verbs

In This Chapter

- Subject pronouns
- Verb families and conjugation
- Common regular Italian verbs
- Taking conjugation a step further: asking questions
- Forming negative statements

Verbs are where the action is, so study them closely. *I verbi (verbs)* are the skeleton of *la lingua* (the language); without *i verbi*, nothing would exist, get done, or happen. Verbs are what move us, shape us, and allow us to convey messages. If you're new to second language learning, prepare yourself for your greatest, and most important, linguistic challenge: understanding verbs.

You'll probably work on this chapter for a while. That's okay. Don't expect to have the verbs mastered before continuing your Italian studies. Go easy on yourself. This is a high mountain, but together we will scale it!

Your Loyal Subject

Before you can begin to use verbs, you need to know your subject pronouns and understand what a subject is.

Determining the subject of a verb is essential to conjugation. As a reminder: to determine the subject, you need to ask the simple question, *"What* or *who* is doing the action?" The subject may be a person (Roberto), a thing (such as the car), or a pronoun replacing the noun (he, she, it, they, and so on).

WHAT'S WHAT

Especially in older texts, you may see the Italian pronouns *egli* (he) and *ella* (she) serving in place of the subject pronouns *lui* and *lei*. You may also hear— depending on gender and number—the pronouns *esso, essi, essa,* and *esse* used in reference to people, animals, and inanimate objects.

Subject Pronouns

Study the Italian subject pronouns in the following table.

Italian Subject Pronouns

Singular	Plural
io (I)	*noi* (we)
tu (you, informal)	*voi* (you)
lui/lei/Lei (he/she/You)	*loro* (they)

ATTENZIONE!

In Italian, the subject pronoun *io* (I) isn't capitalized unless it begins a sentence. The Italian polite form of you, the subject pronoun *Lei,* is always capitalized to distinguish it from *lei,* meaning "she."

How to Use Italian Subject Pronouns

Subject pronouns are useful for several things, including …

Clarity. To differentiate who the subject is in cases when verb forms are the same and when there's more than one subject:

> **He** speaks Italian but **she** speaks French.
> ***Lui*** *parla l'**italiano** ma **lei** parla il francese.*

Emphasis. To clearly underline the fact that the subject will be performing the action:

> **You** stay here; **I** am going to Italy.
> ***Tu*** *stai qui; **io** vado in Italia.*

You may also see the subject pronoun placed after a verb, especially when making comparisons:

> **I** am the most beautiful!
> *Sono **io** la più bella!*

> **You** are the most intelligent!
> *Sei **tu** la più intelligente!*

Politeness. To show respect and maintain a formality with another person:

> **You** are very kind.
> ***Lei** è molto gentile.*

Tu, Lei, Voi, and *Loro:* All You

Italian has a few ways to talk about "you": an informal, a polite, and a plural. Italian uses *tu*, the informal you (second person singular) specifically with friends and family members.

Lei, the polite form of you (third person singular), is used when addressing elders, strangers, and authority figures.

Voi, the plural form of you (third person plural), is used when addressing a group of people. In the southern United States, you'd say, "Y'all." In the North, you might say, "All of you." You may recall an Italian friend or relative referring to a group as *Yous*, and now you know why.

I Verbi Are Where the Action Is

As you know, verbs indicate action. Keep in mind that an infinitive verb is a verb in its unconjugated form, as in *parlare* (to talk), *scrivere* (to write), *dormire* (to sleep), and *capire* (to understand). A conjugated verb is simply a form of the verb that agrees with the subject. You conjugate verbs in English all the time when you say I am, you are, and he is.

All Italian verbs fall into one of two categories. They're either transitive or intransitive. Sometimes, a verb that's transitive in Italian will be intransitive in English and vice versa. Although it's a bit confusing, your dictionary will always indicate whether a verb is transitive or intransitive.

Transitive verbs carry the action from the subject directly to an object. Verbs like *studiare* (to study) and *mangiare* (to eat) are transitive. Even if the direct object is implied, the verb is transitive. They answer the question "what?" There are far more transitive verbs.

Intransitive verbs stand alone, and never have a direct object. Intransitive signifies "nontransitive"; the action does not pass from the subject to the object directly. Verbs like *essere* (to be), *stare* (to stay), *nascere* (to be born), and *morire* (to die) that express a state or condition are also intransitive. Verbs that express movement such as *andare* (to go) and *ritornare* (to return) also fall into this category. They often answer the questions "when?" "where?" and "how long?" Reflexive verbs are also intransitive.

It's important to be able to identify the kind of verb because it's going to affect which auxiliary—or helping—verb to use. We get to helping verbs later.

Verbs: All in the *Famiglia*

Almost all verbs in Italian belong to one of three families, easily identified by their endings. Most of the time, Italian verbs follow certain rules. We call these regular verbs.

Also called the first conjugation, the *-are* family is the largest and most regular family. The *-ere* family, known as the second conjugation, has its own set of rules. The *-ire* family has two methods of conjugation and is referred to as the third conjugation. These verb families include infinitive verbs such as *parlare* (to speak), *scrivere* (to write), *partire* (to depart), and *capire* (to understand).

The rules are the same for each family, so after you've learned the pattern for one verb, you know how to conjugate all the verbs in that family.

The Anatomy of a *Verbo*

Understanding the anatomy of Italian verbs will help you conjugate.

WHAT'S WHAT

The terms *root* and *stem* are sometimes used interchangeably, but there are differences. For our purposes, let's just say that the stem of a word is the base from which other words are formed. In regular verbs, the stem remains the same when conjugated. In irregular verbs, the stem may change form after it has been conjugated. This is called a stem-changing verb, as with the verb *bere* (to drink), whose stem changes to *bev-* when conjugated.

Most Italian infinitive verbs end in *-are*, *-ere*, or *-ire*, making it very easy to distinguish infinitive verbs from other parts of speech.

To conjugate any regular verb in the present tense, you simply drop the infinitive ending and replace it with the appropriate conjugation. Following this formula, you can conjugate any regular verb (whether you understand its meaning or not).

You'll note that there are two groups of *-ire* verbs: *dormire* (to sleep) and *capire* (to understand). Knowing which verbs belong to what group takes a little studying, but after a very short time, you'll be able to *hear* when it's right. Trust your ear!

The Anatomy of a Verb

Conjugation	Infinitive Verb	Stem	Infinitive Ending
First	*parlare* (to speak)	*parl-*	*-are*
Second	*scrivere* (to write)	*scriv-*	*-ere*
Third (Group I)	*dormire* (to sleep)	*part-*	*-ire*
Third (Group II)	*capire* (to understand)	*cap-*	*-ire*

The Present-Tense Conjugations

In English, the present tense can be expressed in three different ways:

> The simple present: I speak.
>
> The present progressive: I am speaking.
>
> The emphatic present: I do speak.

Using the verb *parlare* (to speak) as an example, observe how Italian allows you to express all three of these with one simple conjugation: *parlo.*

For a general overview, the following table outlines the correct endings for all three verb families.

Regular Verb Endings

Subject Pronoun	*Parlare* (*To Speak*)	*Scrivere* (*To Write*)	*Dormire* (to Sleep)	*Capire* (to Understand)
			(Group I)	(Group II)
io	*parlo*	*scrivo*	*dormo*	*capisco*
tu	*parli*	*scrivi*	*dormi*	*capisci*
lui/lei/Lei	*parla*	*scrive*	*dorme*	*capisce*
noi	*parliamo*	*scriviamo*	*dormiamo*	*capiamo*
voi	*parlate*	*scrivete*	*dormite*	*capite*
loro	*parlano*	*scrivono*	*dormono*	*capiscono*

The *-are* Family

The largest *famiglia* in the batch, the *-are* verbs, are also the most regular. These are the most user-friendly verbs because they follow consistent rules.

The sheer number of verbs can be daunting to someone new to the language. Skim through to see which verbs resonate most with you and go from there. You're not going to finish this chapter in one or two reads. Come back as often as you can stand. I realize that conjugating verbs is not the most riveting, dynamic experience, but once you understand them, you'll be so happy you stuck it out. I can't repeat it enough: verbs are where the action is.

P Is for *Parlare*

Study the verb *parlare* (to speak) to see how it conjugates. Substitute the infinitive *-are* with the endings you just saw. The English words *parable*, *paragraph*, and *parlance* all share roots with this verb.

Parlare (to Speak)

Italiano	Pronunciation	English
io parlo	*par-loh*	I speak
tu parli	*par-lee*	you speak
lui/lei/Lei parla	*par-lah*	he/she speaks; You speak
noi parliamo	*par-lee-yamo*	we speak
voi parlate	*par-lah-teh*	you speak
loro parlano	*par-lah-noh*	they speak

AS A *REGOLA*

As you know, pronouncing Italian is easy; the challenge is knowing where to place the stress. When pronouncing all forms of the verbs, note that except for *noi* and *voi,* stress should be placed on the stem of the verb, not the ending. Although there are exceptions, this is particularly helpful to recall when you're pronouncing the third person plural (*loro*) conjugations:

they eat	*mangiano*	**mahn**-*jah-noh*
they speak	*parlano*	**par**-*lah-noh*
they see	*vedono*	**veh**-*doh-noh*

Remember that double consonants should be emphasized but not separated, and all syllables should slide together in a flow of melodic *musica!*

Regular *-are* Verbs

Go to town with these regular *-are* verbs. Many of them are cognates.

Regular *-are* Verbs

Italiano	Pronunciation	English
abbronzare	*abb-brohn-**zah**-reh*	to tan
abitare	*ah-bee-**tah**-reh*	to live
abusare	*ah-boo-**zah**-reh*	to abuse
accompagnare	*ahk-kohm-pah-**nyah**-reh*	to accompany
adorare	*ah-doh-**rah**-reh*	to adore
affermare	*ahf-fer-**mah**-reh*	to affirm
affittare	*ahf-fee-**tah**-reh*	to rent
aggiustare	*ahj-joos-**tah**-reh*	to adjust/to fix
aiutare	*ah-yoo-**tah**-reh*	to help
alzare	*ahl-**tsah**-reh*	to raise/to lift up
amare	*ah-**mah**-reh*	to love
ammirare	*ahm-mee-**rah**-reh*	to admire
anticipare	*ahn-tee-chee-**pah**-reh*	to anticipate
arrestare	*ahr-reh-**stah**-reh*	to stop/to arrest
arrivare	*ahr-ree-**vah**-reh*	to arrive
ascoltare	*ah-skol-**tah**-reh*	to listen
aspettare	*ah-speht-**tah**-reh*	to wait/to expect
avvisare	*ahv-vee-**sah**-reh*	to inform/to advise
ballare	*bahl-**lah**-reh*	to dance
bloccare	*blohk-**kah**-reh*	to block
bussare	*boos-**sah**-reh*	to knock

continues

Italiano	Pronunciation	English
buttare	*boot-**tah**-reh*	to throw
calcolare	*kal-koh-**lah**-reh*	to calculate
camminare	*kahm-mee-**nah**-reh*	to walk
cancellare	*kahn-chel-**lah**-reh*	to cancel
cantare	*kahn-**tah**-reh*	to sing
causare	*kow-**zah**-reh*	to cause
celebrare	*cheh-leh-**rah**-reh*	to celebrate
cenare	*cheh-**nah**-reh*	to dine
chiamare	*kee-ah-**mah**-reh*	to call
comprare	*kohm-**prah**-reh*	to buy
consumare	*kohn-soo-**mah**-reh*	to consume
contare	*kohn-**tah**-reh*	to count
controllare	*kohn-trol-**lah**-reh*	to control/to check
conversare	*kohn-ver-**sah**-reh*	to converse
costare	*koh-**stah**-reh*	to cost
cucinare	*koo-chee-**nah**-reh*	to cook
deliberare	*deh-lee-beh-**rah**-reh*	to deliberate/to resolve
depositare	*deh-poh-zee-**tah**-reh*	to deposit
desiderare	*deh-zee-deh-**rah**-reh*	to desire
determinare	*deh-ter-mee-**nah**-reh*	to determine
detestare	*deh-teh-**stah**-reh*	to detest
dimostrare	*dee-moh-**strah**-reh*	to demonstrate
disegnare	*dee-zen-**yah**-reh*	to draw/design
disgustare	*dee-sgoo-**stah**-reh*	to disgust
disperare	*dee-speh-**rah**-reh*	to despair
diventare	*dee-ven-**tah**-reh*	to become
domandare	*doh-mahn-**dah**-reh*	to question
donare	*doh-**nah**-reh*	to donate/give
elevare	*eh-leh-**vah**-reh*	to elevate
eliminare	*eh-lee-mee-**nah**-reh*	to eliminate
entrare	*ehn-**trah**-reh*	to enter
esaminare	*eh-zah-mee-**nah**-reh*	to examine
evitare	*eh-vee-**tah**-reh*	to avoid
firmare	*feer-**mah**-reh*	to sign
formare	*for-**mah**-reh*	to form/to create
fumare	*foo-**mah**-reh*	to smoke
funzionare	*foon-zee-oh-**nah**-reh*	to function
gettare	*jeht-**tah**-reh*	to throw
gridare	*gree-**dah**-reh*	to scream
guardare	*gwar-**dah**-reh*	to look at something
guidare	*gwee-**dah**-reh*	to drive

Italiano	Pronunciation	English
immaginare	eem-mah-jee-**nah**-reh	to imagine
imparare	eem-pah-**rah**-reh	to learn
informare	een-for-**mah**-reh	to inform
invitare	een-vee-**tah**-reh	to invite
lavare	lah-**vah**-reh	to wash
lavorare	lah-voh-**rah**-reh	to work
liberare	lee-beh-**rah**-reh	to liberate/to set free
limitare	lee-mee-**tah**-reh	to limit
lottare	loht-**tah**-reh	to struggle/to fight
mandare	mahn-**dah**-reh	to send
meritare	meh-ree-**tah**-reh	to deserve
misurare	mee-zoo-**rah**-reh	to measure
modificare	moh-dee-fee-**kah**-reh	to modify
nuotare	nwoh-**tah**-reh	to swim
occupare	ohk-koo-**pah**-reh	to occupy
odiare	oh-dee-**ah**-reh	to hate
operare	oh-peh-**rah**-reh	to operate
ordinare	or-dee-**nah**-reh	to order
organizzare	or-gah-nee-**tsah**-reh	to organize
osservare	ohs-ser-**vah**-reh	to observe
parlare	par-**lah**-reh	to speak
partecipare	par-teh-chee-**pah**-reh	to participate
passare	pahs-**sah**-reh	to pass
pensare	pen-**sah**-reh	to think
perdonare	per-doh-**nah**-reh	to forgive/to pardon
pesare	peh-**zah**-reh	to weigh
pettinare	pet-tee-**nah**-reh	to comb
portare	por-**tah**-reh	to bring/to carry
pranzare	prahn-**zah**-reh	to eat lunch
pregare	preh-**gah**-reh	to pray/to request
prenotare	preh-noh-**tah**-reh	to reserve
preparare	preh-pah-**rah**-reh	to prepare
presentare	preh-zen-**tah**-reh	to present
prestare	preh-**stah**-reh	to lend
provare	proh-**vah**-reh	to try
raccomandare	rah-koh-mahn-**dah**-reh	to recommend
raccontare	rahk-kohn-**tah**-reh	to tell/to recount
rappresentare	rahp-preh-zehn-**tah**-reh	to represent
respirare	reh-spee-**rah**-reh	to breathe
rifiutare	ree-fyoo-**tah**-reh	to refuse/to reject

continues

Italiano	Pronunciation	English
rilassare	*ree-lahs-**sah**-reh*	to relax
riparare	*ree-pah-**rah**-reh*	to repair
riservare	*ree-zer-**vah**-reh*	to reserve
rispettare	*ree-spet-**tah**-reh*	to respect
ritornare	*ree-tor-**nah**-reh*	to return
saltare	*sahl-**tah**-reh*	to jump
salvare	*sahl-**vah**-reh*	to save
scusare	*skoo-**zah**-reh*	to excuse
soddisfare	*sohd-dee-**sfah**-reh*	to satisfy
sognare	*sohn-**yah**-reh*	to dream
sposare	*spoh-**zah**-reh*	to marry
suonare	*swoh-**nah**-reh*	to play an instrument
telefonare	*teh-leh-foh-**nah**-reh*	to telephone
terminare	*ter-mee-**nah**-reh*	to terminate
trovare	*troh-**vah**-reh*	to find
urlare	*oor-**lah**-reh*	to yell
usare	*oo-**zah**-reh*	to use
vietare	*vee-eh-**tah**-reh*	to forbid/to prohibit
visitare	*vee-zee-**tah**-reh*	to visit
volare	*voh-**lah**-reh*	to fly
votare	*voh-**tah**-reh*	to vote

Let's Begin Here

A few verbs deviate from the regular *-are* verb endings you just learned. For many verbs ending in *-iare*, such as *baciare* (to kiss), *cominciare* (to begin), and *studiare* (to study), you must drop the additional *-i* if it occurs during conjugation. This serves to avoid a doubling of the vowel *-i* in the *tu* and *noi* forms.

Subject	*Cominciare* (to Begin)	*Studiare* (to Study)
io	*comincio*	*studio*
tu	*cominci*	*studi*
lui/lei/Lei	*comincia*	*studia*
noi	*cominciamo*	*studiamo*
voi	*cominciate*	*studiate*
loro	*cominciano*	*studiano*

Other verbs falling under this category include the following:

abbracciare (to hug)	*lasciare* (to leave something)
assaggiare (to taste)	*mangiare* (to eat)
baciare (to kiss)	*tagliare* (to cut)
cambiare (to change)	*viaggiare* (to travel)

An exception to this rule is the verb *odiare* (to hate), which retains the double *-ii*. (Try not to hate all these exceptions!)

Let Me Explain

Many verbs ending in *-care* and *-gare* add an *-h* to the stem in front of the vowels *i* and *e* to maintain the hard *c* and *g* sounds. Look at the verbs *cercare* (to search for) and *spiegare* (to explain) to see how this works.

Subject	*Cercare* (to Look for/Search)	Spiegare
io	*cerco*	*spiego*
tu	*cerchi*	*spieghi*
lui/lei/Lei	*cerca*	*spiega*
noi	*cerchiamo*	*spieghiamo*
voi	*cercate*	*spiegate*
loro	*cercano*	*spiegano*

Other verbs falling under this category include the following:

comunicare (to communicate)	*notificare* (to notify)
giocare (to play)	*pagare* (to pay)
indicare (to indicate)	*toccare* (to touch)
navigare (to navigate)	*verificare* (to verify)

Practice Makes *Perfetto*

Use the correct form of the verb in the following sentences. If the subject isn't identified in the sentence, it's given in parentheses. Don't forget to determine what your subject is and whether the verb should be conjugated in its singular or plural form. Translate the sentences.

1. *Paolo _____ (lavorare) in ufficio.*

2. *Luca ed io _____ (aspettare) il treno.*

3. *_____ (abitare) in una casa splendida. (tu)*

4. *_____ (parlare) la lingua italiana. (io)*

5. *_____ (passare) la notte a casa. (loro)*

6. *Antonella e Dina _____ (preparare) la cena.*

Answers: 1. (lavora) Paolo is working at the office. 2. (aspettiamo) Luca and I are waiting for the train. 3. (Abiti) You live in a splendid home. 4. (Parlo) I speak the Italian language. 5. (Passano) They're spending the night at home. 6. (preparano) Antonella and Dina are preparing dinner.

First Person

Here's an easy trick to remember when you start using your verbs: begin with yourself. Whatever the verb family and its rules, to express "I" to do anything (I eat, I open, I sleep), is super simple and the same for all. Just ditch the infinitive ending and add an -*o*. You don't even need to use the subject pronoun *io* (I) because it's inferred by the conjugation. Do the same thing to express "we" by adding -*iamo*.

In grammatical parlance, both of these are called the first person.

Look at the examples in the following table using the verbs *parlare* (to speak), *scrivere* (to write), *dormire* (to sleep), and *finire* (to finish).

Infinitive	"I"	"We"
Parlare (to speak)	*Parl/are* + *o* = *Parlo* (I speak)	*Parl/are* + iamo = Parliamo (we speak)
Scrivere (to write)	*Scriv/ere* + *o* = *Scriv/o* (I write)	*Scriv/ere* + iamo = Scriviamo (we write)
Dormire (to sleep)	*Dorm/ire* + *o* = *Dorm/o* (I sleep)	*Dorm/ire* + iamo = Dormiamo (we sleep)
Finire (to finish)	*Fin/ire* + *isco* = *Finisco* (I finish)*	*Fin/ire* + iamo = Finiamo (we finish)

*The second group of -*ire* verbs uses a different set of endings, but they still all end in -o.*

The *-ere* Verbs

In most cases, *-ere* verbs are conjugated similarly to the *-are* verbs. Drop the infinitive ending from your root and add the endings from the "Regular *-ere* Verbs" table in the following sections. You'll see more of the many irregular *-ere* verbs later.

S Is for *Scrivere*

Notice how easy it is to write in Italian with the verb *scrivere* (to write). The English words *scribe*, *script*, and *scripture* all share common roots with this verb.

Scrivere (to Write)

Italiano	Pronunciation	English
io scrivo	*skree-voh*	I write
tu scrivi	*skree-vee*	you write
lui/lei/Lei scrive	*skree-veh*	he/she writes; You write
noi scriviamo	*skree-vee-yah-moh*	we write
voi scrivete	*skree-veh-teh*	you write
loro scrivono	*skree-voh-noh*	they write

Regular *-ere* Verbs

Whether you believe or still need convincing, you'll find it hard to resist these *-ere* verbs. There are many cognates here, such as *alludere* (to allude, as in allusion), *concludere* (to conclude, as in conclusion), and *dividere* (to divide, as in division).

Regular *-ere* Verbs

Italiano	Pronunciation	English
accendere	*ah-chen-deh-reh*	to light/to turn on
affliggere	*ahf-flee-jeh-reh*	to afflict
aggiungere	*ahj-joon-jeh-reh*	to add
alludere	*ahl-loo-deh-reh*	to allude/to refer
ammettere	*ahm-meh-teh-reh*	to admit
apprendere	*ahp-pren-deh-reh*	to learn
assistere	*ahs-see-steh-reh*	to assist
assumere	*ahs-soo-meh-reh*	to hire
attendere	*aht-ten-deh-reh*	to attend/to wait for

continues

Italiano	Pronunciation	English
cadere	*kah-**deh**-reh*	to fall
chiedere	*kee-**yeh**-deh-reh*	to ask
chiudere	*kee-**yoo**-deh-reh*	to close
commettere	*kohm-**meh**-teh-reh*	to commit/to join
commuovere	*kohm-**mwoh**-veh-reh*	to move/to affect
comprendere	*kohm-**pren**-deh-reh*	to comprehend
concedere	*kohn-**cheh**-deh-reh*	to concede/to grant/to award
concludere	*kohn-**kloo**-deh-reh*	to conclude
confondere	*kohn-**fon**-deh-reh*	to confuse
conoscere	*koh-**noh**-sheh-reh*	to know someone
consistere	*kohn-**see**-steh-reh*	to consist
convincere	*kohn-**veen**-cheh-reh*	to convince
correggere	*kohr-**rej**-jeh-reh*	to correct
correre	***kohr**-reh-reh*	to run
corrispondere	*kohr-ree-**spohn**-deh-reh*	to correspond
credere	***kreh**-deh-reh*	to believe
crescere	***kreh**-sheh-reh*	to grow
decider	*deh-**chee**-deh-reh*	to decide
descrivere	*deh-**skree**-veh-reh*	to describe
difendere	*dee-**fen**-deh-reh*	to defend
dipendere	*dee-**pen**-deh-reh*	to depend
dipingere	*dee-**peen**-jeh-reh*	to paint
discutere	*dee-**skoo**-teh-reh*	to discuss
dissolvere	*dees-**sohl**-veh-reh*	to dissolve
distinguere	*dee-**steen**-gweh-reh*	to distinguish
distruggere	*dee-**strooj**-jeh-reh*	to destroy
divider	*dee-**vee**-deh-reh*	to divide
emergere	*eh-**mer**-jeh-reh*	to emerge
esistere	*eh-**zee**-steh-reh*	to exist
esprimere	*es-**pree**-meh-reh*	to express
fingere	***feen**-jeh-reh*	to pretend
godere	*goh-**deh**-reh*	to enjoy
includere	*een-**kloo**-deh-reh*	to include
insistere	*een-**see**-steh-reh*	to insist
intendere	*een-**ten**-deh-reh*	to intend
interrompere	*een-ter-**rohm**-peh-reh*	to interrupt
invader	*een-**vah**-deh-reh*	to invade
leggere	***lehj**-jeh-reh*	to read
mettere	***meht**-teh-reh*	to put/to place
muovere	***mwoh**-veh-reh*	to move

Italiano	Pronunciation	English
nascondere	*nah-**skon**-deh-reh*	to hide
offendere	*ohf-**fen**-deh-reh*	to offend
perdere	***per**-deh-reh*	to lose
permettere	*per-**met**-teh-reh*	to permit
piangere	*pee-**yahn**-jeh-reh*	to cry
prendere	***pren**-deh-reh*	to take
proteggere	*proh-**tej**-jeh-reh*	to protect
rendere	***ren**-deh-reh*	to render/to give back
resistere	*reh-**zee**-steh-reh*	to resist
ricevere	*ree-**cheh**-veh-reh*	to receive
ridere	***ree**-deh-reh*	to laugh
riflettere	*ree-**flet**-teh-reh*	to reflect
ripetere	*ree-**peh**-teh-reh*	to repeat
risolvere	*ree-**zol**-veh-reh*	to resolve
rispondere	*ree-**spon**-deh-reh*	to respond
rompere	***rom**-peh-reh*	to break
scendere	***shen**-deh-reh*	to descend
scrivere	***skree**-veh-reh*	to write
sorridere	*sor-**ree**-deh-reh*	to smile
sospendere	*sos-**pen**-deh-reh*	to suspend
spendere	***spen**-deh-reh*	to spend
succedere	*soo-**cheh**-deh-reh*	to happen/to occur
uccidere	*oo-**chee**-deh-reh*	to kill
vedere	*veh-**deh**-reh*	to see
vendere	***ven**-deh-reh*	to sell
vincere	***veen**-cheh-reh*	to win
vivere	***vee**-veh-reh*	to live

LA BELLA LINGUA

The regular verb *conoscere* (to know someone; to be acquainted with) is used to talk about a person you know, but you can also use it when referring to a city or place, or even *una lingua*. Students of Italian often confuse this verb with the irregular verb *sapere* (to know something). Related nouns include *conoscente* (acquaintance) and *conoscenza* (knowledge/acquaintance).

Practice Makes *Perfetto* II

Your plate is full, and your eyes are bloodshot from the feast of verbs. Refer to the previous table and provide the correct verb form that best completes the sentences. Translate.

prendere	accendere	risolvere
vendere	spendere	scrivere

1. *(Loro)* _____ *molti soldi.*

2. *(Io)* _____ *una lettera.*

3. *(Tu)* _____ *la luce.*

4. *(Noi)* _____ *la nostra macchina.*

5. *(Lei)* _____ *sempre i suoi problemi.*

6. *(Voi)* _____ *il treno o il pullman?*

Answers: 1. (spendono) They spend a lot of money. 2. (scrivo) I write a letter. 3. (accendi) You turn on the light. 4. (vendiamo) We are selling our car. 5. (risolve) She always resolves her problems. 6. (prendete) Are you taking the train or the coach?

The *-ire* Family

There are two groups of *-ire* verbs. The first group follows conjugation rules similar to those for the *-ere* verbs. As a matter of fact, they're the same except for the second person plural (*voi*), as shown in the following table.

D Is for *Dormire*

It's true, verb conjugations can put you to sleep. As an example of the first group, study the verb *dormire* (to sleep). The English words *dormitory*, *dormant*, and *dormer* are related to this verb.

Dormire (to Sleep)

Italiano	**Pronunciation**	**English**
io dormo	*dor-moh*	I sleep
tu dormi	*dor-mee*	you sleep
lui/lei/Lei dorme	*dor-meh*	he/she sleeps; You sleep

Italiano	Pronunciation	English
*noi dorm**iamo***	*dor-mee-**yah**-moh*	we sleep
*voi dorm**ite***	*dor-**mee**-teh*	you sleep
*loro dorm**ono***	***dor**-moh-noh*	they sleep

The *-ire* Verbs (Group I)

A handful of verbs fall under this *categoria*. The following table shows you some of them. Note the cognates such as *convertire* (to convert), *fuggire* (to escape, as in fugitive or fugue), and *seguire* (to follow, as in sequence).

Group I: Regular *-ire* Verbs

Italiano	Pronunciation	English
aprire	*ahp-**ree**-reh*	to open
bollire	*bohl-**lee**-reh*	to boil
convertire	*kohn-ver-**tee**-reh*	to convert
coprire	*koh-**pree**-reh*	to cover
dormire	*dor-**mee**-reh*	to sleep
fuggire	*fooj-**jee**-reh*	to escape
mentire	*men-**tee**-reh*	to lie
offrire	*ohf-**free**-reh*	to offer
partire	*par-**tee**-reh*	to depart
seguire	*seh-**gwee**-reh*	to follow
servire	*ser-**vee**-reh*	to serve

More *-ire* Verbs (Group II)

The second group of *-ire* verbs is still considered regular but must be conjugated differently from other *-ire* verbs. After you learn the endings, you'll have no problem conjugating them.

C Is for *Capire*

A commonly used verb from this family is the verb *capire* (to understand). Look at the following table to see how this verb conjugates. If you can remember this verb, the others follow quite easily. English words sharing etymological ties include *capitalism*, *capable*, and *capacity*.

Capire (to Understand)

Italiano	Pronunciation	English
io capisco	*kah-**pee**-skoh*	I understand
tu capisci	*kah-**pee**-shee*	you understand
lui/lei/Lei capisce	*kah-**pee**-shay*	he/she understands; You understand
noi capiamo	*kah-pee-**yah**-moh*	we understand
voi capite	*kah-**pee**-teh*	you understand
loro capiscono	*kah-**pee**-skoh-noh*	they understand

The *-ire* Verbs (Group II)

The second group of *-ire* verbs includes interesting verbs such as *capire* (to understand), *impazzire* (to go crazy), and *tradire* (to betray)—all the verbs you'll need for a good juicy opera like *La Traviata*.

Group II: *-ire* Verbs

Italiano	Pronunciation	Verb
aderire	*ah-deh-**ree**-reh*	to adhere
attribuire	*aht-tree-boo-**ee**-reh*	to attribute
capire	*kah-**pee**-reh*	to understand
colpire	*kol-**pee**-reh*	to hit/strike
costruire	*kohs-troo-**wee**-reh*	to construct
definire	*deh-fee-**nee**-reh*	to define
digerire	*dee-jeh-**ree**-reh*	to digest
diminuire	*dee-mee-noo-**wee**-reh*	to diminish
esaurire	*eh-zow-**ree**-reh*	to exhaust
fallire	*fahl-**lee**-reh*	to fail/to go bankrupt
finire	*fee-**nee**-reh*	to finish
garantire	*gah-rahn-**tee**-reh*	to guarantee
gestire	*jeh-**stee**-reh*	to manage/to administrate
guarire	*gwah-**ree**-reh*	to heal/to recover
impazzire	*eem-pah-**tsee**-reh*	to go crazy
istruire	*ee-stroo-**wee**-reh*	to instruct/to teach
obbedire	*ohb-beh-**dee**-reh*	to obey
preferire	*preh-feh-**ree**-reh*	to prefer
proibire	*pro-ee-**bee**-reh*	to prohibit/to forbid
pulire	*poo-**lee**-reh*	to clean
punire	*poo-**nee**-reh*	to punish

Italiano	Pronunciation	Verb
riunire	*ree-yoo-**nee**-reh*	to reunite
spedire	*speh-**dee**-reh*	to send
stabilire	*sta-bee-**lee**-reh*	to establish
suggerire	*sooj-jeh-**ree**-reh*	to suggest
tradire	*trah-**dee**-reh*	to betray/to deceive
trasferire	*tras-feh-**ree**-reh*	to transfer
unire	*oo-**nee**-reh*	to unite

Asking Questions

No one knows everything. The curious mind wants to understand, so it needs to ask questions. In Italian, it's very easy to ask a question. (Understanding the *risposta* [answer] is another story.)

ATTENZIONE!

When asking questions, be sure to change your intonation. Your voice should start out lower and gradually rise until the end of a sentence, as you do in English: *Parla l'**italiano**?* (Do you speak Italian?)

The Tags *Vero? No?* and *Giusto?*

Another way to ask a simple yes/no *domanda* (question) is to add the tags *vero?* (true? or right?), *no?* and *giusto?* (Is that so? or Correct?) to the end of a sentence:

Partiamo alle otto, no?
We're leaving at eight, no?

Capisci la lezione, vero?
You understand the lesson, right?

La classe incomincia alle due, giusto?
The class starts at two o'clock, correct?

And the *Risposta* Is ...

To answer a question affirmatively (yes), use *sì* and give your *risposta* (response).

To answer a question negatively (no), use *no* attached to *non* before the conjugated verb form. This is equivalent to our *don't*, as in "No, I don't smoke." Adverbs generally come after the verb.

Question	Affirmative Answer	Negative Answer
Do you smoke cigarettes? *Lei fuma le sigarette?*	Yes, I smoke cigarettes. *Sì, fumo le sigarette.*	No, I don't **ever** smoke cigarettes. *No, non fumo **mai** le sigarette.*
Do you understand the lesson? *Capisci la lezione?*	Yes, I understand the lesson. *Sì, capisco la lezione.*	No, I don't understand the lesson. *No, non capisco la lezione.*

A Whole Lot of *Niente* (Nothing)

If you're answering a question and starting your sentence with *no*, use the negative adverbs in the following table directly after the conjugated verb.

Italiano	English	Example
mai	never/ever	*No, non fumo **mai**.* I never smoke. (I smoke never.)
niente	nothing/anything	*No, non desidero **niente**.* I don't desire anything. (I desire nothing.)
nulla	nothing/anything	*No, non compro **nulla**.* I don't buy anything. (I buy nothing.)
nessuno	no one	*No, nessuno **arriva**.* No one is arriving.

The Least You Need to Know

- Determining the subject of a verb is essential to conjugation—and therefore, speaking.
- Subject pronouns are used much less frequently in Italian than in English because the verb endings usually indicate the subject; however, you will sometimes hear subject pronouns used for clarity, emphasis, or courtesy.
- There are four forms of *you* in Italian: the second person plural, the second person singular, the third person singular, and the third person plural.
- Any verb that follows a subject noun or pronoun must be properly conjugated.
- There are three verb families: *-are, -ere,* and *-ire.* Each has its own set of conjugation rules. Many verbs are cognates.
- Start using your verbs in the first person (I) form of the verb by attaching *-o* to the stem of any verb.

A State of Being

This chapter deals with the complexities of *being:* I am, you are, they are, we all are. In addition to learning two intransitive verbs that both mean "to be" (*stare* and *essere*), I also show you how to form the present progressive, the *-ing* form of any verb. You also learn how to indicate the existence of something using a tiny, but powerful word, the pronoun *ci*.

The Birds and the Be Verbs

Two different *verbi* are used to express "to be" in Italian: *stare* and *essere*. When you ask someone, "*Come stai?*" (How are you?), you're using the verb *stare*. When you say, "*La vita è bella*" (Life is beautiful), you're using the verb *essere*. Because the two verbs mean the same thing, the difference between the two comes down to usage.

Fortunately, *stare* (which can also mean "to stay") pretty much follows along the lines of the regular verbs. *Essere*, on the other hand, has its own special way of being.

All these verbs can stand on their own, but they can also be used as *helping* or *auxiliary* verbs. You'll need helping verbs when you want to form compound tenses, including the past tense and the progressive tense.

> **ATTENZIONE!**
>
> Don't be confused between *e* (and) and *è* (is): the accent tells you when it's the verb.

The Verb *Essere* (to Be)

The verb *essere* is essential and very useful. When you talk about immutable facts, this is your verb. *Essere* is also used as a helping verb, necessary to create compound tenses like the past. The English words *essence, essential,* and *existence* all share etymological roots with this verb. It's highly irregular and therefore difficult to find in a dictionary. You'll do yourself a big favor by being able to recognize its many different forms.

What's amazing is how much importance one tiny little letter—*è* (is)—can have. Pronounce it with oomph, like a strong *ay*.

The Verb *Essere* (to Be)

Italiano	**Pronunciation**	**English**
io **sono**	*soh-noh*	I am
tu **sei**	say	you are
lui/lei/Lei **è**	ay	he/she (it)* is; You are
noi **siamo**	*see-ah-moh*	we are
voi **siete**	*see-yeh-teh*	you are
loro **sono**	*soh-noh*	they are

*Italian has no neuter "it." It uses the verb form alone to refer to things or animals.

This may seem tricky at first (but it's really not hard): *essere* uses the same conjugation for the first person singular as the third person plural: *sono.* Unless you have something obvious like a subject pronoun (*io* or *loro*), to figure out the subject (I or they), you'll have to infer it through the context of the statement. Study the articles, nouns, or adjective endings, which must always reflect gender and plurality:

(Io) Sono una persona sincera.
I am a sincere person.

(Loro) Sono persone sincere.
They are sincere people (persons).

Essere Versus *Stare:* What's the *Differenza?*

Although the verbs *essere* and *stare* both mean *to be*, each verb follows specific rules of usage. Keep in mind the following basics.

When to Use *Essere*

The verb *essere* is used in several different ways. It can, for example, be used to describe nationalities, origins, and inherent unchanging qualities:

Maurizio è di Verona.
Maurizio is from Verona.

La banana è gialla.
The banana is yellow.

It can be used to identify the subject or describe the subject's character traits and physical attributes:

Maria è bionda.
Maria is blond.

Sono io.*
It's me. (*Literally:* I am I.)

*The subject pronoun can come after the verb in special cases.

Essere is used to talk about the existence of something using the pronoun *ci:*

C'è tempo?
Is there time?

Non ci sono problemi.
There are no problems.

It's used to talk about the time:

Che ore sono?
What time is it?
(*Literally:* What hours are there?)

Sono le tre e mezzo.

It is 3:30.

And to talk about the date:

Natale è il 25 dicembre.
Christmas is December 25.

Oggi è lunedì.
Today is Monday.

It's also used to indicate possession:

Questo è lo zio di Anna.
This is Anna's uncle.
(*Literally:* This is the uncle of Anna.)

Quella è la mia casa.
That is my house.
(*Literally:* That is the my house.)

Finally, *essere* is used for certain impersonal expressions:

È una bella giornata.
It is a beautiful day.

È molto importante studiare.
It is very important to study.

Come Sei Intelligente!

Now, prove how smart you are. Use the correct form of *essere* in the following phrases. Translate the sentences.

1. *Luisa _____ una bella persona.*

2. *Grazie per i fiori! Tu _____ così romantico.*

3. *Noi _____ di Firenze.*

4. *Gli occhi _____ le finestre dell'anima.*

5. *Io _____ contenta.*

6. *Voi _____ molto generosi.*

Answers: 1. (è) Luisa is a beautiful person. 2. (sei) Thank you for the flowers! You're so romantic. 3. (siamo) We are from Florence. 4. (sono) The eyes are the window to the soul. 5. (sono) I am content. 6. (siete) You're very generous.

Using the Adverb *Ci*

For a little word, the adverb *ci* packs a lot of punch. Remember, adverbs always work with either adjectives or verbs. They are "added" onto the verb or adjective as a descriptive.

If you want to indicate the existence of something, like "Is there a God?" you'll use this little word. *Ci* is also used to mean *here* or *there*. (In older texts, you might also see the adverb *vi* used similarly.) It's often used with the verb *essere* to make the declaration "There is," ask "Is there?" or indicate "There are …"

Ci often replaces nouns or prepositional phrases preceded by *a, in,* and *su,* saving the speaker unnecessary repetition.

Study the following examples to better grasp this versatile word. First, let's use *ci* to denote place:

Vai spesso in piazza?	*Sì, ci vado.*
Do you often go to the piazza?	Yes, I go there.
Abiti a New York?	*No, non ci abito.*
Do you live in New York?	No, I don't live there.

Ci can also denote things or ideas:

Credi in Dio?	*Sì, ci credo.*
Do you believe in God?	Yes, I do [believe in God].
Pensi ai tuoi amici?	*Sì, ci penso.*
Do you think about your friends?	Yes, I do [think about them].

C'è and *Ci sono* (There Is, There Are)

When *ci* is used with the third person singular *è,* the contraction *c'è* is created:

C'è tempo; non c'è fretta.	*Ci sono molti turisti a Roma.*
There is time; there is no hurry.	There are many tourists in Rome.

AS A *REGOLA*

Use this formula to express "There is" or "Is there …?": *Ci + è = c'è.*

Using *Ci* to Ask Questions

When using *c'è* in a question, the word order stays the same. Like in English, you should raise your voice at the end of the sentence. This is also useful for when you're making *una telefonata* (a telephone call):

C'è un problema?	*C'è Fabrizio?*
Is there a problem?	Is Fabrizio there?

Making a Negative Statement Using *Non*

To make negative statements, say "no" and add the word *non* in front of the construction:

No, non c'è un problema.
No, there isn't a problem.

No, Fabrizio non c'è.
No, Fabrizio isn't here.

Fill in the Blankety-Blanks

Study the following phrases and fill in the blanks with either *c'è* or *ci sono.* Translate the sentences. Don't forget to look at the endings to determine whether the subject is singular or plural. If you're unsure about the meaning of a word, consult your dictionary or Appendix A at the back of the book.

Example: _____ *un supermercato?*
Answer: _C'è_ *un supermercato?*

1. _____ *un museo vicino?*

2. _____ *ancora due posti.*

3. _____ *un bagno privato in camera?*

4. _____ *molti ristoranti a Roma.*

5. _____ *una festa stasera a casa di Alessandro.*

6. *Non* _____ *tempo.*

Answers: 1. (C'è) Is there a museum nearby? 2. (Ci sono) There are still two places (seats). 3. (C'è) Is there a private bath in the room? 4. (Ci sono) There are many restaurants in Rome. 5. (C'è) There's a party this evening at Alessandro's house. 6. (c'è) There's no time.

The Verb *Stare* (to Be; to Stay)

It's time to switch over to another super handy verb: *stare.* You'll use this verb to ask someone how they are, to discuss temporary situations (like where you're staying), and to form the progressive tense. The English words *stay, state,* and *status* are all cousins to *stare.*

The Verb *Stare* (to Be; to Stay)

Italiano	Pronunciation	English
io **sto**	*stoh*	I am
tu **stai**	*sty*	you are
lui/lei/Lei **sta**	*sta*	he/she (it) is; You are
noi **stiamo**	*stee-**ah**-moh*	we are
voi **state**	***stah**-teh*	you are
loro **stanno**	***stahn**-noh*	they are

When to Use *Stare*

You're already familiar with the most commonly used expression in Italian, *Come sta?* With few exceptions, the verb *stare* is also used in the following ways:

To describe a temporary state or condition of the subject:

Come stai?
How are you?

Sto bene, grazie.
I am well, thanks.

To express a location:

Stiamo in albergo.
We are staying in a hotel.

Patrizia sta a casa.
Patricia is staying at home.

In many idiomatic expressions and to form the imperative (the command form of a verb):

Sta' attento!
Pay attention!

Sta' zitto!
Be quiet!

To form the progressive tenses. We'll get to those in a *minuto:*

With the verb *andare* (to go):

Stiamo andando al cinema.
We are going to the movies.

With the verb *parlare* (to speak):

Sto parlando con mia madre.
I am speaking with my mother.

Chitchat

You're having a *conversazione* with the person sitting next to you on the plane. Should you use the verb *essere* or *stare?* Complete the following *frasi* with the correct form of the necessary *verbo.* Translate.

1. *Noi* _____ *nella pensione Paradiso per due giorni.*

2. *Come* _____ *Lei?*

3. *Io* _____ *bene, grazie.*

4. *Loro* _____ *turisti.*

5. *Il ristorante Caffè Greco* _____ *famoso.*

6. *Lo studente* _____ *studiando.*

Answers: 1. (stiamo) We're staying at Pensione Paradiso for two days. 2. (sta) How are You? 3. (sto) I am well, thanks. 4. (sono) They are tourists. 5. (è) The restaurant Caffè Greco is famous. 6. (sta) The student is studying.

Using *Stare* to Form the Present Progressive Tense (*-ing*)

Aside from asking someone how they're doing, the verb *stare* enables you to create the present progressive tense. Used to describe an action in progress, the progressive is very easy to form. Keep in mind that the progressive is used in Italian differently than in English. However, for the purposes of communicating with ease (especially at this early stage), it's a terrific shortcut to managing your verbs, even if you haven't mastered the various conjugations yet.

Because the Italian present tense can serve as both the simple present and the progressive, native Italian, French, and Spanish speakers have difficulty distinguishing the difference in meaning between "I am going to the store" and "I go to the store." In English, we use the present progressive much more often than the simple present tense.

To create the present progressive, conjugate the helping verb *stare* (to be; to stay) and attach the gerund form of any infinitive verb. What's a gerund? That's the *-ing* form of a verb, like talking, wishing, creating. To create the gerund, slice off the infinitive ending of the verb and add the appropriate endings, as shown in the following table. Notice how the *-ere* and the *-ire* progressive tense endings are the same.

Present Progressive

Infinitive Verb		Gerund	English
parl/**are** (to talk)	→	parl**ando**	talking
scriv/**ere** (to write)	→	scriv**endo**	writing
dorm/**ire** (to sleep)	→	dorm**endo**	sleeping

The following table takes the verbs *parlare, scrivere,* and *dormire* and shows what happens when you attach the auxiliary verb *stare* to the gerund.

Forming the Present Progressive

Italiano	English
io sto + parlando/scrivendo/dormendo	I am + speaking/writing/sleeping
tu stai + parlando/scrivendo/dormendo	you are + speaking/writing/sleeping
lui/lei/Lei sta + parlando/scrivendo/dormendo	he/she is/You are + speaking/writing/sleeping
noi stiamo + parlando/scrivendo/dormendo	we are + speaking/writing/sleeping
voi state + parlando/scrivendo/dormendo	you are + speaking/writing/sleeping
loro stanno + parlando/scrivendo/dormendo	they are + speaking/writing/sleeping

There's another plus to using the progressive: irregular verbs tend to follow the simple rules used to form it. Now that's progress!

Making Progress

Turn the following sentences into the present progressive. (Hint: you need to determine the infinitive of the verb before you can find the appropriate progressive form.) Translate the sentences.

1. *Guardiamo il film.*

2. *Scrivi una lettera.*

3. *Nicola cucina la cena.*

4. *I bambini dormono.*

5. *Leggo il libro* The Complete Idiot's Guide to Learning Italian.

6. *Pulite la camera da letto.*

Answers: 1. (stiamo guardando) We're watching the film. 2. (stai scrivendo) You're writing a letter. 3. (sta cucinando) Nicola is cooking dinner. 4. (stanno dormendo) The children are sleeping. 5. (sto leggendo) I am reading The Complete Idiot's Guide to Learning Italian. *6. (state pulendo) You are cleaning the bedroom.*

Ecco! You Got It!

The word *ecco* is not what you hear when you scream into a canyon. An adverb, *ecco* can mean *here* or *there*. *Ecco* can also be used to express understanding or agreement, and it is very similar to the French word *voilà*, meaning "Here it is!" or "Got it!":

Ecco la stazione!
Here's the station!

Ecco Gabriella!
Here's Gabriella!

Eccomi!
Here I am!

The Least You Need to Know

- The verb *essere* is used to express various states of existence, usually permanent.
- The verb *stare* is generally used to describe a temporary condition such as "How y'all doing?"
- To form the progressive tense, use the conjugated helping verb *stare* + the gerund.
- Use the adverb *ci* (there) to indicate the existence of something, as in *C'è traffico.* (There's traffic.)
- It's not the big words that present a challenge; it's the little ones. Don't be deterred.
- Use *ecco* to indicate "here" or "you got it!"

Having It All

This chapter introduces one of the most useful verbs you'll ever learn, *avere* (to have), along with a bunch of idiomatic expressions you can form with it. In addition to learning your numbers, you develop the lingo to talk about time, dates, and historical periods. Finally, I've given you a primer on Italian punctuation marks.

It's Time to Have Some Fun: *Avere*

The irregular verb *avere* (to have) is used in myriad *situazioni* and idiomatic *espressioni* and is virtually unrecognizable from its infinitive when it has been conjugated. It's also used to form compound tenses, including the past. The following table outlines this practical verb.

The Verb *Avere* (to Have)

Italiano	Pronunciation	English
io **ho**	*oh*	I have
tu **hai**	*eye*	you have
lui/lei/Lei **ha**	*ah*	he/she (it) has; You have
noi **abbiamo**	*ahb-bee-**yah**-moh*	we have
voi **avete**	*ah-**veh**-teh*	you have
loro **hanno**	*__ahn__-noh*	they have

LA BELLA LINGUA

Avere is one of the few verbs that contains a silent letter used primarily to distinguish the conjugations from other Italian words. For example, take the *h* out of *ho*, and you have *o*, meaning "or." Take the *h* out of *hai*, and you have the contraction *ai*, meaning "to the." Take the *h* out of *ha*, and you have the preposition *a*, meaning "to." Take the *h* out of *hanno*, and you have the word *anno*, meaning "year."

When and How to Use *Avere*

Versatile *avere* is used in many idiomatic expressions such as *Ho una fame da lupo!* (I'm hungry as a wolf!) This verb is also used to express when you feel hot, cold, drowsy, hungry, and afraid, not to mention ashamed, sick, needy, and unlucky (and that's on a good day).

You use *avere* to find out how old someone is. In Italian you ask how many years one has:

> *Quanti anni hai?*
> *Literally:* How many years do you have?

Avere can also be used as an auxiliary—or helping—verb and to form the *passato prossimo* (present perfect):

> *Ho mangiato.*
> I have eaten.

Use *avere* if you're feeling hot or cold:

> *Ho freddo.*
> *Literally:* I have cold.

> *Ho caldo.*
> *Literally:* I have warm.

Sharing Your Needs and Feelings

The expressions in the following table help you express your needs and feelings. I've given you the infinitive form of *avere;* it's up to you to conjugate it to reflect the subject of the verb.

Expressing Needs and Feelings

English	Italiano
to be ___ years old	*avere ___ anni*
to be afraid	*avere paura*
to be at fault, to be guilty	*avere colpa*
to be hungry	*avere fame*
to be in the habit of	*avere l'abitudine di*
to be in the mood, to feel like	*avere voglia di*
to be right	*avere ragione*
to be sleepy	*avere sonno*
to be thirsty	*avere sete*
to be wrong	*avere torto*
to feel cold	*avere freddo*
to feel hot	*avere caldo*
to have need of	*avere bisogno di*
to have pain/to be sick	*avere mal di (body part)*
to have the chance to	*avere l'occasione di*
to have the intention of	*avere l'intenzione di*
to have the mis/fortune of	*avere la s/fortuna di*
to have the opportunity to	*avere l'opportunità di*
to have the possibility to	*avere la possibilità di*

Ho bisogno di te.
I need you.
Literally: I have need of you.

Ho sete.
I'm thirsty.
Literally: I have thirst.

Hai fame?
Are you hungry?
Literally: Do you have hunger?

Non adesso; ho mal di testa.
Not now; I've got a headache.

LA BELLA LINGUA

In Italian, you would never ask how *old* someone is. *Old* never enters the equation; Italians know age is an attitude. Instead, ask how many years a person *has: Quanti anni hai?* (How many years do you have?)

\WHAT'S WHAT

A helping verb is used to form other tenses, including compound tenses such as the present perfect tense. In English, we usually use the auxiliary verb *to have,* as in "I have eaten." Italian has three helping verbs: *essere* (to be), *avere* (to have), and *stare* (to be), used principally to create the present progressive tense (as in, "I am leaving").

Bambino, I Got Your *Numero*

26

You don't need to use Roman numerals to do your math. Italians use the euro (EUR), so be ready to manage a lot of coins because there are no bills under 5 euros. Numbers that express amounts are known as cardinal numbers (*numeri cardinali*) in Italian, as shown in the following table.

Numeri Cardinali

English	Italiano	Pronunciation
0	zero	**zeh**-roh
1	uno	**oo**-noh
2	due	**doo**-weh
3	tre	treh
4	quattro	**kwaht**-troh
5	cinque	**cheen**-kweh
6	sei	say
7	sette	**seht**-teh
8	otto	**oht**-toh
9	nove	**noh**-veh
10	dieci	dee-**yay**-chee
11	undici	**oon**-dee-chee
12	dodici	**doh**-dee-chee
13	tredici	**treh**-dee-chee
14	quattordici	kwaht-**tor**-dee-chee
15	quindici	**kween**-dee-chee
16	sedici	**seh**-dee-chee
17	diciassette	dee-chas-**seht**-teh
18	diciotto	dee-**choht**-toh
19	diciannove	dee-chahn-**noh**-veh
20	venti	**ven**-tee
21	ventuno	ven-**too**-noh
22	ventidue	ven-tee-**doo**-weh

English	*Italiano*	Pronunciation
23	*ventitré*	*ven-tee-**treh***
24	*ventiquattro*	*ven-tee-**kwaht**-troh*
25	*venticinque*	*ven-tee-**cheen**-kweh*
26	*ventisei*	*ven-tee-**say***
27	*ventisette*	*ven-tee-**seht**-teh*
28	*ventotto*	*ven-**toht**-toh*
29	*ventinove*	*ven-tee-**noh**-veh*
30	*trenta*	***tren**-tah*

More Numbers

We could count together forever, but it's really not necessary. Use the rules you just learned and apply them *ad infinitum*. These are the essential numbers from which all numbers can be expressed.

Note that in Italian, numbers (especially big ones) are written as one contiguous word.

From 40 to a Million: More Numbers

English	*Italiano*	Pronunciation
40	*quaranta*	*kwah-**rahn**-tah*
50	*cinquanta*	*cheen-**kwahn**-tah*
60	*sessanta*	*sehs-**sahn**-tah*
70	*settanta*	*seht-**tahn**-tah*
80	*ottanta*	*oht-**tahn**-tah*
90	*novanta*	*noh-**vahn**-tah*
100	*cento*	***chen**-toh*
101	*centouno**	*chen-**toh** **oo**-noh*
200	*duecento*	*doo-eh-**chen**-toh*
300	*trecento*	*treh-**chen**-toh*
400	*quattrocento*	*kwaht-troh-**chen**-toh*
500	*cinquecento*	*cheen-kway-**chen**-toh*
1.000	*mille***	*meel-lay*
1.001	*milleuno*	*meel-lay-**oo**-noh*
1.200	*milleduecento*	*meel-lay-doo-eh-**chen**-toh*
2.000	*duemila*	*doo-eh-**mee**-lah*
3.000	*tremila*	*treh-**mee**-lah*
10.000	*diecimila*	*dee-ay-chee-**mee**-lah*

continues

English	*Italiano*	Pronunciation
20.000	*ventimila*	*ven-tee-**mee**-lah*
100.000	*centomila*	*chen-toh-**mee**-lah*
200.000	*duecentomila*	*doo-eh-chen-toh-**mee**-lah*
1.000.000	*un milione*	*oon mee-**lyoh**-neh*
1.000.000.000	*un miliardo*	*oon mee-**lyar**-doh*

*Cento (100) does not have a plural form and retains its final vowel regardless of the following number.

**Mille (1,000) becomes mila *in the plural.*

Number Crunching

Note that Italian uses a period, called *un punto* (literally, "a point"), to indicate units of thousands, not a comma:

English	**Italian**
2,000	2.000

Also, in Italian, you must use a comma, called *una virgola*, in decimal numbers, not a period. The following number could be read as *uno virgola venticinque* (one *comma* twenty-five) or *uno e venticinque* (one and twenty-five) but in general, when pronounced, like English, Italian would not indicate the punctuation:

English	**Italian**
1.25	1,25

Finally, Italian uses a period when writing down the time. Similar to English, Italians don't read the punctuation aloud:

English	**Italian**
3:15	3.15

Practice Using *Avere* and Numbers

Translate the following sentences into Italian. Use your articles and cognates. See Appendix A to find any additional vocabulary you need.

1. I have one sister and one brother.

2. Do you (*tu*) have ten minutes?

3. Italy has a population of sixty million.

4. My daughter is seven years old.

5. They have one cat and two dogs.

6. The month of February has twenty-eight days.

Answers: 1. Ho una sorella e un fratello. 2. Hai dieci minuti? 3. L'Italia ha una popolazione di sessanta milioni. 4. Mia figlia ha sette anni. 5. Loro hanno un gatto e due cani. 6. Il mese di febbraio ha ventotto giorni.

Tick Tock: Telling Time

27

Time is easy to learn. Even if it takes you a while, remember the adage, *Meglio tardi che mai.* (Better late than never.)

When asking what time it is, you use the verb *essere*. You can ask the time in several ways:

Che ore sono?	*Che ora è?*
What time is it?	What time is it?

Sa l'ora?
Do you know what time it is?
Literally: Do you know the hour?

Because they are all considered singular, use *è* when you're talking about noon, midnight, and 1 o'clock. For all other (plural) times, use *sono*:

È l'una.	It is 1 o'clock.
È mezzogiorno.	It is noon.
È mezzanotte.	It is midnight.
Sono le due.	It is 2 o'clock.
Sono le nove e mezzo.	It is 9:30.
Sono le tre.	It is 3 o'clock.

Many Italian movie, train, public transportation, and other schedules use military time, which is based on a 24-hour clock (midnight being the twenty-fourth hour). For example, in Italian military time, 1 o'clock in the morning would be *l'una*. Piece of cake, right? But once you get to the afternoon, things require a little addition. Here, 13.00 would refer to 1 P.M., while 22.00 (*ore ventidue*) would refer to 10 P.M. and so on.

When writing the time, Italian uses a dot, not a colon:

English	Italian
3:30 A.M.	*3.30 del mattino* or *di mattina* ("of the morning")
9:45 P.M.	*9.45 di sera* ("of the evening")

Give Me a *Secondo*

The expressions in the following table help talk about the time.

More Time Expressions

English	Italiano	English	Italiano
At what time?	*A che ora?*	an hour	*un'ora*
in a half hour	*fra una mezz'ora*	a minute	*un minuto*
a quarter past	*e un quarto*	a quarter to	*meno un quarto*
a second	*un secondo*	ago	*fa*
and	*e*	before/after	*prima/dopo*
[to be] early/late	*[essere] in anticipo/in ritardo*	half past	*e mezzo*
[to be] on time	*[essere] in tempo*	since	*da*
in	*fra*	in the afternoon	*di pomeriggio*
... a while	*... un po'*	in the evening	*di sera*
... an hour	*... un'ora*	in the morning	*di mattina*
... a half hour	*... una mezz'ora*	less than/before	*meno*

ATTENZIONE!

The Italian word *tempo*, although used when talking about the weather (as in *temperatura*), can also refer to time.

To express time after the hour, use *e* (without the accent, meaning "and") plus the number of minutes past the hour:

Sono le quattro e dieci.	It is 4:10.
Sono le sei e cinque.	It is 6:05.
È l'una e un quarto.	It is 1:15.

To express time before the next hour (in English, we use "ten to," "quarter to," and so on), use the next hour + *meno* (less) + whatever time remains before the next hour:

> *Sono le otto meno un quarto.*
> It is a quarter to eight (*literally:* eight minus a quarter).
>
> *È l'una meno dieci.*
> It's ten to one (*literally:* one minus ten).

It is not unusual to hear the time expressed as follows:

> *Sono le sette e quarantacinque.*
> It is 7:45.

Minute by Minute, Hour by Hour

The following table spells out exactly how to tell the time minute by minute, hour by hour.

Telling Time

English	*Italiano*
It is 1:00.	*È l'una.*
It is 2:00.	*Sono le due.*
It is 2:05.	*Sono le due e cinque.*
It is 3:10.	*Sono le tre e dieci.*
It is 4:15.	*Sono le quattro e un quarto.*
It is 5:20.	*Sono le cinque e venti.*
It is 6:25.	*Sono le sei e venticinque.*
It is 6:30.	*Sono le sei e trenta.*
It is 7:30.	*Sono le sette e mezzo.*
It is 8:40. (20 minutes to 9)	*Sono le nove meno venti.*
It is 9:45. (a quarter to 10)	*Sono le dieci meno un quarto.*
It is 10:50. (10 minutes to 11)	*Sono le undici meno dieci.*
It is 11:55. (5 minutes to noon)	*È mezzogiorno meno cinque.*
It is noon.	*È mezzogiorno.*
It is midnight.	*È mezzanotte.*

Time Will Tell

Answer the following questions as best you can using complete sentences. The tiny preposition *a* (at; to) is used in the following examples; a contraction of that is *alle* (at the). Remember that the answer is usually in the question. The verb in each sentence is underlined. A time is given at the end of each question.

> *Example: A che ora mangiamo?* (What time do we eat?)
> *Answer: Mangiamo alle otto e mezzo.* (We're eating at eight thirty.)

1. *A che ora <u>andiamo</u> al cinema?* (6:00 P.M.)

2. *A che ora <u>parte</u> il volo?* (8:25 A.M.)

3. *A che ora <u>inizia</u> il programma?* (19:00)

4. *Quando <u>parte</u> l'autobus per Verona?* (noon)

5. *A che ora <u>arriva</u> il treno da Roma?* (22:30)

6. *A che ora <u>andiamo</u> a fare colazione?* (7:30)

Answers: 1. Andiamo al cinema alle sei di sera. 2. Il volo parte alle otto e venticinque.
3. Il programma inizia alle dicianove. 4. L'autobus parte per Verona a mezzogiorno.
5. Il treno arriva alle dieci e mezzo. 6. Andiamo a fare colazione alle sette e mezzo.

Italian Punctuation

A dot, a line, a curve, a star … all these are important punctuation marks, called *segni d'interpunzione*. The usage for many of these symbles is the same between Italian and English, but there are plenty of exceptions. The following table helps you map out the terrain, understand the signs, and ensure you're able to make your point.

Segni d'Interpunzione

Sign	English	*Italiano*
&	ampersand	*e* (literally "and")
@	at sign	*la chiocciola** (literally, "the snail")
'	apostrophe	*l'apostrofo*
*	asterisk	*l'asterisco*
[]	brackets	*le parentesi quadre* (literally, "parenthesis square")
:	colon	*due punti*

Sign	English	*Italiano*
,	comma	*la virgola*
-	dash	*la lineetta*
°	degree	*il grado*
…	ellipsis	*i puntini di sospensione*
!	exclamation point	*il punto esclamativo*
-	hyphen	*il trattino*
( )	parenthesis	*le parentesi tonde* (literally, "parenthesis round")
.	period	*il punto*
#	pound sign	*il cancelletto*
?	question mark	*il punto interrogativo*
« »	quotation marks*	*le virgolette*
;	semicolon	*il punto e virgola*
/	slash	*la sbarretta*

*Italian calls a winding staircase una scala a chiocciola *("a snail stair").*

LA BELLA LINGUA

The logogram &, called ampersand, comes from classical Latin and is a merging of two notions. The term breaks down to mean "and *per se* and"; *per se* translates to "by itself."

Establishing When

The following table offers a selection of time-related vocabulary. Whenever you hear people say *Ancor* at a venue, you now know they're saying "Again!" (This same adverb also means "still" as in *Sei ancora qui?* "Are you still here?")

English	*Italiano*	Pronunciation
after	*dopo; poi*	**doh**-poh; poy
afternoon	*il pomeriggio*	eel poh-meh-**reej**-joh
always	*sempre*	**sehm**-prey
appointment	*l'appuntamento*	lahp-poon-tah-**men**-toh
before	*prima*	**preeh**-mah
calendar	*il calendario*	eel kah-len-**dah**-ree-yoh
century	*il secolo*	eel **seh**-koh-loh
date	*la data*	lah **dah**-tah
day	*il giorno*	eel **jor**-noh

continues

English	*Italiano*	Pronunciation
... every (day)	*ogni (giorno)*	**oh**-nyee (**jor**-noh)
decade	*il decennio*	eel deh-**chen**-nee-yoh
early	*presto*	**prehs**-toh
evening	*la sera*	lah **seh**-rah
... this evening	*stasera*	stah-**seh**-rah
holiday	*la festa*	lah **fes**-tah
in a hurry	*in fretta*	een **fret**-tah
last	*scorso/a; passato/a*	**skor**-soh; pahs-**sah**-toh
... last year	*l'anno scorso*	**lahn**-noh **skor**-soh
late; later	*tardi; più tardi*	**tar**-dee; pyoo **tar**-dee
millennium	*il millennio*	eel meel-**leh**-nee-yoh
month	*il mese*	eel **meh**-zeh
morning	*la mattina*	lah maht-**tee**-nah
... this morning	*stamattina*	stah-maht-**tee**-nah
next	*prossimo/a*	**prohs**-see-moh
now	*adesso; ora*	ah-**dess**-oh; **oh**-rah
often	*spesso*	**spehs**-soh
sometimes	*qualche volta; tavolta*	**kwahl**-key **vol**-tah; **tah**-vol-tah
... at times	*certe volte*	**cher**-teh **vol**-teh
soon; immediately	*subito*	**soob**-bee-toh
still; again	*ancora*	ahn-**koh**-rah
today	*oggi*	**ohj**-jee
tomorrow	*domani*	doh-**mah**-nee
... day after tomorrow	*dopo domani*	doh-poh doh-**mah**-nee
tonight	*stasera*	stah-**seh**-rah
usually	*di solito*	dee **soh**-lee-toh
week	*la settimana*	lah seht-tee-**mah**-nah
... last week	*la settimana scorsa*	lah seht-tee-**mah**-nah **skor**-sah
... next week	*la settimana prossima*	lah seht-tee-**mah**-nah **prohs**-see-mah
within (two weeks)	*fra (due settimane)*	frah (doo-weh seht-tee-**mah**-neh)
yesterday	*ieri*	**yeh**-ree

Time passes quickly.
Il tempo passa velocemente.

We eat dinner everyday at six.
Mangiamo la cena ogni giorno alle sei.

We often stay with friends.
Stiamo spesso con gli amici.

I have an appointment tomorrow morning.
Ho un appuntamento domani mattina.

BUON'IDEA

In Italy, in addition to making a big deal out of birthdays, many people also celebrate their onomastico (Saint's Day), or one's name day. Pick up an Italian calendar and see if there's a day for you! If you can't find your name, don't feel left out:you still get to celebrate your *onomastico* on *Ognissanti* (All Saint's Day).

It's a Date!

To talk about the date requires a particular order. Often this simply means that, in Italian, you must place the day *before* the month—for example, *5 settembre* (September 5).

I Giorni: Days

When pronouncing days of the week, the accent tells you to emphasize the last syllable. Italians have adopted the English way of expressing the end of the week by using the English word *weekend*, but you will also hear *il fine settimana*.

Days of the Week

28

English	*L'Italiano*	Pronunciation
Monday	*lunedì*	loo-neh-**dee**
Tuesday	*martedì*	mar-teh-**dee**
Wednesday	*mercoledì*	mer-koh-leh-**dee**
Thursday	*giovedì*	joh-veh-**dee**
Friday	*venerdì*	veh-ner-**dee**
Saturday	*sabato*	**sah**-bah-toh
Sunday	*domenica*	doh-**meh**-nee-kah
the weekend	*il fine settimana*	eel fee-neh seh-tee-**mah**-nah

With the exception of *domenica* (Sunday), which refers to God's day, the days of the week correspond to planets. Here's how they line up:

lunedì: la luna (the moon)   *giovedì: Giove* (Jupiter)

martedì: Marte (Mars)   *venerdì: Venere* (Venus)

mercoledì: Mercurio (Mercury)   *sabato: Saturno* (Saturn)

I Mesi: **Months**

The original *calendario* (calendar) the Romans used was based on a 10-month year. The original "old-style" Roman calendar, instituted by Julius Caesar in 46 B.C.E., was used until 1583, when Pope Gregory XIII made official the "new-style" calendar— also referred to as the *Gregorian* calendar. The months *luglio* (July) and *agosto* (August) were added in honor of the great Roman Emperors Julius Caesar and Augustus. As with days of the week, Italian does not capitalize names of months.

> **LA BELLA LINGUA**
>
> The word *calendario* originally comes from the Latin word *calends,* signifying the day of the new moon. During the Middle Ages, money lenders referred to their account books as the calendar due to the fact that the monthly interest was due on the *calends.*

I Mesi **(the Months)**

28

English	*Italiano*	Pronunciation
January	*gennaio*	*jen-**ny**-yoh*
February	*febbraio*	*feb-**bry**-yoh*
March	*marzo*	***mar**-tsoh*
April	*aprile*	*ah-**pree**-leh*
May	*maggio*	***mahj**-joh*
June	*giugno*	***joo**-nyoh*
July	*luglio*	***loo**-lyoh*
August	*agosto*	*ah-**goh**-stoh*
September	*settembre*	*set-**tem**-breh*
October	*ottobre*	*oht-**toh**-breh*
November	*novembre*	*noh-**vem**-breh*
December	*dicembre*	*dee-**chem**-breh*

With the exception of the *first* day of the month, dates in Italian require cardinal numbers (1, 2, 3, …). As indicated previously, in Italian, the day comes before the month. This isn't difficult to realize when you're talking about *il 25 dicembre* (December 25), but with some dates, it can get tricky.

For example, if you wrote the abbreviation 4/5, in Italian it would be read as the fourth of May, the fifth month. If you meant the fifth of April, you were off by almost a month! It's crucial that you remember to reverse the two numbers when dealing with any kinds of documents, such as a car lease or apartment contract. Or avoid this problem altogether and always write out the month!

In Italian, the definite article always goes in front of the day, followed by the month. Unless beginning a sentence, months are not capitalized.

il 25 (venticinque) giugno   *l'otto marzo*
June 25   March 8

But if you're talking about the first day of any month, use the ordinal number *primo* (first): *il primo maggio* (May 1).

LA BELLA LINGUA

Here's a who's who of mythological archetypes. The Romans and Greeks shared many of the same gods. The Greek equivalents are in parentheses.

The Gods	The Goddesses
Apollo (Apollo)	Ceres (Demeter)
Jupiter (Zeus)	Diana (Artemis)
Mars (Ares)	Juno (Hera)
Mercury (Hermes)	Minerva (Athena)
Neptune (Poseidon)	Venus (Aphrodite)
Vulcan (Hephaistos)	Vesta (Hestia)

What *Secolo* (Century)?

Talking about centuries can be confusing in both English and Italian. For example, in English when you talk about the *third century*, you're really talking about the century before (200–299). Additionally, you're using an *ordinal* number (first, second, third, …).

Italian, on the other hand, always uses cardinal numbers (1, 2, 3 …), unless referring to the *first* (day, month, year).

A.D.

The basis for today's calendar finds its roots in Christianity. As you probably know, the abbreviation A.D. comes from Latin and literally stands for *Anno Domini*, meaning *in the year of the Lord*. In writing, the Italian language uses both the Latin abbreviation A.D. and the Italian abbreviation D.C. (from *dopo Cristo*, meaning "after Christ") to express time *after* the birth of Christ. (When speaking, the tendency is to use the words *dopo Cristo*.)

In Italian, to talk about dates from 1 A.D. *until* the year 1000 A.D., you must use cardinal numbers plus the words *dopo Cristo* (D.C.):

79 D.C.	*Il Vesuvio distrusse Pompei.*
79 A.D.	*Vesuvius destroyed Pompei.*

You might also see *anno domini* or the abbreviation A.D. written on monuments and tombstones.

121–180 D.C.	*Marco Aurelio, Imperatore*
121–180 A.D.	*Marcus Aurelius, Emperor*

As a general rule, you don't need to use A.D. for dates after the year 1000.

LA BELLA LINGUA

Today, English more commonly uses B.C.E. (before Common Era) and C.E. (in the Common Era).

B.C.

To express time *before* the birth of Christ (B.C.), as in 400 B.C., Italian uses the abbreviation *A.C.* (from *avanti Cristo*, meaning *before Christ*).

753 A.C.	*La fondazione di Roma*
753 B.C.	*The foundation of Rome*
106–43 A.C.	*Cicero, oratore*
106–43 B.C.	*Cicero, orator*

To talk about the year 1965, you would say it like any other number; Italian does not separate the numbers so it becomes *really* long:

millenovecentosessantacinque
one thousand nine hundred sixty-five

1,000 Years Later

To express centuries *after* the year 1000, it gets a little tricky. To talk about the sixteenth century (1500–1599) like an Italian, you must omit the first thousand and say *il Cinquecento* (the five hundred). There is no need to indicate that this occurred after the birth of Christ.

However, it is also possible to use an ordinal number (first, second, third, ...) when referring to centuries, as in *il quindicesimo secolo* (the fifteenth century).

In writing, the apostrophe before the number shows that it's after the year 1000.

> '100—*La Crociata*
> 1100—*the Crusades*
>
> '300–'600—*Il Rinascimento*
> 1300–1600—*the Renaissance*

In addition, you should know that when Italians talk about *il Cinquecento* (*literally:* the five hundred), they are actually referring to the sixteenth century, and not the year 500. Look for the apostrophe before the number. This is especially important if you're in a museum and discussing different artistic or historical periods.

You can always spell out the year using numbers, for example, 1861 (the year Italy was united) would be *milleottocentosessantauno* (one thousand eight hundred sixty one). You would *not* say "eighteen sixty-one."

Check out how this works:

'200 (*il duecento*)	the thirteenth century (1200)
'300 (*il trecento*)	the fourteenth century (1300)
'400 (*il quattrocento*)	the fifteenth century (1400)
'500 (*il cinquecento*)	the sixteenth century (1500)
'600 (*il seicento*)	the seventeenth century (1600)
'700 (*il settecento*)	the eighteenth century (1700)
'800 (*l'ottocento*)	the nineteenth century (1800)
'900 (*il novecento*)	the twentieth century (1900)

To talk about this millennium, you would use one of the following:

2000 (*due mila*)

il ventunesimo secolo   the twenty-first century

The Least You Need to Know

- *Avere* (to have) is an important verb used to express needs and feelings. It's used as an auxiliary verb.
- Telling time is easy. Remember the key words *meno* (less than) and *e* (and).
- To express the date, use the number of the day plus the month and the year.
- Days of the week and months are not capitalized in Italian.
- Italian punctuation marks are often used differently from the English use.
- Use D.C. (*dopo Cristo*) to express A.D. and A.C. (*avanti Cristo*) to express B.C. (before Christ).
- When discussing historical dates—for example to express the seventeenth century (1600)—Italian uses '600.

Doing Things Right

In This Chapter

- Making do with the verb *fare* (to do/to make)
- Using the verb *essere* (to be) to ask about the weather
- Using the verb *stare* (to be/to stay) to talk about something about to happen
- Out of this world: discussing the sky
- Tuning into *l'astrologia* (astrology)

The verb *fare* (to do/make) gives you the language to actually do something about those needs you expressed in Chapter 8. Plus, you get to chitchat about *il tempo* (the weather) with a gorgeous stranger near you.

In this chapter, you also learn how to discuss the stars and, for fun, check out your astrological sign.

Things to Do: The Verb *Fare*

If you're a doer, then *fare* (to do) is the verb for you because it expresses when you want to make or do something. It's also often used like the English verb *to take* and appears in many idiomatic expressions. For example, in Italian, you don't *take* a trip—rather, you *make* a trip (*fare un viaggio*). *Fare* is also used to talk about *il tempo* (the weather) or when you *take* that perfect picture.

With this versatile verb, you can go shopping, pretend, or indicate where something hurts. You'll use it when you take a shower, a walk, or a spin. You'll also use it a lot during your travels. Because *fare* is irregular, you must memorize the different parts shown in the following table.

The Verb *Fare* (to Do; to Make)

Italiano	Pronunciation	English
io **faccio**	**fah**-*choh*	I do/make
tu **fai**	*fy*	you do/make
lui/lei/Lei **fa**	*fah*	he/she (it) does/makes; You do/make
noi **facciamo**	*fah-***chah***-moh*	we do/make
voi **fate**	**fah**-*teh*	you do/make
loro **fanno**	**fahn**-*noh*	they do/make

Let's take a look at some of the idiomatic *espressioni* the verb *fare* is used in. (Your Italian *dizionario* will offer many as well.) In English, you *take* a shower, whereas in Italian you *make* a shower (*fare una doccia*). Conversely, in English you *make* a decision, in Italian you *take* a decision (*prendere una decisione*). It can be hard to *make* sense of everything, but you'll *do* fine. The following table contains some more idiomatic expressions using the verb *fare*. Remember that, like idiomatic expressions using the verbs *avere*, you must conjugate the verb in parentheses.

Expressions Using *Fare*

English	*Italiano*	English	*Italiano*
to ask a question	*fare una domanda*	to make a bad impression	*fare una brutta figura*
to be early	*fare presto*	to make a good impression	*fare una bella figura*
to be late	*fare tardi*	to make a ruckus	*fare baccano*
to do good	*fare del bene*	to make love	*fare l'amore*
to fill it up	*fare il pieno*	to pack/prepare one's bags	*fare le valigie*
to get a tune-up	*fare un controllo*	to pretend	*fare finta*
to get gas	*fare benzina*	to show	*fare vedere*
to give a gift	*fare un regalo*	to take a bath	*fare il bagno*
to go shopping	*fare le spese*	to take a picture	*fare una fotografia*
to have breakfast	*(fare) colazione*	to take a shower	*(fare) la doccia*
to hitchhike	*fare l'autostop*	to take a spin	*fare un giro*
to hurt someone	*fare male a qualcuno*	to take a trip	*(fare) un viaggio*
to take a walk	*fare una passeggiata*		

Can I ask a question?
Posso fare una domanda?
Literally: Can I make a question?

At what time are we having breakfast?
A che ora facciamo colazione?
Literally: At what time are we making breakfast?

Hugo is taking a walk.
Hugo fa una passeggiata.

You may also see and hear the verb as *far,* as in *far le compere* (to do the shopping).
Poems and lyrics often chop off the last *-e.*

Talking About the Weather: *Che Tempo Fa?*

Che tempo fa? literally means "What's the weather doing?" To talk about *il tempo* (the weather), you'll need the verb *fare.* You'll see the *ci + essere* combination here, too, as in *C'è il sole* (*literally:* There is sun).

Weather Expressions

English	*Italiano*
What's the weather?	*Che tempo fa?*
How's the weather?	*Com'è il tempo?*
What's the forecast?	*Quali sono le previsioni?*
What is the temperature today?	*Quanto fa oggi?* (How much is it doing today?)
It's 30° (Celsius).	*Fa trenta gradi.*

There are several very simple ways to talk about the weather using the verbs you've learned so far.

Study the following examples using *fare:*

It's …	*Fa* (it makes) …
hot.	*caldo.*
cold.	*freddo.*
cool.	*fresco.*
nice out.	*bel tempo.*
bad.	*brutto.* (ugly)

You can also use *Ci + essere (C'è/Ci sono)* to talk about the weather:

There's …	*C'è …*
sun.	*il sole.*
rain.	*la pioggia.*
freezing rain.	*la pioggia ghiacciata.*
sleet.	*il nevischio.*
snow.	*la neve.*
fog.	*nebbia.*
frost.	*la brina.*
wind/a bit of wind.	*vento/un venticello.*
a breeze.	*una brezza.*
humidity.	*umidità.*
a storm.	*un temporale.*

It's thundering and lightning.
Ci sono tuoni e fulmini.

It was love at first sight.
È stato un colpo di fulmine. (It was like a bolt of lightning.)

These phrases utilize one simple letter: *È* (again, using *essere*) + an adjective:

It is …	*È …*
beautiful/gorgeous.	*bello/bellissimo.*
ugly/cruddy.	*brutto/bruttissimo.*
clear.	*sereno.* (serene)
humid.	*umido.*
cloudy.	*nuvoloso.*
freezing.	*gelido.*

You can use these invariable verbs in either present tense or present progressive (especially if it's happening right now, this very second):

It's raining.
Piove./Sta piovendo. (from *piovere*, to rain)

It's snowing.
Nevica./Sta nevicando. (from *nevicare*, to snow)

It's hailing.
Grandina./Sta grandinando. (from *grandinare*, to hail)

The verb *stare* (to be/to stay) + *per* can indicate something *about to happen:*

It's about to …	*Sta per …*
rain.	*piovere.*
snow.	*nevicare.*
I'm about to …	*Sto per …*
go out.	*uscire.*
go crazy.	*andare matto(a).*

LA BELLA LINGUA

In Italy, *il ferragosto* refers to the mid-August holidays many Italians take during the hot, humid month. If you're planning a trip during this time, don't be surprised to find many of the smaller businesses closed for *le ferie* (the holidays).

Pizza Quattro Stagioni (the Four Seasons)

Have you ever eaten *pizza quattro stagioni*? Did you realize it was referring to "four season pizza"? Here are the ingredients:

summer	*l'estate*
spring	*la primavera* (literally, first green)
fall	*l'autunno* (autumn)
winter	*l'inverno*

When talking about a particular season, you'll hear used both the prepositions *in* and *di*:

Is it cold in winter?	It rains in spring.
Fa freddo d'inverno?	*Piove in primavera.*

Il Clima (the Climate)

There's a lot more out there than *la pioggia* (rain), *il sole* (sun), and *la neve* (snow). How about *fiocchi di neve* (snowflakes)? A personal favorite, *il tramonto* (sunset), literally translates as "between the mountains." When it rains in Italy, there are no drenched dogs or cats dropping from the sky; we say *Piove a catinelle.* (It's raining buckets.) And is there anything more delightful than *un cielo celeste* (a blue sky), or *il mare azzurro* (the azure sea)?

The following table gives you more climate-related terms.

L'Atmosfera (the Atmosphere)

English	Italiano	English	Italiano
air	*l'aria*	pollution	*l'inquinamento*
atmosphere	*l'atmosfera*	rain	*la pioggia*
climate	*il clima*	rainbow	*l'arcobaleno*
cloud	*la nuvola*	sky	*il cielo*
degree	*grado*	smog	*lo smog*
ice	*il ghiaccio*	snowball	*la palla di neve*
mud	*il fango*	snowflake	*il fiocco di neve*
nature	*la natura*	sunrise	*l'alba*
overcast	*coperto*	sunset	*il tramonto*
ozone	*l'ozono*	thermometer	*il termometro*

The next time you're hanging around the fatalists and doomsdayers, impress them with your knowledge of natural disasters. The terms in the following table will help you talk about *le previsioni del tempo* (the forecast).

Disastri Naturali (Natural Disasters)

English	Italiano	English	Italiano
avalanche	*la valanga*	fire	*il fuoco*
calamity	*la calamità*	flood	*l'alluvione*
disaster	*il disastro*	pestilence	*la pestilenza*
earthquake	*il terremoto*	plague	*la peste*
famine	*la carestia*	volcano	*il vulcano*

La Temperatura: **What's Hot and What's Not**

To refer to *la temperatura* (the temperature), you use the verb *fare* in the third person, as you do with the weather.

If someone asks, *Quanto fa oggi?* they're really asking, "How many degrees (*gradi*) are there today?" The word *gradi* is implied, and the use of *fare* in this case is idiomatic.

If it's **20°** Centigrade, you reply:

> *Fa* ***venti*** *gradi.*
> *Literally:* It's making **twenty** degrees.

If it's 10 **below**, say:

> *Fa dieci* ***sotto*** *zero.*
> *Literally:* It's making ten **under** zero.

Obviously, you can change the numbers in these examples when speaking to reflect the actual temperature.

AS A *REGOLA*

In Italy, as in all Europe, the metric system is used to determine the temperature. To convert Centigrade to Fahrenheit, multiply the Centigrade temperature by 1.8 and add 32. To convert Fahrenheit to Centigrade, subtract 32 from the Fahrenheit temperature and divide the remaining number by 1.8. Here are some basic temperature reference points:

   Freezing: 32°F = 0°C

   Room temperature: 68°F = 18°C

   Body temperature: 98.6°F = 33°C

   Boiling: 212°F = 90°C

Che Segno Sei? (What's Your Sign?)

Of course *you* don't believe in all that astrological mumbo-jumbo … or do you? What better way to learn your *mesi* (months), *elementi* (elements), and develop your ability to describe people than by reading your daily horoscope?

All the Italian words used here are *parole simili* (cognates). Understanding their significance should be easy. Just go with your gut.

Segni Astrologici (Astrological Signs)

Simbolo	Segno	Elemento	Caratteristiche	Periodo	English
♈	ariete	fuoco	indipendente, aggressivo, impulsivo	21 marzo–19 aprile	Aries
♉	toro	terra	determinato, testardo, fedele, tollerante	20 aprile–20 maggio	Taurus
♊	gemelli	aria	intelligente, ambizioso, capriccioso	21 maggio–21 giugno	Gemini
♋	cancro	acqua	sensibile, simpatico, impressionabile	22 giugno–22 luglio	Cancer
♌	leone	fuoco	generoso, nobile, entusiasta	23 luglio–22 agosto	Leo
♍	vergine	terra	intellettuale, passivo, metodico	23 agosto–22 settembre	Virgo
♎	bilancia	aria	giusto, organizzato, simpatico	23 settembre–23 ottobre	Libra
♏	scorpione	acqua	filosofo, fedele, dominante	24 ottobre–21 novembre	Scorpio
♐	sagittario	fuoco	pragmatico, maturo, creativo	22 novembre–21 dicembre	Sagittarius
♑	capricorno	terra	ambizioso, fedele, perseverante	22 dicembre–19 gennaio	Capricorn
♒	acquario	aria	generoso, idealista, originale	20 gennaio–18 febbraio	Aquarius
♓	pesci	acqua	timido, simpatico, sensibile	19 febbraio–20 marzo	Pisces

The Least You Need to Know

- *Fare* (to do or make) is used in many idiomatic expressions such as *fare una foto* (to take a photo), *fare un viaggio* (to take a trip), and *fare benzina* (to get gas).
- To ask about the weather, say *Che tempo fa?* (What's the weather doing?)
- The verb *essere* (to be) can also be used to talk about the weather.
- Use *stare* to talk about something that is *about to happen*.
- Develop your vocabulary while talking about your *segno astrologico* (astrological sign).

The Modal and Other Irregular Verbs

In This Chapter

- Working with modal verbs *volere, potere,* and *dovere*
- Another look at some irregular verbs
- Travel and geography terms
- Making suggestions and plans
- All about animals

In this chapter, you learn about modal verbs. I like to think of these as the ready-and-able superheroes of verbs. You also learn about several very useful, but irregular verbs, many of which are used to make your way around town and ask for directions. You additionally develop the vocabulary you need to talk about countries, nationalities, and religions, and for the fun of it, animals.

Superhero Verbs: The Modals

Do you *want* to learn Italian? You *can,* but you *must* study. The modal verbs *volere* (to want), *potere* (to be able to), and *dovere* (to have to) express a mood, such as when you say, "I want! I can! I must!" They're powerful verbs that describe intention, desire, and potential.

I Want What I Want!

Volere is an important verb you have already been using in its conditional form. When you say *"Vorrei,"* you're saying "I would like." Because you *would like* to express your wants as delicately as possible, you use the conditional. Sometimes, however, you just want what you want and there's no doubt about it. The following table shows you how to express want, pure and simple, in the present tense. The English terms *volunteer* and *volition* are etymological cousins to this verb.

Volere (to Want)

Italiano	English
io **voglio**	I want
tu **vuoi**	you want
lui/lei/Lei **vuole**	he/she/it wants; You want
noi **vogliamo**	we want
voi **volete**	you want
loro **vogliono***	they want

Emphasis should be placed on the first syllable of the third person plural (loro).

I Think I Can, I Think I Can!

You use the verb *potere* (to be able to; can) to express your potential to do something. It's the same as what the little *treno* said as it puffed up the hill—and it's what you use to express that you *can* speak Italian. The *possibilità* are endless, as long as you think you can. The verb *potere* is always used with an infinitive. Linguistic cousins include the words *potential*, *potent*, and *possibility*.

Potere (to Be Able to/Can)

Italiano	English
io **posso**	I can
tu **puoi**	you can
lui/lei/Lei **può**	he/she/it/You can
noi **possiamo**	we can
voi **potete**	you can
loro **possono***	they can

Emphasis should be placed on the first syllable of the third person plural (loro).

I Have to …

Use the modal verb *dovere*, outlined in the following table, to express *to have to* and *must* or to express *to owe*. Like the verb *potere*, *dovere* is almost always used in front of an infinitive, such as when you say, "I must study." Relatives to this word include *debt* and *debit*.

Dovere (to Have to/Must/to Owe)

Italiano	English
io **devo**	I must;
tu **devi**	you must;
lui/lei/Lei **deve**	he/she/it/You must
noi **dobbiamo**	we must
voi **dovete**	you must
loro **devono***	they must

*Emphasis should be placed on the first syllable of the third person plural (loro).

LA BELLA LINGUA

Most modal verbs are followed by an infinitive:

Posso imparare la lingua italiana.
I can learn Italian.

Voglio partire.　　　　　*Devo studiare i verbi.*
I want to leave.　　　　　I must study the verbs.

I'm in the Mood for …

Read through the *frasi* and determine which modal *verbo*—*potere*, *dovere*, or *volere*—is most appropriate to each *situazione*. There may be more than one correct *risposta*. Don't forget to conjugate the verb according to the subject. The Italian pronouns are given in parentheses to help you determine the subject. Read the entire *frase* before giving your *risposta*.

1. *(Io)* _____ studiare **italiano** ogni giorno.

2. *Cinzia (tu),* _____ venire alla festa domani sera?

3. *Pino* _____ fare una prenotazione.

4. *(Io)* _____ una camera singola per favore.

5. *Tiziana e Maria* _____ *incontrare un'amica più tardi.*

6. *(Voi)* _____ *mangiare gli spaghetti al ristorante?*

7. *Giorgio* _____ *parlare il greco.*

8. *Leonardo non* _____ *mai studiare.*

Answers: 1. voglio, posso, devo 2. vuoi, puoi 3. deve, vuole 4. voglio 5. vogliono, devono 6. volete 7. può 8. deve, vuole

More Irregular Verbs

Whoopie! More irregular verbs! If you want to know or say anything, you'll need the verbs *sapere* (to know) and *dire* (to say). If you plan on drinking, you'll need *bere* (to drink). And if you want to get anywhere, you'll need *andare* (to go), and *salire* (to get on). To exit, use *uscire* (to go out). If you feel like hanging out for a minute, use *rimanere* (to remain). You may finally just want to come back home, in which case you'll need the verb *venire* (to come).

LA BELLA LINGUA

If someone asks you a question for which you don't know the answer (like, Do aliens exist?), shrug your shoulders and say, *"Chi sa?"* (Who knows?), *"Non lo so"* (I don't know), or *"Non ho idea!"* (I have no idea!)

B Is for *Bere* (to Drink)

You'll definitely need to use the irregular verb *bere* (to drink) if you plan on enjoying any number of the fine beverages (another etymological cousin), from *il vino* to *un bicchiere d'acqua* (a glass of water).

Bere (to Drink)

Italiano	English
io **bevo**	I drink
tu **bevi**	you drink
lui/lei/Lei **beve**	he/she/it drinks; You drink
noi **beviamo**	we drink
voi **bevete**	you drink
loro **bevono**	they drink

D Is for *Dire* (to Say)

Dire (to say or tell) is another useful irregular verb. Note in the following table that the stem changes to *dic-* in all persons except the second plural. Think *diction, dictate, dictionary.*

Dire (to Say/Tell)

Italiano	English
io **dico**	I say
tu **dici**	you say
lui/lei/Lei **dice**	he/she/it says; You say
noi **diciamo**	we say
voi **dite**	you say
loro **dicono**	they say

Knowing with *Sapere*

The irregular verb *sapere* (to know something) is what you use to talk about all the information you have stuck inside that head of yours. Linguistic cousins include *la sapienza* (knowledge) and *consapevole* (aware, conscious).

Sapere (to Know)

Italiano	English
io **so**	I know
tu **sai**	you know
lui/lei/Lei **sa**	he/she/it knows; You know
noi **sappiamo**	we know
voi **sapete**	you know
loro **sanno**	they know

Getting on with *Salire*

The irregular verb *salire* (to climb) additionally translates to "to get on," "to mount," and "to go up." Use it to get on the bus or train.

Salire (to Climb)

Italiano	English
io **salgo**	I climb
tu **sali**	you climb
lui/lei/Lei **sale**	he/she/it climbs; You climb
noi **saliamo**	we climb
voi **salite**	you climb
loro **salgono**	they climb

Going Out with *Uscire*

You're ready to paint the town red. The verb *uscire* (to go out or exit) gets you out of your hotel room and into the heart of the action.

Uscire (to Go Out/Exit)

Italiano	English
io **esco**	I go out
tu **esci**	you go out
lui/lei/Lei **esce**	he/she/it goes out; You go out
noi **usciamo**	we go out
voi **uscite**	you go out
loro **escono**	they go out

Remember your pronunciation rules: the word *esco* is pronounced *es-koh; esci* is pronounced *eh-she*.

Staying a While with *Rimanere*

The verb *rimanere* (to remain) has similar endings to the verb *venire*.

Rimanere (to Remain)

Italiano	English
io **rimango**	I remain
tu **rimani**	you remain
lui/lei/Lei **rimane**	he/she/it remains; You remain
noi **rimaniamo**	we remain
voi **rimanete**	you remain
loro **rimangono**	they remain

LA BELLA LINGUA

The verb *rimanere* can also be used idiomatically to express a state or condition, as in *rimanere male* (to be disappointed) or *rimanere soddisfatto* (to be satisfied). Among other things, it can also mean to be situated, as in *Dove rimane la stazione?* (Where is the station?)

Rimango in albergo stasera.
I'm remaining in the hotel this evening.

Rimangono in campagna.
They are remaining in the country.

Coming Together with *Venire*

Eventually, you have to come down to Earth. The irregular verb *venire* (to come) might help you find your way.

Venire (to Come)

Italiano	English
io **vengo**	I come
tu **vieni**	you come
lui/lei/Lei **viene**	he/she/it comes; You come
noi **veniamo**	we come
voi **venite**	you come
loro **vengono**	they come

Going Crazy: The Verb *Andare*

The verb *andare* (to go) is an essential irregular verb, so you need to memorize the parts outlined in the following table. (You can cram on the 7-hour plane ride to Italy.) You'll get to use the verbs you've studied so far to talk about getting around.

Andare (to Go)

Italiano	English
io **vado**	I go
tu **vai**	you go
lui/lei/Lei **va**	he/she/it goes; You go
noi **andiamo**	we go
voi **andate**	you go
loro **vanno**	they go

The verb *andare* can come in handy as you make your way around. *Andare* is often followed by a preposition (because you've got to go *to* somewhere).

When using *andare* with the preposition *a* plus a definite article, you must create a contraction:

I am going **to the** university.	We're going **to the** restaurant.
*Vado **all'**università.*	*Andiamo **al** ristorante.*

Andare may also be followed by the preposition *in* (to) to express the English equivalent *by:*

We're going **by** car.	Lorenza is going **by** bicycle.
*Andiamo **in** macchina.*	*Lorenza va **in** bicicletta.*
The tourists are going by train.	I'm going by plane.
*I turisti vanno **in** treno.*	*Vado **in** aeroplano.*

However, When using the verb *andare* to say you're going by foot, you use the preposition *a* to express *by:*

I am going **by** foot.
*Vado **a** piedi.*

Note that the Italians often say *Andiamo!* much in the same way we say *Let's go!*

Let's go …	*Andiamo …*
… abroad.	… *all'estero.*
… around, on tour.	… *in giro.*
… on vacation.	… *in vacanza.*
… to the country.	… *in campagna.*
… to the mountains.	… *in montagna.*
… to the seashore.	… *al mare.*

AS A *REGOLA*

You use the preposition *a* when you want to express going to or staying in a city: *Vado a Roma.* (I'm going to Rome.) The preposition *in* is generally used when you're traveling to a country: *Andiamo in Italia.* (We are going to Italy.)

Going, Going, Gone

Fill in the appropriate form of *andare*. Translate the sentences.

1. *Luisa e Marta _____ in macchina all'aeroporto.*

2. *Io _____ a New York.*

3. *Tu _____ alla stazione.*

4. *Roberto ed io _____ a mangiare una pizza.*

5. *Voi _____ a piedi. Loro _____ in bicicletta.*

Answers: 1. vanno; Luisa and Marta are going by car to the airport. 2. vado; I am going to New York. 3. vai; You're going to the station. 4. andiamo; Robert and I are going to eat a pizza .5. andate; vanno; You're going by foot. They're going by bicycle.

The Power of Suggestion

The gorgeous Italian you sat next to on the plane phoned you at your *albergo* (hotel), and you've made a date to go sightseeing. Although you haven't even left your hotel room, you've already planned your beautiful wedding in your mind. Sometimes a hint won't do; you have to come right out and make a suggestion.

Perché Non?

The easiest way to make a suggestion is to ask this simple question using the words *perché non* ... (why not ...):

> *Perché non* + the verb in the first person plural form (*noi*)?

For example:

> Why don't we take a spin?
> *Perché non facciamo un giro?*

If you want to ask what someone thinks of the idea, these phrases utilize the partitive *ne:*

What do you think (of it)?	What do you say (about it)?
Che ne pensi/pensa?	*Che ne dici/dice?*

LA BELLA LINGUA

Here's a quick *sommario* of question words: *che/cosa/che cosa* (what; which), *chi* (who), *come* (how), *dove* (where), *perché* (why), *quando* (when), *quanto* (how much).

Let's ...

To suggest the English *Let's* ..., use the first person plural form (*noi*) of the verb:

mangiare (to eat):	*Mangiamo!* Let's eat!
partire (to leave):	*Partiamo stasera.* Let's leave this evening.
viaggiare (to travel):	*Viaggiamo in Italia.* Let's travel to Italy.

Talking About Your Trip

You're familiar with all these words but may not have seen them used in these idiomatic expressions related to *la vacanza*. Match up the Italian and English translations. You'll find it's a piece of cake.

1. *Siamo in ferie.*

2. *I bambini sono in vacanza.*

3. *Luigi fa il campeggio.*

4. *Voglio fare un viaggio.*

5. *Perché non facciamo una crociera?*

6. *Gli studenti vanno in giro.*

7. *Il pellegrino va a vedere il Vaticano.*

a) Why don't we go on a cruise?

b) I want to take a trip.

c) We're on holiday.

d) The pilgrim is going to see the Vatican.

e) The children are on vacation.

f) Luigi is camping.

g) The students are taking a spin.

Answers: 1. c 2. e 3. f 4. b 5. a 6. g 7. d

More Review

You've studied verbs until you thought you would go *matto* (crazy) trying to understand the different conjugations, stems, tenses, and persons. Don't try to rush through any of it. You'll learn Italian with perseverance and *pazienza*. Now is a good time to review the first two parts of this book to reinforce what you've studied. In the meantime, the following table offers a quick review of some of the more important *verbi* you've learned so far.

Irregular Verbs

Italiano	**Conjugation (Present Indicative)**
andare (to go)	*vado, vai, va, andiamo, andate, vanno*
avere (to have)	*ho, hai, ha, abbiamo, avete, hanno*
dare (to give)	*do, dai, dà, diamo, date, danno*
dire (to say)	*dico, dici, dice, diciamo, dite, dicono*
dovere* (to have to/must)	*devo, devi, deve, dobbiamo, dovete, devono*
essere (to be)	*sono, sei, è, siamo, siete, sono*
fare (to do/make)	*faccio, fai, fa, facciamo, fate, fanno*
potere (to be able to/can)	*posso, puoi, può, possiamo, potete, possono*
rimanere (to remain)	*rimango, rimani, rimane, rimaniamo, rimanete, rimangono*
salire (to go up/to get on)	*salgo, sali, sale, saliamo, salite, salgono*
sapere (to know)	*so, sai, sa, sappiamo, sapete, sanno*
scendere (to get off/go down)	*scendo, scendi, scende, scendiamo, scendete, scendono*
stare (to be/to stay)	*sto, stai, sta, stiamo, state, stanno*
uscire (to go out/to exit)	*esco, esci, esce, usciamo, uscite, escono*
volere (to want)	*voglio, vuoi, vuole, vogliamo, volete, vogliono*

*Dovere *can also mean "to owe," as in the word* debt.

Practice with a friend and see if you have these verbs memorized. At first you'll probably fumble a bit, but after a while they'll come naturally. It's like doing scales on a musical instrument. After you can play them three times in a row with no mistakes, you've pretty much got them down pat.

Congratulations! More Conjugations!

Fill in the appropriate conjugations for the following irregular verbs. Keep in mind that some may be irregular. These are the kinds of exercises you should be doing on your own as you learn new verbs.

1. *Potere* (can)

   io _____ noi _____

   tu _____ voi _____

   lui/lei/Lei _____ loro _____

2. *Andare* (to go; irregular)

   io _____ noi _____

   tu _____ voi _____

   lui/lei/Lei _____ loro _____

3. *Salire* (to get on; to go up)

   io _____ noi _____

   tu _____ voi _____

   lui/lei/Lei _____ loro _____

4. *Fare* (to do/make; irregular)

   io _____ noi _____

   tu _____ voi _____

   lui/lei/Lei _____ loro _____

5. *Rimanere* (to remain)

   io _____ noi _____

   tu _____ voi _____

   lui/lei/Lei _____ loro _____

Answers: 1. potere: posso, puoi, può, possiamo, potete, possono 2. andare: vado, vai, va, andiamo, andate, vanno 3. salire: salgo, sali, sale, saliamo, salire, salgono 4. fare: faccio, fai, fa, facciamo, fate, fanno 5. rimanere: rimango, rimani, rimane, rimaniamo, rimanete, rimangono

Countries

As one of the world's smallest countries, *La Republica di San Marino* is a land-locked independent city-state located on the slope of Mount Titano (near the Italian city of Rimini). Like any self-respecting country, it has its own mint, postal system, and soccer team.

Some geographical terms, including continents, countries, states, and large islands, require the definite article:

> This summer, we're visiting Italy, Spain, France, and Greece.
> *Quest'estate, noi visitiamo l'Italia, la Spagna, la Francia e la Grecia.*

The only exception occurs when the term comes after the preposition *in:*

> We're going to Italy, Albania, and Africa.
> *Noi andiamo in Italia, in Albania e in Africa.*

AS A *REGOLA*

All countries, regions, states, towns, and so on are capitalized. Nationalities are not capitalized.

We, the People

It's *impossibile* not to meet people from different nationalities and backgrounds when you're traveling. The first thing I notice about someone, like it or not, is his or her shoes. I can—with a fair amount of success—tell who is from where just by looking at their feet.

Are You of Italian origin?	Yes, I am of Italian origin.
Lei è d'origine italiana?	*Sì, sono d'origine italiana.*
Are you of Italian origin?	No, I am of Russian origin.
Sei d'origine italiana?	*No, sono d'origine russa.*

Note: The first example uses the polite form of address, and the second example uses the familiar form.

> **ATTENZIONE!**
>
> Use the preposition *in* before the name of a country and the preposition *a* before the name of a city: *Andiamo in Italia a Venezia.*

I Continenti

As air travel becomes more common, the world shrinks exponentially. How many continents have you hopped?

L'Africa	*L'Asia*	*L'Antartide*
L'America del Nord	*L'Australia*	
L'America del Sud	*L'Europa*	

Italian Regions

In 1492, *Cristoforo Colombo* bumped into North America, thinking he had found a route to India. Ten years later, the Florentine *Amerigo Vespucci*—a skilled navigator and cartographer—was commissioned by King Ferdinand of Spain to do some fact-checking. In addition to the colorful letters he wrote that described his findings, Vespucci's well-charted maps became the rage all over Florence, leading the new continent to be named in his honor. Until his dying day, Columbus refused to accept the possibility that he had not reached India.

Before its unification in 1861, the peninsula now known as Italy was once a cluster of city-states ruled by powerful families. Although Italy is now a unified state, each of its 20 regions has a distinctive character.

These *regioni* (regions) of Italy are …

L'Abruzzo	*Il Molise*	*Il Friuli-Venezia Giulia*	*La Toscana*
La Basilicata	*Il Piemonte*	*Il Lazio*	*Il Trentino-Alto Adige*
La Calabria	*La Puglia*	*La Liguria*	*L'Umbria*
La Campania	*La Sardegna*	*La Lombardia*	*La Val d'Aosta*
L'Emilia-Romagna	*La Sicilia*	*Le Marche*	*Il Veneto*

This map shows Italy's regions. Where do you want to go?

A Matter of Faith

You might be asked about your *religione* when meeting someone new. Some answers are provided in the following table. Similar to the days of the week, and months, Italian does not capitalize religions.

Religioni (Religions)

English	*Italiano*	Pronunciation
agnostic	*agnostico/a*	*ah-**nyoh**-stee-koh/ah*
atheist	*ateo/a*	***ah**-teh-oh/ah*
Buddhist	*buddista*	*boo-**dees**-tah*
Catholic	*cattolico/a*	*kah-**toh**-lee-koh/ah*
Christian	*cristiano/a*	*kree-stee-**ah**-noh/ah*
Jewish	*ebreo/a*	*eh-**breh**-oh/ah*
Hindu	*indù*	*een-**doo***
Muslim	*musulmano/a*	*moo-sool-**mah**-noh/ah*
Protestant	*protestante*	*proh-tes-**tahn**-teh*

Gli Animali (Animals)

I love *gli animali*. You probably won't see too many *alligatori* in Italy, but you might see a *farfalla* (butterfly, and also what Italians call bowtie pasta), a lot of *gatti* (cats), and the occasional *porcospino* (porcupine).

English	*Italiano*	English	*Italiano*
alligator	*l'alligatore*	leopard	*il gattopardo*
ant	*la formica*	lion	*il leone*
antelope	*l'antilope*	lizard	*la lucertola*
bat	*il pipistrello*	mole	*la talpa*
bear	*l'orso*	monkey	*la scimmia*
bird	*l'uccello*	mosquito	*la zanzara*
boar	*il cinghiale*	mouse	*il topo*
bull	*il toro*	ostrich	*lo struzzo*
butterfly	*la farfalla*	owl	*la civetta, il gufo*
cat	*il gatto*	pig	*il maiale*
chicken	*la gallina*	pigeon	*il piccione*
cow	*la mucca*	porcupine	*il porcospino*
crocodile	*il coccodrillo*	rabbit	*il coniglio*
crow	*il merlo*	raccoon	*il procione*
deer	*il cervo*	rooster	*il gallo*
dog	*il cane*	shark	*il pescecane, lo squalo*
dolphin	*il delfino*	sheep	*la pecora*
donkey	*l'asino*	skunk	*la puzzola*
duck	*l'anatra*	snail	*la lumaca*
eagle	*l'aquila*	snake	*il serpente*
elephant	*l'elefante*	spider	*il ragno*
fish	*il pesce*	squirrel	*lo scoiattolo*
fly	*la mosca*	swan	*il cigno*
fox	*la volpe*	tiger	*la tigre*
frog	*la rana*	turkey	*il tacchino*
giraffe	*la giraffa*	turtle	*la tartaruga*
goat	*la capra*	whale	*la balena*
gorilla	*il gorilla*	wolf	*il lupo*
hare	*la lepre*	worm	*il baco, il bruco, il verme*
hippopotamus	*l'ippopotamo*	zebra	*la zebra*
horse	*il cavallo*		

Are you one of herd, one of the flock, or part of a swarm? Here are some animal-related terms that express a group of a certain species:

flock	*un gregge*
herd	*una mandria*
shoal	*un banco*
swarm	*uno sciame*

LA BELLA LINGUA

In Italy, the animals have a saint: St. Francis of Assisi (1182–1226). As Italy's (and the whole of Europe's) patron saint, this gentle man lived during *Il Medioevo* (Middle Ages), before the boom that would later become known as *il Rinascimento* (the Renaissance). In Chapter 21, I've included his poem *Il Cantico delle Creature* (*Canticle of Created Things*).

The Least You Need to Know

- The modal verbs *dovere* (to have to/must), *potere* (to be able to/can), and *volere* (to want) are often followed by a verb.

- To express *I would like* … use *vorrei,* the conditional form of the modal verb *volere* (to want).

- Review the irregular verbs you've learned so far. These include *sapere* (to know) and *dire* (to say or tell). To get up you'll need *salire* and to go you'll need *andare,* not to mention the verbs *venire* (to come), *uscire* (to go out), and *rimanere* (to remain).

- To suggest an activity (*Let's* …), use the first person plural (*noi*) form of the verb.

- Countries and some geographical locations always take the definite article and are capitalized. Nationalities are not capitalized.

- To say you have a particular origin, you must use *sono d'origine* + the nationality in its feminine form.

Testing Your *Riflessivi:* Reflexive Verbs

In This Chapter

- Reflexive verbs and pronouns
- The verb *farsi*
- Naming your body parts
- Talking to *il medico* about what ails you
- Visiting the *ottica, dentista,* and *la profumeria*

Many people more often get sick while in a foreign country than any other time. You're in a new environment, you're eating different foods, your daily rituals have been altered, and you're having a great time. Those little bugs know just when to crash a party. In this chapter, you learn how to feed your cold, starve your fever, and get back on your feet.

But first, you learn about reflexive verbs.

You've Got Good Reflexes

Whenever you tell someone *Mi chiamo …* (I call myself …), you're using a reflexive verb. In Italian, when you enjoy yourself (*divertirsi*), get dressed (*vestirsi*), or comb your hair (*pettinarsi*), you're using a reflexive verb.

Reflexive verbs are easily identified by the *-si* attached at the end of the infinitive. Conjugation of the reflexive verbs follows the same rules as any other Italian verb, with one exception: reflexive verbs require the use of reflexive pronouns. These pronouns show that the subject is performing (or reflecting) an action upon itself. In other words, the subject and the reflexive pronoun both refer to the same persons or things, as in the phrases "We enjoyed ourselves" and "I hurt myself."

The reflexive pronouns differ only from the direct object pronouns in the third person singular and plural. Study the following reflexive pronouns.

Reflexive Pronouns

Italiano	English
mi	myself
ti	yourself
si	himself/herself; Yourself
ci	ourselves
vi	yourselves
si	themselves

The Verb *Chiamarsi*

Look at the reflexive verb *chiamarsi* (to call oneself) in the following table to see how the reflexive pronouns work with the conjugated verb.

Chiamarsi (to Call Oneself)

Italiano	English
mi chiamo	I call myself
ti chiami	you call yourself
si chiama	he/she calls him/herself; You call yourself
ci chiamiamo	we call ourselves
vi chiamate	you call yourselves
si chiamano	they call themselves

What's your dog's name?   My dog's name is Virgil.
Come si chiama il tuo cane?   *Il mio cane si chiama Virgil.*

Flexing Those Muscles

Let's look at some more common reflexive verbs, shown in the following table.

Il Verb Riflessivo (Reflexive Verbs)

Italiano	English	Italiano	English
accorgersi	to notice	lavarsi	to wash
addormentarsi	to fall asleep	mettersi	to put on
alzarsi	to get up	pettinarsi	to comb one's hair
annoiarsi	to be bored	rendersi	to realize
arrabbiarsi	to get angry	ricordarsi	to remember/to remind
chiamarsi	to call oneself	sentirsi	to feel
conoscersi	to know each other	sposarsi	to get married
diplomarsi	to obtain a diploma	svegliarsi	to wake up
divertirsi	to enjoy	truccarsi	to put makeup on
fermarsi	to stop	vestirsi	to get dressed
laurearsi	to graduate		

Have you known each other for a long time?
Vi conoscete da molto tempo?

Federico is graduating in June.
Federico si laurea a giugno.

The children enjoy themselves in the park.
I bambini si divertono al parco.

ATTENZIONE!

In Italian, you are responsible for your own boredom because the verb *annoiarsi* (to be bored) is reflexive, literally translating to I bore myself. The verb *truccarsi* is the verb used to put on makeup. It's interesting to note that the noun *trucco* means "trick" in Italian.

A Little Reflection

Some rules applying to reflexive verbs might make them easier to master. For example, when talking about parts of the body or clothing and using a reflexive verb, a possessive adjective is not required:

My head hurts.
Mi fa male la testa.

He/she takes off the jacket.
Si toglie la giacca.

The reflexive pronoun can be placed before the verb or after the infinitive when preceded by a form of the verb *potere, dovere,* or *volere:*

I want to get married.
Voglio sposarmi.

You must wash your hair.
Ti devi lavarti i capelli.

The reflexive pronoun is attached to the end of the word when it's used with an imperative. The reflexive pronoun can be attached to the end of an infinitive verb when it's preceded by an imperative:

Enjoy yourself!   Remember to wash your face!
Divertiti!*   *Ricordati di lavare la faccia!*

**But to make a statement or ask a question:*
You enjoy yourself.   Do you enjoy yourself?
Ti diverti.   *Ti diverti?*

Reciprocity

Every time you say to someone *Arrivederci!* you're using a reflexive. The expression literally translates to "re-see each other." The same goes for the expression *Ci vediamo!* (We'll see one another!), which comes from the infinitive *vedersi*.

You've seen all the verbs in the following table as nonreflexive verbs. By simply being made reflexive, these verbs can all express reciprocity.

Do Unto Others ...

English	Reflexive Verb
to greet each other	*salutarsi*
to hug one another	*abbracciarsi*
to kiss one another	*baciarsi*
to know one another	*conoscersi*
to look at one another	*guardarsi*
to meet one another/to run into	*incontrarsi*
to see one another	*vedersi*
to understand one another	*capirsi*

We hug one another every time we see each other.
Ci abbracciamo ogni volta che ci vediamo.

Mother and daughter understand one another without words.
Madre e figlia si capiscono senza parole.

To Reflect or Not

Some verbs greatly change their meaning when made reflexive. The regular verb *sentire*, for example, can mean *to hear* or *to smell*.

I hear the music.	He smells the perfume.
Sento la musica.	*Sente il profumo.*

As a reflexive verb, however, *sentirsi* means *to feel*:

I feel well.	How does he feel?
Mi sento bene.	*Come si sente?*

The verbs in the following table exemplify the pliable nature of such verbs.

Flexible Reflexives

Italiano	English	*Italiano*	English
annoiare	to annoy	*annoiarsi*	to get bored
arrabbiare	to become rabid (to get rabies; seldom used)	*arrabbiarsi*	to get angry
arrestare	to arrest	*arrestarsi*	to pause, to stop
battere	to beat	*battersi*	to fight
chiedere	to ask	*chiedersi*	to wonder
comportare	to entail	*comportarsi*	to behave
conoscere	to know someone	*conoscersi*	to know oneself
giocare	to play	*giocarsi*	to risk
lamentare	to mourn	*lamentarsi*	to complain
licenziare	to dismiss/to fire	*licenziarsi*	to resign/to quit
offendere	to offend	*offendersi*	to take offense (at)
onorare	to honor	*onorarsi*	to take pride (in)
perdere	to lose	*perdersi*	to get lost
scusare	to excuse	*scusarsi*	to apologize
sentire	to hear/to smell	*sentirsi*	to feel

I get lost (I lose myself) in new cities.
Mi perdo nelle città nuove.

Giovanni is bored when he goes to the opera.
Giovanni si annoia quando va all'opera.

Test Your Reflexes

In the following sentences, use the reflexive verbs in parentheses with the appropriate reflexive pronoun.

Example: Noi _____ spesso. (vedersi)
Answer: Noi ci vediamo spesso.

1. *Io _____ alle nove. (alzarsi)*

2. *Luciano e Marcello _____ da nove anni. (conoscersi)*

3. *Tu _____ in palestra? (divertirsi)*

4. *Giulia deve _____ i capelli ogni giorno. (lavarsi)*

5. *Tu, come _____? (chiamarsi)*

6. *Noi _____ una volta la settimana. (telefonarsi)*

7. *Come _____ la nonna di Sandra? (sentirsi)*

8. *Antonella e Marco _____ lunedì prossimo. (sposarsi)*

Answers: 1. mi alzo 2. si conoscono 3. ti diverti 4. lavarsi 5. ti chiami 6. ci telefoniamo 7. si sente 8. si sposano

AS A REGOLA

Reflexive verbs always take *essere* as their helping verb when forming compound tenses. As a result, the past participle acts like an adjective and reflects the gender and the number of the subject. Study the examples to see the two ways verbs can be modified in the present perfect, a past tense that always requires a helping verb. (You learn more about forming the past in Chapter 16.)

I woke up at 7:00.
(alzarsi) Mi sono alzato(a) alle 7,00.

We saw each other yesterday.
(vedersi) Ci siamo visti ieri.

What a Bod!

You've only got one *corpo* (body), so you might as well love it and all of its imperfections. The names of body parts (and their plurals) are often irregular. Start at your toes and work up. Try to decipher the Italian idiom *Dai una mano e si prende il braccio.**

Il Corpo (the Body)

English	*Italiano*	English	*Italiano*
ankle	*la caviglia*	hand	*la mano (le mani)*
appendix	*l'appendice*	head	*la testa*
arm	*il braccio (le braccia)*	heart	*il cuore*
back	*la schiena*	joint	*l'articolazione*
bladder	*la vescica*	knee	*il ginocchio (le ginocchia)*
blood	*il sangue*	leg	*la gamba*
body	*il corpo*	ligament	*il legamento*
bone	*l'osso (le ossa)*	mouth	*la bocca*
brain	*il cervello*	muscle	*il muscolo*
breast	*il seno*	nail	*l'unghia*
buttock	*il sedere*	neck	*il collo*
chest	*il petto*	nose	*il naso*
chin	*il mento*	skin	*la pelle*
ear	*l'orecchio*	shoulder	*la spalla*
elbow	*il gomito*	stomach	*lo stomaco*
eye	*l'occhio*	throat	*la gola*
face	*il viso*	toe	*il dito (le dita)*
finger	*il dito (le dita)*	tongue	*la lingua*
foot	*il piede*	tooth	*il dente*
gland	*la ghiandola*	wrist	*il polso*

*Literally: Give a hand and s/he'll take an arm = Give an inch and they'll take a yard.

LA BELLA LINGUA

A little schmoozing can go a long way. To give someone a compliment, use the word *che* + the appropriate form of *bello* + the body part:

What beautiful eyes!   What a great physique!
Che begli occhi!   *Che bel fisico!*

Farsi: Where Does It Hurt?

The reflexive and highly idiomatic verb *farsi* comes from the verb *fare* (to do/to make) and can be used in several manners. *Farsi* is used to talk about when something hurts. In this case, the subject of the sentence is the troublesome body part (or parts). If what's hurting you is singular—for example, your head—so is your verb; if your feet hurt you, because they are plural, your verb must also be plural.

My head hurts.
Mi fa male la testa.

My feet hurt.
Mi fanno male i piedi.

A doctor or pharmacist will ask you what hurts by changing the indirect object pronoun. The verb stays the same:

Does your arm hurt?
Ti fa male il braccio? (familiar)

Does your stomach hurt?
Le fa male lo stomaco? (polite)

Do your feet hurt?
Le fanno male i piedi? (polite)

What Ails You?

29

Sickness can be especially exasperating in a foreign country where you don't know the names of your medicines and you have to explain to a *dottore* or *farmacista* exactly what the problem is. If you're traveling with medications you're currently taking, it's not a bad idea to make a list of them, just in case.

There's no need to be shy about what you're experiencing. Italians have the same kinds of ailments you do. The doctor will ask you a few questions. Naturally, the *Lei* form of the verb is used to maintain a professional relationship.

What's Wrong?

English	Italiano
What is the problem?	*Qual è il problema?*
How do you feel?	*Come si sente?*
How old are you?	*Quanti anni ha?*
(For) How long have you been suffering?	*Da quanto tempo soffre?*
Are you taking any medications?	*Prende delle medicine?*
Do you have any allergies?	*Ha delle allergie?*
Do you suffer from ...?	*Soffre di ...?*
Have you had ...?	*Ha avuto ...?*
What hurts you?	*Che cosa Le fa male?*

When talking about your body, use the verb *avere* to describe any kind of ache, whether it's in your head or your stomach. You'll also use the reflexive verb *sentirsi* (to feel) to describe your various ailments, as in, *Mi sento male* (I feel bad). When using the idiomatic expression *avere mal di*, the final -*e* is dropped from the word *male*.

Describe Your Pain

English	Italiano
I have …	*Ho …*
… a headache	*… mal di testa.*
… a stomachache.	*… mal di stomaco/pancia.*
… a sore throat	*… mal di gola.*
(The body part) … hurts me.	*Mi fa male (body part) …*
My knee hurts.	*Mi fa male il ginocchio.*
My feet hurt.	*Mi fanno male i piedi.*
I feel bad.	*Mi sento male.*
I don't feel well.	*Non mi sento bene.*

Tell Me Where It Hurts

Imagine you're telling a doctor about your aches and pains. If you're using the expression *mi fa male*, don't forget to account for number if what hurts you is plural.

> *Example:* your head
> *Answer: Mi fa male la testa* or *Ho mal di testa.*

1. your knee _____

2. your shoulders _____

3. your feet _____

4. your throat _____

5. your tooth _____

6. your ankle _____

Answers: 1. Mi fa male il ginocchio. 2. Mi fanno male le spalle. 3. Mi fanno male i piedi. 4. Mi fa male la gola./Ho mal di gola. 5. Mi fa male il dente./Ho mal di denti. 6. Mi fa male la caviglia.

LA BELLA LINGUA

There's a saint for just about every ailment. Got a hangover? Pray to Saint Bibiana, a virgin who was martyred in Rome in c. 361 C.E. She is also invoked against epilepsy and headaches. Here are a few more saints you may want to invoke should the need arise:

St. Ignatius: sore throats   St. Aldegonda: cancer

St. Antoninus: fever   St. Lucy: blindness

St. Stephen: headaches   St. Valentine: heartache

At *la Farmacia*

A visit to the *farmacia* (pharmacy) will provide you with prescriptions, vitamins, and assorted sundries. Pick up some *vitamina C* to get your system back in sync, buy some *aspirina* for your head, or smooth some *moisturizer* all over your body.

Drugstore Items

English	*Italiano*	English	*Italiano*
ace bandage	*la fascia elastica*	needle and thread	*ago e filo*
antibiotics	*gli antibiotici*	nose drops	*le gocce per il naso*
antiseptic	*l'antisettico*	pacifier	*il ciuccio*
aspirin	*l'aspirina*	pills	*le pastiglie*
Band-Aids	*i cerotti*	prescription	*la ricetta medica*
baby bottle	*il biberon*	razor	*il rasoio*
body lotion	*la lozione*	safety pin	*la spilla di sicurezza*
castor oil	*l'olio di ricino*	sanitary napkins	*gli assorbenti*
condoms	*i preservativi, i profilattici*	scissors	*le forbici*
cotton balls	*i batuffoli di ovatta*	shaving cream	*la crema da barba*
cotton swabs (for ears)	*i tamponi per le orecchie*	sleeping pill	*il sonnifero*
cough syrup	*lo sciroppo per la tosse*	soap	*il sapone*
deodorant	*il deodorante*	syringe	*la siringa*
depilatory wax	*la ceretta depilatoria*	talcum powder	*il talco*
diapers	*i pannolini*	tampons	*i tamponi*
eye drops	*le gocce per gli occhi*	thermometer	*il termometro*
floss	*il filo interdentale*	tissues	*fazzolettini di carta*
gauze bandage	*la fascia*	toothbrush	*lo spazzolino da denti*
heating pad	*l'impacco caldo*	toothpaste	*il dentifricio*
ice pack	*la borsa del ghiaccio*	tweezers	*le pinzette*
laxative	*il lassativo*	vitamins	*le vitamine*
mirror	*lo specchio*		

The Least You Need to Know

- Reflexive verbs, identified by the pronoun *-si* attached to the end of the infinitive, require the use of one of the reflexive pronouns: *mi, ti, si* (singular), *ci, vi,* and *si* (plural).

- Many regular verbs can become reflexive. In some cases, the meaning changes dramatically. The verbs *annoiare* (to annoy) and *annoiarsi* (to be bored) are good examples.

- Reflexive pronouns are attached at the end of an infinitive verb when preceded by a modal verb such as *potere, dovere,* or *volere.* The pronoun is also attached at the end of an imperative, such as *Divertiti!* (Enjoy yourself!)

- Reflexive verbs always take *essere* as their helping verb when forming compound tenses.

- To tell someone that a certain part of your body doesn't feel well, use *Mi fa male* plus the body part.

- Certain body parts are irregular in the plural.

The Nitty Gritty

Part 3 pays attention to more sophisticated concepts and brings you deeper into the language. First you learn the imperative, the command form of a verb, like when your grandmother used to tell you *Mangia!* (Eat!). To whet your appetite, I show you how to conjugate the verb *piacere* (used to describe when you like something). This is all accompanied by a rich lesson on dining and includes loads of vocabulary related to food.

Then you can go to town and do a little shopping. This is when you want to know how to use object pronouns, those little words used to substitute for nouns.

Finally, you learn how to talk about the past using the present perfect and imperfect tenses.

In the meantime, you also learn about Italian holidays, the arts, music, film, sports, and much more.

On the Road: Using the Imperative

In This Chapter

- Using the imperative
- Modes of transportation you'll use in *Italia*
- Talking about travel
- The *Si impersonale*
- Using prepositions and contractions
- A look at prepositions and infinitive verbs

This chapter gives you all the *vocabolario* you need to be as *indipendente* as *possibile* as you travel and successfully get from point A to point B. To help you get what you need, you learn about the imperative mood (particularly used by bossy types).

We also take a look at prepositions in this chapter. These little connectors tie everything together.

The Imperative: Bossing People Around

The *imperativo* is used for giving suggestions, orders, and directions. It's the command form of a verb, like when your mamma told you, "Brush your teeth!" or your *nonna* told your *nonno*, "Quit talkin' nonsense!"

The Regular Imperative Endings

Look at the following imperative endings to see how they work. You're already familiar with at least one imperative, such as when you tell your child to eat, *Mangia!* Obviously there's no first-person imperative. (I've been known to yell at myself, but I'm still doing so in second person.)

Imperative Endings

Subject	-are	-ere	-ire
tu (you; familiar)	-a	-i	-i
Lei (You; polite)	-i	-a	-a
noi ("Let's…")	-iamo	-iamo	-iamo
voi (you; plural)	-ate	-ete	-ite

The Imperative Using *Tu* and *Lei*

The imperatives are always followed by an exclamation point, but YOU DON'T HAVE TO SHOUT! Salespeople in stores rarely ask you if they can help. Instead, they'll say simply, *Mi dica!* (Tell me … [what you want/need]). When giving directions, the imperative is used.

The *voi* (you; plural) form of the imperative is identical to the present indicative tense. In other words, telling your kids *Mangiate!* (Eat!) is the same as making a simple statement, *Mangiate.* (You eat.)

The following table offers some of the most common commands you'll hear, using the familiar *tu* (you; familiar) along with the polite form *Lei* (You; polite). Irregular forms are indicated by the * along with the negative forms.

Imperative Forms

Imperative	Verb	Familiar (*Tu*)	Polite (*Lei*)
Be!	*essere**	*Sii!/Non essere!*	*(Non) Sia!*
Come!	*venire**	*Vieni!/Non venire!*	*(Non) Venga!*
Continue!	*continuare*	*Continua!/Non continuare!*	*(Non) Continui!*
Cross!	*attraversare*	*Attraversa!/Non attraversare!*	*(Non) Attraversi!*
Do!	*fare**	*Fa'! or Fai!/Non fare!*	*(Non) Faccia!*
Excuse me!	*scusarsi*	*Scusami!/Non scusarmi!*	*(Non) Mi scusi!*
Finish!	*finire*	*Finisci!/Non finire!*	*(Non) Finisca!*
Follow!	*seguire*	*Segui!/Non seguire!*	*(Non) Segua!*
Get off! Go down!	*scendere*	*Scendi!/Non scendere!*	*(Non) Scenda!*
Get on! Go up!	*salire**	*Sali!/Non salire!*	*(Non) Salga!*
Go!	*andare**	*Va!/Non andare!*	*(Non) Vada!*
Have!	*avere**	*Abbi!/Non avere!*	*(Non) Abbia!*
Pass!	*passare*	*Passa!/Non passare!*	*(Non) Passi!*
Say!/Tell!	*dire**	*Di'!/Non dire!*	*(Non) Dica!*

Imperative	Verb	Familiar (*Tu*)	Polite (*Lei*)
Speak!	*parlare*	*Parla!/Non parlare!*	*(Non) Parli!*
Stay!	*stare**	*Sta'!* or *Stai!/Non stare!*	*(Non) Stia!*
Take!	*prendere*	*Prendi!/Non prendere!*	*(Non) Prenda!*
Turn!	*girare*	*Gira!/Non girare!*	*(Non) Giri!*
Wait!	*aspettare*	*Aspetta!/Non aspettare!*	*(Non) Aspetti!*
Walk!	*camminare*	*Cammina!/Non camminare!*	*(Non) Cammini!*

Have patience! (polite)
Abbia pazienza!

Tell me! (polite)
Mi dica!

Tell me everything! (familiar)
Dimmi tutto!

Do what you want! (familiar)
Fai quello che vuoi.

To form a negative command is so simple in the *tu* (you; familiar) form. Just add *non* in front of your infinitive verb. If the verb is reflexive, the appropriate reflexive pronoun attaches to the end of the infinitive (minus the final -*e*).

Don't eat that cookie!
Non mangiare quel biscotto!

Don't worry!
Non preoccuparti!

The negative command in the *Lei* (You; polite) form utilizes the regular imperative form. If the verb is reflexive, the pronoun comes before the conjugation.

Don't tell me! (You don't say!)
Non mi dica!

Don't worry!
Non si preoccupi!

Tell Me What to Do

Use the imperative form with the following nondirectional verbs:

	Tu	Lei
1. *finire* (to finish)	_____	_____
2. *lasciare* (to leave alone/to leave something behind)	_____	_____
3. *mangiare* (to eat)	_____	_____
4. *portare* (to bring)	_____	_____

5. *preparare* (to prepare)   _____ _____

6. *telefonare* (to telephone)   _____ _____

Answers: 1. finisci/finisca 2. mangia/mangi 3. lascia/lasci 4. porta/porti 5. prepara/prepari 6. telefona/telefoni

Go Straight and Then Take a Right ... Directions

30

Ask three different Italians for *indicazioni* (directions), and you'll probably get three different answers. The next time you stop and ask a stranger for directions, you'll more than likely hear the imperatives used with the directives in the following table (given in the You, polite form).

Indicazioni (Directions)

English	*Italiano*	English	*Italiano*
Follow ...	*Segua* ...	below/above	*sotto/sopra*
Go ...	*Vada* ...	down/up	*giù/su*
Remain ...	*Rimanga* ...	far/near	*lontano/vicino*
Return ...	*Ritorni* ...	inside/outside	*dentro/fuori*
Take ...	*Prenda* ...	opposite/in front of	*di fronte a*
Turn ...	*Giri* ...	straight	*sempre diritto*
left/right	*a sinistra/a destra*	to the end of the street	*giù in fondo*
before/after	*prima/dopo*	until; up to	*fino a*

I Mezzi Pubblici: Public Transportation

In Italy, public transportation is quite efficient, with buses, trains, and *la metro* (subway) available to take you just about anywhere you want to go. It's a good idea to purchase bus tickets at a *cartoleria* or *tabacchi* to keep in your wallet because buses do not accept cash or coins. You can also buy *biglietti* (tickets) at train stations and from automated machines using your *carta di credito.*

After you get on *l'autobus,* you must *convalidare* your ticket by punching it into a small box located on the back of the bus. Hold on to your ticket in case of a surprise check by stern-faced inspectors eager to find transgressions.

When using *la metro*, you must also buy a ticket either from one of the automated machines or from a ticket booth. It's possible to buy daily, weekly, and monthly tickets.

All Aboard!

The terms in the following table are essential to traveling through Italy.

Get Your *Biglietti* Ready

English	*Italiano*
bus	*l'autobus*
bus stop	*la fermata dell'autobus*
connection	*la coincidenza*
information	*l'ufficio informazioni*
taxi	*il tassì*
train	*il treno*
... by train (railway)	... *in treno*
... train station	... *la stazione ferroviaria*
ticket	*il biglietto*
... one-way ticket	... *il biglietto di corsa semplice*
... first/second class	... *di prima/seconda classe*
... round-trip ticket	... *il biglietto di andata e ritorno*
ticket counter	*la biglietteria*
schedule	*l'orario, la tabella*
seat	*il sedile/il posto*
track	*il binario*
waiting room	*la sala d'aspetto*
window	*il finestrino*

Here are some other handy phrases:

At what times does the train leave?
A che ora parte il treno?

I would like a round-trip ticket.
Vorrei un biglietto di andata e ritorno.

Is there a connection?
C'è la coincidenza?

Is there a seat near the window?
C'è un posto vicino al finestrino?

May I open the window?
Posso aprire il finestrino?

On which track does the train leave?
Da quale binario parte il treno?

Take this bus.
Prenda quest'autobus.

The planes (are running) on time.
I voli sono in orario.

We're leaving immediately.
Partiamo subito.

Where is the bus stop?
Dov'è la fermata dell'autobus?

Behind the Wheel

The following phrases help you get some wheels:

I would like to rent a car.
Vorrei noleggiare una macchina.

I prefer a car with automatic transmission.
Preferisco una macchina con il cambio automatico.

How much does it cost per day (per week)?
Quanto costa al giorno (alla settimana)?

How much does automobile insurance cost?
Quanto costa l'assicurazione per l'auto?

What (which) form of payment do you prefer?
Quale tipo di pagamento preferite?

Do you accept credit cards?
Accettate carte di credito?

Automobile Parts

If you've decided to rent *una macchina,* carefully inspect it inside and out before driving off in it. Be sure it has *il cricco* or *cric* (a jack) and *la ruota di scorta* (a spare tire) in the trunk, in case you get a *gomma a terra* (flat tire). It doesn't hurt to check for any preexisting damages such as scratches and dents you could unfairly be charged for later.

The following table gives you the Italian words for car parts and predicaments. You never know—that cherry-red Ferrari you rent could turn out to be a *limone.*

Automobile Parts and Predicaments

English	*Italiano*	Pronunciation
antenna	*l'antenna*	*lahn-**ten**-nah*
battery	*la batteria*	*lah baht-teh-**ree**-yah*
breakdown	*un guasto*	*oon **gwah**-stoh*
carburetor	*il carburatore*	*eel kar-boor-ah-**toh**-reh*
door	*la portiera*	*lah por-tee-**yeh**-rah*
door handle	*la maniglia*	*lah mah-**nee**-lyah*
fan belt	*la cinghia del ventilatore*	*lah **cheen**-ghee-yah del ven-tee-lah-**toh**-reh*
fender	*il parafango*	*eel pah-rah-**fahn**-goh*
filter	*il filtro*	*eel **feel**-troh*
flat tire	*una gomma a terra, una ruota bucata*	*oo-nah **gohm**-mah ah **ter**-rah, oo-nah **rwoh**-tah boo-**kah**-tah*
fuse	*un fusibile*	*oon foo-**see**-bee-leh*
gas tank	*il serbatoio*	*eel ser-bah-**toy**-oh*
headlights	*i fari*	*ee **fah**-ree*
hood	*il cofano*	*eel **koh**-fah-noh*
license	*la patente*	*lah pah-**ten**-teh*
license plate	*la targa*	*lah **tar**-gah*
motor	*il motore*	*eel moh-**toh**-reh*
muffler	*la marmitta*	*lah mar-**mee**-tah*
radiator	*il radiatore*	*eel rah-dee-yah-**toh**-reh*
sign	*il segnale*	*eel sen-**yah**-leh*
spark plug	*la candela d'accensione*	*lah kahn-**deh**-lah dah-chen-see-**oh**-neh*
tail light	*la luce di posizione*	*lah **loo**-cheh dee poh-zee-tsee-**oh**-neh*
tire	*la ruota*	*lah **rwoh**-tah*
traffic officer	*il/la vigile*	*eel/lah **vee**-jee-leh*
trunk	*il bagagliaio*	*eel bah-gahl-**yiy**-yoh*
window	*il finestrino*	*eel fee-neh-**stree**-noh*
windshield	*il parabrezza*	*eel pah-rah-**breh**-tsah*
windshield wiper	*il tergicristallo*	*eel ter-jee-kree-**stah**-loh*

LA BELLA LINGUA

Tools might be the last thing you think of when learning a second language, but if you're stranded, the following might be helpful: *le pinze* (pliers), *il cacciavite* (screwdriver), *il martello* (hammer), *la chiave inglese* (monkey wrench).

The Road Less Traveled

The following table contains more useful verbs and expressions related to travel on the road.

Macchina Speak

English	Italiano	English	Italiano
to break down	*guastarsi*	to get gas	*fare benzina*
to change a tire	*cambiare la ruota*	to get a ticket	*prendere una multa*
to check	*controllare*	to give a ride	*dare un passaggio*
... the oil	*... l'olio*	to go	*andare*
... the tires	*... le ruote*	to obey traffic signs	*rispettare i segnali*
... the water	*... l'acqua*	to park	*parcheggiare*
to drive	*guidare*	to run/function	*funzionare*
to fill it up	*fare il pieno*	to run out of gas	*rimanere senza benzina*

> **LA BELLA LINGUA**
>
> There are several types of roads in Italy. *L'autostrada* is just like the throughway, so expect to pay high tolls on these fast-paced lanes. *La superstrada* is like a local highway. These roads are well maintained and can be quite scenic. *La statale* is a state road and is slower than a superstrada but faster than the *strada comunale*. *La strada comunale* is local road. Watch out for slow-moving tractors and the occasional flock of sheep on these!

Follow the Signs!

As you're driving through *Italia*, be sure you follow the signs.

Road Signs

English	Italiano
Detour	*Deviazione*
No Entrance	*Divieto di Ingresso*
No Passing	*Divieto di Sorpasso*
No Parking	*Divieto di Sosta*
Parking Permitted	*Sosta Autorizzata*
One-Way Traffic	*Senso Unico*
Two-Way Traffic	*Doppio Senso*

The *Si Impersonale*

The *si impersonale* is used to talk in general terms about something, without there being a specific subject of the verb, like when someone might say, "You just have to go straight, then you take a right, and you should see a big building …." When the person speaking refers to *you* in this case, it could be anyone, not just you (nothing personal).

To form the *si impersonale* is easy: simply add the pronoun *si* (not to be confused with the word *sì*, yes) in front of the third-person conjugation of a verb.

The *si impersonale* can be used with any tense. Check out how it works:

How does one arrive at …?   How does one get to …?
Come si arriva a …?   *Come si va …?*

When the *si impersonale* is used with an adjective, the adjective uses the masculine, plural form, even though you're using a singular form of the verb. Go figure! (Not *you* personally.)

You're always tired after a long trip.
Si è sempre stanchi dopo un lungo viaggio.

When used with reflexive verbs and the the third person reflexive pronoun *si*, the first *si* becomes a *ci*. This avoids repetition.

You have fun at the park.
Ci si diverte al parco.

More Travel Verbs and Expressions

You'll be surprised to see how quickly you begin to understand the following, even if it all seems like a lot of gobbledygook.

Viaggio Speak

English	*Italiano*	English	*Italiano*
to be (running) early	*essere in anticipo*	to change	*cambiare*
to be (running) late	*essere in ritardo*	to commute	*fare il pendolare*
to be (running) on time	*essere in orario*	to get off (to go down)	*scendere da*

continues

English	*Italiano*	English	*Italiano*
to get on (to go up)	*salire su*	to stop	*fermare*
to leave	*partire*	to take	*prendere*
to miss, to lose	*perdere*	to turn	*girare*
to return	*tornare, ritornare*	to turn around (to go back)	*tornare indietro*

What, When, and How Much?

Remember that in Italy, schedules are given in military time. If you're leaving at 2 P.M., for example, you are told 14:00 hours. This may be tricky at first, so confirm that you understand correctly by asking if it is A.M. (*di mattina*) or P.M. (*di sera*).

The following table contains a list of words and expressions that help you get what you want, find out where you want to go, and meet the people you'd like to meet.

Information Questions

English	*Italiano*
how?	*come?*
how much?	*quanto?*
what?	*che cosa?* (can be broken up as *che?* or *cosa?*)
what time?	*a che ora?*
when?	*quando?*
where?	*dove?*
where is …?	*dov'è …?*
who?	*chi?*
why?	*perché?*

It's one thing to ask for directions and another to understand the response. First, know that in Italian, the cognate for direction—*direzione*—is used primarily to talk about compass points, as in *nord/sud* (north/south), *est/ovest* (east/west). To ask for help to get somewhere, you need to ask for *indicazioni* (indications).

It's easy to ask questions in Italian. You don't even have to change the word order. Just take any phrase (following the usual rules of conjugation), and instead of making it sound like a statement, raise the intonation of your voice at the end of the phrase. Try practicing with the following two examples. Note that they are exactly the same phrase, but pronounced differently:

As a statement:

> This train goes to Rome.
> *Questo treno va a Roma.*

As a question:

> Does this train go to Rome?
> *Questo treno va a Roma?*

When asking a question using the word *dove* (where) with the third person of the verb *essere* (*è*), elide the two words, as in *dov'è* (where's), to avoid a double vowel and maintain the flow of the pronunciation.

Are there many tourists at this hour?
Ci sono molti turisti a quest'ora?

At what hour does the museum open?
A che ora apre il museo?

For how long are you in Italy? (you, plural)
Per quanto tempo state in Italia?

How much does this cost?
Quanto costa?

Is there a hospital nearby?
C'è un ospedale qui vicino?

When is the train for Rome?
Quando c'è il treno per Roma?

Where are you from? (informal)
Di dove sei?

Where are you from? (polite)
Di dov'è Lei?

Where is the bus stop?
Dov'è la fermata dell'autobus?

With whom are you traveling? (polite)
Con chi viaggia Lei?

Prepositions: Sticky Stuff

You've used these words thousands of times and probably never knew they were all prepositions. Just like the name implies, a preposition is situated *before* a word (*pre*position) to tell you its relationship to other words. These little commonly used words pack a lot of punch, connecting everything together.

You've already seen a lot of prepositions because they're the glue of a *frase* and tie the words together. The following table provides a comprehensive list of Italian prepositions and their meanings. Those in bold are the most commonly used.

Preposizioni (Prepositions)

English	*Italiano*	English	*Italiano*
about, around (when making an estimation)	*circa*	from, by	*da*
above	*sopra*	in front of, before, ahead	*avanti, davanti*
after	*dopo*	in, into, by, on	*in*
against, opposite to	*contro*	inside of	*dentro a*
around	*attorno a*	near	*vicino a*
before	*davanti a*	of, from, about	*di*
behind	*dietro a*	on, upon	*su*
beside	*accanto a*	outside	*fuori di*
besides, beyond	*oltre*	to, at, in	*a*
between, among, in, within	*fra, tra*	under	*sotto*
except, save	*eccetto*	until, as far as	*fino a*
far from	*lontano da*	with	*con*
for, in order to	*per*	without	*senza*

A Few Points on Prepositions

It's the little words that will drive you nuts! Does the Italian preposition *in* mean "to" or "by" or "in"? Does *a* mean "at" or "in"? It might help to go over a few rules about the most commonly used prepositions, all of which can be used to form contractions. (I'll get to those next.)

Use the preposition *a* (at, to, in) with cities and towns and both before and after verbs.

Use the preposition *da* (from, at, by) to express when you've been *at* somewhere, whether an office, the doctor's, or far away.

The preposition *da* (from, by, of, since) can also mean "since" or describe an amount of time. For example, use the present tense of the verb *essere* + *da* to create the following:

> For how long are you in Italy?   I am [have been] in Italy since October.
> *Da quanto tempo sei in Italia?*   *Sono in Italia da ottobre.*

Use the preposition *di* (of, from, about) to express possession; it's also used in many idiomatic expressions.

To express an unspecified quantity or "some" of a greater amount, use the preposition *di* plus an article:

I am eating some pasta.
Mangio della pasta.

I am drinking some wine.
Bevo del vino.

Do You want some fruit?
Vuole della frutta?

Use the preposition *in* (at, in, to) before the names of countries, when talking about modes of transportation, and when talking about what street you live *on*.

In Italian there's no need to express the preposition *on* before the names of days; just say the day:

We are arriving (on) Monday.
Arriviamo lunedì.

Giuseppe is arriving (on) Saturday.
Giuseppe arriva sabato.

Use either *in* or *a* to express *in* with months:

My birthday is in June.
Il mio compleanno è a giugno.

It's still cold in March.
Fa ancora freddo in marzo.

Use either *in* or *di* to express the notion of being in with seasons:

We are going to Italy in the winter.
Andiamo in Italia d'inverno.

It's beautiful in the spring.
In primavera fa bello.

From Prepositions to Contractions

No one is having a baby here. A contraction, in linguistic terms, is a single word made out of two words. The prepositions in the following table form contractions when followed by a definite article. Notice that the endings remain the same as the definite article. A contraction can be as simple as *alla* (to the) or *sul* (on the).

The prepositions *per, tra,* and *fra* are never contracted. *Con* is sometimes contracted, especially in older texts.

Preposizioni Articolati (Contractions)

Preposition	Masculine				Feminine			
	Singular		Plural		Singular		Plural	
	il	*lo*	*l'*	*i*	*gli*	*la*	*l'*	*le*
a	*al*	*allo*	*all'*	*ai*	*agli*	*alla*	*all'*	*alle*
in	*nel*	*nello*	*nell'*	*nei*	*negli*	*nella*	*nell'*	*nelle*
di	*del*	*dello*	*dell'*	*dei*	*degli*	*della*	*dell'*	*delle*
su	*sul*	*sullo*	*sull'*	*sui*	*sugli*	*sulla*	*sull'*	*sulle*
da	*dal*	*dallo*	*dall'*	*dai*	*dagli*	*dalla*	*dall'*	*dalle*

The Ol' Switcharoo

Replace the bold words with the words in parentheses, changing the preposition or contraction as necessary. Accommodate any changes in gender or plurality.

1. *Silvia ed io andiamo **al cinema**. (festa)*

2. *Il tassì va **in centro**. (piazza)*

3. *Andate **a piedi?** (macchina)*

4. *La giacca è **sulla tavola**. (sedia)*

5. *Mangiamo **del riso**. (spaghetti)*

6. *Dobbiamo andare **dal dottore**. (dentista)*

Answers: 1. alla festa 2. in piazza 3. in macchina 4. sulla sedia 5. degli spaghetti 6. dal dentista

Infinitive Verbs and Prepositions

The infinitive of a verb, as you know, is a verb before it has been conjugated, or the *to* form of a verb, as in *to study, to laugh,* and *to cry.* Sometimes an infinitive takes a different form, as in this sentence:

I plan on *studying* a lot this summer.

In Italian, when a verb doesn't have a subject, it's usually in its infinitive form, even if this form resembles the gerund (-*ing* form) of the verb in English.

Some Italian verbs are preceded by a preposition, others are followed by a preposition, and some take none at all. Knowing when to use a preposition is often a question of usage, because the meaning of a verb can change when used with one. This applies in English as well. Compare these two sentences, and see how the meaning changes by changing the preposition:

> I want to go *on* the plane.   I want to go *to* the plane.

Italian prepositions sometimes change while their English counterparts do not:

> **pensare di**   *Penso **di** andare in italia.*
>   I am thinking **of** going to Italy.
>
> **pensare a**   *Penso **a** te.*
>   I'm thinking **of** you.

Alone at Last

For some verbs, you don't have to worry about the preposition at all. The following verbs are followed by an infinitive without a preposition.

Verbs Without a Preposition

English	*Italiano*	English	*Italiano*
to be able	*potere*	to listen	*sentire*
to be necessary	*occorrere*	to love	*amare*
to desire	*desiderare*	to prefer	*preferire*
to do/make	*fare*	to see	*vedere*
to have to	*dovere*	to seem	*parere/sembrare*
to know (something)	*sapere*	to suffice	*bastare*
to leave (something behind)	*lasciare*	to want	*volere*

> I want to speak Italian.
> *Voglio parlare l'**italiano**.*

Oddballs

There are always going to be peculiarities that cannot be translated. The verbs and idiomatic expressions used in the following table require the preposition *di* when followed by an infinitive.

Verbs and Idiomatic Expressions Taking *di* Before an Infinitive

English	*Italiano*	English	*Italiano*
to accept from	*accettare di …*	to intend to	*avere intenzione di …*
to admit to	*ammettere di …*	to offer to	*offrire di …*
to ask for	*chiedere di …*	to order to	*ordinare di …*
to be afraid of	*avere paura di …*	to permit to	*permettere di …*
to be in the mood for	*avere voglia di …*	to pray to	*pregare di …*
to be right about	*avere ragione di …*	to remember to	*ricordare di …*
to believe in	*credere di …*	to repeat to	*ripetere di …*
to decide to	*decidere di …*	to respond to	*rispondere di …*
to dream of	*sognare di …*	to say to	*dire di …*
to expect to	*aspettare di …*	to search for	*cercare di …*
to finish	*finire di …*	to speak of	*parlare di …*
to forget to	*dimenticare di …*	to stop/quit	*smettere di …*
to have need of	*avere bisogno di …*	to think of	*pensare di …*
to hope to	*sperare di …*		

I hope to see you soon.
Spero di vederti presto.

Quit swearing!
Smetti di bestemmiare!

Children need to sleep.
I bambini hanno bisogno di dormire.

The Preposition *a*

Some verbs, as in the following table, take the preposition *a* before an infinitive. Pay attention to how the preposition in the English changes from one verb to the next. Although you *help to protect someone,* you *succeed at your job.* (This flexible nature of prepositions is what makes them as annoying as fruit flies.)

The Preposition *a* Before an Infinitive

English	*Italiano*	English	*Italiano*
to be at	*stare a …*	to help to	*aiutare a …*
to be careful to	*stare attento a …*	to invite to	*invitare a …*
to be ready to	*essere pronto a …*	to learn to	*imparare a …*
to begin to	*cominciare a …*	to pass to	*passare a …*
to bring to	*portare a …*	to prepare for/to	*preparare a …*
to come to	*venire a …*	to return to	*tornare a …*
to enter into	*entrare a …*	to run to	*correre a …*
to exit to	*uscire a …*	to succeed at	*riuscire a …*
to go to	*andare a …*	to teach to	*insegnare a …*

Let's go see a movie.   You're learning how to speak Italian.
Andiamo a vedere un film.   *Impari a parlare l'**italiano**.*

Learning by Example

Complete the sentences using the subjects provided. Translate the sentences.

> *Example:* _____ *essere brava. (io/cercare di)*
> *Answer: Cerco di essere brava. (I try to be good.)*

1. _____ *soldi. (voi/avere bisogno di)*

2. _____ *parlare l'**italiano**. (tu/imparare a)*

3. _____ *lavorare mentre sta a scuola. (Cristoforo/continuare a)*

4. _____ *dormire presto. (noi/andare a)*

5. _____ *fumare le sigarette. (io/smettere di)*

6. _____ *mangiare alle 8,00. (Loro/finire di)*

Answers: 1. Avete bisogno di (You need money.) 2. Impari a (You are learning how to speak Italian.) 3. Cristoforo continua a (Cristoforo is continuing to work while he's in school.) 4. Andiamo a (We are going to sleep early.) 5. Smetto di (I'm quitting smoking.) 6. Finiscono di (They're finishing eating at 8:00.)

The Least You Need to Know

- Traveling in Italy using the *mezzi pubblici* (public transportation) is efficient and safe.
- The imperative is used to give directions and is especially helpful when offering unsolicited advice. (Listen to me, will ya?)
- Many idiomatic expressions are used in travel.
- Prepositions are the glue that ties words together and are frequently used with an article, forming a contraction.

Pane, Vino, e Cioccolata: Expressing Pleasure

In This Chapter

- Foods and where to buy them
- Using *ne* and expressing quantity
- Food-related verbs and idiomatic expressions
- The verb *piacere* (to be pleasing to)

In this chapter, we're going to look at the verb *piacere*, used to talk about when something pleases you. There's no better way to express pleasure than when discussing food.

Cooking. Italy. The two are inseparable. It's *gastronomia* (gastronomy) brought to the level of *arte*. What makes Italy so special is the *attenzione* it gives to the everyday elements of successful living. Italians know fine cuisine is a precursor to living *la dolce vita*.

Be sure you eat something before reading this chapter, or you won't be able to *concentrare* on anything. *Buon appetito!*

To Market! To Market!

Imagine you're staying with your *famiglia* in a rented villa for a month. The tomatoes are ripe, and the *basilico* is fresh. Maybe you want to *fare un picnic*. Whatever your *preferenza*, in Italy, there's something *delizioso* for everyone.

Here are some food-oriented verbs you might find useful:

assaggiare (to taste)	*fare* colazione* (to have breakfast, lunch)
cenare (to dine)	*mangiare* (to eat)
comprare (to buy)	*pranzare* (to eat lunch)
cucinare (to cook)	*preparare* (to prepare)

*The idiomatic expression fare la prima colazione *(to eat breakfast) differs slightly from* fare colazione. *Both can be used to eat breakfast, while the latter can also be used to eat lunch in some regions. Don't forget* fare la spesa *(to go food shopping).*

Going Shopping

The words in the following table should help you on your next shopping expedition. To tell someone you would like to take something, use the verb *prendere* (to take), as in *Prendo un chilo di pomodori.* (I'll take a kilo of tomatoes.)

Atil Negozio (at the Store)

Store	The Product	Negozio	Il Prodotto
bakery	bread	*il fornaio*	*il pane*
bar	coffee, liquors, alcohol	*il bar*	*il caffè, i liquori, gli alcolici*
butcher	meat, chicken	*la macelleria*	*la carne, il pollo*
dairy store	cheese, milk, eggs	*la latteria*	*il formaggio, il latte, le uova*
fish store	fish	*la pescheria*	*il pesce*
green grocer	fruit, vegetables, legumes	*il fruttivendolo*	*la frutta, le verdure, i legumi*
grocery store	everything	*la drogheria*	*tutto*
ice-cream shop	ice cream	*la gelateria*	*il gelato*
market	everything	*il mercato*	*tutto*
pastry shop	pastries, sweets	*la pasticceria*	*le paste, i dolci*
supermarket	everything	*il supermercato*	*tutto*
wine bar	wine	*l'enoteca*	*il vino*
wine store	wine	*il vinaio*	*il vino*

At *il Fruttivendolo* (at the Green Grocer)

L'agriturismo is an increasingly popular way for families to vacation abroad. Guests stay in the countryside on working farms or vineyards and eat the cheeses, meats, and vegetables produced there. Why not take a cooking vacation? Eat, live, and drink Italian as you go from the market to the kitchen to the vineyard to the table!

The following table gives you the terms to express your needs.

Le Verdure (Vegetables)

English	Italiano	Pronunciation
anise	*l'anice*	*lah-nee-cheh*
artichoke	*il carciofo*	*eel kar-choh-foh*
asparagus	*gli asparagi*	*ylee ahs-pah-rah-jee*
beans	*i fagioli*	*ee fah-joh-lee*
cabbage	*il cavolo*	*eel kah-voh-loh*
carrots	*le carote*	*leh kah-roh-teh*
cauliflower	*il cavolfiore*	*eel kah-vol-fyoh-reh*
corn	*il mais*	*eel myss*
eggplant	*la melanzana*	*lah meh-lan-zah-nah*
garlic	*l'aglio*	*lah-lyoh*
green beans	*i fagiolini*	*ee fah-joh-lee-nee*
legumes	*i legumi*	*ee leh-goo-mee*
lettuce	*la lattuga*	*lah laht-too-gah*
mushrooms	*i funghi*	*ee foon-ghee*
olive	*l'oliva*	*loh-lee-vah*
onion	*la cipolla*	*lah chee-pohl-lah*
peas	*i piselli*	*ee pee-zel-lee*
potato	*la patata*	*lah pah-tah-tah*
rice	*il riso*	*eel ree-zoh*
spinach	*gli spinaci*	*ylee spee-nah-chee*
tomato	*il pomodoro*	*eel poh-moh-doh-roh*
vegetable/greens	*la verdura*	*lah ver-doo-rah*
zucchini	*gli zucchini*	*ylee zoo-kee-nee*

In Rome, a favorite summertime treat is *il cocomero,* also called *l'anguria* (watermelon), which can be bought at brightly lit *bancarelle* (stands). It's so sweet your teeth will hurt and as wet as a waterfall. (Get extra napkins!) Somehow, the Italians manage to eat the thickly sliced pieces with a plastic spoon.

Another fruit fact: Italians rarely bite into apples. They peel them with a knife in one long curl and then slice them into bite-size chunks to share with everyone at the table.

The following table provides a list of the Italian for various fruits and nuts.

La Frutta e Le Noci (Fruits and Nuts)

English	*Italiano*	Pronunciation
almond	*la mandorla*	*lah **mahn**-dor-lah*
apple	*la mela*	*lah **meh**-lah*
apricot	*l'albicocca*	*lal-bee-**kohk**-kah*
banana	*la banana*	*lah bah-**nah**-nah*
cherry	*la ciliegia*	*lah cheel-**yeh**-jah*
chestnut	*la castagna*	*lah kah-**stah**-nyah*
date	*il dattero*	*eel **daht**-teh-roh*
figs	*i fichi*	*ee **fee**-kee*
fruit	*la frutta*	*lah **froot**-tah*
grapefruit	*il pompelmo*	*eel pom-**pehl**-moh*
grapes	*l'uva*	***loo**-vah*
hazelnut	*la nocciola*	*lah **noh**-choh-lah*
lemon	*il limone*	*eel lee-**moh**-neh*
melon	*il melone*	*eel meh-**loh**-neh*
orange	*l'arancia*	*lah-**rahn**-chah*
peach	*la pesca*	*lah **pes**-kah*
pear	*la pera*	*lah **peh**-rah*
pineapple	*l'ananas*	***lah**-nah-nas*
pistachio nut	*il pistacchio*	*eel pee-**stah**-kee-yoh*
pomegranate	*la melagrana*	*lah meh-lah-**grah**-nah*
raisin	*l'uva secca*	***loo**-vah **sehk**-kah*
raspberry	*il lampone*	*eel lam-**poh**-neh*
strawberry	*la fragola*	*lah **frah**-goh-lah*
walnut	*la noce*	*lah **noh**-cheh*

At *la Macelleria* (at the Butcher)

Italian food is fresh, and most perishables are bought and cooked immediately. You will find the terms for different types of meat in the following table.

La Carne e il Pollame (Meat and Poultry)

English	*Italiano*	Pronunciation
beef	*il manzo*	*eel **mahn**-zoh*
chicken	*il pollo*	*eel **pohl**-loh*
cold cuts	*i salumi*	*ee sah-**loo**-mee*
cutlet	*la costoletta*	*lah koh-stoh-**leht**-tah*
duck	*l'anatra*	***lah**-nah-trah*
fillet	*il filetto*	*eel fee-**leht**-toh*
ham	*il prosciutto*	*eel proh-**shoot**-toh*
lamb	*l'agnello*	*lah-**nyehl**-loh*
liver	*il fegato*	*eel **feh**-gah-toh*
meat	*la carne*	*lah **kar**-neh*
meatballs	*le polpette*	*leh pol-**peht**-teh*
pork	*il maiale*	*eel mah-**yah**-leh*
pork chop	*la braciola di maiale*	*lah **brah**-choh-lah dee mah-**yah**-leh*
quail	*la quaglia*	*lah **kwah**-lyah*
rabbit	*il coniglio*	*eel koh-**nee**-lyoh*
salami	*il salame*	*eel sah-**lah**-meh*
sausage	*la salsiccia*	*lah sal-**see**-chah*
steak	*la bistecca*	*lah bee-**stehk**-kah*
tripe	*la trippa*	*lah **treep**-pah*
turkey	*il tacchino*	*eel tahk-**kee**-noh*
veal	*il vitello*	*eel vee-**tehl**-loh*
veal shank	*lo stinco di vitello*	***lo** steen-**koh** **dee** vee-**tehl**-**loh***

At *la Pescheria* (at the Fish Store)

Ahh, *i frutti di mare!* Go to any seaside village in Italy, and you're guaranteed to eat some of the best seafood you've ever had. The following table gives you a little taste.

I Pesci e I Frutti di Mare (the Fruit of the Sea: Fish and Seafood)

English	*Italiano*	Pronunciation
anchovies	*le acciughe*	*leh ach-**choo**-gheh*
cod	*il merluzzo*	*eel mer-**loo**-tsoh*
crab	*il granchio*	*eel **gran**-kee-yoh*
fish	*il pesce*	*eel **peh**-sheh*
flounder	*la passera*	*lah **pahs**-seh-rah*

continues

English	*Italiano*	Pronunciation
halibut	*l'halibut*	***lah****-lee-boot*
herring	*l'aringa*	*lah-****reen****-gah*
lobster	*l'aragosta*	*lah-rah-****gohs****-tah*
mussel	*la cozza*	*lah **koh***-tsah*
oyster	*l'ostrica*	***loh****-stree-kah*
salmon	*il salmone*	*eel sahl-****moh****-neh*
sardines	*le sardine*	*leh sar-****dee****-neh*
scallop	*la cappasanta*	*lah kahp-pah-****sahn****-tah*
shrimp	*i gamberetti*	*ee gahm-beh-****reht****-tee*
sole	*la sogliola*	*lah **sohl***-yoh-lah*
squid	*i calamari*	*ee kah-lah-****mah****-ree*
swordfish	*il pesce spada*	*eel **peh***-sheh **spah***-dah*
trout	*la trota*	*lah **troh***-tah*
tuna	*il tonno*	*eel **tohn***-noh*

In Vino Veritas

As is the Italian way, certain times befit certain beverages. *Il cappuccino* is generally consumed in the morning with a *cornetto* (similar to a croissant). *L'espresso* can be consumed any time of the day, but is usually taken after meals (never *cappuccino*).

The word *cappuccino* shares roots with the word *cappuccio* (mantle, cloak) both because of its color, and for the fact of it having a "hood" of foam, the yummy fluffy stuff that makes you want to lick your spoon clean!

To whet your appetite, you can have an *aperitivo* (aperitif), and to help you digest, a *digestivo* (digestive) or *amaro* (bitter). As an afternoon pick-me-up, you can indulge in a *spremuta* (freshly squeezed juice). The following table lists different beverages. You should be able to pronounce these words without the guide—just sound them out like you see them.

Le Bibite (Drinks)

English	*Italiano*
beer	*la birra*
coffee	*il caffè*
drink	*la bibita, la bevanda*
freshly squeezed juice	*la spremuta*
freshly squeezed orange/grapefruit juice	*la spremuta d'arancia/di pompelmo*

English	Italiano
fruit juice	*il succo di frutta*
hot chocolate	*la cioccolata calda*
iced tea	*il tè freddo*
lemon soda	*la limonata*
milk	*il latte*
mineral water	*l'acqua minerale*
nonalcoholic beverage	*l'analcolico*
noncarbonated mineral water	*l'acqua minerale naturale*
orange soda	*l'aranciata*
sparkling mineral water	*l'acqua minerale gassata/frizzante*
sparkling wine	*lo spumante*
tea	*il tè*
wine (red/white)	*il vino (rosso/bianco)*

More Talk of Food

The Italians have a saying for everything. A million *modi di dire* (ways of saying) are used around food. The following table gives you several.

Idioms Related to Food

English	Italiano
a good mouth (a good eater)	*di bocca buona*
good natured	*di pasta buona* (of good pasta)
I could give a darn.	*Non me ne importa un fico secco.* (I don't care a dry fig's worth.)
One thing leads to another.	*Una ciliegia tira l'altra.* (One cherry pulls the other.)
red as a beet	*rosso come un peperone* (red as a pepper)
smooth as oil	*liscio come l'olio*
to be a little slow in the head	*avere poco sale nella zucca* (to have little salt in the pumpkin)
to be a sack of potatoes	*essere un sacco di patate*
to be stubborn as nails	*essere un osso duro* (to be a hard bone)
to be a wet noodle	*avere lo spirito di patata* (to have a potato's sense of humor)
to call a spade a spade	*dire pane al pane e vino al vino* (to call bread bread and wine wine)

continues

English	*Italiano*
to drink like a fish	*bere come una spugna* (to drink like a sponge)
to give the shirt off your back	*togliersi il pane di bocca* (to give bread from your mouth)
to live on bread and water	*mangiare pane e cipolla* (to eat bread and onion)
to mess things up big time	*fare la frittata* (to make an omelette of things)
to make mincemeat of ...	*fare polpette di ...* (to make meatballs ...)
to the core	*fino al midollo* (to the marrow)

What's in a Name?

When you're talking about food, what often sounds slightly exotic almost invariably derives from a simple description of its shape or taste.

Look at the word *capellini*, for example, referring to a type of spaghetti that's as thin as *capelli* (in English, you call this angel-hair pasta), or *orecchiette*, which literally means *little ears*. The pasta shapes known as *conchiglie* are named after the seashells they resemble. *Le bombarde* (bombs) describe the huge "bomblike" tubes of pasta that are stuffed with cheese and meat fillings. The word for the popular *ziti* may find its origins in the word *zitellone*, referring to an old bachelor. (*Zitella* was used to describe a spinster.) And let's not forget the corkscrew-shape pasta *fusilli*, perhaps finding its origins in the word *fusello*, meaning *spindle* or *bobbin*. Finally, note the similarities between the words *lasagna* and *lenzuolo* (bed sheet). Ah ha!

Expressing *Quantità*

You want a little of this and a little of that. You'll take some olives, a loaf of bread, and a couple boxes of pasta. Maybe you'll also get a slice of cheese, and since you're there, why not a chicken cutlet or two?

When you're out shopping, you need to know how to express how much you want of something. There are a few ways of doing this.

It's the *Quantità* That Counts

Italy uses the metric system, which you might not be all that familiar with, coming from the U.S. standard system. The following table helps make the metric system much easier to follow. These comparisons are approximate but close enough to get roughly the right amount.

Measuring

Solid Measures		Liquid Measures	
U.S. System	*Metrico*	U.S. System	*Metrico*
1 ounce	*28 grammi*	1 ounce	*30 millilitri*
¼ pound	*125 grammi (un etto)**	16 ounces (1 pint)	*475 millilitri*
½ pound	*250 grammi*	32 ounces (1 quart)	*circa un litro*
¾ pound	*375 grammi*	1 gallon	*3.75 litri*
1.1 pounds	*500 grammi*		
2.2 pounds	*1 chilogrammo (un chilo)*		

*Prices are often quoted by the etto *(a hectogram).*

It might be just as easy to indicate a little of this and a little of that and then say when enough is enough using the expression *Basta così* (That's good./That's enough). Because Italy uses the metric system, instead of asking for a dozen, you can also ask for "10 of." Some helpful ways of expressing quantity are listed in the following table.

Le Quantità (Amounts)

English	*Italiano*	English	*Italiano*
a bag of	*un sacchetto di*	a kilo of	*un chilo di*
a bottle of	*una bottiglia di*	a pack of	*un pacchetto di*
a box of	*una scatola di*	a piece of	*un pezzo di*
a can of	*una lattina di*	a quarter pound of	*un etto di*
a container of	*un barattolo di*	a sack (lot) of	*un sacco di*
a dozen of	*una dozzina di*	a slice of	*una fetta di*
a drop of	*una goccia di*	a ten of	*una decina di*
a jar of	*un vasetto di*		

LA BELLA LINGUA

The words *qualche* and *alcuni* (or *alcune* [f.]) can mean "some" or "any" and can be used when there are a few or several. Note that *qualche* and the noun it modifies is always used in the singular, even if the meaning is plural.

qualche volta	sometimes
alcuni amici	some friends
alcune lingue	a few languages

Give Me Some!

To indicate that you'd like *some of* a larger quantity, you can use the preposition *di* + the noun (with its appropriate definite article) to create the partitive. (See Chapter 12 to refresh your memory of contractions.) Take a look at the following examples:

*Vorrei **del** pane.*	I'd like some bread.
*Prendo **della** frutta.*	I'll take some fruit.
*Ho anche bisogno **dello** zucchero.*	I also need some sugar.

A Riddle

Try to figure out the subject of this *indovinello toscano* (Tuscan riddle) and determine the identity of "la bella del palazzo."

Son la bella del palazzo;
Casco in terra e non mi ammazzo;
Faccio lume al gran Signore,
Son servita con amore.

(Hint: I'm edible.)

The following is an adaptation of the poem, altered slightly to re-create the rhyme:

I am the beauty of the palace;
I fall on the ground without malaise;
I shine for the Grand Lord above,
I am always served with love.

Answer: un'oliva (an olive)

Some or Any: The Partitive *Ne*

Imagine that someone asks you whether you want some ice cream. You're stuffed to the gills, though, and if you eat one more bite, you'll explode. So you say, "Nah, I don't want any, thanks." It's assumed that *any* refers to the ice cream.

You've learned how to indicate "some" or "any" by using the preposition *di* plus *l'articolo*. The partitive pronoun *ne* comes in handy when used to ask for a part of or some of a greater quantity. It can be translated to mean "some," "any," "of it," "of them," "some of them," "any of it," and "any of them." It's especially used in response to a question, when the object has already been indicated.

Like most object pronouns, *ne* usually precedes the verb but attaches itself to the infinitive form (minus the final *-e*).

Would You like some fruit?   No, thanks; I don't want any.
Vuole della frutta?   *No grazie, non ne voglio.*

I don't want to eat any.
Non voglio mangiarne.

Now for Some Practice

Answer the following questions with the pronoun *ne* using the affirmative and the negative.

> *Example: Vuole un frutto?* (Do You want a piece of fruit?)
> *Answer: No, non ne voglio.* (No, I don't want any.)

1. *Hanno dei soldi?* (Do they have money?) *Sì,* _____.

2. *Avete del pane?* (Do you [all] have some bread?) *Sì,* _____.

3. *Bevi vino?* (Do you drink wine?) *Sì,* _____.

4. *Mangi del gelato?* (Are you eating ice cream?) *No,* _____.

Answers: 1. ne hanno 2. ne abbiamo 3. ne bevo 4. non ne mangio

What's Your Pleasure? The Verb *Piacere*

One of the first things an Italian will ask is *Le piace l'Italia?* (Do you like Italy?) What's not to like? What they're really asking is whether Italy pleases you or not. If you've ever studied Spanish, you're familiar with this concept from the Spanish verb *gustar.*

In Italian, you wouldn't say, "I like pizza." Using the verb *piacere*, you would say "*Mi piace la pizza.*" The English equivalent of this would be "Pizza pleases me." If you were talking about spaghetti, because the word is plural in Italian, you would say, "*Mi piacciono gli spaghetti.*" ("Spaghetti please me.")

On rare occasions, you might find it necessary to use the verb in the first or second person, in which case it is conjugated as shown in the following table.

Piacere (to Please)

Italiano	English
io **piaccio**	I am pleasing
tu **piaci**	you are pleasing
lui/lei/Lei **piace**	he/she (it) is pleasing; You are pleasing
noi **piacciamo**	we are pleasing
voi **piacete**	you are pleasing
loro **piacciono**	they are pleasing

Do you like me?
Ti piaccio? (Am I pleasing to you?)

I like you.
Mi piaci. (You please me.)

Keep in mind these points about *piacere:*

Unlike English, in Italian, the thing that is pleasing is the subject of the sentence. The person who is pleased is the indirect object.

Because the subject of the sentence dictates how the verb is conjugated, *piacere* is rarely used in anything other than the third person singular and plural. Those two forms are shown here:

piace (it pleases)

piacciono (they please)

Piacere is used with your indirect object pronouns. In the first few examples, the **indirect object** (or pronoun) is in **bold:**

I like pizza.
Mi piace la pizza. (Pizza pleases **me.**)

I like spaghetti.
Mi piacciono gli spaghetti. (Spaghetti please **me.**)

Children, do you like pizza?
Bambini, vi piace la pizza? (Does pizza please **you?**)

Yes, we like pizza and spaghetti.
*Sì, **ci** piacciono la pizza e gli spaghetti!* (Yes, pizza and spaghetti please **us.**)

AS A *REGOLA*

Piacere is almost always used in third person (singular and plural) and is always used with an indirect object or indirect object pronoun. I've reworded the English in these examples to help you see how this verb works in the Italian.

When used as the subject, the infinitive is singular:

I like to eat pizza.
Mi piace mangiare la pizza. (Eating pizza pleases me.)

Do you like to study?
Ti piace studiare? (Does studying please you?)

When you're not using an indirect object pronoun, you must use the preposition *a* (or its contraction, *a* + the article) before the noun:

Marcello likes to drink wine.
A Marcello piace bere il vino. (Drinking wine is pleasing **to** Marcello.)

The children like chocolate.
***Ai** bambini piace la cioccolata.* (Chocolate is pleasing **to the** children.)

The word order is somewhat flexible. The indirect object (the recipient of the verb's action) of the verb can come before or after the conjugated form of *piacere:*

Giovanni likes bread.
***A Giovanni** piace il pane.* (To Giovanni, bread is pleasing.)

Does Giovanni like bread?
*Piace il pane **a Giovanni?*** (Is bread pleasing to Giovanni?)

To make a negative statement, put *non* in front of the indirect object pronoun:

I don't like to eat liver.
***Non** mi piace mangiare il fegato.* (Eating liver does not please me.)

However, when the indirect object of the verb is a noun (and not a pronoun), put *non* in front of the conjugated form of *piacere:*

> The children don't like to eat liver.
> *Ai bambini **non** piace mangiare il fegato.* (Eating liver does not please the children.)

When *loro* (to them) is being used, it's the only pronoun to always follow the verb:

> They like the candies.
> *Piacciono loro le caramelle.* (Candies please them.)

The verb *dispiacere* means "to be sorry" (not "to be displeasing") as well as "to mind." It's used exactly like the verb *piacere:*

> I'm sorry.
> *Mi dispiace.*

Practice Using the Verb *Piacere*

Ask someone if he or she likes the following. Remember that the thing that is liked is the subject and the verb *piacere* must reflect number.

> *Example: Le _____ il vino bianco?*
> *Answer: Le <u>piace</u> il vino bianco?*

1. *Ti _____ la frutta?*   4. *Ti _____ cucinare?*

2. *Signora, Le _____ il vino?*   5. *Mamma, ti _____ le caramelle?*

3. *Vi _____ le paste?*   6. *L'Italia _____ loro?*

Answers: 1. piace 2. piace 3. piacciono 4. piace 5. piacciono 6. piace

Practice Using the Verb *Piacere* II

Imagine that you're asking your partner if he or she likes something from the following list. Give both an affirmative and a negative response.

> *Example: Ti piacciono i biscotti?*
> *Answer: Sì, mi piacciono i biscotti.*
> *No, non mi piacciono i biscotti.*

1. *i dolci* _____

2. *la pasta* _____

3. *i bambini* _____

4. *le acciughe* _____

5. *i fichi* _____

6. *il fegato* _____

Answers: 1. (Non) mi piacciono 2. (Non) mi piace 3. (Non) mi piacciono 4. (Non) mi piacciono 5. (Non) mi piacciono 6. (Non) mi piace

The Least You Need to Know

- The pronoun *ne* is used to express that you want a *part of* or *some of* a greater quantity.
- To say that you like something, you must use the verb *piacere* (to be pleasing).
- To easily grasp the verb *piacere,* reframe your thinking. Instead of saying, "I like boys," say "Boys please me" and then try to conjugate your verb.
- You must use indirect object pronouns with *piacere.*

Buon Appetito: Dining Out

In This Chapter

- First things first: ordinal numbers
- Dining out
- Ordering food for special diets
- Determining "which" one with *quale*
- Making comparisons

In this chapter, we cover a few different things. First, we talk about ordinal numbers. Second, we discuss ordering in a *ristorante*. Finally, we talk about how to compare things. Which is better, and what's the best?

For a change, you won't be given any verb lessons.

Who's on First?: Ordinal Numbers

When you *ordini* your dinner in a *ristorante*, you start with your *primo piatto* (first course). Maybe you order *pasta primavera* (which means *springtime* and translates literally as "first green"). You move along to your *secondo piatto* (second course), and afterward, you might have *per ultimo* (for last)—a nice *tiramisù*, so sweet and light and lovely you feel like you died and went to heaven.

What do all these things have in common (other than they are *deliziose*)? They all use ordinal numbers.

Ordinal numbers specify the order of something in a series. The word *primo* is similar to the English word *primary*, *secondo* is like *secondary*, *terzo* is like *tertiary*, *quarto* is like *quarter, quinto* is like *quintuplets,* and so on. The following table gives you a rundown of useful ordinal numbers you need to know and how to recognize them in both the masculine and feminine abbreviated forms.

Ordinal Numbers

English	*Italiano*	Masculine	Feminine
first	*primo*	1°	1a
second	*secondo*	2°	2a
third	*terzo*	3°	3a
fourth	*quarto*	4°	4a
fifth	*quinto*	5°	5a
sixth	*sesto*	6°	6a
seventh	*settimo*	7°	7a
eighth	*ottavo*	8°	8a
ninth	*nono*	9°	9a
tenth	*decimo*	10°	10a
eleventh	*undicesimo*	11°	11a
twelfth	*dodicesimo*	12°	12a
twentieth	*ventesimo*	20°	20a
twenty-first	*ventunesimo*	21°	21a
twenty-third*	*ventitreesimo*	23°	23a
sixty-sixth*	*sessantaseiesimo*	66°	66a
seventy-seventh	*settantasettesimo*	77°	77a
hundredth	*centesimo*	100°	100a
thousandth	*millesimo*	1000°	1000a

*Note: The final vowel of the cardinal number is not dropped with numbers ending in 3 (-tre) and 6 (-sei).

Like any adjective, ordinal numbers must agree in gender and number with the nouns they modify. As in English, they precede the nouns they modify. Notice how they are abbreviated: 1° (1st), 2° (2nd), and 3° (3rd), etc.—much easier than in English. The feminine abbreviation reflects the ending *-a*, as in *1a, 2a,* and *3a*:

la prima volta (1a)   *il primo piatto (1°)*
the first time   the first course

The first 10 ordinal numbers all have separate forms, but after the tenth ordinal number, they simply drop the final vowel of the cardinal number and add the ending *-esimo:*

13th

tredici → *tredicesimo*

25th

venticinque → *venticinquesimo*

You need to use ordinal numbers whenever you reference a Roman numeral, as in *Enrico V* (*quinto*) or *Papa Giovanni Paolo II* (*secondo*).

Unlike in English, dates in Italian require cardinal numbers, unless you're talking about the first day of a month, as in *il primo ottobre.* My brother's birthday, June 8th, is *l'otto (di) giugno* because the day always comes before the month. The use of the preposition *di* is optional. Therefore, it's important to remember that in Italian, 8/6/98 is actually June 8, 1998 (and not August 6, 1998). (See Chapter 8 to review dates.)

LA BELLA LINGUA

In Italian, the word for "floor" is *piano* (just like the instrument). The *primo piano* (first floor) is actually the floor *above* the *pianterreno* (ground floor) and equal to what's considered the second floor in the United States. So if someone says he lives on the *terzo piano,* he actually lives on the fourth floor.

What's the House Special?

The following expressions help you ask for what you want at a restaurant or eatery.

31

Dal Ristorante

English	Italiano
Waiter!	*Cameriere!*
I'd like to make a reservation ...	*Vorrei prenotare ...*
... for this evening.	*... per stasera.*
... for tomorrow evening.	*... per domani sera.*
... for Saturday evening.	*... per sabato sera.*
... for two people.	*... per due persone.*
... for 8:00.	*... per le otto.*

continues

English	*Italiano*
May we sit ...	*Possiamo sederci ...*
... near the window?	*... vicino alla finestra?*
... on the terrace?	*... sul terrazzo?*
Is there a nonsmoking section?	*C'è una zona per non fumatori?*
How long is the wait?	*Quanto tempo si deve aspettare?*
What is the house special?	*Qual è la specialità della casa?*
What is the special for the day?	*Qual è il piatto del giorno?*
What do you recommend?	*Che cosa ci consiglia?*
I'd like one portion of	*Vorrei una porzione di ....*
The check, please.	*Il conto, per favore.*
We ate very well.	*Abbiamo mangiato molto bene.*

A Table Setting

Prior to the fifteenth century, most food was eaten with *le mani* (the hands) or from the point of a knife. Although it didn't come to be commonly used until the seventeenth century, it appears that *i napoletani* created the four-pronged *forchetta* to aid them in eating *gli spaghetti*. Nowadays, it's considered *maleducato* (rude) to eat with your hands unless you're eating *il pane* (bread).

The following table provides terms for eating implements and other useful items.

A Tavola (at the Table)

English	*Italiano*	Pronunciation
bottle	*la bottiglia*	*lah boht-**teel**-yah*
bowl	*la ciotola, la scodella*	*lah **choh**-toh-lah, lah skoh-**dehl**-lah*
carafe	*la caraffa*	*lah kah-**raf**-fah*
cup	*la tazza*	*lah **tah**-tsah*
dinner plate	*il piatto*	*eel pee-**aht**-toh*
fork	*la forchetta*	*lah for-**keht**-tah*
glass	*il bicchiere*	*eel bee-kee-**yeh**-reh*
knife	*il coltello*	*eel kohl-**tel**-loh*
menu	*il menù*	*eel meh-**noo***
napkin	*il tovagliolo*	*eel toh-vah-**lyoh**-loh*
oil	*l'olio*	***lohl**-yoh*
pepper	*il pepe*	*eel **peh**-peh*
pitcher	*la brocca*	*lah **brohk**-kah*
salad bowl	*l'insalatiera*	*leen-sah-lah-tee-**yeh**-rah*

English	*Italiano*	Pronunciation
salt	*il sale*	*eel **sah**-leh*
silverware	*l'argenteria*	*lar-jen-teh-**ree**-ah*
spoon	*il cucchiaio*	*eel kook-kee-**ay**-yoh*
sugar bowl	*la zuccheriera*	*lah zook-keh-ree-**yeh**-rah*
table	*il tavolo*	*eel **tah**-voh-loh*
tablecloth	*la tovaglia*	*lah toh-**vah**-lyah*
teapot	*la teiera*	*lah teh-**yeh**-rah*
teaspoon	*il cucchiaino*	*eel kook-kee-ay-**ee**-noh*
vinegar	*l'aceto*	*lah-**cheh**-toh*

LA BELLA LINGUA

Il tavolo refers to a table in a restaurant; *la tavola* refers to a table at home. You may already be familiar with the term *Buon appetito!* When you want to make a toast (*fare un brindisi*) you say: *Alla salute!* (To your health!) or *Cincin!* (Cheers! pronounced *cheen-cheen*).

In the Kitchen

There's no better way than to eat your way to fluency! Why not tape the following kitchen-related terms to your refrigerator?

Nella Cucina (in the Kitchen)

English	*Italiano*	English	*Italiano*
basket	*il cesto*	frying pan	*la padella*
bowl	*la ciotola*	funnel	*l'imbuto*
box/container	*la scatola*	grill	*la griglia*
can opener	*l'apriscatole*	measuring cup	*il misurino*
canister	*il barattolo*	microwave oven	*il forno a microonde*
colander	*il colapasta*	oven	*il forno*
corkscrew	*il cavatappi*	oven mitt	*il guanto da forno*
counter	*il piano di lavoro*	pitcher	*la caraffa*
cupboard	*l'armadietto*	pot	*la pentola*
curtains	*le tende, le tendine*	recipe	*la ricetta*
cutting board	*il tagliere*	recipe book	*il libro di cucina*
dishwasher	*la lavastoviglie*	refrigerator	*il frigorifero*
faucet	*il rubinetto*	rolling pin	*il matterello*

continues

English	*Italiano*	English	*Italiano*
saucepan	*la padella*	straw	*la cannuccia*
saucer	*il piattino*	toaster	*il tostapane*
sink	*il lavandino*	tray	*il vassoio*
stove	*la cucina a gas o elettrica*	vase	*il vaso*
stove burner	*il fornello*		

Il Caffè

In Italy, people take their *caffè* very seriously, and it's served in a variety of manners. If you must drink American coffee—which by Italian standards is considered weak and without flavor—ask for *un caffè americano*. If you're in a small town, you should indicate this as *un caffè molto lungo*.

Coffee, Coffee Everywhere

Kind of Coffee	Description	*Il Tipo di Caffè*	*La Descrizione*
an espresso	normal coffee	*un espresso*	*caffè normale*
a caffé americano	like *un espresso* but with a lot of water, equivalent to an American double espresso	*un espresso lungo*	*caffè con molta acqua*
a tight espresso	concentrated coffee	*un espresso ristretto*	*caffè concentrato*
a cappuccino	espresso with steamed milk	*un cappuccino*	*un espresso con latte vaporizzato*
a stained milk	a lot of milk, little coffee	*un latte macchiato*	*molto latte, poco caffè*
a stained coffee	coffee with a drop of milk	*un caffè macchiato*	*caffè con una goccia di latte*
a coffee milk	coffee made at home with heated milk	*un caffè latte*	*caffè fatto a casa con latte*
a corrected coffee	coffee with booze	*un caffè corretto*	*caffè con un liquore*
a decaf coffee	coffee without caffeine	*un caffè decaffeinato*	*caffè senza caffeina*
a Hag coffee*	coffee without caffeine	*un caffè Hag*	*caffè senza caffeina*
an iced coffee	cold coffee	*un caffè freddo*	*caffè freddo*

*Like Sanka.

A Little Dining Etiquette

Italians aren't big snackers; when they eat, they really eat. Although nothing is written in stone, to enhance your dining *esperienza*, a few guidelines won't hurt.

For example, in Italy, almost everything is *alla carta*—that is, ordered individually. If you want *un contorno* (a side) of veggies, you'll get a separate *piattino* because Italians almost never have more than one kind of food on a plate unless they're eating from a buffet, usually referred to as either *la tavola fredda* (the cold table) or *la tavola calda* (the hot table).

 WHAT'S WHAT

Contrary to popular belief, Marco Polo wasn't the first to introduce *gli spaghetti* to Italy. Evidence that the Romans had various forms of pasta predates Marco Polo's adventure, although tomatoes weren't introduced to Italy until the fifteenth century. Found growing in South America, t was believed that the yellow and red fruit (yes, the tomato is a fruit—the Italian word *pomodoro* literally means golden apple) was poisonous unless cooked for a long time.

The order of the meal is important. Generally, you order a *primo piatto* (first course), which is usually a pasta dish or soup, and then you eat your *secondo piatto* (main course). *L'insalata* is usually eaten with *il secondo piatto*. Finally, when you order *un caffè*, it's assumed that you mean *espresso*. (Remember, Italians drink espresso, not cappuccino, after a meal, and grated cheese is never offered for pasta dishes that include fish.)

 BUON'IDEA

Collect menus from your favorite Italian *ristorante* and study the *ingredienti* for each *piatto*. Often, what sounds exotic is simply a description of the food. Angel-hair pasta, called *capellini*, literally means thin hairs. The ear-shape pasta called *orecchiette* refers to little ears. *Calzone* comes from the word *calza*, due to its resemblance to a cheese-filled sock.

That's the Way I Like It

Do you want your eggs scrambled or poached? Your meat cooked rare, or well done? A poached egg is called *le uova in camicia* because the white of the egg surrounds the yolk, like a shirt. Italians generally eat eggs for lunch or dinner as a *secondo piatto*.

The terms in the following table enable you to express exactly how you want your food prepared.

Cooked to Order

Preparation	*La Preparazione*
baked	*al forno*
boiled	*bollito*
breaded	*impanato*
fried	*fritto*
fried (eggs)	*le uova fritte*
grilled	*alla griglia*
hard-boiled (eggs)	*le uova bollite*
marinated	*marinato*
medium	*normale*
omelette	*la frittata*
poached	*in camicia*
poached (eggs)	*le uova in camicia*
rare	*al sangue*
scrambled (eggs)	*le uova strapazzate*
soft-boiled (eggs)	*le uova alla coque*
steamed	*al vapore*
well done	*ben cotto*

Special People Have Special Dietary Needs

You're in great shape and have eliminated certain things from your *dieta*. There's no reason to destroy all your hard work with one visit to Italy. The phrases in the following table help you stick to your *dieta* or express your special dietary needs.

WHAT'S WHAT

In Italy, each region has its own bread. For example, *il pane toscano* is found throughout Tuscany and Umbria. This bread has no salt, stemming back to the thirteenth century when a salt tax was imposed on the people who then began to bake their breads without it.

For those with allergies to nuts, it's important to know that in Italian, the term *noci* translates specifically to "walnuts"; a variation of this, *nocciole*, refers to "hazelnuts";

and the term *noccioline* refers to "peanuts" (also called *arachidi*). Not to mention *mandorle* (almonds), *pinoli* (Pignoli), or *pistacchi* (pistaccios). To refer to nuts in general, it's best to use the term *alla frutta secca e/o con guscio* ("dried fruit and/or with shells"). Remember, too, that many restaurants cook with peanut oil. For those who are lactose intolerant, keep an eye out for warnings on labels such as *Può contenere tracce di latte e nocciole* (May contain traces of milk and nuts), or a variation *Può contenere frutta a guscio e derivati* (May contain dried fruits and nuts and derivatives).

Special Dietary Needs

English	Italiano
I am allergic to …	*Sono allergico/a a …*
dried fruit and/or nuts	*alla frutta secca e/o con guscio*
I am on a diet.	*Faccio la dieta/Sono in dieta.*
No nuts.	*Niente noci.*
I'm on a …	*Faccio …*
… diabetic diet.	*… la dieta per diabetici.*
… light diet.	*… la dieta leggera.*
… low-calorie diet.	*… la dieta ipocalorica.*
… low-carb diet.	*… la dieta povera di carboidrati.*
… low-salt diet.	*… la dieta povera di sale.*
… macrobiotic diet.	*… la dieta macrobiotica.*
I'm a vegetarian.	*Sono vegetariano(a).*
Do you serve kosher food?	*Servite del cibo kosher?*
I can't have any …	*Non posso prendere …*
… dairy products.	*… i latticini.*
… alcohol.	*… l'alcol.*
… saturated fat.	*… i grassi saturi.*
… shellfish.	*… i frutti di mare.*
I'm looking for a dish …	*Cerco un piatto …*
… high in fiber.	*… con molta fibra.*
… low in cholesterol.	*… con poco colesterolo.*
… low in fat.	*… con pochi grassi.*
… low in sodium.	*… poco salato.*
… without preservatives.*	*… senza conservanti.*

*Be sure to use the Italian word conservanti *and not the false cognate* preservativi, *which means "prophylactics"!*

You Call This Food?

You asked for a rare steak, but you received what looks like a *scarpa*, or there's a small nail in your pizza (don't worry, you won't be charged extra) and a hair in your spaghetti. The following table gives you the terms you need to deal with these and other problems.

Take It Away!

English	Italiano
This is ...	*Questo è ...*
... burned.	*... bruciato.*
... dirty.	*... sporco.*
... overcooked.	*... troppo cotto.*
... spoiled.	*... andato a male.*
... too cold.	*... troppo freddo.*
... too rare.	*... troppo crudo.*
... too salty.	*... troppo salato.*
... too spicy.	*... troppo piccante.*
... too sweet.	*... troppo dolce.*
... unacceptable.	*... inaccettabile.*

AS A *REGOLA*

Italian standards for wine are very high. The next time you go for a *degustazione vini* (wine tasting), it might help you to know a little about how Italian wines are classified. Finer wines are classified as *denominazione di origine controllata* (DOC; denomination of controlled origins) or *denominazione di origine controllata e garantita* (DOCG; denomination of controlled origins and guaranteed), which you'll see on the wine label. Other wines are simply classified as *vino da tavola* (table wine), which range in quality and are served by many restaurants as *il vino della casa* (the house wine).

A *Bellini* Please

One of Italy's most popular cocktails is the *Bellini*, created by Giuseppe Cipriani of Harry's Bar in Venice. This light, refreshing drink is perfect before a meal.

Bellini

²/₃ tazza (160 ml.) di purè di pesca

1 cucchiaino di purè di lampone

1 bottiglia di Prosecco (o Asti Spumante o champagne)

1. *In ogni bicchiere di vino o spumante, versate 7 cucchiaini di purè di pesca.*

2. *Aggiungete 2 o 3 goccie di purè di lampone.*

3. *Aggiungete il vino, e servite subito.*

Translation:

Bellini

²/₃ cup (160 ml.) of peach purée

1 teaspoon of raspberry purée

1 bottle of Prosecco (or Asti Spumante or champagne)

1. In every glass of wine or sparkling wine, mix 7 teaspoons of the peach purée.

2. Add 2 or 3 drops of the raspberry purée.

3. Add wine, and serve immediately.

Which One?

The interrogative pronoun and adjective *quale* means "which" or "what" and is also used to ask questions. There are two forms: *quale* (which one), and *quali* (which ones).

Qual è …? expresses the question "What is …?":

> *Ecco la lista; quale antipasto preferisci?*
> Here's the menu; which appetizer do you prefer?

> *Quali cafè ti piacciono?*
> What caffés do you like?

Qual è il numero di telefono per il ristorante?
What is the telephone number of the restaurant?

LA BELLA LINGUA

Quale refers to a choice between two or more alternatives. *Che* (what) can be substituted for *quale* in almost any given situation: *Quale (che) ristorante avete scelto?* (Which restaurant did you choose?)

Comparatives and Superlatives

In addition to describing nouns and verbs, you use adjectives and adverbs to compare things. Often, you can add *-er* or *-est* to an adjective in English to indicate that something is more (or less) beautiful, big, sweet, tall, and so on, as in "She is sweeter than honey; in fact, she is the sweetest person I have ever met." Use the following table to help you compare things.

Comparison of Adjectives: Inequality

	English	***Italiano***
Adjective	sweet	*dolce*
Comparative	sweeter	*più dolce*
	less sweet	*meno dolce*
Superlative	the sweetest	*il/la* più dolce*
	the least sweet	*il/la* meno dolce*

*The same rules apply using the plural articles i, gli, *and* le.

To compare one thing as being either more or less than another, place the word *più* (more) or *meno* (less) before the adjective:

This restaurant is more expensive.
Questo ristorante è più caro.

That restaurant is less expensive.
Quel ristorante è meno caro.

To express the English *than*, use the preposition *di* (or its contraction) in front of nouns and pronouns. Watch how the same word can serve two different functions in one sentence:

> I have more Facebook friends than you.
> *Ho più amici di Facebook di te.*

> Laura's dog is smaller than the cat.
> *Il cane di Laura è più piccolo del gatto.*

> Dogs are bigger than cats.
> *I cani sono più grandi dei gatti.*

The comparative and superlative forms of the adjectives must agree in gender and number with the nouns they describe:

> The moon is smaller than the earth.
> *La luna è meno grande della terra.*

> Your eyes are the most beautiful.
> *I tuoi occhi sono i più belli.*

Che is used when making comparisons of quantity, when comparing two qualities pertaining to the same person or thing, or when comparing two infinitive verbs:

> more/less … than
> *più/meno … di (che)*

> You are taller than I.
> *Tu sei più alto di me.*

> The evening is colder than the day.
> *Di sera fa più freddo che di giorno.*

> It's easier to play than study.
> *È più facile giocare che studiare.*

> I am less tall than you.
> *Io sono meno alta di te.*

> Better late than never.
> *Meglio tardi che mai.*

To make a relative comparison between two things, simply add *più* (more) or *meno* (less) before the adjective or adverb:

> This restaurant is the most expensive.
> *Questo è il ristorante più caro.*

> That restaurant is the least expensive.
> *Quello è il ristorante meno caro.*

Better Than the Best

In addition to having regular forms, some adjectives have irregular comparative and superlative forms. Are you good? Getting better? Or the best?

Good, Better, Best: Adjective Comparatives and Superlatives

Adjective	Comparative	Relative Superlative
buono (good)	*migliore* (better)	*il/la migliore* (the best)
cattivo (bad)	*peggiore* (worse)	*il/la peggiore* (the worst)
grande (big/great)	*maggiore* (bigger/greater)	*il/la maggiore* (the biggest/greatest)
piccolo (small)	*minore* (smaller/lesser)	*il/la minore* (the smallest/least)

Maggiore and *minore* are often used to reference family members, such as younger sister or older brother. The superlative is used to indicate the oldest or the youngest. Although possessives involving immediate family members normally do not take a definite article, they do when the thing being possessed is modified by an adjective:

> My younger brother is called Robert.
> *Il mio fratello minore si chiama Roberto.*

The superlatives *migliore, peggiore, maggiore,* and *minore* drop the final *-e* before nouns, except with nouns beginning with *s* + consonant or *z:*

> You're my best friend!
> *Tu sei la mia miglior amica!*

Irregular Comparisons

How are you doing? Well? A perfect illustration of an irregular adverb is the English word *well.* In Italian, irregular adverbs are easily learned. The following table outlines some of the most commonly used adverbs.

Irregular Adverb Comparatives and Superlatives

Adverb	Comparative	Absolute Superlative
bene (well)	*meglio* (better)	*benissimo* (best)
male (badly)	*peggio* (worse)	*malissimo* (really bad)
molto (much/a lot)	*più, di più* (more)	*moltissimo* (very much)
poco (little)	*meno, di meno* (less)	*pochissimo* (very little)

To make the relative superlative, simply add the definite article in front of the comparative:

> I'm arriving as soon as possible.   I'm doing my best.
> *Arrivo il prima possibile.*   *Faccio del mio meglio.*

LA BELLA LINGUA

Give all you have to give! To say this in Italian, use the following espressione: *Farò del mio meglio.* (I will do my best.)

Comparisons of Equality

To say that something is as good as another is called a comparison of equality. To say that two things are *as equal as* something else:

> *tanto … quanto* + adjective or adverb
> *as … as* + adjective or adverb
>
> *così … come* + adjective or adverb
> *as … as* + adjective or adverb

Jessica is as tall as Gabriella.
Jessica è tanto alta quanto Gabriella.

You are as handsome as your father.
Tu sei così bello come tuo padre.

I like skiing as much as playing tennis.
Mi piace sciare tanto quanto giocare a tennis.

The teacher learns as much as she teaches.
L'insegnante impara tanto quanto insegna.

Personal pronouns following *come* or *quanto* are always stressed:

I am as intelligent as you are.
Io sono intelligente come te.

You are like me.
Tu sei come me.

Absolutely, Totally Superlative

If something is really extraordinary, you can use the adverb *veramente* (truly) or *molto* (very) in front of your adjective or adverb. Or to show the extreme of something, a poetic, commonly used ending is *-issimo*. The following table lists a few adjectives (which must always reflect gender and number) used in this manner.

Above Average

Adjective	Very	Extremely
bello (beautiful)	*molto bello*	*bellissimo*
buono (good)	*molto buono*	*buonissimo/ottimo**
cattivo (bad)	*molto cattivo*	*cattivissimo/pessimo**
grande (big)	*molto grande*	*grandissimo*
piccolo (small)	*molto piccolo*	*piccolissimo*
vecchio (old)	*molto vecchio*	*vecchissimo*
veloce (fast)	*molto veloce*	*velocissimo*

*Irregular.

Ottimo is often used in addition to *buonissimo* when something is really great, as in the best. *Pessimo* is used to describe something that is as bad as bad can get, as in *Questo ristorante è pessimo*. (This restaurant is the worst.)

The Least You Need to Know

- Ask to make a reservation using the expression *Vorrei fare una prenotazione* or *Vorrei prenotare un tavolo.* Do not use the cognate *riservare,* which means *to keep* or *to put aside.*
- There are several parts to an Italian meal: *gli antipasti, i contorni, i primi piatti, i secondi piatti,* and *i dolci.*
- Use *meno* (less) or *più* (more) before adjectives and adverbs to make comparisons or express the superlative.
- Use *(tanto) quanto* or *(così) come* to express that things are equal.
- *Che* and *quale* are used to ask *what?* and *which?*
- Use the ending *-issimo* to form the absolute superlative of adverbs and adjectives.
- Use *molto* for "very" and *moltissimo* for "extremely much."

Made in *Italia:* Using Object Pronouns and Shopping

In This Chapter

- Stores and their wares
- Bejeweled and bedazzled, Italian style
- Clothing colors, sizes, and materials
- Direct and indirect object pronouns
- Double object and disjunctive pronouns

Italians understand style—they practically invented it! Whether you bring back hand-blown wine glasses from the famous Venetian island Murano, a Fendi bag from Milano, or an expressive cameo made in Florence, Italy is a place you definitely want to shop!

Stores Galore (*I Negozi*)

As you meander through the *strade* of Italia, you might find some *liquirizia* lozenges in a small *tabaccheria*, a silk scarf gently blowing in the wind at the *mercato*, or a hand-painted porcelain doll staring blankly in a *vetrina*.

If you find something you must have (or should I say *when* you find something?), most stores will ship major purchases home for you. Some purchases made with a credit card will be covered for loss or damage. The I.V.A. (value-added tax) is a sales tax attached to all major purchases. Save your receipts—non-European travelers receive I.V.A. (which stands for "Imposta sul Valore Aggiunto") refunds when they leave the country.

In Italy, by law, consumers must be given a receipt and have it when leaving the store. Otherwise, you and the store could be fined by the Department of Finance—not a great way to end your trip.

> May I have a receipt, please?
> *Posso avere lo scontino, per favore?*

The cognate *ricevuta* (receipt) is used when you're given an invoice for services rendered, such as with the plumber or electrician.

The following table helps you find your way to the stores that carry the merchandise you're looking for. Italian terms are given with the appropriate definite article.

I Negozi (Stores)

The Store	The Merchandise	*Il Negozio*	*La Merce*
shop	everything	*la bottega*	*tutto*
stationery store	paper, postcards, toys, cigarettes	*la cartoleria*	*la carta, le cartoline, i giochi, le sigarette*
pharmacy	medicine	*la farmacia*	*le medicine*
florist	flowers, plants	*il fioraio*	*i fiori, le piante*
jewelry store	jewelry	*la gioielleria*	*i gioielli*
newspaper stand	newspapers, magazines, postcards	*il giornalaio*	*i giornali, le riviste, le cartoline*
department store	jewelry, toys, magazines, furnishings, perfumes, clothing	*il grande magazzino*	*i gioielli, i giochi, le riviste, i mobili, i profumi, i vestiti*
bookstore	books	*la libreria*	*i libri*
market	everything	*il mercato*	*tutto*
clothing store	clothing	*il negozio d'abbigliamento*	*l'abbigliamento, i vestiti*
furniture store	furniture	*il negozio d'arredamento*	*i mobili*
shoe store	shoes	*il negozio di scarpe*	*le scarpe*
pastry shop	pastries, cakes, cookies	*la pasticceria*	*le paste, le torte, i biscotti*
leather store	jackets, purses, luggage	*la pelletteria*	*le giacche, le borse, le valigie*
cosmetics shop	perfumes, cosmetics	*la profumeria*	*i profumi, i cosmetici*
tobacco shop	cigarettes, cigars, matches	*la tabaccheria*	*le sigarette, i sigari, i fiammiferi*

La Cartoleria

In addition to office supplies, stationery, candy, and cigarettes, *la cartoleria* often sells stamps and bus tickets. It's also a good place to find inexpensive gift items.

La Cartoleria (the Stationery Store)

English	*Italiano*	English	*Italiano*
candy	*le caramelle*	pen	*la penna*
gift	*il regalo*	pencil	*la matita*
a guidebook	*una guida*	postcard	*la cartolina*
lighter	*l'accendino*	stamp	*il francobollo*
map	*la pianta, la cartina, la mappa*	ticket	*il biglietto*
matches	*i fiammiferi*	… for the bus	*… per l'autobus*
notebook	*il quaderno*	… for the metro	*… per la metro*
paper	*la carta*		

It's in the Jeans: Clothing

Italians seem to be born knowing how to dress. If the body is a blank canvas, they sure know how to paint! Maybe it's in part because Italians are used to being watched—and to watching each other. Some would say it's all in *le scarpe* (the shoes), the finely woven fabrics, and the tailoring. Whatever the reason, *la moda* is a refined *eleganza* that has deep and powerful roots, permeating Italian culture. If you're hoping some of that Italian style will rub off on you, the following table gives you some helpful words to get you started.

L'Abbigliamento (Clothing)

English	*Italiano*	Pronunciation
article	*l'articolo*	*lahr-**tee**-koh-loh*
bathing suit	*il costume da bagno*	*eel kohs-**too**-meh dah bahn-yoh*
bra	*il reggiseno*	*eel reh-jee-**seh**-noh*
clothing	*l'abbigliamento*	*lah-beel-yah-**men**-toh*
… women's	*… per donna*	*per **dohn**-nah*
… men's	*… per uomo*	*per **woh**-moh*
… children's	*… per bambini*	*per bam-**bee**-nee*

continues

English	*Italiano*	Pronunciation
coat	*il cappotto/il giubbotto*	*eel kah-__poht__-toh/eel joob-__boht__-toh*
dress	*l'abito*	*__lah__-bee-toh*
evening dress	*l'abito da sera*	*__lah__-bee-toh dah seh-rah*
jacket	*la giacca*	*lah __jahk__-kah*
jeans	*i jeans*	*ee jeens*
lining	*la fodera*	*lah __foh__-deh-rah*
model	*il modello*	*eel moh-__dehl__-loh*
pajamas	*il pigiama*	*eel pee-__jah__-mah*
pants	*i pantaloni*	*ee pahn-tah-__loh__-nee*
pullover	*il golf*	*eel golf*
raincoat	*l'impermeabile*	*leem-per-meh-__ah__-bee-leh*
robe	*l'accappatoio*	*lah-kahp-pah-__toh__-yoh*
skirt	*la gonna*	*lah __gohn__-nah*
suit	*il completo*	*eel kom-__pleh__-toh*
sweat suit	*la tuta da ginnastica*	*lah too-tah dah jee-__nah__-stee-kah*
sweater	*la maglia*	*lah __mah__-lyah*
T-shirt	*la maglietta*	*lah mah-__lyeh__-tah*
undershirt	*la canottiera*	*lah kan-oht-tee-__yeh__-rah*
underwear	*gli slip*	*ylee sleep*
panties	*le mutandine*	*leh moo-tahn-__dee__-neh*
briefs	*le mutande*	*leh moo-__tahn__-deh*
boxers	*i boxer*	*ee __box__-er*

Accessories

By adding *gli accessori* that best complement your wardrobe, you can look like a million bucks without spending a million *euros*.

Gli Accessori (Accessories)

English	*Italiano*	Pronunciation
accessories	*gli accessori*	*ylee ah-chess-__oh__-ree*
belt	*la cintura*	*lah cheen-__too__-rah*
boots	*gli stivali*	*ylee stee-__vah__-lee*
cosmetics	*i cosmetici*	*ee kos-__meh__-tee-chee*
gloves	*i guanti*	*ee __gwahn__-tee*
handkerchief	*il fazzoletto*	*eel fah-tsoh-__let__-toh*

English	*Italiano*	Pronunciation
hat	*il cappello*	*eel kahp-**pehl**-loh*
lingerie	*la biancheria intima*	*lah bee-an-keh-**ree**-yah **een**-tee-mah*
pantyhose	*i collant*	*ee **kohl**-lant*
purse	*la borsa*	*lah **bor**-sah*
sandals	*i sandali*	*ee **sahn**-dah-lee*
scarf	*la sciarpa*	*lah **shar**-pah*
shoes	*le scarpe*	*leh **skar**-peh*
slippers	*le pantofole*	*leh pahn-**toh**-foh-leh*
sneakers	*le scarpe da tennis*	*leh **skar**-peh dah **ten**-nees*
socks	*le calze*, i calzini*	*leh **kal**-zeh, ee kal-**zee**-nee*
stockings	*le calze*	*leh **kal**-zeh*
umbrella	*l'ombrello*	*lohm-**brel**-loh*

*Do you see this word in calzone *(the kind you eat)?*

How Do I Look?

The helpful expressions in the following table will make your shopping even more enjoyable. If someone isn't exactly as they appear to be, you can use the expression, *È un lupo nelle vesti di una pecora!* (He's a wolf in sheep's clothing.)

Shop 'Til You Drop!

English	*Italiano*
What size do You wear?	*Che taglia porta? (formal)*
I wear size …	*Porto il/la …* trentotto*
What size shoe?	*Che numero di scarpe?*
Where is the fitting room?	*Dov'è il camerino?*
I'm just looking.	*Sto solo dando un'occhiata.*
This is (too) …	*Questo è (troppo) …*
… expensive, dear.	*… caro.*
… classical.	*… classico.*
… short.	*… corto.*
… in fashion.	*… di moda.*
… inexpensive.	*… economico.*
… out of season.	*… fuori stagione.*
… big.	*… grande.*

continues

English	Italiano
… long.	… *lungo.*
… tight.	… *stretto.*
discount	*lo sconto*
sale	*la svendita*
shop window	*la vetrina*
size: small, medium, large	*la taglia: piccola, media, grande*
the price	*il prezzo*
the sales clerk	*il commesso/la commessa*
the shoe size	*il numero di scarpe*
the size	*la misura, la taglia***

There are two words for "size": il taglio (literally, "the cut"), and la misura (literally, "the measure"), but the word size is always implied.

***Like the pasta tagliatelle.*

LA BELLA LINGUA

Note the subtle shift in meaning when the noun (and its article) is made plural: *Fare la spesa* (singular) generally means you are shopping for the household (groceries). *Fare spese* (plural) refers to shopping in general, as in "shop 'til you drop!"

Objection!

In this chapter, you've learned all about shopping and how to ask for what you want. While we're on the subject of precious objects, this is as good an *opportunità* as any to introduce objects and object pronouns. Although not as exciting as shopping for new shoes, understanding object pronouns can certainly help you purchase them. (I want them, and these and those ….)

A Little Objective Review

Sorry, in this case, we're not talking about a UFO. Remember, an object pronoun sits in place of the object in a sentence. In Italian, it must agree in gender and number with the noun it's replacing. There are direct and indirect object pronouns.

A direct object indicates who or what is affected by the verb's action. When you say, "I love *my mother*," the object of your love (and the verb) is Mommie Dearest. You can replace the object *my mother* with a direct object pronoun and simply say, "I love *her*."

An indirect object answers the question *to whom* or *for whom*. Indirect objects refer only to people (and pets) and are generally preceded by the preposition *to* or *for*. When you say, "I talk *to my parents* every week," you could replace *to my parents* with an indirect object pronoun, as in "I talk *to them* every week."

In Italian, you also use double object pronouns, like when you say, "Give it to her." Stressed pronouns are used to emphasize and highlight certain nouns or pronouns.

Objectify Me, Baby

The object pronouns may be confusing for a non-native speaker because of their similarity to each other as well as to the articles and other words in Italian. This is why it's so important to listen to the context of a sentence. One trick is to remember that direct and indirect object pronouns are all the same except in the third person singular and plural forms. As shown in the following table, *gli* is commonly used to replace *loro* primarily in the spoken language.

The following table also outlines the subject, direct object, and indirect object pronouns in Italian. It might help you to see how the direct and indirect object pronouns correspond to the subject pronouns.

Subject, Direct, and Indirect Object Pronouns

Subject	Direct Object	Indirect Object
io (I)	*mi* (me)	*mi* (to/for me)
tu (you)	*ti* (you)	*ti* (to/for you)
lui (he)	*lo* (him/it)	*gli* (to/for him)
lei (she)	*la* (her/it)	*le* (to/for her)
Lei (You)	*La* (You)	*Le* (to/for You)
noi (we)	*ci* (us)	*ci* (to/for us)
voi (you)	*vi* (you)	*vi* (to/for you)
loro (they)	*li/le* (them [*m./f.*])	*loro/gli** (to/for them)

**Loro is the only pronoun that follows the verb instead of preceding it.*

All Italian object pronouns agree in gender and number with the nouns they replace. The referred object is given in parentheses. There's no way to translate word for word without changing the word order, so I've also given you the literal translation:

Direct object pronouns:

I see **her** every day. (Maria)
La vedo ogni giorno. (Maria)
(Her I see every day.)

I see **them** every week. (the boys)
Li vedo ogni settimana. (i ragazzi)
(Them I see every week.)

Indirect object pronouns:

I offer **him** a hand. (to my brother)
Gli offro una mano. (a mio fratello)
(Him I offer a hand.)

I send **her** a kiss. (the girl)
Le mando un bacio. (alla ragazza)
(Her I send a kiss.)

Both direct and indirect object pronouns are usually placed immediately before a conjugated verb:

Leopoldo buys the newspaper and **reads it** to Mario. (direct)
Leopoldo compra il giornale e lo legge a Mario.
(Leopoldo buys the newspaper and it reads to Mario.)

Giulia **reads him** a story. (indirect)
Giulia gli legge una storia.
(Giulia him reads a story.)

There are two ways the object pronouns can work when an infinitive verb depends on the modal verbs *dovere* (to have to, to must), *potere* (to be able to), or *volere* (to want). The object pronoun can come either before the conjugated verb, or it can be attached to the end of the infinitive (minus the final *-e*):

I want to accompany you to the movies.
Ti voglio accompagnare al cinema.
Voglio accompagnarti al cinema.

When to Use the Direct Object Pronoun

"The next time I go to Italy, my friend Sofia asked me to buy a book for Sofia." You would probably never say something so awkward. You'd say something like, "The next time I go to Italy, my friend Sofia asked me to buy a book for *her*." As you can see, direct object pronouns can make your life a lot easier when you use them to replace the direct object in a sentence:

I kiss **the boy**.	→	I kiss **him**.
Bacio il ragazzo.	→	*Lo bacio*. (Him I kiss.)
I read **the books**.	→	I read **them**.
Leggo i libri.	→	*Li leggo*. (Them I read.)

Easy, right? You don't even have to add a preposition (as in to look *at* or to wait *for*). In Italian, the commonly used verbs *guardare* (to look at), *cercare* (to look for), and *aspettare* (to wait for) have a built-in preposition:

I am searching for **the theater**.	→	I am searching for **it**.
Cerco il teatro.	→	*Lo cerco*. (It I am searching for.)
I am looking at **the girl**.	→	I am looking at **her**.
Guardo la ragazza.	→	*La guardo*. (Her I am looking at.)

Whenever you hear someone use the expression *Non lo so* (I don't know it), the speaker is using the direct object pronoun *lo*.

When to Use Indirect Object Pronouns

"Congratulazioni! If you have the winning number, a check for $1 billion will be sent *to you!"* Lucky you! You're the indirect object of the billion-dollar sweepstakes! As you can see here, the indirect object of a sentence tells to whom or for whom the action is done. Indirect objects are often replaced by indirect object pronouns:

Marco offers a glass of wine **to Marina**.   → Marco offers **her** a glass of wine.
Marco offre un bicchiere di vino a Marina.   → *Marco le offre un bicchiere di vino*.
(Marco her offers a glass of wine.)

Elisabetta writes a letter **to Francesco**.   → Elisabetta writes **him** a letter.
Elisabetta scrive una lettera a Francesco.   → *Elisabetta gli scrive una lettera*.
(Elisabetta him writes a letter.)

Verbs That May Use an Indirect Object

Some verbs that take a direct object in English take an indirect object in Italian:

I am calling **Dario** this evening.	→	I am calling **him** this evening.
*Telefono **a Dario** stasera.*	→	***Gli** telefono stasera.*

The following table lists Italian verbs that may use an indirect object or its pronoun in Italian. The preposition *a* (meaning "to" or "at") is your bridge.

Verbs Using Indirect Objects and Pronouns

English	*Italiano*	English	*Italiano*
to ask	*chiedere*	to render	*rendere*
to bring	*portare*	to respond	*rispondere*
to donate	*donare*	to say	*dire*
to give	*dare; regalare*	to sell	*vendere*
to lend	*prestare*	to send	*mandare*
to let know	*fare sapere*	to show	*mostrare*
to offer	*offrire*	to speak	*parlare*
to prepare	*preparare*	to teach	*insegnare*
to present	*presentare*	to telephone	*telefonare*
to question	*domandare*	to write	*scrivere*
to read	*leggere*		

I'm letting **Silvia** know the date.	→	I'm letting **her** know the date.
*Faccio sapere **a Silvia** la data.*	→	***Le** faccio sapere la data.*
Joel telephones **his friends.**	→	Joel telephones **them.**
*Joel telefona **ai suoi amici.***	→	*Joel telefona **loro.***

In this case, you can also use what's called *un pronome tonico* (a stressed pronoun), which then requires a preposition before the pronoun. The tonic pronouns are covered later in this chapter.

*Joel telefona **ai suoi amici**.* → *Joel telefona **a loro**.*

> **ATTENZIONE!**
>
> The indirect object pronoun *loro* is often replaced with *gli* in modern spoken Italian:
>
> *Giovanni telefona **loro**.* → *Giovanni **gli** telefona.*
>
> *Chiede **loro** di uscire.* → ***Gli** chiede di uscire.*
>
> In an imperative, *gli* is attached to the end of the verb:
>
> *Telefona **loro**!* → *Telefona**gli**!*

Using Indirect Object Pronouns to Suggest

Shape the phrases in the following table to make suggestions. After each *espressione*, simply add the infinitive of the verb that best expresses your suggestion.

Note how the indirect object pronouns change, depending on who's being addressed. The pronouns most commonly used are *ti* (you, familiar), *Le* (You, polite), and *vi* (you, plural).

Getting Suggestive

Italiano	English
Ti interessa …?	Are you interested in …?
Le va di …?	Are You in the mood to …?
Vi piacerebbe …?	Would you (plural) like …?

Notice how the previous examples apply in the following suggestions:

Are you in the mood to try on this skirt?
Ti va di provate questa gonna?

Are You interested in taking a trip to Italy?
Le interessa fare un viaggio in Italia?

Who's in Command?

The indirect object pronoun follows the imperative (a command) when you use the *tu*, *noi*, or *voi* form of the verb and can usually be attached to the end of the verb to form one word:

*Compra il libro per **Giovanni!***	→	*Compra**gli** il libro!*
Buy the book for **Giovanni!**	→	Buy **him** the book!
*Invitate **la vostra amica** a casa!*	→	*Invitate**la** a casa!*
Invite **your friend** home!	→	Invite **her** home.

The exception is *loro*, which must always remain separate:

*Telefona ai tuoi **amici!***	→	*Telefona **loro**.*
Call your **friends!**	→	Call **them!**
*Non date una risposta **a Carlo e Maria**.*	→	*Non date **loro** una risposta.*
Don't give a response to **Carlo and Maria**.	→	Don't give **them** a response.

A Review of Object Pronouns

Keep in mind the following, and you'll find it much easier to master the object pronouns. Don't forget that all object pronouns agree in gender and number with the nouns they replace. In a negative sentence, the word *non* always comes before the object pronoun:

*Non **la** voglio.*	*Non **lo** bacio.*
I don't want **it**.	I don't kiss **him**.

When object pronouns are attached to the end of an infinitive, the final *-e* of the infinitive is omitted:

*Devo da**rti** un bacio.*	*Vorrei invita**rli** alla festa.*
I must give **you** a kiss.	I'd like to invite **them** to the party.

Singular object pronouns should be contracted in front of verbs that begin with a vowel:

L'ascolto. (la musica)
I'm listening to **it**. (the music)

In monosyllabic imperatives, such as with the verbs *dire* and *fare*, you add an extra *m* when using the familiar form (*tu*) of the imperative with an object pronoun:

Dimmi!   *Fammi sapere!*

Tell me!   Let me know!

WHAT'S WHAT

Verbs that take a direct object and can answer the question "what?" are called *transitive* (I eat an apple, you speak Italian). Verbs that do not take a direct object are called *intransitive* (I go, you return).

Who's Who I

Replace the direct object in each sentence with the direct object pronoun. Translate the sentences.

> *Example: Leggo **il giornale.***
> *Answer: Lo leggo.*

1. *Mangiamo **la pasta.** _____*

2. *Dante e Boccaccio vogliono mangiare **la pizza.** _____*

3. *Prendo **l'autobus.** _____*

4. *Mario scrive **un libro.** _____*

5. *Vedo **Giuseppe e Mario.** _____*

6. *Giovanni bacia **la sua ragazza.** _____*

7. *Comprate **una macchina nuova?** _____*

8. *Lei (You) capisce **la lezione?** _____*

*Answers: 1. **La** mangiamo. (We're eating it.) 2. Dante e Boccaccio vogliono mangiar**la** (or **La** vogliono mangiare.) (Dante and Boccaccio want to eat it.) 3. **Lo** prendo. (I'm taking it.) 4. Mario **lo** scrive. (Mario writes it.) 5. **Li** vedo. (I see them.) 6. **La** bacia. (Giovanni kisses her.) 7. **La** comprate? (Are you buying it?) 8. **La** capisce? (Do You understand it?)*

Who's Who II

Replace the indirect object with its appropriate pronoun.

> *Example: Beatrice scrive una lettera **a Dante**.* (Beatrice writes a letter to Dante.)
> *Answer: Beatrice gli scrive una lettera.* (Beatrice writes him a letter.)

1. *Desideriamo parlare **a voi**.* _____

2. *Maria e Giorgio danno un regalo **a te**.* _____

3. *Carlo telefona **ad Anna**.* _____

4. *Lo studente fa una domanda **al professore**.* _____

5. *Offro un caffè **a Caterina**.* _____

6. *I nonni danno le caramelle **ai bambini**.* _____

7. *Offro una birra **a Domenico**.* _____

8. *Augurano **a noi** una buona notte.* _____

*Answers: 1. Desideriamo parlar**vi**. (We want to speak to you.) 2. Mario e Giorgio **ti** danno un regalo. (Maria and Giorgio are giving you a present.) 3. Carlo **le** telefona. (Carlo is calling her.) 4. Lo studente **gli** fa una domanda. (The student asks him a question.) 5. **Le** offro un caffè. (I offer a coffee to her.) 6. I nonni danno loro le caramelle. (The grandparents give them candy.) 7. **Gli** offro una birra. (I offer him a beer.) 8. **Ci** augurano una buona notte. (They wish us a good night.)*

Who's Who—Final Round

Determine which kind of object pronoun should go in the following sentences where it is bold. Translate the sentences.

1. *Guardate **il film**.* _____

2. *Regalo a Lorenzo **un mazzo di fiori**.* (bunch of flowers) _____

3. *Vede **la bella ragazza**?* _____

4. *Regalo **a Lorenzo** un mazzo di fiori.* _____

5. *Danno i libri **ai bambini**.* _____

6. *Conosco **il signor Spadone** molto bene.* _____

7. *Danno **i libri** ai bambini.* _____

8. *Accettiamo **l'invito** con piacere.* _____

*Answers: 1. **Lo** guardate. (You watch it.) 2. **Lo** regalo a Lorenzo. (I'm giving it to Lorenzo.) 3. **La** vede? (Do you see her?) 4. **Gli** regalo un mazzo di fiori. (I'm giving a bunch of flowers to him.) 5. Danno **loro** i libri. (They're giving them the books.) 6. **Lo** conosco molto bene. (I know him well.) 7. **Li** danno ai bambini. (They're giving them to the children.) 8. **Lo** accettiamo con piacere. (We accept it with pleasure.)*

Double Object Pronouns

You've learned your object pronouns and remember that they must reflect the gender and number of the objects they replace. In Italian, unlike English, it's possible to join the object pronouns together to form one word. In the following table, notice how the indirect object pronouns *mi, ti, ci, vi,* and *si* change to *me, te, ce, ve,* and *se.* Also note that the indirect object pronouns *gli, le,* and *Le* change to *glie-* before direct object pronouns, creating one word.

Double Object Pronouns

	Direct Object			
Indirect Object	*lo*	*la*	*li*	*le*
mi	*me lo*	*me la*	*me li*	*me le*
ti	*te lo*	*te la*	*te li*	*te le*
gli, le, Le	*glielo*	*gliela*	*glieli*	*gliele*
ci	*ce lo*	*ce la*	*ce li*	*ce le*
vi	*ve lo*	*ve la*	*ve li*	*ve le*

When the same verb has two object pronouns, the indirect object always precedes the direct object:

Are you sending the letter to Mr. Rossi? Yes, I'm sending **it to him**.
*Mandi la lettera al signor Rossi? Sì, **gliela** mando.*

Are they giving back the money to the woman? Yes, they are giving it back to her.
*Restituiscono i soldi alla signora? Sì, **glieli** restituiscono.*

After an infinitive, the final *-e* is dropped and the double object pronoun is attached to the end of the infinitive forming one word:

Can I send it to you? He wants to give it to us.
Posso spedirtela? *Vuole darcelo.*

When dealing with double object pronouns, it's assumed that the speaker has already referred to the object of the sentence. In certain cases, the gender of the indirect object is not always obvious:

Are you lending the car to Silvia? Yes, I'm lending it to her.
Presti la macchina a Silvia? Sì, **gliela** *presto.*

Stressed Out

As if you haven't had enough of pronouns, here are a few more. Disjunctive, or stressed, pronouns—called *i pronomi tonici* ("tonic pronouns") in Italian—are used after prepositions and verbs for emphasis. They're also used to emphasize certain facts and highlight or replace certain nouns or pronouns. Study how they correspond to the pronouns you've learned so far. The stressed pronoun *sè* is used as a reflexive and also can mean "oneself" when used with the passive tense.

Disjunctive Pronouns

Subject	Direct Object	Indirect Object	Disjunctive (Stressed)
io	*mi*	*mi*	*me* (me)
tu	*ti*	*ti*	*te* (you)
lui	*lo*	*gli*	*lui/esso/sé* (him/it/himself)
lei	*la*	*le*	*lei/essa/sé* (her/it/herself)
Lei	*La*	*Le*	*Lei/ sè* (You/Yourself)
			sè (oneself)
noi	*ci*	*ci*	*noi* (us)
voi	*vi*	*vi*	*voi* (you)
loro	*li/le*	*a loro/gli*	*loro/sè* (them/themselves)

Feeling a Little Disjointed

Some disjunctive pronouns resemble the subject pronouns (which doesn't make things any easier). However, when used disjunctively, they're not subjects.

Disjunctive pronouns must always follow a verb or preposition:

<table>
<tr>
<td>Do you want to come **with me**?
Vuoi venire con me?</td>
<td>I am proud **of you**.
Sono fiero di te.</td>
</tr>
<tr>
<td>I am waiting for a phone call **from her**.
Aspetto una telefonata da lei.</td>
<td>These flowers are **for you**.
Questi fiori sono per voi.</td>
</tr>
<tr>
<td>He is leaving **before me**.
Lui parte prima di me.</td>
<td></td>
</tr>
</table>

The disjunctive pronoun *sé* is used to indicate *oneself, himself, herself,* and *themselves* as well as *itself:*

<table>
<tr>
<td>Giovanni always talks about himself.
Giovanni parla sempre di sé.</td>
<td>Anna works for herself.
Anna lavora per sé.</td>
</tr>
<tr>
<td>The light goes out by **itself**.
La luce si spegne da sé.</td>
<td></td>
</tr>
</table>

The disjunctive pronoun is most commonly used when there are two direct or indirect objects in a phrase:

<table>
<tr>
<td>Daniela writes **to me** and **to you**.
Daniela scrive a me e a te.</td>
<td>They are telephoning **him and her**.
Telefonano a lui e a lei.</td>
</tr>
</table>

Disjunctive pronouns are used after a verb to emphasize the object (direct or indirect), as shown in the following table.

English	Emphatic	Unemphatic
I'm waiting **for him**.	*Aspetto lui.*	*Lo aspetto.*
I give **you** a gift.	*Do un regalo a te.*	*Ti do un regalo.*
Call (telephone) **me**.	*Telefona a me.*	*Mi telefona.*

An Exercise in Stress Management

Use the appropriate stressed pronoun in the following sentences and then translate.

1. *Senza di* _____, *non posso vivere.* (you, informal)

2. *Mario parla sempre di* _____. (himself)

3. *Vuole parlare a* _____? (me)

4. *Questa lettera è per* _____. (Cristina)

5. *Passiamo la sera a casa di* _____. (Robert)

6. *Viene con* _____ *o va con* _____? (me, her)

Answers: 1. te (Without you, I cannot live.) 2. sé (Mario always talks about himself.) 3. me (Do you want to speak to me?) 4. lei (This letter is for her.) 5. lui (We're spending the evening at Robert's house.) 6. me, lei (Are you coming with me or her?)

The Least You Need to Know

- The verb *portare* means *to carry, to bring,* and *to wear.*
- A direct object answers the question *what* or *whom* is the subject acting upon.
- An indirect object answers the question *to what* or *to whom* is the subject acting for.
- Use object pronouns to replace the object in a sentence. Object pronouns are usually placed before the conjugated verb, except in an affirmative command, when they come after the verb.
- When dealing with double object pronouns, the indirect object pronoun always precedes the direct object pronoun. In certain cases, the gender of the indirect object is not always obvious.
- Use stressed pronouns when you want to emphasize a point or after verbs and prepositions. Until you understand them, they have the potential of stressing you out. Don't let them.

Forming the Past with the Present Perfect

In This Chapter

- Fun with sports and games
- Another look at the helping verbs *avere* and *essere*
- Forming the *passato prossimo* (present perfect)
- Using double object pronouns
- Talking about the past

This chapter covers many of the pastimes that make up the Italian lifestyle. Whether you're a sports buff, a film fanatic, an opera lover, or an art appreciator, there's a little bit of everything and something for everyone.

In addition, you'll learn a very important new verb tense: *il passato prossimo* (called the present perfect tense in English), which requires the use of the two *verbi ausiliari* (auxiliary verbs) *avere* (to have) and *essere* (to be). Using this tense enables you to talk about what you've been up to lately.

Name Your Game

In Italian, *il football*—also known as *il calcio*—refers to soccer. The rough-and-tumble version played in the Super Bowl is aptly called *football americano*. Italians refer to baseball, golf, hockey, tennis, and windsurfing, however, in English.

There are three things you should never dare take away from an Italian: *la mamma*, *la pasta*, and *il calcio*. Expect anarchy if you dare. (For more on anarchy, try reading the translated works of Nobel Prize winner Dario Fo.)

Keep in mind that the Italian terms in the following table are offered with the appropriate definite articles.

Game Time

Sport	Lo Sport	Pronunciation
aerobics	l'aerobica	lay-eh-**roh**-bee-kah
basketball	la pallacanestro	lah **palh**-lah-kah-**neh**-stroh
bicycling	il ciclismo	eel chee-**kleez**-moh
boating	il canottaggio	eel kah-noht-**tah**-joh
boxing	il pugilato	eel poo-jee-**lah**-toh
fencing	la scherma	lah **sker**-mah
fishing	pescare	peh-**skah**-reh
game	la partita	lah par-**tee**-tah
horseback riding	l'equitazione	leh-kwee-tah-zee-**oh**-neh
karate	il karatè	kah-rah-**tay**
rock climbing	l'alpinismo	lahl-pee-**neez**-moh
sailing	la vela	lah **veh**-lah
score	il punteggio	eel poon-**tehj**-joh
skating	il pattinaggio	eel paht-tee-**nah**-joh
skiing	lo sci	loh shee
... cross-country skiing	... lo sci di fondo	loh shee dee **fon**-doh
... water skiing	... lo sci acquatico	loh shee ak-**wah**-tee-koh
soccer	il calcio, il football	eel **kahl**-choh
swimming	il nuoto	eel **nwoh**-toh
team	la squadra	lah **skwah**-drah
volleyball	la pallavolo	lah **pahl**-lah-**voh**-loh
wrestling	la lotta libera	lah **loht**-tah **lee**-beh-rah

You're Playing with My Head

If you're looking for less exertion, a few games allow you to use more brain power than brawn. *Briscola* and *Scopa* are two popular card games. *Giochiamo!*

Games for the Brain

English	*Italiano*	English	*Italiano*
backgammon	*backgammon*	dominoes	*domino*
briscola	*briscola*	hide-and-seek	*nascondino*
cards	*carte*	poker	*poker*
checkers	*dama*	scopa (a popular card game)	*scopa*
chess	*scacchi*	tarot	*tarocchi*
dice	*dadi*		

LA BELLA LINGUA

To play *scacchi* (chess), you need to know some terminology to get you started understanding *i pezzi* (the pieces) on your *scacchiera* (chessboard):

Check!	Checkmate!	the rook	the bishop
Scacco!	*Scacco Matto!*	*la torre* (the tower)	*l'alfiere*

the king	the knight	the queen	the pawn
il re	*il cavallo* (the horse)	*la regina*	*il pedone*

Don't Play with My Head!

In Italian, there are many ways of expressing *to play:*

- The verb *giocare* (to play) is used when playing sports or games. (Think of the English word *joker.*)
- The verb *suonare* (to play) is used when playing an instrument. (Think of the English word *sound.*)
- The verbs *andare* (to go) and *fare* (to do/to make) are often used when participating in a sport or activity.
- The idiomatic expression *prendere in giro* (to take for a spin; to tease) is especially useful if you want to play with someone's head.

Il Passato Prossimo (the Present Perfect)

The *passato prossimo* (present perfect) lets you communicate something that has recently occurred and is now over. "I have forgotten," "I have eaten," and "I have been" are the English equivalents to the *passato prossimo*, as are "I forgot," "I ate," and "I was." This tense, literally translated as "the near past," enables you to talk about what you ate for dinner, where you were last night, and what you have done about something.

The *passato prossimo* is a compound tense and requires the use of the helping verbs *avere* and *essere*.

In Italian, all *transitive verbs* (verbs that take a direct object) require the use of the auxiliary verb *avere*. Transitive verbs answer the questions "who?" and "what?" and include verbs such as *invitare* (to invite), *lavare* (to wash), *leggere* (to read), *mangiare* (to eat), and *studiare* (to study). Transitive verbs also answer the question of "whom?" and include the verbs *cercare* (to look for), *conoscere* (to be acquainted with), and *invitare* (to invite).

All *intransitive verbs* (verbs taking an indirect object) require the use of *essere*. Intransitive verbs use *essere* as an auxiliary verb. Included in this category are verbs of locomotion such as *andare* (to go), *arrivare* (to arrive), *entrare* (to enter), *uscire* (to go out/exit), and *venire* (to come). Other intransitive verbs include *morire* (to die) and *nascere* (to be born), and *sedersi* (to sit). If you're not sure whether a verb is transitive or intransitive, go back to the questions "who?" and "what?" Does the verb answer that question? If not, it's more than likely intransitive.

This will make more sense as you move forward.

Constructing the Past Participle

When you use the *passato prossimo*, you need a past participle. For example, in English you use the helping verb *have* plus the participle (wished/finished/studied). Most of the time this is regular, but English also has several irregular past participles (had/been/sang). The same goes for Italian.

As you recall, Italian has three principal verb families (*-are*, *-ere*, and *-ire*). To form the past participle from an infinitive, hold on to the stem and add the appropriate ending, as shown in the following table.

Regular Endings for the Past Participle

	Endings		Infinitive Example		Participle
-are	→	*-ato*	*lavare*	→	*lavato*
-ere	→	*-uto*	*potere*	→	*potuto*
-ire	→	*-ito*	*capire*	→	*capito*

Forming the Present Perfect with *Avere*

It's easy to construct the *passato prossimo*. After you understand how this works, you'll have no trouble learning all the other compound tenses. It all starts with the helping verb *avere*. When you've determined your subject, you only have to conjugate *avere* in the present tense. The past participle stays the same, regardless of the subject (unless accompanied by a direct object pronoun, which will be discussed in a bit). Study the verb *lavare* (to wash) to better understand how this works.

The Present Perfect of *Lavare* (to Wash)

Italiano	English
io ho lavato	I have washed
tu hai lavato	you have washed
lui/lei Lei ha lavato	he/she has washed; You have washed
noi abbiamo lavato	we have washed
voi avete lavato	you have washed
loro hanno lavato	they have washed

Notice that the participle *lavato* did not change. The helping verb is the only thing you need to conjugate.

In their efforts to determine the subject, and create the past participle from the infinitive, many of my students forget to use their helping verbs. You can learn from their mistakes and always remember to use your helping verb. (*Capisco* … there's a lot to remember!)

Irregular Past Participles Used with *Avere*

Some commonly used irregular past participles are shown in the following table. All of these are generally used with the helping verb *avere*.

Commonly Used Irregular Past Participles with *Avere*

Verb	Past Participle	Meaning
accendere	*acceso*	to turn on, to light
aprire	*aperto*	to open
ardere	*arso*	to burn
bere	*bevuto*	to drink
chiedere	*chiesto*	to ask

continues

Verb	Past Participle	Meaning
chiudere	*chiuso*	to close
conoscere	*conosciuto*	to know someone
correggere	*corretto*	to correct
correre	*corso*	to run
decidere	*deciso*	to decide
dire	*detto*	to say
leggere	*letto*	to read
mettere	*messo*	to put, to place, to wear
offrire	*offerto*	to offer
perdere	*perso*	to lose
permettere	*permesso*	to permit
prendere	*preso*	to take
rispondere	*risposto*	to respond
rompere	*rotto*	to break
scrivere	*scritto*	to write
spegnere	*spento*	to turn off, to extinguish
spendere	*speso*	to spend
togliere	*tolto*	to take from
vedere	*visto*	to see
vincere	*vinto*	to win

We won the game.
Abbiamo vinto la partita.

Did you write to Mom?
Hai scritto alla mamma?

The restaurant closed early.
Il ristorante ha chiuso presto.

They asked us for a favor.
Ci hanno chiesto un favore.

BUON'IDEA

When things go wrong, your Italian will probably go out the window. Consult this section ahead of time and see how useful the *passato prossimo* is when you have lost something, like your *passaporto*:

I lost …	Ho perso …
… my passport.	… *il passaporto.*
… my wallet.	… *il portafoglio.*
… my purse.	… *la borsa.*
… my head.	… *la testa.*

Forming the Present Perfect with *Essere*

Some verbs, called *intransitive verbs*, always require the use of *essere* as their auxiliary. How can you remember what those verbs are? Think of a *scoiattolo* (squirrel) living in a tree, and imagine all the motions he does in and around his home, high up in the branches of a great old *quercia* (oak): he comes and he stays a while before he goes again, then he returns, departs, and so on.

Whenever *essere* is used as the auxiliary verb, the participle is still formed by adding the appropriate ending to the stem of the verb. However, in addition to conjugating your helping verb *avere*, your past participle must reflect both gender and number of the subject. Participles act very much like adjectives in this case.

You'll understand better by studying the verb *andare* (to go) in the following table.

The Present Perfect Using *Essere: Andare* (to Go)

Italiano	English	*Italiano*	English
io **sono andato(a)**	I have gone	noi **siamo andati(e)**	we have gone
tu **sei andato(a)**	you have gone	voi **siete andati(e)**	you have gone
lui/lei Lei **è andato(a)**	he/she has gone; You have gone	loro **sono andati(e)**	they have gone

Oriana went to the university of Bologna.
Oriana è andata all'università di Bologna.

AS A *REGOLA*

When forming the *passato prossimo* (present perfect), the verb *avere* takes itself as an auxiliary verb: *Ho avuto un'idea.* (I had an idea.) Likewise, the verb *essere* also takes itself as an auxiliary verb: *Sono stato(a) dal dentista oggi.* (I was at the dentist today.)

Verbs Taking *Essere*

The following table contains a list of the most commonly used intransitive verbs conjugated with *essere*. Irregular participles are indicated with an asterisk.

Intransitive Verbs Commonly Used with *Essere*

Verb	Past Participle	Meaning
andare	*andato*	to go
apparire	*apparso**	to appear
arrivare	*arrivato*	to arrive
bastare	*bastato*	to be enough
cadere	*caduto*	to fall
dimagrire	*dimagrito*	to lose weight
dispiacere	*dispiaciuto**	to be sorry
diventare	*diventato*	to become
entrare	*entrato*	to enter
esistere	*esistito*	to exist
essere	*stato**	to be
ingrassare	*ingrassato*	to gain weight
morire	*morto**	to die
nascere	*nato**	to be born
partire	*partito*	to leave
piacere	*piaciuto**	to be pleasing
rimanere	*rimasto**	to remain
ritornare	*ritornato*	to return
salire	*salito*	to go up/to get on
scendere	*sceso**	to get off
sembrare	*sembrato*	to seem
stare/restare	*stato/restato*	to stay
succedere	*successo**	to happen
tornare	*tornato*	to return
uscire	*uscito*	to go out
venire	*venuto*	to come
vivere	*vissuto**	to live

*Irregular participle.

Additional Applications of the *Passato Prossimo*

I realize that juggling all these new concepts can be confusing. Keep in mind the following rules when using the *passato prossimo*.

All reflexive verbs require *essere* as their auxiliary verb. Reflexives are most easily identified by their endings and include the verbs *alzarsi* (to get up), *arrabbiarsi* (to get angry), and *chiamarsi* (to call oneself).

Reflexive verbs always take *essere* as their auxiliary verb, such as when forming the passato prossimo (present perfect):

The baby enjoyed himself.	I woke up very early.
Il bambino si è divertito.	*Mi sono svegliata prestissimo.*
We kissed each other.	
Ci siamo baciati.	

When forming compound tenses, the verb *piacere* always takes the helping verb *essere*:

Do you like the show?	I like animals.
Ti piace lo spettacolo?	*Mi piacciono gli animali.*
Did you like the show?	I liked animals.
*Ti **è piaciuto** lo spettacolo?*	*Mi **sono piaciuti** gli animali.*
Do You like Italy?	You like cars.
Le piace l'Italia?	*Vi piacciono le macchine.*
Did You like Italy?	You liked the cars.
*Le **è piaciuta** l'Italia?*	*Vi **sono piaciute** le macchine.*

Certain verbs can go both ways. For instance, the verb *correre* generally takes *avere* as its helping verb, because it can answer the question "what?":

Ho corso la maratona.
I ran the marathon.

But if you simply ran, then you would use *essere* as the helping verb:

Sono corso via.
I ran away.

Adverbs in Compound Tenses

Most adverbs are placed after the past participle in compound sentences, such as in the *passato prossimo* (present perfect):

We ate **well.**	Isabella studied **regularly.**
*Abbiamo mangiato **bene.***	*Isabella ha studiato **regolarmente.***

Adverbs related to time, such as *ancora*, *già*, *mai*, and *sempre*, are placed between the auxiliary verb and the past participle:

> Have you **already** eaten? (formal)   Have you **ever** seen a lion? (informal)
> *Ha **già** mangiato?*   *Hai **mai** visto un leone?*

> We **always** passed the summer by the sea.
> *Abbiamo **sempre** passato l'estate al mare.*

When negating something in the past, the word *non* comes before the helping verb:

> I did **not** eat much.
> ***Non** ho mangiato molto.*

Unlike English, double negatives are mandatory in Italian:

> I have never seen a lion.
> ***Non** ho **mai** visto un leone.*

Direct Object Pronouns in Compound Tenses

Transitive verbs take a direct object and are conjugated with the verb *avere*. When using direct object pronouns in compound tenses, including the *passato prossimo*, the ending of the participle must reflect gender and plurality of the direct object. Note that the singular direct object pronouns meaning *it* (*lo/la*) drop the final vowel and elide with the auxiliary verb *avere*. The plural object pronouns don't change. The following table illustrates this for you. The direct object and direct object pronouns are in bold.

Passato Prossimo with Direct Object Pronouns

Question	Direct Object Pronoun	Answer
*Hai spedito **la lettera?*** (Did you send the letter?)	*la* (it)	*Sì, **l'ho** spedita.* (Yes, I sent it.)
*Hai mangiato **il pane?*** (Did you eat the bread?)	*lo* (it)	*Sì, **l'ho** mangiato.* (Yes, I ate it.)
*Hai ricevuto **le lettere?*** (Did you receive the letters?)	*le* (them)	*No, non **le** ho ricevute.* (No, I didn't receive them.)
*Hai letto **i libri?*** (Did you read the books?)	*li* (them)	*Sì, **li** ho letti.* (Yes, I read them.)

Indirect Object Pronouns and the *Passato Prossimo*

Both transitive and intransitive verbs can take an indirect object pronoun. In compound tenses, to distinguish the indirect and direct object pronouns from one another, the gender and number of indirect object pronouns—unlike the direct object pronouns—do not affect the participle. In the following table, the indirect object and indirect object pronouns are in bold.

Passato Prossimo with Indirect Object Pronouns

Question	Indirect Object Pronoun	Answer
Hai parlato alla ragazza? (Did you speak to the girl?)	*le* (to her)	*Sì, le ho parlato.* (Yes, I spoke **to her.**)
Hai spedito la lettera a Paolo? (Did you send the letter to Paolo?)	*gli* (to him)	*Sì, gli ho spedito la lettera.* (Yes, I sent the letter **to him.**)
Hai offerto ai signori un caffè? (Did you offer the men coffee?)	*loro/gli* (to them)	*Sì, ho offerto loro un caffè.** *Sì, gli ho offerto un caffè.** (Yes, I offered coffee **to them.**)
Hanno mandato un pacco a noi? (Did they send a package to us?)	*ci* (to us)	*Sì, ci hanno mandato un pacco.* (Yes, they sent a package **to us.**)

*Both of these are correct. If you recall, loro *can be replaced with the pronoun* gli.

The *Passato Prossimo* and Double Object Pronouns

Everything here is detail. If you don't always remember to make things agree, you won't be locked into a tower and fed stale *pane*. However, if you want to be a master, you've got to pay special attention to the little things.

When the same verb has two object pronouns, the indirect object pronoun always precedes the direct object pronoun. The following examples illustrate how double object pronouns work with the *passato prossimo*. Notice how the participle ending reflects the number and gender of the direct object even when the helping verb is *avere*.

When dealing with double object pronouns, it's necessary to infer the gender of the indirect object (to him/to her).

Did you send the letter to Mr. Rossi?	Yes, I sent it to him.
Hai mandato la lettera al signor Rossi?	*Sì, gliel'ho mandata.*

Did they give back the money to the woman?
Hanno restituito i soldi alla signora?

Yes, they gave it back to her.
Sì, glieli hanno restituiti.

Did you give the letter to the lady?
Hai dato la lettera alla signora?

Yes, I gave it to her.
Sì gliel'ho data.

Talking About the Past

These timely words help you talk about the past.

Way Back When

English	*Italiano*	Pronunciation
ago	*fa*	*fah*
next week	*la prossima settimana*	*la **probs**-see-mah set-tee-**mah**-nah*
last week	*la settimana scorsa*	*lah set-tee-**mah**-nah **skor**-sah*
next year	*l'anno prossimo*	***lahn**-noh **probs**-see-moh*
last year	*l'anno scorso*	***lahn**-noh skor-soh*
last night	*ieri notte*	***yeh**-ree **noht**-teh*
this morning	*stamattina**	*stah maht-**tee**-nah*
this evening	*stasera**	*stah **seh**-rah*
tonight	*stanotte*	*stah **noht**-teh*
yesterday	*ieri*	***yeh**-ree*
yesterday evening	*ieri sera*	***yeh**-ree **seh**-rah*

*The terms stamattina, stasera, *and* stanotte *are abbreviated from* questa mattina, questa sera, *and* questa notte.

LA BELLA LINGUA

When referring to the day after tomorrow, Italians use *dopodomani* (literally, after tomorrow). To talk about the day before yesterday, Italians use *l'altro ieri* (literally, the other yesterday).

The Least You Need to Know

- The verbs *andare* and *fare* are often used to describe participation in a sport. Use the verb *giocare* to play games and the verb *suonare* to play an instrument.
- The past participle is created by adding the appropriate ending to the stem of a verb. The three regular forms are *-ato, -uto,* and *-ito.*
- Many past participles are irregular, such as *aperto* (open), *chiuso* (closed), and *stato* (from *essere,* "been").
- The two helping verbs used to form the *passato prossimo* are *essere* and *avere.*
- Transitive verbs take *avere* as their auxiliary verb and answer the question "what?" or "whom?"
- Intransitive verbs and reflexive verbs require *essere* as their auxiliary verb.
- The past participle must agree in gender and number with the preceding direct object pronoun. Double object pronouns form one word when used in the third person singular and are used to refer to something already mentioned.

Forming the Past with the Imperfect

In This Chapter

- Enjoying cinema, music, and art
- Using the imperfect
- The imperfect versus the present perfect
- Forming the pluperfect

In this chapter, you learn about the arts and the imperfect tense, another way to talk about the past. You may not feel up to learning yet another tense, and ask, "When does it end?"

Mai, I say. Never.

Scherzavo! I was just kidding! You'll get it, I promise.

Carnevale! Festeggiamo!

The word *carnevale* (meaning "carnival" and source of the English word *carnal*) is no different from the infamous Mardi Gras (in Italian, *Martedì Grasso*—literally, *fat Tuesday*). This was the last night one was permitted to eat *la carne* (meat) before beginning the period of Lent (called *la quaresima* in Italian).

In Italy, two of the most famous *carnevale* celebrations take place in Venice and Viareggio, where tens of thousands show up to participate in the festivities and watch the parades.

Many of the more important Christian holidays coincide with the major Roman celebrations of Bacchanalia and Saturnalia.

The Arts

Ah, *la Madre Patria!* The Italians have an emotional relationship to *la politica*, *la famiglia*, and *l'amore*. It's no surprise that their art reflects these powerful forces.

Let's Go to the Movies!

There's no better way to practice your Italian than by watching films (next to visiting Italy, that is). Italy started as one of the world's major film producers. *Cinecittà* (the Hollywood of Italy), in *Roma*, has spawned some of the best filmmakers, including Bernardo Bertolucci, Vittorio De Sica, Federico Fellini, Pier Paolo Pasolini, and Luchino Visconti, to name a few.

Il Cinema (the Cinema)

English	*Italiano*	English	*Italiano*
actor	*l'attore*	plot	*la trama*
actress	*l'attrice*	producer	*il produttore*
camera	*la cinepresa, la macchina fotografica*	scene	*la scena*
cinema	*il cinema*	screen	*lo schermo*
close-up	*il primo piano*	theater	*la sala cinematografica*
director	*il/la regista*	to hear	*sentire, udire*
dissolve	*la dissolvenza*	to listen	*ascoltare*
film	*il film, la pellicola*	to see	*vedere*
long-shot	*il campo lungo*	to watch/look	*guardare*
panning	*la panoramica*	video camera	*la telecamera*

La Musica

Nothing soothes the savage beast like music. The great violin maker Antonio Stradivari (1644–1737) came from Cremona, Italy. Is there a musical instrument that makes you swoon every time you hear it? Find it in the following table.

GliStrumenti (Instruments)

English	Italiano	English	Italiano
accordion	*la fisarmonica*	oboe	*l'oboe*
cello	*il violoncello*	piano	*il pianoforte*
clarinet	*il clarinetto*	piccolo	*il piccolo*
drum	*il tamburo, la batteria*	saxophone	*il sassofono*
flute	*il flauto*	trombone	*il trombone*
guitar	*la chitarra*	trombone	*la tromba*
harp	*l'arpa*	viola	*la viola*
horn	*il corno*	violin	*il violino*

LA BELLA LINGUA

Venetian composer Giovanni Gabrielli (1557–1612) was one of the first to use the term *concerto* (bringing into agreement), a classical term describing music that uses many different voices to form one.

La Vita Imita L'Arte (Life Imitates Art)

Le belle arti (the beautiful arts) attempt to interpret the real world, glorify *Dio* (God), or express something without words. As ideas about the world have changed, so has the *arte* that depicts these notions. Ultimately, you know what you like and what you don't, and that's often the only criterion necessary to appreciate a piece.

You may have seen countless reproductions of Botticelli's *Birth of Venus* on everything from greeting cards to coffee mugs, but there's still nothing like seeing her up close.

And if you want to be an artist, these verbs can help: *disegnare* (to draw/to design), *dipingere* (to paint), and *scolpire* (to sculpt).

Adding to Your Palette

English	Italiano	English	Italiano
abstract	*astratto*	masterpiece	*il capolavoro*
acrylic	*acrilico*	the Middle Ages	*il Medioevo*
architecture	*l'architettura*	mosaic	*il mosaico*
background	*lo sfondo*	oil	*olio*
Baroque	*il Barocco*	painter	*il pittore*
bronze	*il bronzo*	painting	*il quadro*
ceramic	*la ceramica*	pen	*la penna*
classical	*classico*	pencil	*la matita*
cubism	*il cubismo*	perspective	*la prospettiva*
depth	*la profondità*	picture	*la pittura, il quadro*
drawing	*il disegno*	pigments	*i colori*
Etruscan	*etrusco*	portrait	*il ritratto*
figure	*la figura*	realism	*il realismo*
foreground	*il primo piano*	the Renaissance	*il Rinascimento*
fresco	*l'affresco*	restoration	*il restauro*
futurism	*il futurismo*	sculpture	*la scultura*
geometric	*geometrico*	shadow	*l'ombra*
granite	*il granito*	sketch	*lo schizzo*
human figure	*la figura umana*	statue	*la statua*
landscape	*il paesaggio*	still-life painting	*la natura morta*
light	*la luce*	symbol	*il simbolo*
marble	*il marmo*	visual arts	*le belle arti*
master	*il maestro*	work of art	*un'opera d'arte*

I Was What I Was: The Imperfect

L'imperfetto (the imperfect) tense describes repeated, ongoing actions that occurred in the past. If a verb involves *-ing* (doing, working, …) in the past, you're probably using the imperfect. Whenever you refer to something that used to be or describe a habitual pattern, you use the imperfect. Why is it called imperfect? Because the action that occurred never ended.

Key words used to identify when the imperfect is being used include: *Mentre* (while), *quando* (when), *sempre* (always), *spesso* (often), and *di solito* (usually).

The imperfect also expresses actions we were doing when something else happened. For example, I was studying when the telephone rang.

AS A *REGOLA*

Which tense should you use? The present perfect expresses an action that was completed at a specific time in the past: you did it once, and now it's over and done with. The imperfect represents an action that continued to occur, that was happening, that used to happen, or that would (meaning used to) happen: *Andavamo al mare ogni estate.* (We used to go to the sea every summer.)

Formation of the Imperfect

The imperfect tense is one of the easiest tenses to remember. With the exception of the verb *essere*, there are hardly any irregularities—and when there are, they are usually consistent with stem changes in the present. The best part is that the endings are the same for all three verb families. Just drop the final *-re* from any infinitive and add the endings shown in the following table.

Imperfect Endings

Subject	Imperfect Endings
io	*-vo*
tu	*-vi*
lui/lei/Lei	*-va*
noi	*-vamo*
voi	*-vate*
loro	*-vano*

Take a look at the verbs *parlare* (to speak), *scrivere* (to write), and *capire* (to understand) to see how they work in the imperfect. The English can be translated in two ways: "I used to speak" and "I was speaking."

Imperfect Examples

Subject	*Parlare* (to speak)	*Scrivere* (to write)	*Capire* (to understand)
io	*parlavo* (I used to speak)	*scrivevo* (I used to write)	*capivo* (I used to understand)
tu	*parlavi* (you used to speak)	*scrivevi* (you used to write)	*capivi* (you used to understand)
lui/lei/Lei	*parlava* (he/she/You used to speak)	*scriveva* (he/she/You used to write)	*capiva* (he/she/You used to understand)

continues

Subject	*Parlare* (to speak)	*Scrivere* (to write)	*Capire* (to understand)
noi	*parlavamo* (we used to speak)	*scrivevamo* (we used to write)	*capivamo* (we used to understand)
voi	*parlavate* (you used to speak)	*scrivevate* (you used to write)	*capivate* (you used to understand)
loro	*parlavano* (they used to speak)	*scrivevano* (they used to write)	*capivano* (they used to understand)

The Helping Verbs *Avere* and *Essere* in the Imperfect

The same idiomatic expressions used with avere in the present tense can be used in the imperfect. For example, to talk about when you were 10 years old, using the imperfect, you would say, *Quando avevo dieci anni. (Literally:* When I had 10 years.

The Imperfect with *Avere* (to Have)

Italiano	English
io **avevo**	I had/used to have
tu **avevi**	you had/used to have
lui/lei/Lei **aveva**	he/she/You (it) had/used to have
noi **avevamo**	we had/used to have
voi **avevate**	you had/used to have
loro **avevano**	they had/used to have

The only verb that completely changes form in the imperfect is the highly irregular verb *essere*, shown in the following table.

The Imperfect with *Essere* (to Be)

Italiano	English
io **ero**	I was/used to be
tu **eri**	you were/used to be
lui/lei/Lei **era**	he/she (it) was/used to be; You were/used to be
noi **eravamo**	we were/used to be
voi **eravate**	you were/used to be
loro **erano**	they were/used to be

When to Use the Imperfect

Several instances call for the *imperfetto*. Use it when talking about age:

> **I was** 18 when I went to Italy alone.
> *Avevo 18 anni quando sono andata in Italia da sola.*

Time also requires the *imperfetto:*

> **It was** seven thirty when the film began.
> *Erano le sette e mezzo quando è iniziato il film.*

Feelings, because they're ongoing, take the imperfect:

> **I was** sad because it was raining.
> *Ero triste perché pioveva.*

Because they remain constant, descriptions use the imperfect:

> The house **was** small but very light.
> *La casa era piccola ma molto luminosa.*

Things related to *il tempo* (weather) take the imperfect:

> It always rained in spring.
> *Pioveva sempre in primavera.*

Fill in the *Spazio*

Take a look at these stem-changing verbs, and fill in the rest of the chart using the endings you just learned.

Subject Pronoun	*Dire* (to Say)	*Fare* (to Do/Make)	*Bere* (to Drink)
io	_____	*facevo*	_____
tu	*dicevi*	_____	_____
lui/lei/Lei	_____	_____	*beveva*
noi	*dicevamo*	_____	_____
voi	_____	*facevate*	_____
loro	_____	_____	*bevevano*

Answers: dire: dicevo, diceva, dicevate, dicevano; fare: facevi, faceva, facevamo, facevano; bere: bevevo, bevevi, bevevamo, bevevate

La Pratica

Fill in the blanks with the verb in parentheses, using the imperfect.

1. *Quando hai telefonato, (io) _____ (guardare) la televisione.*

2. *Quando (noi) _____ (essere) bambini, _____ (andare) spesso al mare.*

3. *Mentre Maria _____ (lavorare), Luigi _____ (preparare) la cena.*

4. *Io _____ (ascoltare) la radio ogni notte.*

5. *Quando Katerina _____ (avere) 18 anni, è andata in Italia per la prima volta.*

6. *(Loro) _____ (abitare) in Via Condotti quando è nata la loro figlia.*

7. *Mio nonno _____ (fare) una passeggiata ogni giorno. Lui _____ (essere) un uomo forte.*

8. *Io _____ (tornare) a casa quando ho visto l'incidente.*

9. *(Noi) Ci _____ (vedere) spesso al lavoro.*

10. *Maurizio _____ (alzarsi) sempre tardi la mattina.*

Answers: 1. guardavo 2. eravamo, andavamo 3. lavorava, preparava 4. ascoltavo 5. aveva 6. abitavano 7. faceva, era 8. tornavo 9. vedevamo 10. si alzava

What's Done Is Done

It's awkward trying to speak in the present tense all the time. Replace the underlined verbs with the appropriate form of the past tense (present perfect or imperfect).

Arriviamo il 21 settembre, il primo giorno d'autunno. Il sole brilla e fa bel tempo. Viaggiamo spesso ma questa è la nostra prima volta in Italia. Prima andiamo a Roma dove vediamo il Vaticano, il Foro Romano e il Colosseo. Poi andiamo a Firenze per una settimana.

Answers: siamo arrivati, brillava, faceva, viaggiavamo, era, siamo andati, abbiamo visto, siamo andati

Remember, sometimes it's possible to use either the *passato prossimo* or the *imperfetto*. I've provided my answers, but your answers might be just as appropriate, whichever tense you use!

Forming the Pluperfect (the Past Perfect)

You probably learned about the birds and bees long before *you had spoken* with your parents about the facts of life. The *trapassato prossimo* (pluperfect) is used to talk about an action that happened before another past action.

The pluperfect is a compound tense, and just like with the present perfect, you'll need a helping verb, which will be either *avere* or *essere*. The big difference is that your helping verb must be conjugated in the imperfect tense.

The Pluperfect Using *Avere: Lavare* (to Wash)

Italiano	English
io avevo lavato	I had washed
tu avevi lavato	you had washed
lui/lei Lei aveva lavato	he/she/You had washed
noi avevamo lavato	we had washed
voi avevate lavato	you had washed
loro avevano lavato	they had washed

The Pluperfect Using *Essere: Andare* (to Go)

Italiano	English
io ero andato(a)	I had gone
tu eri andato(a)	you had gone
lui/lei Lei era andato(a)	he/she/You had gone
noi eravamo andati(e)	we had gone
voi eravate andati(e)	you had gone
loro erano andati(e)	they had gone

The Least You Need to Know

- The imperfect tense is used to indicate something that occurred in the past over a period of time or something you *used to do.* It is also used to talk about a mental, emotional, or physical condition that happened in the past.
- The present perfect is used to indicate an isolated event that occurred in the past.
- Intransitive verbs and reflexive verbs require *essere* as their auxiliary verb.
- The past participle must agree in gender and number with the preceding direct object pronoun.
- The pluperfect is a compound tense formed by conjugating the helping verbs *avere* and *essere* in the imperfect and then adding the past participle.

Minutiae

Part 4 focuses on the little details. In the following chapters, I show you how to "speak computer," write a text or a letter, make a phone call, navigate through the *ufficio postale* (post office), and make plans for the *futuro*.

I discuss the conditional, used to talk about what you would, could, and should be doing. I talk about the subjunctive, the "if only" mood used to talk about how things *might* be. In the business section, I share all the practical lingo for real life—banking, professions, and trades.

The final chapter offers a look at the *passato remoto* (past absolute), used to talk about things that happened—you guessed it—a *looooong* time ago. It also offers suggestions on translation and a poem by St. Francis of Assisi.

If at first Part 4 feels a bit daunting, remember that it's not you! Certain grammatical concepts require a great deal of practice and application. Go easy with yourself and find ways to apply your new skills. By the time you study this section, you've already come quite the distance. Be proud of your accomplishment! Think more about how much you have already learned, and less about what you still need to learn.

Che Sarà, Sarà: Communicating in the *Futuro*

Chapter

18

In This Chapter

- Using *il telefono*
- Decoding technobabble and computer talk
- Writing *una lettera* and visiting *l'ufficio postale*
- *Amore* Italian style
- *Il futuro* (the future) and *il futuro anteriore* (the future perfect)

Without the future, we probably wouldn't do much in the present. For most of us, it's difficult to think too far ahead without feeling a little anxious. After all, if I imagine my young daughter growing up, I'm forced to think about myself growing old, too. Yikes!

But if you want to map out your journey as opposed to winging it, you've got to plan. In this chapter, you learn how to form the future tense and the future perfect. The thrills don't stop there! To round out your studies, I've also added a section on computers to give you the latest *terminologia*. I've also included a few of the more entertaining and commonly used emoticons Italians use when they're *ciattando* (chatting) online.

You'll also learn how to make a phone call, decipher a basic text message, decode your Facebook page, and tell your sweetheart how you feel.

Il Telefono (the Telephone)

Most telephone numbers in Italy start with 0 + the area code (which can be either 2 or 3 digits) followed by the 6- to 8-digit phone number. As more and more people require new numbers, it's likely the numbers will reach 11 digits. To get an operator, you must dial 15; to get an international operator, dial 170. Your best option is to use a prepaid telephone card called a *scheda telefonica*. Most public telephones also still accept coins.

Telefonate (Telephone Calls)

Making *una telefonata* is especially challenging because you don't have the advantage of body language and facial expressions to interpret what's being said. When speaking to an international operator, you can probably speak in English. What happens if you're in a small village and need to call back home? The *vocabolario* in the following table should help you reach out and touch someone.

Telephone Talk

English	Italiano
I'd like to make ...	*Vorrei fare ...*
a local call	*una telefonata urbana*
a long-distance call	*una telefonata interurbana*
a collect call	*una telefonata a carico del destinatario*
a conference call	*una teleconferenza*
a credit-card call	*una telefonata con carta di credito*
an intercontinental call	*una telefonata intercontinentale*
an international call	*una telefonata internazionale*
a person-to-person call	*una telefonata con preavviso*
a Skype call	*una telefonata Skype*

In case of an emergency while in Italy, keep these helpful contact numbers handy:

General SOS (free from any telephone): 113

Carabinieri (police; free): 112

Automobile Club d'Italia (car accidents and breakdowns): 116

Modern Communications

Ever since the Italian Antonio Meucci invented one of the first voice communicating devices—the *telettrofono*—in 1854, we haven't been the same. Use the following terminology to stay connected whether via the telephone or your computer.

Le Comunicazioni (Communications)

English	*Italiano*	English	*Italiano*
* asterisk/star	*l'asterisco*	landline	*un telefono fisso*
# pound sign	*il cancelletto*	line	*la linea*
800 number (free)	*il numero verde*	message	*il messaggio*
access	*l'accesso; il permesso*	network	*la rete informatica*
answering machine	*la segreteria telefonica*	off-peak	*non di punta*
area code	*il prefisso*	peak	*il periodo di punta*
bandwidth	*la larghezza di banda*	phone card	*la scheda telefonica*
booth	*la cabina telefonica*	PIN (personal identification number)	*il numero di identificazione personale/il codice* ("code")
broadband	*la banda*	public phone	*il telefono pubblico*
cell phone	*il telefonino/il cellulare*	receiver	*il ricevitore; la cornetta*
charges	*i costi*	roaming	*la telefonia roaming*
cordless phone	*il telefono senza fili*	service	*il servizio*
email	*la posta elettronica; l'email*	signal	*il segnale*
email address	*l'indirizzo elettronico*	Sim card	*la Sim telefonica/la carta SIM*
fax/fax machine	*il facsimile/il fax*	SMS (short message service)	*SMS* (it's the same in Italian, except you pronounce it *ess-say em-meh ess-say*)
fax number	*il numero di fax*	telephone book	*l'elenco telefonico*
... to send a fax	*inviare un fax/"faxare"*	telephone call	*la telefonata*
... fax modem	*il fax modem*	telephone operator	*l'operatore*
hot spot	*la zona calda; il punto di accesso*	touch-tone phone	*il telefono a tastiera*
internet	*l'internet*	wireless	*la connessione wireless; la connessione senza fili*
interruption of service	*l'interruzione di servizio*	wireless access point	*il punto di accesso senza fili*
keypad	*la tastiera*	Yellow Pages	*le pagine gialle*

Say What?

The following dialogue should help you get your point across. When answering the phone, put on your best Italian voice and work on your accent. Say *Pronto?* (This word is invariable and does not change according to gender.)

Icebreakers

English	Italiano
(telephone ring)	*(squillo di telefono)*
Hello?	*Pronto?*
Hello.	*Buongiorno.*
With whom do I speak?	*Con chi parlo?*
This is Gabriella. Is Fabrizio there?	*Sono Gabriella. C'è Fabrizio?*
Just a minute.	*Un momento.*

If the party you're trying to reach isn't there, you'll want to leave *un messaggio* (a message). Try to improvise using the following. Practice with a friend. Make it *un gioco* (a game). Pretend to be Italian long enough, and you might surprise yourself.

English	Italiano
No, s/he's not here, I'm sorry.	*Non c'è adesso, mi dispiace.*
Would you like to leave a message?	*Vorrebbe lasciare un messaggio?*
When can I call back?	*Quando posso richiamare?*
I'll call back later.	*Richiamerò più tardi.*

Please Leave a Message

32

You're busy (studying Italian, for example) and don't want to interrupt the flow of your studies. When you can't take a call, use one of these standard, no-nonsense Italian voicemail greetings. Listen to the audio to hear how these should sound in Italian:

> The person you are calling cannot answer the phone. Leave a message after the tone. Thank you.
> *La persona che stai chiamando non può rispondere al telefono. Lascia un messsaggio dopo il segnale acustico. Grazie.*

> Please leave your number after the beep.
> *Per favore lasciate il vostro numero dopo il bip.*

Hello, Operator?

Making phone calls can be tough if you're not prepared. You may dial the wrong number or hear a recording telling you the number is no longer in service. The following are some phrases you might hear or want to say to an operator. They may be in the past tense, so keep an ear out for the auxiliary verbs and their participles.

What you might say:

> I can't get a line.
> *Non posso prendere la linea.*

> The line is always busy.
> *La linea è sempre occupata.*

> May I speak with an international operator?
> *Posso parlare con un operatore internazionale?*

> Can you connect me with …?
> *Mi può mettere in comunicazione con …?*

> Excuse me, I dialed the wrong number.
> *Mi scusi, ho sbagliato numero.*

> I need assistance.
> *Ho bisogno d'assistenza.*

What a recording (or operator) might say:

> The line was disconnected.
> *È caduta la linea.*

> Hold please.
> *Attendere prego.*

> What number did you dial?
> *Che numero ha fatto?*

> No one is answering.
> *Non risponde.*

> This (that) number is out of service.
> *Questo (quel) numero di telefono è fuori servizio.*

> This (that) number does not work.
> *Questo (quel) numero non funziona.*

LA BELLA LINGUA

When calling home from Italy, it's always cheaper to charge your calls to your home phone, better still to Skype or invest in Magic Jack and the call is free!

Texting, Italian Style

Italians are texters. Rather than spell out each word, texters use abbreviations. You may want to use a couple of these if you're texting someone. Please, don't text and drive … especially in Italy. (Someone has to keep an eye on the road.)

Texting

English	*Italiano*	Abbreviation
always	*sempre*	*smpr*
excuse me	*scusa*	*scs*
for	*per*	*x*
how	*come*	*km*
I am	*sono*	*sn*
left	*sinistra*	*sx*
many kisses	*tanti baci*	*xxx*
message	*messaggio*	*sms*
next	*prossimo*	*prox*
not	*non*	*nn*
number	*numero*	*nm*
respond	*rispondi*	*rsp*
right	*destra*	*dx*
that; what	*che*	*ke*
what; thing	*cosa*	*ks*
when	*quando*	*qnd*
where are you	*dove sei*	*dv 6*
who	*chi*	*ki*
with	*con*	*kn*

Il Computer

Computer terms in Italian are *per la maggior parte* (for the most part) borrowed from English and often *un salto* (jump) from their English counterparts. Take *downloadare*, for instance. To look at it, you might not immediately recognize it as "to download," yet it becomes quite obvious when you say it.

The following terms should get you *navigando/surfando sulla rete* (surfing the internet) in no time.

Vocabulary for the Information Superhighway

English	*Italiano*	English	*Italiano*
adapter	*l'adattatore*	keyboard	*la tastiera*
address	*l'indirizzo*	laptop computer	*il computer portable*
at (@)	*la chiocciola*	memory stick	*la chiavetta USB/la pennetta USB*
battery	*la batteria, la pila*	mouse	*il mouse*
computer	*il computer*	online	*in linea*
dialogue box	*la finestra di dialogo*	page	*la pagina*
discs	*i dischetti*	password	*la parola d'acceso/il codice/la password*
email	*la posta elettronica*	printer	*la stampante*
folder	*la cartella*	screen	*lo schermo*
icon	*l'icona*	search engine	*il motore di ricerca*
internet	*la rete*	website	*il sito internet; il sito*

Computer- and Internet-Related Verbs

In the constant *evoluzione* and intermingling of languages, many of these computer-related verbs have been assimilated from English and Italianized.

Il Computer

English	*Italiano*	English	*Italiano*
to back up a file	*backuppare*	to crash	*andare in bomba*
to burn (a CD or DVD)	*masterizzare*	to debug	*debuggare*
to chat online	*chattare*	to download	*downloadare*
to click	*cliccare*	to format	*formattare*
to compact	*compattare*	to scan	*scannarizzare or scandire*
to compress a series of files	*zippare*	to surf the web for fun	*surfare/navigare*
to connect	*connettersi*		

Italian Emoticons

Tell them you heard it here first. Italians are no strangers to chatting, and the Internet provides no exception. Try using the following emoticons to express yourself the next time you're online:

:-(	*Triste* (sad)
:-)	*Contento* (content)
:-/	*Indeciso, hummm …* (undecided)
%-)	*Confuso* (confused)
:-c	*Molto dispiaciuto* (very disappointing)
:-O	*Molto stupito* (very surprised)
:-?	*Non capisco* (I don't get it.)
:~i	*Fumando* (smoking)
:~j	*Fumando e sorridendo* (smoking and smiling)
(:-*	*Bacio* (kiss)
;*)	*Bacio sulla punta del naso* (kiss on the point of your nose)
'-)	*Strizzatina d'occhio* (wink of an eye)
:-B	*Dire sciocchezze (o cose strane)* (to talk nonsense)
:---)	*Grossa bugia* (a really big lie)
:^)	*Piccola bugia* (a little lie)
:*)	*Forse ho bevuto troppo* (maybe I drank too much)
(:-)	*Sono calvo* (I am bald)
8-)	*Porto gli occhiali* (I wear glasses)
:/i	*Vietato fumare* (no smoking)
@---	*Una rosa* (a rose)
*<|:-)	*Babbo Natale* (Santa Claus)

Facebook

Why not take advantage of the time you spend on Facebook to improve your Italian-language skills? Facebook can be read in any number of languages, including Italian. Additionally, you can find, with a little sleuthing, some great pages that are specifically geared toward students of Italian.

Fun with Facebook

English	Italiano	English	Italiano
answer a request	*rispondi a una richiesta*	friend request	*la richiesta di amicizia*
cancel	*annulla*	like	*mi piace*
change (profile)	*modifica (profilo)*	message	*messaggio*
comment	*commenta*	notifications	*notifiche*
common (friend)	*(amico/a) in comune*	share	*condividi*
confirm	*conferma*	wall	*la bacheca*
contact information	*le informazioni di contatto*	What's on your mind?	*A cosa stai pensando?*

Rain or Shine: *L'Ufficio Postale*

A visit to *l'ufficio postale* (the post office) can bring the most reasonable person to the verge of insanity. All you want is a stamp, but you've got to wait in *la fila* (line) for what seems like hours. If you want to send a *pacco*, you wait in one line only to find out you need to go to the other *sportello* (counter).

Take a deep breath and remember: you're not just in the post office, you're in the post office *in Italy*. Things could be worse.

L'Ufficio Postale (the Post Office)

English	Italiano	English	Italiano
addressee	*il destinatario*	package	*il pacco*
cardboard box	*la scatola di cartone*	packing paper	*la carta da pacchi*
counter/window	*lo sportello*	post office	*l'ufficio postale*
envelope	*la busta*	post office box	*la cassetta postale*
extra postage	*la soprattassa postale*	postage	*la tariffa postale*
letter	*la lettera*	postal worker	*l'impiegato(a) postale*
line	*la fila*	postcard	*la cartolina*
mail	*la posta*	receipt	*la ricevuta*
mail carrier	*il postino*	to send	*spedire, mandare*
mailbox	*la buca delle lettere, la cassetta della posta*	sender	*il mittente*
		stamps	*i francobolli*
money transfer	*il vaglia postale, il vaglia telegrafico*	telegram	*il telegramma*

Il Postino: **Special Delivery!**

There are many different ways to send something—some costing more, some taking longer than others. If you don't indicate how you want something to be shipped, chances are good it'll take the longest route. *Vorrei mandare questa lettera ...* (I'd like to send this letter ...).

Letter Perfect

English	*Italiano*
by airmail	*per posta aerea/per via aerea*
by C.O.D.	*con pagamento alla consegna*
by express mail	*per espresso*
by special delivery	*per corriere speciale*
by registered mail	*per posta raccomandata*

Dear Gianni ...

Pick up some beautiful handmade marbleized paper from a *cartoleria* in Firenze. You don't have to write a lot; a couple lines letting someone know you appreciate him or her goes a long way.

Le Lettere (Letters)

English	*Italiano*	English	*Italiano*
Dear (formal)	*Egregio/a*	Yours (informal)	*tuo/tua*
Dear (informal)	*Caro/a*	Sincerely (formal)	*Sinceramente*
Dearest	*Carissimo/a*	A hug (informal)	*Un abbraccio*
Affectionately (informal)	*Affettuosamente*	A big kiss (informal)	*Un bacione*
	Cordialmente	Soon! (informal)	*A presto!*
Cordially (formal)			

L'Amore e le Consequenze (Love and Consequences)

A *roman* was originally a medieval tale whose origins derive from the ancient epic poems that told of adventure and conquest. Later, as love ballads (told by the traveling storytellers, the medieval equivalent of today's comedians) swept through Europe in the twelfth and thirteenth centuries, the "romantic" tales began to take on the meaning we now associate with the word *romance*. The difference now is that in

Italian, when you speak of *un romanzo*, you're talking about a novel—a made-up story with fictitious characters.

LA BELLA LINGUA

Learn these Italian proverbs about love:

Love is blind.
L'amore è cieco.

Love rules without rules.
L'amore domina senza regole.

Out of sight, out of mind.
Lontano dagli occhi, lontano dal cuore.

I'm a hopeful romantic, which is probably why I love languages so much. They allow us to express the realm that lives within our minds and hearts, to reach out and connect with another through our words. Listen to the CD to hear how these things should be pronounced.

Love, Italian Style

English	Italiano
You're beautiful.	*Sei bellissimo/a.*
You're fascinating.	*Sei affascinante.*
Are you married?	*Sei sposato/a?*
I (don't) have a boyfriend/girlfriend.	*(Non) ho un fidanzato/fidanzata.*
What about dinner tonight?	*Vuoi andare a cena insieme stasera?*
Can we meet again?	*Possiamo vederci ancora?*
Can I give you a kiss?	*Posso darti un bacio?*
Give me a kiss!	*Dammi un bacio!*
Will you marry me?	*Mi vuoi sposare?*
I care for you.	*Ti voglio bene.*
I love you.	*Ti amo.*
I hate you.	*Ti odio.*
You drive me crazy.	*Mi fai impazzire.*

Che Sarà Sarà: The Future

The future tense is quite easy. It's used in Italian in exactly the same manner as English uses it. Some irregular verbs may change their stem (such as *potere*, *fare*, and *andare*), but future endings are all the same for all three verb families.

Unlike most verb conjugations, where you add the appropriate conjugated ending to the infinitive stem, the future endings are added to the end of the infinitive minus its final *-e*. Regular *-are* verbs must also change the final *-a* of the future stem to *-e*, except the verbs *dare*, *fare*, and *stare*.

Future Endings

Subject	Future Endings	Subject	Future Endings
io	*-ò*	*noi*	*-emo*
tu	*-ai*	*voi*	*-ete*
lui/lei/Lei	*-à*	*loro*	*-anno*

Watch how the future works in all three verb families. Pay attention to what happens to the *-are* verb *parlare*. Remember to stress the third accented syllable.

Il Futuro (the Future)

Subject	*Parlare*	*Scrivere*	*Capire*
io	*parlerò* (I'll speak)	*scriverò* (I'll write)	*capirò* (I'll understand)
tu	*parlerai* (you'll speak)	*scriverai* (you'll write)	*capirai* (you'll understand)
lui/lei/Lei	*parlerà* (he/she/You'll speak)	*scriverà* (he/she/You'll write)	*capirà* (he/she/You'll understand)
noi	*parleremo* (we'll speak)	*scriveremo* (we'll write)	*capiremo* (we'll understand)
voi	*parlerete* (you'll speak)	*scriverete* (you'll write)	*capirete* (you'll understand)
loro	*parleranno* (they'll speak)	*scriveranno* (they'll write)	*capiranno* (they'll understand)

I'll speak to you tomorrow.
Ti parlerò domani.

During her vacation, Mary will write many letters.
Durante la sua vacanza, Maria scriverà molte lettere.

AS A *REGOLA*

In Italian, you can express the probability of something by using the future tense. Use the future perfect to express "must have" (when you're not sure of something):

Where is Robert?	He must be around.	He must have gone away.
Dov'è Roberto?	*Sarà in giro.*	*Sarà andato via.*

Avere in the Future

The following table shows how the irregular verb *avere* is conjugated in the future.

Avere (to Have)

Italiano	English	Italiano	English
io **avrò**	I'll have	*noi* **avremo**	we'll have
tu **avrai**	you'll have	*voi* **avrete**	you'll have
lui/lei/Lei **avrà**	he/she/You/it'll have	*loro* **avranno**	they'll have

Essere in the Future

You may already be familiar with the old Italian adage *Che sarà sarà!* (What will be, will be!) As usual, the irregular verb *essere* has its own set of rules.

Essere (to Be)

Italiano	English	Italiano	English
io **sarò**	I'll be	*noi* **saremo**	we'll be
tu **sarai**	you'll be	*voi* **sarete**	you'll be
lui/lei/Lei **sarà**	he/she/You/it'll be	*loro* **saranno**	they'll be

Look for the Pattern

Verbs that end in *-care* or *-gare* (such as *cercare*, *giocare*, and *pagare*) add an *-h* before the *-er* base in order to maintain the original sound of their infinitives.

Forming the Future I

Verb	Stem	Future Conjugations
cercare (to look for)	*cercher-*	*cercherò, cercherai, cercherà, cercheremo, cercherete, cercheranno*
giocare (to play)	*giocher-*	*giocherò, giocherai, giocherà, giocheremo, giocherete, giocheranno*
pagare (to pay)	*pagher-*	*pagherò, pagherai, pagherà, pagheremo, pagherete, pagheranno*

Many verbs that end in *-iare* (such as *cominciare*, *lasciare*, *mangiare*, and *noleggiare*) change *-ia* to *-e*.

Forming the Future II

Verb	Stem	Future Conjugations
cominciare (to begin)	*comincer-*	*comincerò, comincerai, comincerà, cominceremo, comincerete, cominceranno*
lasciare (to leave)	*lascer-*	*lascerò, lascerai, lascerà, lasceremo, lascerete, lasceranno*
mangiare (to eat)	*manger-*	*mangerò, mangerai, mangerà, mangeremo, mangerete, mangeranno*

Irregular Stems

The following table shows a list of commonly used verbs with irregular future stems. However, after the stem has been changed, these verbs use regular future endings.

AS A *REGOLA*

Often it's not the endings that are irregular in the future tense, but the stems of the infinitives. After you've memorized the stem, you'll have no problem conjugating a verb into the future.

Forming the Future III

Verb	Stem	Future
andare (to go)	*andr-*	*andrò, andrai, andrà, andremo, andrete, andranno*
bere (to drink)	*berr-*	*berrò, berrai, berrà, berremo, berrete, berranno*
dare (to give)	*dar-*	*darò, darai, darà, daremo, darete, daranno*
dovere (to have to)	*dovr-*	*dovrò, dovrai, dovrà, dovremo, dovrete, dovranno*
fare (to do/make)	*far-*	*farò, farai, farà, faremo, farete, faranno*
giocare (to play)	*giocher-*	*giocherò, giocherai, giocherà, giocheremo, giocherete, giocheranno*
potere (to be able to)	*potr-*	*potrò, potrai, potrà, potremo, potrete, potranno*
rimanere (to remain)	*rimarr-*	*rimarrò, rimarrai, rimarrà, rimarremo, rimarrete, rimarranno*
sapere (to know)	*sapr-*	*saprò, saprai, saprà, sapremo, saprete, sapranno*
stare (to stay)	*star-*	*starò, starai, starà, staremo, starete, staranno*
tenere (to hold)	*terr-*	*terrò, terrai, terrà, terremo, terrete, terranno*
vedere (to see)	*vedr-*	*vedrò, vedrai, vedrà, vedremo, vedrete, vedranno*
vivere (to live)	*vivr-*	*vivrò, vivrai, vivrà, vivremo, vivrete, vivranno*

I'll give you the money in a week.
Ti darò i soldi fra una settimana.

We will be on vacation for 10 days.
Saremo in vacanza per dieci giorni.

The Future's a Blank

Fill in the blanks with the proper future conjugation of the following verbs. Look at the stems to determine the rest.

Looking Forward with the Future I

	Andare	*Dovere*	*Potere*	*Sapere*	*Vedere*
io	andrò	dovrò	potrò	saprò	vedrò
tu	_____	_____	_____	_____	_____
lui/lei/Lei	_____	_____	potrà	_____	_____
noi	andremo	_____	_____	_____	_____
voi	_____	_____	_____	_____	vedrete
loro	_____	_____	_____	sapranno	_____

Answers: andrai, andrà, andrete, andranno; dovrai, dovrà, dovremo, dovrete, dovranno; potrai, potremo, potrete, potranno; saprai, saprà, sapremo, saprete; vedrai, vedrà, vedremo, vedranno

Verbs such as *bere, rimanere, tenere, venire,* and *volere* double the final -*r* before the endings. See if you can fill in the conjugation for them.

Looking Forward with the Future II

	Bere	*Rimanere*	*Tenere*	*Venire*	*Volere*
io	berrò	rimarrò	terrò	verrò	vorrò
tu	berrai	_____	_____	_____	_____
lui/lei/Lei	_____	_____	_____	_____	_____
noi	_____	rimarremo	_____	_____	_____
voi	_____	rimarrete	_____	_____	_____
loro	_____	_____	_____	verranno	_____

Answers: berrà, berremo, berrete, berranno; rimarrai, rimarrà, rimarranno; terrai, terrà, terremo, terrete, terranno; verrai, verrà, verremo, verrete; vorrai, vorrà, vorremo, vorrete, vorrano

Now let's put it all together. Replace the underlined verbs with the future tense:

> *Domani* <u>*ho*</u> *molto da fare.* <u>*Devo*</u> *fare la spesa per la cena. Prima* <u>*voglio*</u> *comprare la frutta al mercato, poi* <u>*compro*</u> *il pane alla panetteria.* <u>*Vado*</u> *al supermercato per comprare la pasta e poi* <u>*vado*</u> *alla pescheria per comprare del pesce. Probabilmente* <u>*sono*</u> *stanca; allora* <u>*prendo*</u> *l'autobus per tornare a casa. I miei amici* <u>*arrivano*</u> *alle otto.*

Answers: avrò, dovrò, vorrò, comprerò, andrò, andrò, sarò, prenderò, arriveranno

Il Futuro Anteriore (the Future Perfect)

By the time you've finished this book, *you will have learned* a lot about verbs. The future perfect is a compound tense that indicates something *will have happened* in the future before another future action. You form the future perfect by conjugating the auxiliary verb in the future and tacking on the past participle of a verb:

> I will have learned Italian by next year.
> *Per l'anno prossimo avrò imparato l'**italiano**.*

> Will you have returned from work by 8:00?
> *Sarai tornato dal lavoro alle otto?*

Study the following tables to see how the future perfect works.

Parlare (to Speak)

Italiano	English
*io **avrò parlato***	I'll have spoken
*tu **avrai parlato***	you'll have spoken
*lui/lei/Lei **avrà parlato***	he/she/You'll have spoken
*noi **avremo parlato***	we'll have spoken
*voi **avrete parlato***	you'll have spoken
*loro **avranno parlato***	they'll have spoken

Tornare (to Return)

Italiano	English
io **sarò tornato/a**	I'll have returned
tu **sarai tornato/a**	you'll have returned
lui/lei/Lei **sarà tornato/a**	he/she/You'll have returned
noi **saremo tornati/e**	we'll have returned
voi **sarete tornati/e**	you'll have returned
loro **saranno tornati/e**	they'll have returned

The future perfect is also used to deduce something in the past:

> I must have gone to Italy ten times.
> *Sarò andata in Italia dieci volte.*

The Least You Need to Know

- Most telephone numbers in Italy start with 0 + the area code (which can be either 2 or 3 digits) followed by the 6- to 8-digit phone number.
- Many computer terms are brought over from the English, like *downlodare* (to download) and *ciattare* (to chat).
- A visit to the post office shouldn't take all day, but don't be surprised if it takes you all morning!
- *L'amore è cieco.* (Love is blind.)
- The future endings are the same for all three verb families.
- Many verbs have irregular stems in the future tense.
- The verbs *avere* and *essere* are irregular in the future and must be memorized (as usual).
- To create the future perfect, use the helping verb in the future + the participle.

Conditionally Yours: The Conditional

In This Chapter

- Hotels, houses, and apartments
- Rooms, furnishings, and amenities
- The conditional tense: I would
- The conditional past: I would have

Every human shares a basic need for a safe haven. Of course, most of us content ourselves with what we have, but we also imagine how *we'd like things* to be.

To do so, we need to understand how to use the conditional, a verb form that allows us to express things as they could, should, and would be (if things were different). If you're a dreamer, or simply deluded (like me), the conditional *could* be your tense.

This chapter also gives you the language to talk about your hotel, your home, and your hopes.

At the Hotel: *Una Camera, Per Favore*

Are you the type that makes a *prenotazione* (reservation) several months in advance, or are you more comfortable winging it? Use the following phrases to ask for what you need.

Hotel Expressions

English	Italiano
Do you have any rooms?	*Avete delle camere?*
I'd like to make a reservation.	*Vorrei fare una prenotazione.*
... for one night.	*... per una notte.*
... for one week.	*... per una settimana.*
At what time is check-out?	*Qual è l'ora per lasciare la camera?*
Is breakfast included?	*Colazione compresa?* or
	La colazione è compresa?
I'll take it (the room).	*La prendo.*
I need ...	*Ho bisogno di ...*
Compliments!	*Complimenti!*
Did I receive any messages?	*Ho ricevuto dei messaggi?*
Could I leave a message?	*Potrei lasciare un messaggio?*
Thank you so much.	*Grazie tanto.*
This room is too ...	*Questa camera è troppo ...*
... small.	*... piccola.*
... dark.	*... buia.*
... noisy.	*... rumorosa.*
I could use ...	*Mi servirebbe ...*
I'd like ...	*Vorrei ...*
a room	*una camera*
a double room	*una doppia*
... with a double bed	*... con letto matrimoniale*
a single room	*una singola*
... on the garden	*... sul giardino*
... on the sea	*... sul mare*

You'll have a much better chance at practicing your new language skills at a small, family-run *pensione* than you would if you were staying at a major hotel where the staff speak English. If you make a *prenotazione* (reservation) and tell them it's for two people, you'll get two beds *unless* you specifically indicate that you want a double bed, called *un letto matrimoniale* (a marriage bed). Here you'll want to use the conditional to express what you *would* like.

When you check out, you should be given a *fattura* (invoice), *conto* (bill), or *ricevuta* (receipt).

Your Home Away from Home

Pick up a local paper and comb through the real estate section to search for your perfect home. How many bedrooms does it have? Is there a balcony? The following table lists the various features people look for in a home. Use the expression *Ce l'ha …?* (Does it have …?) to ask if it has what you're looking for.

Real Estate Essentials

English	*Italiano*	English	*Italiano*
air conditioning	*l'aria condizionata*	gas	*il gas*
apartment	*l'appartamento*	ground floor	*il pianterreno*
attic	*la soffitta*	hallway	*il corridoio*
balcony	*il balcone*	heating	*il riscaldamento*
basement	*la cantina*	house	*la casa*
bathroom	*il bagno*	kitchen	*la cucina*
bathtub	*la vasca da bagno*	laundry room	*la lavanderia*
bedroom	*la camera da letto*	lease	*il contratto di affitto*
building	*il palazzo, l'edificio*	living room	*il soggiorno*
ceiling	*il soffitto*	maintenance	*la manutenzione*
closet	*l'armadio, il guardaroba*	owner/landlord	*il padrone di casa*
condominium	*il condominio*	rent	*l'affitto*
courtyard	*il cortile*	roof	*il tetto*
day room	*il soggiorno*	room	*la stanza, la camera*
dining room	*la sala da pranzo*	security deposit	*il deposito cauzionale*
electricity	*l'elettricità, la corrente*	shower	*la doccia*
elevator	*l'ascensore*	stairs	*le scale*
entrance	*l'ingresso*	storage room	*la cantina*
fireplace	*il camino*	tenant	*l'inquilino, l'affittuario*
floor	*il pavimento*	terrace	*la terrazza*
floor (story)	*il piano*	villa	*la villa*
garage	*il garage*	window	*la finestra*
garden	*il giardino*		

I Mobili (Furniture)

Without a doubt, if you're an Italian, you value your heirlooms. (This includes your great-grandmother's carved oak chest of drawers that weighs as much as a Fiat Cinquecento.)

Italians also love modern, simple, clean lines, and many urban homes look like pages from an IKEA catalog. Clothes dryers are quite uncommon in Italy; you'll have to *stendere* (hang) your clothes on a line or drape them all over the house. The following table gives you the names of the basics you need to live comfortably.

I Mobili Etcetera (Furniture, Etcetera)

English	*Italiano*	English	*Italiano*
armchair	*la poltrona*	microwave oven	*il forno a microonde*
bed	*il letto*	mirror	*lo specchio*
bookcase; shelf	*la libreria; lo scaffale*	outlet	*la presa; l'attacco*
chair	*la sedia; la poltrona*	oven	*il fornello*
chest of drawers	*il cassettone*	refrigerator	*il frigorifero*
closet	*l'armadio; il guardaroba*	rug	*il tappeto*
connection (water)	*lo scarico*	sideboard	*la credenza*
desk	*la scrivania*	sofa	*il divano*
dishwasher	*la lavapiatti; la lavastoviglie*	stereo	*lo stereo*
dresser	*la cassettiera*	stove	*il fornello*
freezer	*il freezer*	table	*il tavolo*
furniture	*i mobili*	television	*la televisione, il televisore*
glass case	*la cristalliera*	trunk	*il baule*
hotplate	*il forno elettrico*	VCR/DVD	*il videoregistratore/il DVD*
lamp; chandelier	*la lampada; il lampadario*	washing machine	*la lavatrice*

Forming *Il Condizionale* (the Conditional Tense)

The conditional is the dreamer's tense, used to describe what things could be like. When *should* you use the conditional tense? You *would* use it whenever you *would* like to express what *would* happen or what you *would* do under certain circumstances.

That Would Be Nice

The conditional tense follows simple, idiot-proof rules that make it one of the easier tenses to learn. Verbs that are irregular in the present tense tend to be regular in the conditional. Keep in mind these basics:

The same stems you learned for the future tense apply to the conditional tense. As you saw with the future tense, simply drop the final *-e* of the infinitive and add the endings.

Regular *-are* verbs must again change the final *-a* of their base to *-e:*

> *parlare → parle-*

The conditional tense is often used in conjunction with the subjunctive.

To form the conditional past, conjugate your helping verb in the conditional and add the past participle:

> *Avrei voluto*
> I would've wanted

Conditional Endings

Subject	Conditional Endings
io	*-ei*
tu	*-esti*
lui/lei/Lei	*-ebbe*
noi	*-emmo*
voi	*-este*
loro	*-ebbero*

The following examples illustrate how the conditional works. Listen to how the conditional sounds, paying particular attention to the *loro* form of the verb. I've noted where the stressed syllable goes.

Il Condizionale (the Conditional)

Subject	*Parlare*	*Vendere*	*Capire*
io	*parlerei* (I'd speak)	*venderei* (I'd sell)	*capirei* (I'd understand)
tu	*parleresti* (you'd speak)	*venderesti* (you'd sell)	*capiresti* (you'd understand)
lui/lei/Lei	*parlerebbe* (he/she/You'd speak)	*venderebbe* (he/she/You'd sell)	*capirebbe* (he/she/You'd understand)
noi	*parleremmo* (we'd speak)	*venderemmo* (we'd sell)	*capiremmo* (we'd understand)
voi	*parlereste* (you'd speak)	*vendereste* (you'd sell)	*capireste* (you'd understand)
loro	*parlerebbero* (they'd speak)	*venderebbero* (they'd sell)	*capirebbero* (they'd understand)

AS A *REGOLA*

The conditional tense uses the same stems as the future. After you've learned the stems, you simply add the appropriate conditional ending. Note that the first person plural in the future should not be confused with the conditional, which has an extra -*m*:

Future: *Vorremo* (we will want)

Conditional: *Vorremmo* (we would like)

Avere in the Conditional: What Would You Have?

The following table shows how the verb *avere* is conjugated in the conditional.

Forming the Conditional with *Avere* (to Have)

Italiano	English
io **avrei**	I'd have
tu **avresti**	you'd have
lui/lei/Lei **avrebbe**	he/she/You'd have
noi **avremmo**	we'd have
voi **avreste**	you'd have
loro **avrebbero**	they'd have

Essere in the Conditional: What Would You Be?

In our dreams, I'd be, you'd be, we'd all be … so happy because we'd be living in a dream of unconditional reality. Think of the conditional of *essere* (to be) as the dreamer's tense.

The consistently irregular verb *essere* maintains the same stem as it did for the future tense.

Forming the Conditional with *Essere* (to Be)

Italiano	English
io **sarei**	I'd be
tu **saresti**	you'd be
lui/lei/Lei **sarebbe**	he/she/You'd be
noi **saremmo**	we'd be
voi **sareste**	you'd be
loro **sarebbero**	they'd be

Look for the Pattern

Just like you saw in the future tense, verbs that end in *-care* or *-gare* (such as *cercare*, *giocare*, and *pagare*) add an *-h* before the *-er* base to maintain the original sound of their infinitives.

Verb	Stem	Conditional Conjugations
cercare (to look for)	*cercher-*	*cercherei, cercheresti, cercherebbe, cercheremmo, cerchereste, cercherebbero*
pagare (to pay)	*pagher-*	*pagherei, pagheresti, pagherebbe, pagheremmo, paghereste, pagherebbero*

Many verbs that end in *-iare* (such as *cominciare*, *lasciare*, *mangiare*, and *noleggiare*) change *-ia* to *-e*.

Verb	Stem	Conditional Conjugations
baciare (to kiss)	*bacer-*	*bacerei, baceresti, bacerebbe, baceremmo, bacereste, bacerebbero*
mangiare (to eat)	*manger-*	*mangerei, mangeresti, mangerebbe, mangeremmo, mangereste, mangerebbero*

Stem-Changing Verbs in the Conditional

Let's look at some of those irregular verbs again.

Verb	Stem	Conditional Conjugations
andare (to go)	*andr-*	*andrei, andresti, andrebbe, andremmo, andreste, andrebbero*
bere (to drink)	*berr-*	*berrei, berresti, berrebbe, berremmo, berreste, berrebbero*
dare (to give)	*dar-*	*darei, daresti, darebbe, daremmo, dareste, darebbero*
fare (to do/make)	*far-*	*farei, faresti, farebbe, faremmo, fareste, farebbero*
rimanere (to remain)	*rimarr-*	*rimarrei, rimarresti, rimarrebbe, rimarremmo, rimarreste, rimarrebbero*
sapere (to know)	*sapr-*	*saprei, sapresti, saprebbe, sapremmo, sapreste, saprebbero*
stare (to stay)	*star-*	*starei, staresti, starebbe, staremmo, stareste, starebbero*
tenere (to hold)	*terr-*	*terrei, terresti, terrebbe, terremmo, terreste, terrebbero*
vedere (to see)	*vedr-*	*vedrei, vedresti, vedrebbe, vedremmo, vedreste, vedrebbero*
venire (to come)	*verr-*	*verrei, verresti, verrebbe, verremmo, verreste, verrebbero*

It Would Be a Pleasure

The verbs *piacere* (to please) and *interessare* (to interest) are often used in the conditional and the conditional past:

> Would you like to go to the movies?
> *Ti piacerebbe andare al cinema?*

> Yes, I'd like to go [there].
> *Sì, mi piacerebbe andar[ci].*

> I would have liked to live in Italy.
> *Mi sarebbe piaciuto vivere in Italia.*

Add *non* to make a suggestion:

> Wouldn't you all like to see the castle?
> *Non vi interessebbe vedere il castello?*

> Wouldn't you be interested in watching the game?
> *Non Le interessebbe guardare la partita?*

Modal Verbs in the Conditional: Coulda, Shoulda, Woulda

The modal verbs *dovere* (to have to), *potere* (to be able to), and *volere* (to want) are often used in the conditional tense. When *you should* do something, use the verb *dovere*. When *you could* do something, use the verb *potere*. When *you'd like* something, use *volere*. These verbs in the conditional are often used with the infinitive form of another verb.

Dovere, Potere, and *Volere*

Subject	*Dovere* (to Have to; Must)	*Potere* (to Be Able to; Can)	*Volere* (to Want)
io	*dovrei* (I should)	*potrei* (I could)	*vorrei* (I'd like)
tu	*dovresti* (you should)	*potresti* (you could)	*vorresti* (you'd like)
lui/lei/Lei	*dovrebbe* (he/she/You should)	*potrebbe* (he/she/You could)	*vorrebbe* (he/she/You'd like)
noi	*dovremmo* (we should)	*potremmo* (we could)	*vorremmo* (we'd like)
voi	*dovreste* (you should)	*potreste* (you could)	*vorreste* (you'd like)
loro	*dovrebbero* (they should)	*potrebbero* (they could)	*vorrebbero* (they'd like)

You should work out more.
Dovresti fare più ginnastica.

We could go next year.
Potremmo andare l'anno prossimo.

I'd like to quit smoking.
Vorrei smettere di fumare.

Modal Verbs in the Conditional Past

To express something you should have done, or could have done, or would have liked to have done, you'll need your modal verbs. Again, your helping verb is doing all the work. Study the examples given for each verb.

I should have called.
Avrei dovuto telefonare. (dovere)

I could have called.
Avrei potuto telefonare. (potere)

I would have wanted to speak.
Avrei voluto parlare. (volere)

LA BELLA LINGUA

When speaking, Italians often use the imperfect tense of the modal verb *dovere* + an infinitive as a way of expressing the conditional past, like when you should have done something … but didn't:

I should have called.
Dovevo telefonare.

They should have listened.
Dovevano ascoltare.

Things Could Have Been Worse: The Conditional Perfect

When you have a close call with something, you might marvel at your good luck over *what could have been.* Or maybe, you simply ate too much and now lament, "I shouldn't have finished the cookies!"

Like the future perfect, the conditional perfect uses both *avere* and *essere* as helping verbs and is equivalent to talking about how things *could have been* (but weren't). It is often used in conjunction with the subjunctive mood. It's tough to translate this tense word for word, because the construction is so different from English. Watch what happens with the different helping verbs used to form the conditional perfect of *parlare* (to speak) and *andare* (to go).

The Conditional Past Using *Avere* + *Parlare*

Italiano	English
io **avrei parlato**	I'd have spoken
tu **avresti parlato**	you'd have spoken
lui/lei Lei **avrebbe parlato**	he/she/You'd have spoken
noi **avremmo parlato**	we'd have spoken
voi **avreste parlato**	you'd have spoken
loro **avrebbero parlato**	they'd have spoken

The Conditional Past Using *Essere* + *Andare*

Italiano	English
io **sarei andato/a**	I'd have gone
tu **saresti andato/a**	you'd have gone
lui/lei Lei **sarebbe andato/a**	he/she/You'd have gone
noi **saremmo andati/e**	we'd have gone
voi **sareste andati/e**	you'd have gone
loro **sarebbero andati/e**	they'd have gone

I would have called you but there wasn't time.
Ti avrei telefonato ma non c'era tempo.

It would have been a disaster!
Sarebbe stato un disastro!

WHAT'S WHAT

The verb *mancare* (to miss or to be missing) is used in the conditional expression *Ci mancherebbe altro!* (*literally:* other would be missing) to express "God forbid!" It's useful for pessimists waiting for the other shoe to drop, as well as for optimists taking stock of their good fortune over how things *could be* (because they could always be much worse).

Practice Makes *Perfetto*

Translate the following sentences into Italian:

1. I'd like to go to Italy for the summer.

2. We should leave; it's getting late.

3. I could come later.

4. Sofia, would you like to see a film?

5. We'd like a bottle of red wine.

6. I would have been rich with a million dollars.

Answers: 1. Vorrei andare in Italia per l'estate. 2. Dovremmo partire. (or andare via); é tardi 3. Potrei venire più tardi. 4. Sofia, vorresti vedere un film? 5. Vorremmo una bottiglia di vino rosso. 6. Sarei stato ricco con un milione di dollari.

The Least You Need to Know

- The conditional is formed by adding the conditional endings to the stem of the verbs.

- Many irregular stems are the same as those used in the future tense.

- To express that you should, could, or would like, you must use the conditional form of the modal verbs *dovere, potere,* and *volere.*

- The verb *piacere* is used in the conditional to indicate something would be pleasing to you and is used like the verb *volere,* as in *would like.*

Serious Business: The Subjunctive

In This Chapter

- Speaking of professions
- Banking and business terms and titles
- *Il congiuntivo:* the subjunctive
- Practicing different forms of the subjective

Money can't buy you *l'amore,* but you sure can salve your broken heart with it. For people doing business in Italy or staying in Italy for an extended *periodo,* this chapter gives you the terms you need to open a bank account, take out a mortgage, or make an investment.

This chapter also deals with the *subjunctive,* a somewhat unique tense (actually, it's called a mood) used to express uncertainty, opinions, hopes, fears, and with impersonal forms (It's important that … it's necessary to …, etc.) and hypothetical situations.

Professionally Speaking

Modern Italian professionals, regardless of their gender, tend toward the once typically masculine titles: *avvocato* (lawyer), *dottore* (doctor), *attore* (actor), and *professore* (professor), to name a few. Other titles must reflect the gender of the subject. Exceptions include professions ending in *-a,* such as *dentista* (dentist) and *artista* (artist). In these cases, you have to pay attention to the article preceding the *professione* to know whether the subject is *maschile* or *femminile.*

Many professions ending in *-o* or *-e* often change to *-a* to reflect gender:

> *l'archeologo/l'archeologa* (archaeologist)
>
> *lo scienziato/la scienziata* (scientist)

Certain Italian professions have gender-specific endings such as *-ice* that may or may not be used, depending on the specific individual and regional influences:

> *l'attore/l'attrice* (actor/actress)
>
> *lo scrittore/la scrittrice* (writer)

Other professions may end in *-essa*:

> *il dottore/la dottoressa* (doctor)
>
> *il poeta/la poetessa* (poet)
>
> *il professore/la professoressa* (professor)

AS A REGOLA

Note that some titles can be used for either gender; only the article changes:

il/la contabile   the accountant

il/la dentista   the dentist

In My Professional Opinion ...

The following table lists several of the more common professions. If there's only one entry, it can be used for both genders.

Professioni (Professions)

English	*Italiano*	Pronunciation
accountant	*contabile (m./f.)*	*kon-**tah**-bee-leh*
actor/actress	*attore/attrice*	*aht-**toh**-reh/aht-**tree**-cheh*
archaeologist	*archeologo/a*	*ar-keh-**oh**-loh-goh/gah*
architect	*architetto/a*	*ar-kee-**tet**-toh/tah*
artist	*artista (m./f.)*	*ar-**tees**-tah*
banker	*bancario/a*	*bahn-**kah**-ree-yoh/yah*

English	*Italiano*	**Pronunciation**
barber	*barbiere (m.)*	*bar-bee-**yeh**-reh*
cashier	*cassiere/a*	*kah-see-**yeh**-reh/rah*
consultant	*consulente (m./f.)*	*kon-soo-**len**-teh*
dentist	*dentista (m./f.)*	*den-**tees**-tah*
doctor	*dottore/dottoressa*	*doh-**toh**-reh/doh-toh-**rehs**-sah*
editor	*editore/editrice*	*eh-dee-**toh**-reh/eh-dee-**tree**-cheh*
electrician	*elettricista (m./f.)*	*eh-leh-tree-**chee**-stah*
environmentalist	*ecologo/a*	*eh-**koh**-loh-goh/gah*
firefighter	*vigile del fuoco (m./f.)*	***vee**-jeh-leh del fwoh-koh*
fireman	*pompiere (m.)*	*pom-pee-**yeh**-reh*
hair dresser	*parrucchiere/a*	*par-roo-kee-**yeh**-reh/rah*
housewife	*casalinga (f.)*	*kah-zah-**leen**-gah*
jeweler	*gioielliere (m./f.)*	*joh-yehl-lee-**yeh**-reh*
journalist	*giornalista (m./f.)*	*jor-nah-**lee**-stah*
lawyer	*avvocato/avvocatessa*	*ahv-voh-**kah**-toh/ahv-voh-kah-**tes**-sah*
manager	*dirigente (m./f.)*	*dee-ree-**jen**-teh*
mechanic	*meccanico/a*	*mek-**kah**-nee-koh/kah*
musician	*musicista (m./f.)*	*moo-zee-**chee**-stah*
nurse	*infermiere/a*	*een-fer-mee-**yeh**-reh/rah*
plumber	*idraulico (m.)*	*ee-**drow**-lee-koh*
police officer	*agente di polizia (m./f.)*	*ah-**jen**-teh dee poh-lee-**zee**-yah*
professor	*professore/professoressa*	*proh-fehs-**soh**-reh/proh-fehs-soh-**res**-sah*
scientist	*scienziato/a*	*shee-en-zee-**ah**-toh/tah*
secretary	*segretario/a*	*seh-greh-**tah**-ree-oh/ah*
stock broker	*agente di borsa (m./f.)*	*ah-**jen**-teh dee bor-sah*
student	*studente/studentessa (m.)*	*stoo-**den**-teh/stoo-den-**tes**-sah*
teacher	*insegnante (m./f.)*	*een-sen-**yahn**-teh*
waiter	*cameriere/a*	*kah-meh-ree-**yeh**-reh/rah*
worker	*operaio/a*	*oh-per-**ay**-yoh/yah*
writer	*scrittore/scrittrice*	*skreet-**toh**-reh/skreet-**tree**-cheh*

LA BELLA LINGUA

If you're lucky enough to be self-employed, you can say *Lavoro in proprio* (I work for myself).

Industries

These days, with multitasking as the norm, it's more difficult to pinpoint professions. The terms in the following table help you talk about where you fit in.

Le Attività (Trades)

English	*Italiano*	English	*Italiano*
banking	*banca*	insurance	*assicurazioni*
communications	*comunicazioni*	law	*legge*
computers	*computer*	manufacturing	*produzione*
construction	*costruzioni*	marketing	*marketing*
design	*design*	medicine	*medicina*
development	*sviluppo*	public relations	*pubbliche relazioni*
education	*istruzione, pedagogia*	publishing	*editoria*
engineering	*ingegneria*	real estate	*immobiliari*
fashion	*moda*	retail	*vendita al dettaglio*
finance	*finanza*	sales	*vendite*
food services	*alimentazione*	software	*software*
government	*governo*		

Everyone Has Needs: *Il Congiuntivo*

Il congiuntivo is not pink eye; it's the subjunctive. The subjunctive is a mood that expresses wishes, feelings, and doubt. It's the mood you use to express your hunches and your musings. As opposed to describing what is, the subjunctive covers the unrealized potential and the hypothetical.

Use the subjunctive after you offer an opinion. The cue for the subjunctive is often the word *che,* in this case meaning "that":

> I believe that it's going to rain. Is it raining? No. It's an opinion.

> I think that you're cute. Are you cute? Doesn't matter. It's what I think.

When the fiddler on the roof starts singing, he's using the subjunctive mood in the imperfect tense: "If I *were* a rich man …."

LA BELLA LINGUA

If the subject doesn't change, you can avoid the subjunctive altogether. For example:

I'm thinking [that] I'll go.
Penso di andare.

Virgil thinks [that] he's a big dog.
Virgil crede di essere un cane grande.

Using the Subjunctive

The subjunctive is most often used in dependent clauses introduced by *che*. The present subjunctive is formed by adding the subjunctive endings to the stem of the verb. Unlike future and conditional stems, most subjunctive stems change little from the infinitive.

Unless you're using a proper noun, you need to use the singular subject pronouns (*io*, *tu*, *lui/lei/Lei*) to distinguish the singular forms from one another. The pronouns aren't necessary for the plural forms. The examples presented in the following table are given with *che* (that) to familiarize you with this construction. Typical phrases that use the subjunctive include *Credo che* … (I believe that …), *Immagino che* … (I imagine that …), and *Penso che* … (I think that …).

Present Subjunctive Examples

Parlare	*Vendere*	*Offrire*	*Capire*
che io parli	*che io venda*	*che io offra*	*che io capisca*
che tu parli	*che tu venda*	*che tu offra*	*che tu capisca*
che lui/lei/Lei parli	*che lui/lei/Lei venda*	*che lui/lei/Lei offra*	*che lui/lei/Lei capisca*
che parliamo	*che vendiamo*	*che offriamo*	*che capiamo*
che parliate	*che vendiate*	*che offriate*	*che capiate*
che parlino	*che vendano*	*che offrano*	*che capiscano*

È difficile che lui venda la casa a quel prezzo.
It's unlikely that he'll sell the house at that price.

Non penso che Maria capisca.
I don't think that Maria understands.

WHAT'S WHAT
The present subjunctive can be used to refer to either the present or the future. The past subjunctive talks about the unrealized potential of things you "wished had happened." As well as expressing your opinion about whether or not something happened or not, such as:

I believe that the train arrived on time.
Credo che il treno sia arrivato in tempo.

When to Use the Subjunctive

The subjunctive is used when two different clauses exist (dependent and independent) pertaining to two different subjects or when those clauses are joined by *che*. (In English, "that" is sometimes dropped but always implied.) You also use the subjunctive when one of these clauses expresses need, doubt, an opinion, or emotion:

Need:

It's necessary that he goes to the doctor.
È necessario che lui vada da un dottore.

Doubt:

I doubt that our team will win.
Dubito che vinca la nostra squadra.

Opinion:

I think that you are the most beautiful woman in the world.
Credo che tu sia la più bella donna del mondo.

Emotion:

I am afraid that the politician is a liar.
Ho paura che il politico sia un bugiardo.

Helping Verbs in the Subjunctive

The verbs *essere* and *avere* are both irregular. Nothing new there.

Essere (to Be)

Italiano	English
che io **sia**	that I am
che tu **sia**	that you are
che lui/lei/Lei **sia**	that he/she (it) is; that You are
che noi **siamo**	that we are
che voi **siate**	that you are
che loro/essi **siano**	that they are

I think that Luisa is beautiful.
Penso che Luisa sia bella.

I believe that they are at home.
Credo che siano a casa.

Avere (to Have)

Italiano	English
che io **abbia**	that I have
che tu **abbia**	that you have
che lui/lei/Lei **abbia**	that he/she (it) has; that You have
che noi **abbiamo**	that we have
che voi **abbiate**	that you have
che loro/essi **abbiano**	that they have

I think that Tiziana is right.
*Penso che Tiziana **abbia** ragione.*

It's a shame that they don't have time to come.
*È un peccato che non **abbiano** il tempo di venire.*

Oh, So Moody

Oh, those irregularities. It should be no surprise at this point that there are several verbs with irregular subjunctive forms. Notice how the singular subjunctive conjugations are all identical, whether referencing *io*, *tu*, or *lui/lei* and *Lei*.

Irregular Verbs in the Present Subjunctive

Verb	Irregular Present Subjunctive
andare (to go)	*vada, vada, vada, andiamo, andiate, vadano*
dare (to give)	*dia, dia, dia, diamo, diate, diano*
dire (to say)	*dica, dica, dica, diciamo, diciate, dicano*
dovere (to have to; must)	*debba, debba, debba, dobbiamo, dobbiate, debbano*
fare (to do; make)	*faccia, faccia, faccia, facciamo, facciate, facciano*
mantenere (to maintain)	*mantenga, mantenga, mantenga, manteniamo, manteniate, mantengano*
piacere (to be pleasing)	*piaccia, piaccia, piaccia, piacciamo, piacciate, piacciano*
potere (to be able; can)	*possa, possa, possa, possiamo, possiate, possano*
rimanere (to remain)	*rimanga, rimanga, rimanga, rimaniamo, rimaniate, rimangano*
salire (to go up; to get on)	*salga, salga, salga, saliamo, saliate, salgano*
sapere (to know something)	*sappia, sappia, sappia, sappiamo, sappiate, sappiano*
stare (to stay)	*stia, stia, stia, stiamo, stiate, stiano*
tenere (to hold)	*tenga, tenga, tenga, teniamo, teniate, tengano*
venire (to come)	*venga, venga, venga, veniamo, veniate, vengano*
volere (to want)	*voglia, voglia, voglia, vogliamo, vogliate, vogliano*

Dependent Clauses and the Subjunctive

The following expressions are all independent clauses requiring the subjunctive mood. *I think …* is the independant (main) clause that works closely with the dependent clause … *that it is raining.* You use the subjunctive when you're not sure of something. It could be raining or not.

Express Yourself

English	*Italiano*	English	*Italiano*
I am happy that …	*Sono contento che …*	It's easy that …	*È facile che …*
I am sorry that …	*Mi dispiace che …*	It's good/bad that …	*È bene/male che …*
I believe that …	*Credo che …*	It's important that …	*È importante che …*
I desire that …	*Desidero che …*	It's incredible that …	*È incredibile che …*
I doubt that …	*Dubito che …*	It's likely (probable) that …	*È probabile che …*
I imagine that …	*Immagino che …*	It's necessary that …	*Bisogna che …*
I think that …	*Penso che …*	It's not important that …	*Non importa che …*
I want that …	*Voglio che …*	It's possible/impossible that …	*È possibile/impossibile che …*

English	*Italiano*	English	*Italiano*
although …	*sebbene …*	It's strange that …	*È strano che …*
before …	*prima che …*	provided that …	*purché …*
even though …	*benché …*	so that …	*affinché …*
in case …	*nel caso che …*	unless …	*a meno che …*
It seems that …	*Sembra che …*	until …	*finché non …*
It's difficult that …	*È difficile che …*	without …	*senza che …*

It seems to me that you are intelligent.
Mi sembra che tu sia intelligente.

Although I can't play the violin, I like listening to it.
Sebbene io non possa suonare il violino, mi piace ascoltarlo.

Cara Silvia—Practice Makes *Perfetto*

Paola hopes she can go to Italy this summer to study the language. She wants her friend Silvia to join her on an excursion. Fill in the blanks with the appropriate form of the subjunctive.

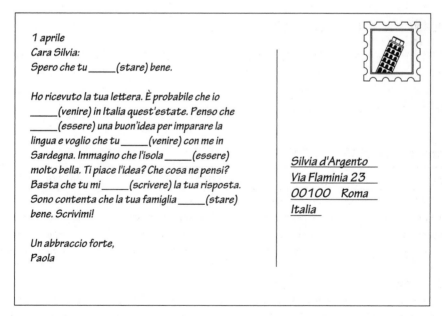

1 aprile
Cara Silvia:
Spero che tu _____ (stare) bene.

Ho ricevuto la tua lettera. È probabile che io _____ (venire) in Italia quest'estate. Penso che _____ (essere) una buon'idea per imparare la lingua e voglio che tu _____ (venire) con me in Sardegna. Immagino che l'isola _____ (essere) molto bella. Ti piace l'idea? Che cosa ne pensi? Basta che tu mi _____ (scrivere) la tua risposta. Sono contenta che la tua famiglia _____ (stare) bene. Scrivimi!

Un abbraccio forte,
Paola

Silvia d'Argento
Via Flaminia 23
00100   Roma
Italia

Answers: 1. stia 2. venga 3. sia 4. venga or vorrei (the imperfect subjunctive) *5. sia 6. scriva 7. stia*

April 1

Dear Silvia:

I hope that everything is going well.

I received your letter. I will probably come to Italy this summer. I think it's necessary for learning the language. I would be so pleased if you came with me to Sardegna. I imagine the island is very beautiful. What do you think? Do you like the idea? It's enough if you write me your response. I am happy your family is well.

Write me!

A big hug,
Paola

The Past (Present Perfect) Subjunctive

To make the past subjunctive (*passato del congiuntivo*), you'll need to use the present subjunctive form of the auxiliary verbs *avere* or *essere* + the past participle of your verb. Remember that verbs requiring *essere* as their auxiliary reflect gender and number in the participle. You use the past (or perfect) subjunctive when the action expressed by the verb of the dependent clause occurred before the action expressed by the verb in the independent clause. Study the following examples.

Past Subjunctive

Avere + Telefonare	*Essere + Andare*
che io abbia telefonato (that I called)	*che io sia andato(a)* (that I went)
che tu abbia telefonato (that you called)	*che tu sia andato(a)* (that you went)
che lui/lei/Lei abbia telefonato (that he/she/You called)	*che lui/lei/Lei sia andato(a)* (that he/she/You went)
che noi abbiamo telefonato (that we called)	*che siamo andati(e)* (that we went)
che voi abbiate telefonato (that you called)	*che siate andati(e)* (that you went)
che loro abbiano telefonato (that they called)	*che siano andati(e)* (that they went)

I am happy that you telephoned.
Sono contenta che tu abbia telefonato.

It seems that he has gone crazy.
Sembra che lui sia diventato pazzo.

Purely Speculation: The Imperfect Subjunctive

By the time you're comfortable using this tense, you probably won't need me anymore. In any case, the imperfect subjunctive (*imperfetto del congiuntivo*) is most often used when someone is talking about what they *would have done if.* Consequently, the imperfect subjunctive is almost always used after the word *se* (if) *unless you're stating a fact.*

Congiuntivo Imperfetto

Parlare	*Vendere*	*Offrire*	*Capire*
che io parlassi	*che io vendessi*	*che io offrissi*	*che io capissi*
che tu parlassi	*che tu vendessi*	*che tu offrissi*	*che tu capissi*
che lui/lei/Lei parlasse	*che lui/lei/Lei vendesse*	*che lui/lei/Lei offrisse*	*che lui/lei/Lei capisse*
che parlassimo	*che vendessimo*	*che offrissimo*	*che capissimo*
che parlaste	*che vendeste*	*che offriste*	*che capiste*
che parlassero	*che vendessero*	*che offrissero*	*che capissero*

I thought that you were selling your motorcycle.
Pensavo che tu vendessi la tua moto.

He hoped that she understood.
Sperava che lei capisse.

The Imperfect Subjunctive with *Avere* and *Essere*

Avere	*Essere*
che io avessi	*che io fossi*
che tu avessi	*che tu fossi*
che lui/lei/Lei avesse	*che lui/lei/Lei fosse*
che avessimo	*che fossimo*
che aveste	*che foste*
che avessero	*che fossero*

If I had the time, I'd learn all languages.
Se avessi il tempo, imparerei tutte le lingue.

If I were you, I'd never complain.
Se io fossi in te, non mi lamenterei mai.

The Past Was Perfect

The possibilities are endless when you start mixing and matching auxiliary verbs in compound tenses. The past perfect subjunctive (*trapassato del congiuntivo*) is created by using the imperfect subjunctive of your auxiliary verb (*avere* or *essere*) + the past participle of the verb you are conjugating. I've given you the two verbs *avere* and *essere*. You can easily substitute the participles presented in the following table with the verbs of your choice. Like with the imperfect subjunctive you just learned, the past perfect subjunctive is often used with the conditional past and with the word *se* (if).

Trapassato with *Avere* and *Essere*

Avere	*Essere*
che io avessi avuto	*che io fossi stato(a)*
che tu avessi avuto	*che tu fossi stato(a)*
che lui/lei/Lei avesse avuto	*che lui/lei/Lei fosse stato(a)*
che avessimo avuto	*che fossimo stati(e)*
che aveste avuto	*che foste stati(e)*
che avessero avuto	*che fossero stati(e)*

If we had had the time, we would have stayed a week longer.
Se avessimo avuto il tempo, saremmo rimasti ancora una settimana.

If you hadn't been there, I don't know what I would have done.
Se tu non ci fossi stato, non so cosa avrei fatto.

The Least You Need to Know

- Certain Italian professions have gender-specific endings.
- The subjunctive is a mood, not a tense, and it is used to express opinions, thoughts, feelings, and desires.
- The subjunctive past is used to desribe what might have happened *if* circumstances were different.
- The past perfect subjunctive (*trapassato del congiuntivo*) is created by using the imperfect subjunctive of your auxiliary verb (*avere* or *essere*) + the past participle of the verb you are conjugating.
- Learning Italian will improve your life. Enjoy the process—it's a short *viaggio*.

Once Upon a Time: The *Passato Remoto*

In This Chapter

- Talking about the distant past with *Il passato remoto*
- Regular forms of the past absolute
- Irregular forms of the past absolute
- Tricks for translation

The *passato remoto* (also called the past definite and the past absolute) is a tense that goes so far back it doesn't even have an equivalent in English. Let's just say it's a verb tense used to describe a *loooooooonnnng* time ago. Although it translates to the simple past, as in *I went*, the *passato remoto* requires you to look at time differently.

C'era Una Volta (Once Upon a Time)

The *passato remoto* is used in *letteratura* (literature), *fiabe* (fables), and *racconti* (stories). Except for particular regions (generally in the south), you'll rarely hear the *passato remoto* used in spoken Italian. This highly irregular verb tense is used to describe a historical event that took place at a specific time in the distant past. At times, it's difficult to determine the infinitive of a conjugation. Although rarely used in daily speech, an understanding of the *passato remoto* is necessary in order to read Italian literature and poetry (which you definitely don't want to miss!).

Regular Past Absolute Examples

Subject	Parlare	Vendere	Capire
io	*parlai* (I spoke)	*vendei/vendetti** (I sold)	*capii* (I understood)
tu	*parlasti* (you spoke)	*vendesti* (you sold)	*capisti* (you understood)
lui/lei/Lei	*parlò* (he/she/You spoke)	*vendè/vendette** (he/she/You sold)	*capì* (he/she/You understood)
noi	*parlammo* (we spoke)	*vendemmo* (we sold)	*capimmo* (we understood)
voi	*parlaste* (you spoke)	*vendeste* (you sold)	*capiste* (you understood)
loro	*parlarono* (they spoke)	*venderono* (they sold)	*capirono* (they understood)

Many of the regular -ere verbs have two forms for io *and* lui/lei.

These ancient forms of the helping verbs *essere* and *avere* are virtually unrecognizable from the present-tense conjugations. Two other verbs commonly used in this tense are *stare* and *fare*.

The *Passato Remoto* with *Essere*

Italiano	English
io **fui**	I was
tu **fosti**	you were
lui/lei/Lei **fu**	he/she was; You were
noi **fummo**	we were
voi **foste**	you were
loro **furono**	they were

The *Passato Remoto* with *Avere*

Italiano	English
io **ebbi**	I had
tu **avesti**	you had
lui/lei/Lei **ebbe**	he/she/You had
noi **avemmo**	we had
voi **aveste**	you had
loro **ebbero**	they had

The *Passato Remoto* with *Stare*

Italiano	English
io **stetti**	I was
tu **stesti**	you were
lui/lei/Lei **stette**	he/she was; You were
noi **stemmo**	we were
voi **steste**	you were
loro **stettero**	they were

The *Passato Remoto* with *Fare*

Italiano	English
io **feci**	I did
tu **facesti**	you did
lui/lei/Lei **fece**	he/she/You did
noi **facemmo**	we did
voi **faceste**	you did
loro **fecero**	they did

Irregular Verbs in the *Passato Remoto*

Yes, you've heard me talk about them *mille volte* (a thousand times), and you're probably used to them by now: more irregular verbs. This is the polish stage of your linguistic journey.

Here's how some irregular verbs act in the *passato remoto*:

bere (to drink):	*bevvi, bevesti, bevve, bevemmo, beveste, bevvero*
chiedere (to ask):	*chiesi, chiedesti, chiese, chiedemmo, chiedeste, chiesero*
chiudere (to close):	*chiusi, chiudesti, chiuse, chiudemmo, chiudeste, chiusero*
dare (to give):	*diedi, desti, diede, demmo, deste, diedero*
dire (to say):	*dissi, dicesti, disse, dicemmo, diceste, dissero*

Dante wrote *The Divine Comedy* in 1307.
Dante scrisse La Divina Commedia *nel 1307.*

Cose Da Vedere

The following has been excerpted from a travel brochure promoting *la bellissima città di* San Gimignano. See if you can identify the use of the *passato remoto*:

> **Cose da vedere**
>
> *San Gimignano prende il nome dal vescovo di Modena morto nel 387. Nel 1099 divenne libero Comune. Combattè contro i vescovi di Volterra e le città vicine. La peste del 1348 e la successiva crisi portarono San Gimignano nel 1353 alla sottomissione a Firenze.*

Translation:

> San Gimignano takes its name from the Bishop of Modena who died in 387 A.D. In 1099, it became a free township. It fought against the bishops of Volterra and bordering cities. The plague of 1348 and successive crisis led to the submission of San Gimignano to Florence in 1353.

Before Once Upon a Time: *Il Trapassato Remoto*

As if you couldn't go any further back in time, there's one more version of the past used to talk about something that happened *before* "once upon a time": the *trapassato remoto* (a.k.a. the past anterior).

It's very easy to form the *trapassato remoto*, even if there's no English equivalent for this particular past tense. Just conjugate your helping verb in the *passato remoto* and attach your past participle.

You might see something like *fu stato* (he/she had been), or *ebbe mangiato* (he/she had eaten).

What's the *Storia* (History)?

If you're going to talk about the many notable historical and artistic periods of Italy's long *storia* (history), you'll need to know a few more terms, offered here chronologically:

Greek	*il periodo ellenistico*
Etruscan	*il periodo etrusco*
Roman	*il periodo romano*
Medieval	*il Medioevo*
Renaissance	*il Rinasciamento*
Byzantine	*il periodo bizantino*
Baroque and Rococo	*il Barocco e Roccocò*
Italy's unification	*il Risorgimento*
Twentieth century	*il Novecento*
Twenty-first century	*il ventunesimo secolo*

If you were to stretch out these times on a timeline, you'd begin to see how different periods correspond to each other. Now's as good a time as ever to seriously sit down and read up on *la storia d'arte* (the history of art). It's a massive undertaking, but if you break things down, it all starts to fit. History buffs don't have to have all the fun!

Advanced Study: Analyzing Ancient Texts

Auguri! You've come a long way! Now, enjoy the fruits of your labors. Let's analyze the following text written by San Francis d'Assisi and see how well you can decipher the intended meaning. You probably know a great deal more than what you might have expected when you began your studies with me.

LA BELLA LINGUA

Poet, animal advocate, and ecologist San Francis d'Assisi was a pensive, thoughtful man who felt his way through the world around him. The patron saint of animals, in Italy, and all of Europe, Francis is also known for having written his poems in the vernacular at a time when texts were all written in Latin and accessible to only those with means or power. (If you were low on the totem pole of medieval society, chances were you couldn't even write your name.) He was also alive and preaching when the Sufi poet Rumi was a boy. At a time when ideology and what side of the mountain you came from mattered greatly, both poets shared similar ideas about love, religion, color, and foot size. Whether you were a human or animal shouldn't matter; they believed we were all God's children.

Tips for Reading and Analyzing Translations

When analyzing Italian texts, especially older poems, it's difficult to translate for even the most accomplished of translators. Enjoy the sound of language as you read aloud. Use a pencil and mark the words that seem to make sense to you. Don't use a dictionary at first. Eventually, you'll come to appreciate the nuances of translation, and how much is up for interpretation. Translation is a true art form, but the translator is rarely given the accolades he or she deserves.

Then, after you've given it your best shot, read through the English translation.

Go back to the Italian and read through again, this time keeping in mind the gist of what you read in the translation. You want to savor the experience of chewing over texts that have transcended time and distance. Isolate the verbs; read through to the end of the Italian, and notice how the word order sometimes differs between the two languages.

The word count ratio to say the same thing between Italian and English is about 20 percent. Yes, that's right. It doesn't just sound like the Italians are speaking more, and longer, they *are*. English is essentially more efficient when it comes to conveying the same concepts.

As you read, enjoy your deepening awareness of the power of language and its ability to connect us all!

Il Cantico delle Creature (*The Canticle of Creatures*)

During the Middle Ages, there were still few or no rules about Italian grammar; every poet attempting to write in the language that was spoken around them (as opposed to Latin) had to make it up as they went along. The simplicity and straightforward quality of the following poem resonates even today. Note that back then, they wrote *ke* for *che* (that; what).

> *Il Cantico delle Creature*
>
> *Altissimu, onnipotente, bon, Signore,*
> *Tue so' le laude, la gloria, l'honore*
> *et onne benedictione.*
> *Ad te solo, Altissimo se konfano et nullo homo ene dignu te mentovare.*
> *Laudato sie, mi' Signore, cum tucte le tue creature,*
> *specialmente messer lo frate sole,*
> *lo quale iorno et allumini noi per loi;*

Et ellu è bellu e radiante cum grande splendore:
de te, altissimo, porta significatione.
Laudato si', mi' Signore, per sora luna e le stelle;
in celu l'ài formate clarite et pretiose et belle.
Laudato si', mi' Signore, per frate vento,
et per aere et nubilo et sereno et onne tempo,
per lo quale a le tue creature dai sustentamento.
Laudato si', mi' Signore, per sora acqua,
la quale è multo utile et humile
et pretiosa et casta.
Laudato si', mi' Signore, per frate focu,
per lo quale enallumini la nocte;
ed ello è bello et iocundo et robustoso et forte.
Laudato si', mi' Signore, per sora nostra matre terra,
la quale ne sustenta et governa,
et produce diversi fructi con coloriti fiori et herba.
Laudato si', mi' Signore, per quelli ke perdonano
per lo tuo amore,
et sostengo' infirmitate et tribulatione;
beati quelli kel sosterrano in pace,
ka da te, Altissimo, sirano incoronati.
Laudato si', mi' Signore, per sora
nostra morte corporale, da la quale nullu homo vivente po skappare:
guai acquelli ke morranno ne le peccata mortali;
beati quelli ke trovarà ne le tue
sanctissime voluntati,
ka la morte secunda nol farrà male.
Laudate et benedicete mi' Signore,
et reingratiate et serviateli
cum grande humiltate.

Here is the Saint's beautiful poem translated in English. When translating poetry, it's often necessary to interpret the poem in order to extract the precise meaning. There are many different translations with subtle differences among them:

The Canticle of Creatures

Most high, all powerfull, all good Lord
All praise is yours, all glory, all honour
and all blessing.
To you alone, Most High, do they belong and no human being is worthy to
pronounce your name.
Praised be You, my Lord, through all that you have made,
and first my lord brother Sun,
who brings the day and light you give us through him;
How beautiful is he, how radiant in all his splendour:
of you, Most High, he bears the likeness.
Praised be You, my Lord, through sister Moon and Stars; in the heaven you
have made them, bright, and precious and fair.
Praised be You, my Lord, through brother Wind,
and air and stormy and fair in all weather moods,
by which You cherish all that you have made.
Praised be You, my Lord, through sister Water,
so useful, humble, precious
and pure.
Praised be You, my Lord, through brother Fire,
through whom You light the night;
and he is beautiful and playful and robust and strong.
Praised be You, my Lord, through our sister mother Earth,
who sustains and governs us,
producing varied fruits with colored flowers and herbs.
Praised be You, my Lord, through those who grant pardon
for love of You,
and bear sickness and trial;
blessed are those who endure in peace,
by You, most High, they will be crowned.
Praised be You, my Lord, through our corporal sister Death,
from whom no mortal can escape:
woe to those who die in mortal sin;
blessed are they she finds doing
your will,
no second death can do them harm.
Praise and bless my Lord,
and give him thanks and serve him
with great humility.

Addio!

In Italian, to augur someone well, you can say *Addio*, which breaks down to "to God." It's used for saying good-bye with the distinct possibility you'll never see that person again, usually someone you've met on an airplane, on a *treno*, or in a waiting room. (Not excluding the occasional jilted lover!)

It's time for you to fly away, *uccellini miei*. Fly high, live well, love with a full heart, and drop me a line once in a while. Just be sure it's in **italiano***!* A hearty *mille grazie* to you for allowing me the *piacere* of accompanying you on this *viaggio*.

The Least You Need to Know

- The absolute past is used primarily in the written language and is very irregular.
- Translation should begin with identification of the verbs. Study the language in context.
- The word count ratio between Italian and English is about 20 percent. (Translation: It takes more words in Italian to say the same thing in English.)
- *The Canticle of Creatures* is one of the earliest poems written in the vernacular.
- *Addio* is used to say good-bye and wish someone well.

In the following word list, key elements are identified to help maximize your studies. Here's the key:

(f.) feminine noun

(m.) irregular masculine noun (includes nouns ending in -e, -a, and foreign words)

(pl.) irregular plural noun

(adj.) adjective

English to Italian

A

a, an *un, uno, un', una*

abandon, to *abbandonare*

abbey *abbazia (f.)*

able *capace*

able, to be (can) *potere*

aboard *bordo, a*

abolish, to *abolire*

about *circa*

about *di*

above, on *sopra*

above all *soprattutto*

abroad *all'estero*

absolutely *assolutamente*

academy *accademia (f.)*

accent *accento*

accept, to *accettare*

access *accesso*

accident *incidente (m.)*

accompany, to *accompagnare*

accomplish, to *compiere, superare*

accountant *contabile (m./f.)*

achieve, to *realizzare*

acoustic *acustico*

acquire, to *acquistare*

across *attraverso*

action *azione (f.)*

active *attivo*

activity *attività (f.)*

actor *attore*

actress *attrice (f.)*

ad *annuncio pubblicitario*

add, to *aggiungere (aggiunto)*

address *indirizzo*

adjective *aggettivo*

admire, to *ammirare*

admission charge *prezzo d'entrata*

adorable *adorabile*

adult *adulto*

advance, in *in anticipo*

advantage *vantaggio*

adventure *avventura (f.)*

adverb *avverbio*

advise, to *consigliare*

aerobics *aerobica (f.)*

affection *affetto*

affectionate *affettuoso, affezionato*

affirm, to *affermare*

after *dopo*

afternoon *pomeriggio*

again *ancora*

against *contro*

age *età (f.)*

agency *agenzia (f.)*

agent *agente (m./f.)*

aggressive *aggressivo*

agile *agile*

ago *fa*

agreement *accordo*

agriculture *agricoltura (f.)*

air *aria (f.)*

air conditioning *aria condizionata (f.)*

airplane *aereo*

airport *aeroporto*

alarm clock *sveglia (f.)*

alcohol *alcol (m.)*

alcoholic *alcolico*

alive *vivo*

All Saint's Day (November 1) *Ognissanti*

allergic *allergico*

allergy *allergia (f.)*

alley *vicolo*

almost *quasi*

alms *elemosina (f.)*

alone *solo*

alphabet *alfabeto*

already *già*

also *anche, inoltre, pure*

although *benché, sebbene*

always *sempre*

ambition *ambizione (f.)*

ambulance *ambulanza (f.)*

American *americano*

amphitheater *anfiteatro*

ample *ampio*

analysis *analisi (f.)*

ancestor *antenato*

anchovy *acciuga (f.)*

ancient *antico*

and *e, ed*

angry *arrabbiato*

animal *animale (m.)*

animated, lively *animato*

announce, to *annunciare*

answer *risposta (f.)*

antibiotics *gli antibiotici (m. pl.)*

antiques *antiquariato*

any *qualsiasi*

any *qualunque*

apartment *appartamento*

aperitif *aperitivo*

apologize, to *scusarsi*

appearance *aria (f.), apparizione (f.), apparenza (f.)*

appetizer *antipasto*

applaud, to *applaudire*

apple *mela (f.)*

appreciate, to *apprezzare*

approach, to *avvicinarsi*

approve of, to *approvare*

apricot *albicocca (f.)*

April *aprile*

aquarium *acquario*

archaeology *archeologia (f.)*

architect *architetto*

architecture *architettura (f.)*

area *area (f.)*

area code *prefisso*

argue, to *discutere (discusso), litigare*

aria *aria (f.)*

aristocratic *aristocratico*

arm *braccio (pl. le braccia)*

aroma *aroma (m.), odore (m.)*

around *intorno a*

arrival *arrivo*

arrive, to *arrivare*

art *arte (f.)*

arthritis *artrite (f.)*

artichoke *carciofo*

article *articolo*

artist *artista (m./f.)*

ashtray *portacenere (m.)*

ask, to *chiedere (chiesto)*

aspirin *aspirina (f.)*

assault, to *assaltare; assalire*

assistance *assistenza (f.)*

association *associazione (f.)*

Assumption Day (August 15) *Ferragosto*

astrology *astrologia (f.)*

astronaut *astronauta (m./f.)*

at *a, in*

at least *almeno*

athlete *atleta (m./f.)*

athletics *atletica (f.)*

ATM *Bancomat*

atrium *atrio (m.)*

attach, to *attaccare*

attack *attacco (m.)*

attention!/warning! *attenzione!*

attitude *atteggiamento*

attract, to *attirare*

attribute, to *attribuire*

August *agosto*

aunt *zia (f.)*

Australian *australiano*

Austrian *austriaco*

authoritarian *autoritario*

automatic *automatico*

automobile *macchina (f.), automobile (f.), auto (f.)*

autumn *autunno (m.)*

available *disponibile*

avalanche *valanga (f.)*

avoid, to *evitare*

awaken, to *svegliarsi*

away *via*

B

baby *bambino*

baby bottle *biberon (m.)*

bachelor *scapolo*

back, behind *indietro*

backpack *zaino*

backward *arretrato*

bacon *pancetta (f.)*

bad *male*

bag (purse) *borsa (f.)*

baker *fornaio*

balcony *balcone (m.)*

ball *palla (f.)*

bank *banca (f.)*

bar *bar (m.)*

barber *barbiere (m.)*

Baroque *barocco*

bartender *barista (m./f.)*

base *base (f.)*

basement *cantina (f.)*

basketball *pallacanestro, basket*

bathroom *bagno*

battery *batteria (f.), pila (f.)*

bay *baia (f.)*

be, to *essere (stato), stare (stato)*

beach *spiaggia (f.)*

bean *fagiolo*

bear *orso*

beard *barba (f.)*

beast *bestia (f.)*

beat, to *battere*

beauty *bellezza (f.)*

because *perché*

bed *letto*

beef *manzo*

beer *birra (f.)*

before *prima*

begin, to *iniziare, cominciare*

beginning *inizio*
behave, to *comportarsi*
behavior *comportamento*
behind *dietro*
believe, to *credere*
bell *campana (f.)*
bell pepper *peperone (m.)*
bell tower *campanile (m.)*
belong, to *appartenere*
belt *cintura (f.)*
bench *panchina (f.)*
beneath *sotto*
berth *cuccetta (f.)*
beside, next to *accanto a*
best *migliore*
best wishes! *auguri!*
bet, to *scommettere (scommesso)*
better *meglio*
between *tra*
beverage *bibita (f.)*
Bible *Bibbia (f.)*
big, large *grande*
bill *conto*
biodegradable *biodegradabile*
biology *biologia (f.)*
bird *uccello*
birth *nascita (f.)*
birthday *compleanno*
bishop *vescovo*
bitter *amaro*
black *nero*
blanket *coperta (f.)*
blind *cieco*
blond *biondo*
blood *sangue (m.)*
blouse *camicetta (f.)*
blue *blu*
boarding *imbarco*
boat *barca (f.)*
body *corpo*
boil, to *bollire*
bone *osso (pl. le ossa)*
book *libro*
bookstore *libreria (f.)*
boot *stivale (m.)*

border *frontiera (f.)*
boring *noioso*
born, to be *nascere (nato)*
boss *padrone/padrona (f.)*
both *entrambi, tutt'e due*
bottle *bottiglia (f.)*
bottom *fondo*
boulevard *viale (m.)*
box *scatola (f.)*
box (theater) *palco*
boy *ragazzo*
bra *reggiseno*
bracelet *braccialetto*
brain *cervello*
brand *marca (f.)*
brass *ottone (m.)*
bread *pane (m.)*
break, to *rompere (rotto)*
breakdown *guasto*
breakfast *prima colazione (f.)*
breath *respiro*
bridge *ponte (m.)*
brief *breve*
briefs *gli slip (m. pl.)*
bring, to *portare*
British *inglese*
broadcast, to *trasmettere (trasmesso)*
broken *rotto*
bronchitis *bronchite (f.)*
bronze *bronzo*
brooch *spilla (f.)*
broth *brodo*
brother *fratello*
brother-in-law *cognato*
brown *castano, marrone*
bruise *contusione (f.), livido*
brush *spazzola (f.)*
buffoon *buffone (m.)*
build, to *costruire*
building *edificio, palazzo*
bulletin *bollettino*
burn, to *bruciare*
bus *autobus (m.), corriera (f.), pullman (m.)*

busy *impegnato, occupato*
but *ma, però*
butcher *macellaio*
butcher shop *macelleria (f.)*
butter *burro*
button *bottone (m.)*
buy, to *comprare*
by *da, in*

C

cabin *cabina (f.)*
cable *cavo*
cable car *funivia (f.)*
cafeteria *mensa (f.)*
cake *torta (f.)*
call, to *chiamare*
call oneself, to *chiamarsi*
calm *calmo, sereno*
calm, to *calmare*
camera *macchina fotografica (f.)*
camping *campeggio*
Canadian *canadese*
cancer *cancro*
candidate *candidato*
candle *candela (f.)*
candy *caramella (f.)*
canyon *burrone (m.)*
cap *berretto*
capable *capace*
cape *mantello*
car *See* automobile.
car rental *autonoleggio*
card *carta (f.)*
care *cura (f.)*
career *carriera (f.), lavoro*
careful *attento*
carnation *garofano*
carpenter *falegname (m.)*
carriage *vagone (m.)*
carrot *carota (f.)*
cash *contanti (m. pl.)*
cash register *cassa (f.)*
castle *castello*
cat *gatto*
catalogue *catalogo*

category   *categoria (f.)*
cathedral   *cattedrale (f.)*
Catholic   *cattolico*
cave   *grotta (f.)*
CD   *cd* (pronounced *chee-dee*)
ceiling   *soffitto*
celebrate, to   *celebrare, festeggiare*
cemetery   *cimitero*
center   *centro*
central   *centrale*
century   *secolo*
ceramic   *ceramica (f.)*, *terracotta (f.)*
certain   *certo*
certificate   *certificato*
chain   *catena (f.)*
chair   *sedia (f.)*
challenge, to   *sfidare*
championship   *campionato*
change, to   *cambiare*
channel   *canale (m.)*
chaotic   *caotico*
chapel   *cappella (f.)*
character   *carattere (m.)*, *personaggio*
characteristic   *caratteristico*
check   *assegno*
check, to   *controllare*
cheek   *guancia (f.)*
cheese   *formaggio*
cherry   *ciliegia (f.)*
chess   *gli scacchi (m. pl.)*
chest   *petto*
chimney   *camino*
chin   *mento*
China   *Cina*
Chinese   *cinese*
chocolate   *cioccolata (f.)*
choose, to   *scegliere (scelto)*
chorus (choir)   *coro*
Christian   *cristiano*
Christmas, Merry   *Natale, Buon*
church   *chiesa (f.)*
cigar   *sigaro*
cigarette   *sigaretta (f.)*

cinema   *cinema (m.)*
circle   *circolo*
circus   *circo*
citizen   *cittadino*
citizenship   *cittadinanza (f.)*
city   *città*
civic   *civico*
civil   *civile*
class   *classe (f.)*
classical   *classico*
classification   *classificazione (f.)*
clause   *clausola (f.)*
clean, to   *pulire*
clear   *chiaro*
clever   *furbo (slang), intelligente*
client   *cliente (m./f.)*
cliff   *costiera (f.), rupe (f.)*
climate   *clima (m.)*
cloakroom   *guardaroba (m.)*
clock   *orologio*
close, to   *chiudere (chiuso)*
closed   *chiuso*
clothing   *abbigliamento*
cloud   *nuvola (f.)*
coast   *costa (f.)*
coat   *cappotto, giubbotto*
coffee   *caffè (m.)*
coin   *moneta (f.)*
cold   *freddo (adj.), raffreddore (m.)*
collaborate, to   *collaborare*
colleague   *collega (m./f.)*
colony   *colonia (f.)*
color   *colore (m.)*
comb, to   *pettinare*
come, to   *venire*
comfort   *conforto*
commandment   *comandamento*
communicate, to   *comunicare*
communism   *comunismo*
community   *comunità (f.)*
company   *azienda (f.), ditta (f.), società (f.)*
comparison   *paragone (m.)*
complain, to   *lamentarsi*

compliment   *complimento*
compose, to   *comporre (composto)*
composition   *composizione (f.)*
concentration   *concentrazione (f.)*
concept   *concetto*
conception   *concezione (f.)*
concert   *concerto*
conclude, to   *concludere (concluso)*
condition   *condizione (f.)*
condom   *profilattico, preservativo*
condominium   *condominio*
conference   *conferenza (f.), congresso*
confess, to   *confessare*
conflict   *conflitto*
congratulations!   *congratulazioni! auguri!*
conjugate, to   *coniugare*
conjugation   *coniugazione (f.)*
connection   *coincidenza (f.)*
conquest, to   *conquistare*
consecutive   *consecutivo*
consequence   *conseguenza (f.)*
consider, to   *considerare*
console, to   *consolare*
consonant   *consonante (f.)*
constitution   *costituzione (f.)*
consumption   *consumo*
contact   *contatto*
contact, to   *contattare*
contain, to   *contenere*
contemporary   *contemporaneo*
contest   *concorso, gara (f.)*
continent   *continente (m.)*
continue, to   *continuare*
contraceptive   *contraccettivo*
contrast   *contrasto*
convenient   *comodo, pratico*
convent   *convento*
conversation   *conversazione (f.)*
convince, to   *convincere (convinto)*
cook, to   *cucinare, cuocere (cotto)*
cooked   *cotto*
cookie   *biscotto*
copper   *rame (m.)*

copy   *copia (f.)*

cork   *tappo*

corkscrew   *cavatappi (m.)*

corn   *mais (m.)*

cornmeal   *polenta (f.)*

correct   *corretto*

correct, to   *correggere (corretto)*

correspond, to   *corrispondere (corrisposto)*

cosmetics   *cosmetici (m. pl.)*

cosmetics shop   *profumeria (f.)*

cost   *costo, prezzo*

cost, to   *costare*

costly   *costoso*

costume   *costume (m.)*

cotton   *cotone (m.)*

cough   *tosse (f.)*

count   *conte, conto*

count, to   *contare*

counter   *banco, sportello*

countess   *contessa (f.)*

country   *campagna (f.), paese (m.)*

couple   *coppia (f.)*

courage   *coraggio*

course   *corso*

court   *corte (f.)*

courteous   *cortese*

cousin   *cugino/cugina (f.)*

cover charge   *coperto*

cow   *mucca (f.), vacca (f.)*

crazy   *matto, pazzo*

cream   *crema (f.), panna (f.)*

create, to   *creare*

creation   *creazione (f.)*

credit   *credito*

credit card   *carta di credito (f.)*

crib   *culla (f.)*

crisis   *crisi (f.)*

cross   *croce (f.)*

cross, to   *attraversare*

cross-country skiing   *sci di fondo*

crossing   *incrocio*

crowded   *affollato*

cruise   *crociera (f.)*

crunchy   *croccante*

cry, to   *piangere (pianto)*

Cuban   *cubano*

cube   *cubo*

cultivate, to   *coltivare*

cultural   *culturale*

culture   *cultura (f.)*

cup   *coppa (f.), tazza (f.)*

curiosity   *curiosità (f.)*

curious   *curioso*

curly   *riccio*

currency   *valuta (f.), moneta (f.)*

current event   *attualità (f.)*

curtain   *tenda (f.)*

curve   *curva (f.)*

customs   *dogana (f.)*

cut, to   *tagliare*

cute, pretty   *carino*

cutlet   *cotoletta (f.), costoletta (f.)*

cycling   *ciclismo*

D

daddy   *papà*

dairy store   *latteria (f.)*

dam   *diga (f.)*

damaged   *danneggiato*

damned   *dannato*

dance   *ballo, danza (f.)*

danger   *pericolo*

dangerous   *pericoloso*

dark   *buio, scuro (adj.)*

darn!   *accidenti!*

date   *data (f.); appuntamento*

daughter   *figlia (f.)*

daughter-in-law   *nuora (f.)*

day   *giorno, giornata*

dead   *morto*

deaf   *sordo*

dear   *caro*

death   *morte (f.)*

December   *dicembre*

decide, to   *decidere (deciso)*

decision   *decisione (f.)*

declare, to   *dichiarare*

decrease, to   *diminuire*

dedicate, to   *dedicare*

defect   *difetto*

defend   *difendere (difeso)*

define, to   *definire*

definition   *definizione (f.)*

degree   *grado (temp.), laurea (f.)—also diploma (m.)*

delay   *ritardo*

delicious   *delizioso*

democracy   *democrazia (f.)*

democratic   *democratico*

demonstrate, to   *dimostrare*

Denmark   *Danimarca (f.)*

density   *densità (f.)*

dentist   *dentista (m./f.)*

depart, to   *partire*

department   *dipartimento*

department store   *grande magazzino*

departure   *partenza (f.)*

depend, to   *dipendere (dipeso)*

descend, to (get off)   *scendere (sceso)*

deserve, to   *meritare*

desk   *scrivania (f.)*

dessert   *dolce (m.)*

destination   *destinazione (f.)*

destiny   *destino*

destroy, to   *distruggere (distrutto)*

detergent   *detersivo*

detour   *deviazione (f.)*

develop, to   *sviluppare*

diabetes   *diabete (m.)*

dialogue   *dialogo, discorso*

diamond   *diamante (m.)*

diaper   *pannolino*

diarrhea   *diarrea (f.)*

dictatorship   *dittatura (f.)*

diction   *dizione (f.)*

dictionary   *dizionario*

die, to   *morire (morto)*

diet   *dieta (f.)*

difference   *differenza (f.)*

different   *differente, diverso*

difficult   *difficile*

digest, to *digerire*

digestion *digestione (f.)*

dine, to *cenare*

dining room *sala da pranzo (f.)*

dinner *cena (f.)*

direct *diretto*

direction *direzione (f.),
indicazione (f.)*

director *direttore (m.)/direttrice
(f.), regista (m./f.)*

dirt *terra (f.)*

dirty *sporco*

discothèque *discoteca (f.)*

discount *sconto*

discover, to *scoprire (scoperto)*

discuss, to *discutere(discusso)*

discussion *discorso, discussione
(f.)*

distance *distanza (f.)*

distinguish, to *distinguere
(distinto)*

distracted *distratto*

dive *tuffo*

divide, to *dividere (diviso)*

division *divisione (f.)*

divorced *divorziato*

do, to *fare (fatto)*

dock *molo*

doctor *dottore (m.)/dottoressa (f.)
medico*

document *documento*

dog *cane (m.)*

dollar *dollaro*

dolphin *delfino*

dome *cupola (f.), duomo*

door *porta (f.)*

doorbell *campanello*

double *doppio*

down *giù*

dozen *dozzina (f.)*

draw, to (design) *disegnare*

drawing *disegno*

dream, to *sognare*

dress *vestito*

dress oneself, to *vestirsi*

drink, to *bere (bevuto)*

drive, to *guidare*

driver's license *patente (f.)*

drown, to *annegare*

drug *droga (f.)*

druggist *droghiere (m.)*

drugstore *drogheria (f.)*

drum *tamburo*

dry *asciutto, secco*

dry cleaner *lavanderia a secco,
tintoria (f.)*

dub, to *doppiare*

duchess *duchessa (f.)*

duck *anatra (f.)*

duke *duca (m.)*

during *durante, mentre*

dust *polvere (f.)*

DVD *DVD* (pronounced
dee-vu-dee)

E

each *ciascuno, ogni, ognuno*

eagle *aquila (f.)*

ear *orecchio*

earn, to *guadagnare*

earrings *gli orecchini (m. pl.)*

earth *terra (f.)*

east *est, Oriente*

Easter, Happy *Pasqua, Buona*

Easter Monday *lunedì
dell'Angelo, Pasquetta (f.)*

easy *facile*

eat, to *mangiare*

eat breakfast, to *fare la prima
colazione, fare colazione*

eat dinner, to *cenare*

eat lunch, to *pranzare*

economy *economia (f.)*

effect *effetto*

efficient *efficiente*

effort *fatica (f.), sforzo*

egg *uovo (pl. le uova)*

eggplant *melanzana (f.)*

Egypt *Egitto*

eight *otto*

eighteen *diciotto*

eighth *ottavo*

eighty *ottanta*

elderly *anziano*

election *elezione (f.)*

electricity *elettricità (f.)*

elegant *elegante*

element *elemento*

elevator *ascensore (m.)*

eleven *undici*

eliminate, to *eliminare*

embassy *ambasciata (f.)*

embroider, to *ricamare*

emergency *emergenza (f.)*

emigrate, to *emigrare*

empire *impero*

empty *vuoto*

end *fine (f.)*

enemy *nemico*

energetic *dinamico*

engineer *ingegnere*

England *Inghilterra (f.)*

English *inglese*

engraved *inciso*

enjoy oneself, to *divertirsi*

enormous *enorme*

enough *abbastanza, basta!*

enter, to *entrare*

entrance *entrata (f.), ingresso*

entrepreneur *imprenditore (m.)*

envelope *busta (f.)*

environment *ambiente (m.)*

Epiphany (January 6) *Befana
(f.), Epifania (f.)*

equipped *attrezzato*

error *errore (m.)*

escape, to *scappare*

essay *saggio*

essence *essenza (f.)*

essential *essenziale*

establish, to *stabilire*

et cetera *eccetera*

Europe *Europa (f.)*

even *persino*

evening *sera (f.), serata*

event *avvenimento, evento*

ever *mai*
every *ogni*
everybody *ognuno*
everyone *tutti*
everything, all *tutto*
everywhere *dappertutto*
evil *cattivo, male*
evoke, to *evocare*
exact *esatto*
exactly *esattamente*
exaggerate, to *esagerare*
exam *esame (m.)*
examine, to *esaminare*
excavate, to *scavare*
excellent *eccellente, ottimo*
except *eccetto*
excerpt *estratto*
exchange *cambio, scambio*
exchange, to *scambiare*
exclude, to *escludere (escluso)*
excursion *escursione (f.), gita (f.)*
excuse, to *scusare*
excuse me! *permesso!*
exercise *ginnastica (f.)*
exist, to *esistere (esistito)*
exit *uscita (f.)*
exit, to *uscire*
exotic *esotico*
expense *spesa (f.)*
expensive *caro*
experience *esperienza (f.)*
expiration *scadenza (f.)*
explain, to *spiegare*
explode, to *esplodere (esploso)*
export, to *esportare*
express *espresso*
express, to *esprimere (espresso)*
expression *espressione (f.)*
eye *occhio (pl. gli occhi)*
eyeglasses *occhiali (m. pl.)*

F

fable *favola (f.), fiaba (f.)*
fabric *stoffa (f.), tessuto*
face *faccia (f.), viso*

fact *fatto*
factory *fabbrica (f.)*
fair *fiera (f.)*
faith *fede (f.)*
fall, to *cadere*
fall in love, to *innamorarsi*
family *famiglia (f.)*
famous *famoso*
fantasy *fantasia (f.)*
far *lontano*
far-sighted *presbite*
fare *tariffa (f.)*
farm *fattoria (f.)*
farmer *contadino/contadina (f.)*
fascinate, to *affascinare*
fascism *fascismo*
fasten, to *allacciare*
fat *grasso*
father *padre (m.)*
father-in-law *suocero*
faucet *rubinetto*
fear *paura (f.)*
Feast of the
  Assumption *Assunzione (f.)*
feather *piuma (f.)*
February *febbraio*
feel, to *sentirsi*
feeling *sentimento, sensazione (f.)*
felt *feltro*
ferry *traghetto*
fever *febbre (f.)*
fiancé *fidanzato*
fiancée *fidanzata (f.)*
field *campo, prato*
fifteen *quindici*
fifth *quinto*
fifty *cinquanta*
fight, to *combattere*
filet *filetto*
fill out, to (a form) *riempire*
fill up, to (a gas tank) *fare il
  pieno*
film *film (m.), pellicola (f.)*
filter *filtro*
finally *finalmente*

finance *finanza (f.)*
finance, to *finanziare*
find, to *trovare*
fine *multa (f.)*
finger *dito (pl. le dita)*
finish, to *finire*
fire *fuoco*
fire, to *licenziare*
firefighter *pompiere (m.), vigile
  del fuoco (m.)*
fireplace *caminetto*
firm *azienda (f.), fisso (adj.)*
first *primo*
first aid *pronto soccorso*
fiscal *fiscale*
fish *pesce (m.)*
fish store *pescheria (f.)*
fist *pugno*
five *cinque*
flea *pulce (f.)*
flight *volo*
floor *pavimento, piano*
Florence *Firenze*
florist *fioraio*
flour *farina (f.)*
flower *fiore (m.)*
flu *influenza (f.)*
fly *mosca (f.)*
fly, to *volare*
foam *schiuma (f.)*
fog *nebbia (f.)*
follow, to *seguire*
food *cibo*
foot *piede (m.)*
for *per*
foreigner *straniero/straniera (f.)*
forest *foresta (f.)*
forgive, to *perdonare*
fork *forchetta (f.)*
form *forma (f.), modulo*
formal *formale*
formulate, to *formulare*
fortress *fortezza (f.), rocca (f.)*
fortune *fortuna (f.)*
forty *quaranta*

forward   *avanti*
founded   *fondato*
fountain   *fontana (f.)*
four   *quattro*
fourteen   *quattordici*
fourth   *quarto*
fox   *volpe (f.)*
fragile   *fragile*
France   *Francia (f.)*
free   *libero*
free of charge   *gratis*
French   *francese*
frequent, to   *frequentare*
fresh   *fresco*
friar   *frate (m.)*
Friday   *venerdì*
fried   *fritto*
friend   *amico/amica (f.)*
friendship   *amicizia (f.)*
frighten, to   *spaventare*
frog   *rana (f.)*
from   *di, da*
fruit   *frutta (f.)*
frying pan   *padella (f.)*
fulfillment   *adempimento*
full   *pieno*
function, to   *funzionare*
funeral   *funerale (m.)*
funny   *buffo*
fur   *pelliccia (f.)*
furnishings   *arredamento*
furrier shop   *pellicceria (f.)*
future   *futuro*

G

gain weight, to   *ingrassare*
game   *gioco, partita (f.)*
game room   *salagiochi (f.)*
garage   *garage (m.)*
garden   *giardino, orto*
garlic   *aglio*
gas pump   *distributore di benzina (m.)*
gas tank   *serbatoio*
gasoline   *benzina (f.)*

gate   *cancello*
generous   *generoso*
genesis   *genesi (f.)*
genre   *genere (m.)*
geography   *geografia (f.)*
German   *tedesco*
Germany   *Germania*
gerund   *gerundio*
get drunk, to   *ubriacarsi*
get on, to (climb)   *salire*
get up, to   *alzarsi*
ghost   *anima, fantasma (m.)*
gift   *regalo, dono*
girl   *ragazza (f.), fanciulla (f.)* (Tuscany)
give, to   *dare*
give, to (a present)   *regalare, donare*
glad   *contento*
gladly!   *volentieri!*
glance   *occhiata (f.)*
glass (drinking)   *bicchiere (m.)*
glass (material)   *vetro*
gloves   *guanti (m. pl.)*—also singular *guanto*
go, to   *andare*
goat   *capra (f.)*
god; God   *dio; Dio*
goddess   *dea (f.)*
godfather   *padrino*
gold   *oro*
good   *bravo (adj.)* (a good person); *buono (adj.)*
good day   *buongiorno*
gothic   *gotico*
government   *governo*
grace   *grazia (f.)*
grade   *voto*
gram   *grammo*
grammar   *grammatica (f.)*
granddaughter   *nipote (f.)*
grandfather   *nonno*
grandmother   *nonna (f.)*
grandson   *nipote (m.)*
grapefruit   *pompelmo*
grapes   *uva (f.)*

grappa   *grappa (f.)*
gravity   *gravità*
gray   *grigio*
Greek   *greco*
green   *verde*
greengrocer's   *fruttivendolo*
greet, to   *salutare*
grill   *griglia (f.)*
grilled   *alla griglia*
groceries   *alimentari (m. pl.)*
ground   *terra*
ground floor   *pianterreno*
group   *gruppo*
grow, to   *crescere (cresciuto)*
guarantee, to   *garantire*
guess, to   *indovinare*
guest   *ospite (m./f.)*
guide   *guida (f.)*
guitar   *chitarra (f.)*
gym   *palestra (f.)*
gym suit   *tuta da ginnastica (f.)*
gynecologist   *ginecologo/ ginecologa (f.)*

H

habit   *abitudine (f.)*
hair   *pelo*
hair (on head)   *capelli (m. pl.)*
hair dryer   *fon (m.)*
half   *metà, mezzo (adj.)*
hall   *sala (f.)*
ham   *prosciutto cotto*
hand   *mano (f.) (pl. le mani)*
handle   *maniglia (f.)*
hanger   *gruccia (f.), stampella (f.)*
happen, to   *capitare, succedere (successo)*
happiness   *allegria (f.), felicità (f.)*
happy   *allegro, felice*
Happy birthday!   *Buon compleanno!*
Happy Easter!   *Buona Pasqua!*
Happy holidays!   *Buone Feste!*
Happy New Year!   *Buon Anno!*
harbor   *porto*

hard *duro*

haste *fretta (f.)*

hat *cappello*

hate, to *odiare*

have, to *avere*

have to, to (must) *dovere*

hazel nut *nocciola (f.)*

he *lui, egli*

head *testa (f.)*

headlight *faro*

health *salute (f.)*

healthy *sano*

hear, to *sentire, udire*

heart *cuore (m.)*

heart attack *infarto*

heat *riscaldamento*

heaven *cielo, paradiso*

heavy *pesante*

hectogram *ettogrammo (abb. etto)*

height *altezza (f.)*

helicopter *elicottero*

hell *inferno*

hello *ciao, buongiorno, Pronto? (telephone)*

helmet *casco, elmetto*

help, to *aiutare*

help! *aiuto!*

hen *gallina (f.)*

here *ecco, qua, qui*

hernia *ernia (f.)*

hide, to *nascondere (nascosto)*

highway *autostrada (f.)*

hill *collina (f.)*

hire, to *assumere (assunto)*

history *storia (f.)*

hitchhiking *autostop (m.)*

hobby *hobby (m.), passatempo*

holiday *festa (f.)*

Holland *Olanda*

homeland *patria (f.)*

homemade *della casa, fatto in casa*

homework *compito*

honest *onesto*

honey *miele (m.)*

honeymoon *luna di miele (f.)*

honor *onore (m.)*

hope *speranza (f.)*

hope, to *sperare*

horoscope *oroscopo*

horse *cavallo*

horse riding *equitazione (f.)*

hospital *ospedale (m.)*

hostel *ostello*

hot *caldo*

hotel *albergo, hotel (m.)*

hour *ora (f.)*

house *casa (f.)*

housewife *casalinga (f.)*

how *come*

how much? *quanto?*

however *comunque, tuttavia*

hug, to *abbracciare*

human *umano*

humble *umile*

humidity *umidità (f.)*

humor *umore (m.)*

hunger *fame (f.)*

husband *marito*

hymn *inno*

I

I *io*

ice *ghiaccio*

ice cream *gelato*

ice-cream parlor *gelateria (f.)*

idea *idea (f.)*

ideal *ideale (m.)*

identification card *carta d'identità (f.)*

identify, to *identificare*

identity *identità (f.)*

idiom *idioma (m.)*

idol *idolo*

if *se*

ignorant *ignorante*

ignore, to *ignorare*

illness *malattia (f.)*

illustrate, to *illustrare*

illustration *illustrazione (f.)*

image *immagine (f.)*

imagination *immaginazione (f.)*

imagine, to *immaginare*

imitation *imitazione*

immaculate *immacolato*

immediately *subito*

immense *immenso*

immigration *immigrazione (f.)*

imperative *imperativo*

imperfect *imperfetto*

import, to *importare*

important *importante*

impossible *impossibile*

impression *impressione (f.)*

improve, to *migliorare*

in *a, in*

in a hurry *in fretta*

in care of (c/o) *presso*

in fact *infatti*

in front of *davanti a*

in season *di stagione*

include, to *includere (incluso)*

increase, to *aumentare*

incredible *incredibile*

indefinite *indefinito*

independence *indipendenza (f.)*

index *indice (m.)*

India *India*

Indian *indiano*

indicate, to *indicare*

indigestion *indigestione (f.)*

indirect *indiretto*

indispensable *indispensabile*

indoor *dentro, al coperto*

industry *industria (f.)*

inexpensive *economico*

infection *infezione (f.)*

inferior *inferiore*

infinitive *infinito*

inflammation *infiammazione (f.)*

inflation *inflazione (f.)*

inform, to *informare*

information *informazione (f.)*

information office *ufficio informazioni*

ingredient *ingrediente (m.)*

inhabitant *abitante (m./f.)*

injection *iniezione (f.), puntura (f.)*

injury *danno, ferita (f.)*

inn *pensione (f.), locanda (f.)*

insect *insetto*

insect bite *puntura (f.)*

insecure *insicuro*

insert, to *inserire*

inside *dentro*

insist, to *insistere*

inspiration *ispirazione (f.)*

instead *invece*

institute *istituto*

instruction *istruzione (f.)*

insulin *insulina (f.)*

insurance *assicurazione (f.)*

insure, to *assicurare*

intelligent *intelligente*

intend, to *intendere (inteso)*

intention *intenzione (f.)*

interesting *interessante*

intermission *intermezzo, intervallo*

internal *interno, dentro*

international *internazionale*

interpret, to *interpretare*

interpreter *interprete (m./f.)*

interrupt, to *interrompere (interrotto)*

interval *intervallo*

interview *intervista (f.); colloquio*

introduce, to *introdurre (introdotto)*

invitation *invito*

invite, to *invitare*

Ireland *Irlanda (f.)*

Irish *irlandese*

iron *ferro* (steel), *ferro da stiro*

irregular *irregolare*

is *è*

island *isola (f.)*

issue *questione (f.)*

issued *rilasciato*

Italian ***italiano***

Italy *Italia (f.)*

itinerary *itinerario*

ivy *edera (f.)*

J

jack (car) *cric (m.)*

jacket *giacca (f.)*

jail *carcere (m.)*

January *gennaio*

Japan *Giappone*

Japanese *giapponese*

jeans *jeans*

Jesus *Gesù*

jeweler's *oreficeria (f.)*

jewelry store *gioielleria (f.)*

Jewish *ebreo*

joke *barzelletta (f.)*

joke, to *scherzare*

journalist *giornalista (m./f.)*

joy *gioia (f.)*

judge, to *giudicare*

juice *succo*

July *luglio*

June *giugno*

just *giusto, proprio*

K

keep, to *tenere*

ketchup *ketchup (m.)*

key *chiave (f.)*

kill, to *uccidere (ucciso)*

kilogram *chilogrammo (abb. chilo)*

kilometer *chilometro*

kind *gentile*

kindergarten *asilo*

kindness *gentilezza (f.)*

king *re*

kiss *bacio*

kiss, to *baciare*

knife *coltello*

knock, to *bussare*

know, to (someone) *conoscere (conosciuto)*

know, to (something) *sapere*

knowledge *conoscenza (f.)*

kosher *kosher*

L

lace *merletto*

lack, to (be missing) *mancare*

lake *lago*

lamb *agnello*

lamp *lampada (f.)*

land, to *sbarcare*

landing *atterraggio*

landlord *padrone di casa (m.)*

lane *corsia (f.)*

language *lingua*

large *grande, grosso*

last *scorso, ultimo*

last, to *durare*

late *tardi*

Latin *latino*

laugh, to *ridere (riso)*

laundry *bucato*

laundry service *lavanderia (f.)*

law *Diritto, giurisprudenza (f.), legge (f.)*

lawyer *avvocato*

lazy *pigro*

lead, to *condurre (condotto)*

leaf *foglia (f.)*

learn, to *imparare*

leather *cuoio, pelle (f.)*

leave, to *partire*

leave (behind), to *lasciare*

left *sinistro*

leg *gamba (f.)*

lemon *limone (m.)*

lemonade *limonata (f.)*

lend, to *prestare*

length *lunghezza (f.)*

leopard *leopardo*

less *meno*

lesson *lezione (f.)*

letter *lettera (f.)*

lettuce *lattuga (f.)*
level *livello*
liberty *libertà (f.)*
license *patente (f.)*
license plate *targa (f.)*
lie down, to *sdraiarsi*
life *vita (f.)*
light *luce (f.)*
light, to *accendere (acceso)*
lightbulb *lampadina (f.)*
lightning flash *lampo, fulmine (m., weather)*
line *linea (f.)*
linen *lino*
linguistics *linguistica (f.)*
lip *labbro; le labbra (pl.)*
liquor *liquore (m.)*
list *elenco*
listen to, to *ascoltare*
liter *litro*
literature *letteratura (f.)*
little *piccolo, (a little) un po'*
live, to *abitare, vivere (vissuto)*
lively *vivace*
liver *fegato*
living room *salotto, soggiorno*
load, to *caricare*
loaf *pagnotta (f.)*
loan *mutuo*
lobster *aragosta (f.)*
local *locale*
lodge, to *alloggiare*
logistics *logistica (f.)*
long *lungo*
long-distance call *interurbana (f.)*
look, to *guardare*
lose, to *perdere (perso)*
lose weight, to *dimagrire*
lost and found *ufficio oggetti smarriti*
lotion *lozione (f.)*
love *amore (m.)*
love, to *amare*
lunch *pranzo*

lung *polmone (m.)*
luxury *lusso*

M

magazine *rivista (f.)*
magic *magia (f.); magico (adj.)*
magnificent *magnifico*
maid *domestica (f.)*
maiden name *nome da nubile*
mail *posta (f.)*
mail, to *inviare, spedire*
mailbox *cassetta postale (f.)*
maintain, to *mantenere*
majority *maggioranza (f.)*
man *uomo*
manage, to *dirigere (diretto)*
management *amministrazione (f.)*
manager *dirigente (m./f.)*
manner *maniera (f.), modo*
manufacture, to *fabbricare*
map *carta (f.), mappa (f.)*
marble *marmo*
March *marzo*
marina *marina (f.), lido*
mark, to *segnare*
market *mercato*
marmalade *marmellata (f.)*
married *sposato*
marry, to *sposare*
marvelous *meraviglioso*
masculine *maschile*
Mass *messa (f.)*
matches *fiammiferi (m. pl.)*
mathematics *matematica (f.)*
matrimony *matrimonio*
maximum *massimo*
May *maggio*
maybe *forse*
mayor *sindaco*
me *mi, a me*
meadow *prato*
meal *pasto*
meaning *significato, senso*
means *mezzo*

measure *misura (f.)*
meat *carne (f.)*
meatball *polpetta (f.)*
mechanic *meccanico*
medicine *medicina (f.)*
meet, to *incontrare*
meeting *congresso, riunione (f.)*
melon *melone (m.)*
mentality *mentalità (f.)*
menu *lista (f.), menù*
merchandise *merce (f.)*
merchant *mercante (m./f.)*
message *messaggio*
messenger *corriere*
metal *metallo*
method *metodo*
Mexico *Messico*
Middle Ages *Medioevo*
midnight *mezzanotte (f.)*
migraine *emicrania (f.)*
mile *miglio (pl. le miglia)*
milk *latte (m.)*
mind *mente (f.)*
minister *ministro*
minority *minoranza (f.)*
mint *menta (f.)*
minute *minuto*
mirror *specchio*
misfortune *disgrazia (f.)*
misfortune, bad luck *sfortuna (f.)*
miss, young lady *signorina (f.)*
mix, to *mischiare*
model *modello*
modern *moderno*
modest *modesto*
mom, mother *mamma (f.); madre*
moment *momento; attimo*
monastery *monastero*
Monday *lunedì*
money *denaro, i soldi (m. pl.)*
money exchange office *ufficio cambio*
money order *vaglia postale (m.)*

month   *mese (m.)*
monthly   *mensile*
monument   *monumento*
moon   *luna (f.)*
more   *più*
more than, in addition to   *oltre a*
morning   *mattina (f.)*
morsel, nibble   *boccone (m.)*
mosaic   *mosaico*
mosquito   *zanzara (f.)*
mother   *madre (f.)*
mother-in-law   *suocera (f.)*
motive   *motivo*
motor   *motore (m.)*
motorcycle   *motocicletta (f.)*
mountain   *montagna (f.)*
mourn, to   *lamentare*
mouse   *topo*
mouth   *bocca (f.)*
movie director   *regista (m./f.)*
Mr.   *signore (m.)*
Mrs.   *signora (f.)*
much   *molto*
municipality   *comune (m.)*
muscle   *muscolo*
museum   *museo*
mushroom   *fungo*
music   *musica (f.)*
musician   *musicista (m./f.)*
Muslim   *musulmano*
mustard   *senape (f.)*
mute   *muto*
myth   *mito*

N

name   *nome (m.)*
name of spouse   *nome del coniuge*
napkin   *salvietta (f.), tovagliolo*
narrative   *narrativa (f.)*
nation   *nazione (f.)*
nationality   *nazionalità (f.)*
native language   *lingua madre (f.)*
natural   *naturale*

nature   *natura (f.)*
nature preserve   *riserva naturale (f.)*
nausea   *nausea (f.)*
near   *vicino*
near-sighted   *miope*
necessary   *necessario*
necessity   *necessità (f.)*
neck   *collo*
necklace   *collana (f.)*
need   *bisogno*
need, to   *avere bisogno di*
negative   *negativo*
neighbor   *vicino/vicina (f.)*
neighborhood   *quartiere (m.)*
neither   *neppure*
neither ... nor   *né ... né*
nephew   *nipote*
nervous   *nervoso*
nest   *nido*
never   *mai*
new   *nuovo*
news   *notizia (f.)*
news program   *telegiornale (m.)*
newspaper   *giornale (m.), quotidiano*
newspaper vendor   *giornalaio*
newsstand   *edicola (f.)*
next   *prossimo*
nice   *simpatico*
niece   *nipote*
night   *notte (f.)*
nightmare   *incubo*
nine   *nove*
nineteen   *diciannove*
ninety   *novanta*
ninth   *nono*
no entrance   *vietato l'ingresso*
no one   *nessuno*
no parking   *divieto di sosta*
nocturne   *notturno*
noisy   *rumoroso*
noon   *mezzogiorno*
normal   *normale*
north   *nord*

Norway   *Norvegia*
nose   *naso*
not   *non*
not even   *neanche, nemmeno*
notebook   *quaderno*
nothing   *niente, nulla*
notwithstanding   *nonostante*
noun   *nome (m.)*
novel   *romanzo*
November   *novembre*
now   *adesso, ora*
number   *numero*
nurse   *infermiera (f.)*

O

object   *oggetto*
obligation   *obbligo*
oblige, to   *obbligare*
obsession   *mania (f.)*
obtain, to   *ottenere*
obvious   *ovvio*
occasion   *occasione (f.)*
occupy, to   *occupare*
ocean   *oceano*
October   *ottobre*
of   *di*
offer   *offerta (f.)*
office   *ufficio*
often   *spesso*
oil   *olio*
old   *vecchio*
olive   *oliva (f.)*
on   *su*
on board   *a bordo*
on purpose   *apposta*
one   *uno*
one hundred   *cento*
one-way street   *senso unico*
onion   *cipolla (f.)*
only   *solamente*
open   *aperto*
open, to   *aprire (aperto)*
operation   *operazione (f.)*
opinion   *opinione (f.)*
opposite   *opposto; contrario*

optician *ottico*

or *o, oppure*

orange *arancia (f.)*

order *ordine (m.)*

order, to *ordinare*

ordinal *ordinale*

oregano *origano*

origin *origine (f.)*

original *originale*

other *altro*

outdoor *all'aperto*

outfit *abito*

outside *fuori*

oven *forno*

overcoat *cappotto, soprabito*

overdone *scotto, troppo cotto*

owner *proprietario*

P

package *pacco*

page *pagina (f.)*

pain *dolore (m.)*

paint *vernice (f.)*

paint, to *dipingere (dipinto)*

painter *pittore/pittrice (f.)*

painting *pittura (f.), quadro*

pair *paio (pl. le paia)*

panorama *panorama (m.)*

pants *pantaloni (m. pl.)*

paper *carta (f.)*

paradise *paradiso*

parents *genitori (m. pl.)*

park *parco*

parking lot *parcheggio*

parsley *prezzemolo*

part *parte (f.)*

participate, to *partecipare*

pass, to *passare*

passing *sorpasso*

passion *passione (f.)*

passport *passaporto*

past *passato*

pasta *pasta (f.)*

pastry shop *pasticceria (f.)*

path *sentiero, via (f.)*

paw *zampa (f.)*

pay, to *pagare*

payment *pagamento*

pea *pisello*

peace *pace (f.)*

peach *pesca (f.)*

peak *picco*

peanut *nocciolina (f.)*

pear *pera (f.)*

pedagogy *didattica (f.)*

pen *penna (f.)*

penalty *multa (f.), pena (f.)*

pencil *matita (f.)*

peninsula *penisola (f.)*

people *gente (f.)*

pepper *pepe (m.)*

percentage *percento, percentuale (f.)*

perception *percezione (f.)*

perfume *profumo*

period *periodo, punto*

permit, to *permettere (permesso)*

person *persona (f.)*

pharmacy *farmacia (f.)*

phase *fase (f.)*

philosophy *filosofia (f.)*

phonetics *fonetica (f.)*

photocopy *fotocopia (f.)*

photograph *fotografia (f.)*

phrase *frase (f.)*

physics *fisica (f.)*

pie *torta (f.)*

piece *pezzo*

piece of furniture *mobile (m.)*

pig *maiale (m.)*

pill *pillola (f.)*

pillow *cuscino*

pink *rosa*

pistol *pistola (f.)*

place *locale (m.), luogo, posto*

plain *pianura (f.)*

plan *programma (m.)*

planet *pianeta (m.)*

plant *pianta (f.)*

plastic *plastica (f.)*

plate *piatto*

plateau *altopiano*

play, to *giocare*

play (an instrument), to *suonare or giocare*

please *per favore, per piacere*

please, to (to like) *piacere (piaciuto)*

please hold! *attendere prego!*

pleasing *piacevole*

pleasure *piacere (m.)*

plural *plurale (m.)*

pocket *tasca (f.)*

poem, poetry *poesia (f.)*

poet *poeta (m.), poetessa (f.)*

poison *veleno*

police *polizia (f.)*

police headquarters *questura (f.)*

police officer *carabiniere (m.), poliziotto*

political party *partito*

politics *politica (f.)*

polluted *inquinato*

pollution *inquinamento*

pond *stagno*

poor *povero*

pope *papa (m.)*

population *popolazione (f.)*

pork *maiale (m.), porco*

portion *porzione (f.)*

portrait *ritratto*

Portugal *Portogallo*

position *posizione (f.)*

possibility *possibilità*

possible *possibile*

post office *ufficio postale*

postage stamp *francobollo*

postal carrier *postino*

postcard *cartolina (f.)*

potato *patata (f.)*

poultry *pollame (m.)*

poverty *miseria (f.), povertà (f.)*

practice *pratica (f.)*

praise, to *lodare*

pray, to *pregare*

prayer   *preghiera (f.)*
precise   *preciso*
prefer, to   *preferire*
preference   *preferenza (f.)*
pregnant   *incinta*
prepare, to   *preparare*
prescription   *ricetta (f.)*
present   *presente*
present, to   *presentare*
preservatives   *conservanti (m. pl.)*
president   *presidente (m.)*
price   *prezzo*
priest   *prete (m.)*
prince   *principe (m.)*
princess   *principessa (f.)*
principal   *principale*
print   *stampa (f.)*
printing   *tipografia (f.)*
prison   *carcere (m.), prigione (f.)*
private property   *proprietà privata (f.)*
problem   *problema (m.)*
produce, to   *produrre (prodotto)*
product   *prodotto*
production   *produzione (f.)*
profession   *professione (f.)*
professor   *professore (m.)/ professoressa (f.)*
progress   *progresso*
progressive   *progressivo*
prohibited   *vietato, proibito*
prohibition   *divieto, proibizione (f.)*
project   *progetto*
promise, to   *promettere (promesso)*
pronoun   *pronome (m.)*
pronounce, to   *pronunciare*
pronunciation   *pronuncia (f.)*
propose, to   *proporre (proposto)*
protect, to   *proteggere (protetto)*
Protestant   *protestante*
proud   *orgoglioso*
proverb   *proverbio*
provided that   *purché*

psychology   *psicologia (f.)*
public   *pubblico*
publicity   *pubblicità (f.)*
pull, to   *tirare*
punctual   *puntuale*
pupil   *allievo, scolaro*
pure   *puro*
purple   *viola*
purse   *borsa (f.)*
push, to   *spingere (spinto)*
put, to   *mettere (messo)*
pyramid   *piramide (f.)*

Q

quality   *qualità (f.)*
quantity   *quantità (f.)*
queen   *regina (f.)*
question, to   *domandare*
quickly, early   *presto*
quit, to   *smettere (smesso)*
quote, to   *citare*

R

rabbi   *rabbino*
rabbit   *coniglio*
race   *corsa (f.)*
racket   *racchetta (f.)*
radiator   *radiatore (m.)*
radio   *radio (f.)*
railroad   *ferrovia (f.)*
rain   *pioggia (f.)*
rain, to   *piovere*
raincoat   *impermeabile (m.)*
raise, to   *alzare*
rare   *raro, al sangue* (meat)
rarely   *raramente*
raspberry   *lampone (m.)*
rather   *piuttosto*
raw   *crudo*
razor   *rasoio*
read, to   *leggere (letto)*
ready   *pronto*
really   *davvero, veramente*
receipt   *ricevuta (f.), scontrino*

receive, to   *ricevere*
recent   *recente*
reception   *ricevimento*
recipe   *ricetta (f.)*
recite, to   *recitare*
record   *disco*
red   *rosso*
reflect, to   *riflettere (riflesso)*
reflexive   *riflessivo*
refreshment   *bevanda (f.)*
refrigerator   *frigorifero*
refuge   *rifugio*
refund   *rimborso*
region   *regione (f.)*
regret (be sorry), to   *dispiacersi (dispiaciuto)*
relationship   *rapporto*
relative   *parente (m./f.)*
relaxing   *rilassante*
religion   *religione (f.)*
remain, to   *rimanere (rimasto)*
remainder   *resto*
remember, to   *ricordare*
Renaissance   *Rinascimento*
render, to   *rendere (reso)*
rent   *affitto*
rent, to   *affittare, noleggiare*
repair, to   *riparare*
repeat, to   *ripetere*
report   *cronaca (f.), rapporto*
represent, to   *rappresentare*
reptile   *rettile (m.)*
republic   *repubblica (f.)*
request   *richiesta (f.)*
reservation   *prenotazione (f.)*
reserve, to   *prenotare*
reserved   *riservato*
reservoir   *riserva d'acqua (f.)*
residence   *domicilio, residenza (f.)*
resident   *abitante (m./f.)*
resign, to   *licenziarsi*
resistance   *resistenza (f.)*
resolve, to   *risolvere (risolto)*
respect, to   *rispettare*

respond, to *rispondere (risposto)*
responsible *responsabile*
restaurant *ristorante (m.)*
result *risultato*
return, to *ritornare, tornare*
revision *revisione (f.)*
rheumatism *reumatismo*
rhythm *ritmo*
rib *costola (f.)*
rice *riso*
rich *ricco*
riddle *indovinello*
right *destro*
right (legal) *diritto*
ring *anello*
ripe *maturo*
river *fiume (m.)*
roasted *arrosto*
robbery *rapina (f.)*
rock *pietra (f.), roccia (f.)*
roll of film *rullino*
romantic *romantico*
roof *tetto*
room *camera (f.), stanza (f.)*
root *radice (f.)*
rope *corda (f.)*
rose *rosa (f.)*
round-trip (ticket) *biglietto d'andata e ritorno*
route *percorso, via*
row *fila (f.)*
ruckus *baccano*
ruins *rovine (f. pl.)*
run, to *correre (corso)*
rush hour *ora di punta (f.)*
Russia *Russia (f.)*
Russian *russo*

S

sack *sacco; sacchetto*
sad *triste*
safe *sicuro*
sailboat *barca a vela (f.)*
saint *santo/santa (f.)*
salad *insalata (f.)*

salary *salario*
sale *saldi (m. pl.), svendita (f.)*
sales clerk *commesso/commessa (f.)*
salmon *salmone (m.)*
salt *sale (m.)*
same *stesso*
sand *sabbia (f.)*
sandwich *panino*
Saturday *sabato*
sauce *salsa (f.)*
saucepan *casseruola (f.), tegame (m.)*
sausage *salsiccia (f.)*
say, to *dire (detto)*
scarf *sciarpa (f.)*
scene *scena (f.)*
schedule *orario, tabella (f.)*
school *scuola (f.)*
science *scienza (f.)*
science fiction *fantascienza (f.)*
scissors *forbici (f. pl.)*
scooter *motorino*
Scotland *Scozia*
screwdriver *cacciavite (m.)*
sculpture *scultura (f.)*
sea *mare (m.)*
search, to *cercare*
seashell *conchiglia (f.)*
season *stagione (f.)*
seat *posto, sedile (m.)*
seat belt *cintura di sicurezza (f.)*
second *secondo*
secretary *segretario/segretaria (f.)*
sedative *sedativo*
see, to *vedere (visto)*
see you later! *arrivederci! ci vediamo!*
seem, to *sembrare*
sell, to *vendere*
semester *semestre (m.)*
Senate *Senato*
send, to *inviare, mandare, spedire*
sender *mittente (m./f.)*

sensation *sensazione (f.)*
sentence *frase (f.)*
sentiment *sentimento*
separate, to *separare*
separated *separato*
September *settembre*
serenade *serenata (f.)*
serious *grave, serio*
service *servizio*
set *fisso, fissato*
set, to *apparecchiare*
seven *sette*
seventeen *diciassette*
seventh *settimo*
seventy *settanta*
severe *severo*
sex *sesso*
sexuality *sessualità*
shadow *ombra (f.)*
shame *vergogna (f.)*
share, to *condividere (condiviso)*
shave, to *radersi*
she *lei, ella*
sheet *lenzuolo*
sheet of paper *foglio*
shingle *tegola (f.)*
ship *nave (f.)*
shirt *camicia (f.)*
shoe *scarpa (f.)*
shoe store *negozio di scarpe; calzoleria (f.)*
shop *bottega (f.), negozio*
shop window *vetrina (f.)*
short *basso, corto*
shorten, to *accorciare*
shorts *calzoncini (m. pl.); pantaloncini (m. pl.)*
shout, to *gridare, urlare*
show *spettacolo, mostra (f.)* (art)
shower *doccia (f.)*
shrimp *gambero*
shy *timido*
Sicilian *siciliano*
Sicily *Sicilia*
sick *ammalato*

side *lato, fianco*

side dish *contorno*

sidewalk *marciapiede (m.)*

sign *cartello, segno*

signal *segnale (m.)*

signature *firma (f.)*

signify, to *significare*

silence *silenzio*

silk *seta (f.)*

silver *argento*

simple *semplice*

since *poiché, da quando*

sincere *sincero*

sing, to *cantare*

singer *cantante (m./f.)*

single *singolo*

single room *monolocale (m.)*

singular *singolare*

sink *lavandino*

sister *sorella (f.)*

sister-in-law *cognata (f.)*

sit, to *sedersi*

situation *situazione (f.)*

six *sei*

sixteen *sedici*

sixty *sessanta*

size *misura (f.), taglia (f.)*

sketch *schizzo*

ski, to *sciare*

skiing *sci (m.)*

skirt *gonna (f.)*

sky *cielo*

sled *slittino*

sleep *sonno*

sleep, to *dormire*

sleeping bag *sacco a pelo*

sleeping pill *sonnifero*

slender *magro, snello*

slide *diapositiva (f.)*

slope *pista (f.), discesa (f.)*

slow down *rallentare*

small *piccolo*

smell, to *odorare, sentire*

smile, to *sorridere (sorriso)*

smoke, to *fumare*

snack *spuntino*

snake *serpente (m.)*

snob *snob*

snow *neve (f.)*

so *così*

so-so *così così*

soap *sapone (m.)*

soccer *calcio, football*

soccer player *calciatore (m.)*

socks *calze (f. pl.), calzini (m. pl.)*

sofa *divano*

soft *soffice*

sold out *esaurito*

soldier *soldato*

some *alcuni/alcune, qualche*

some of *ne, un po' di*

someone *qualcuno*

something *qualcosa*

sometimes *qualche volta, talvolta*

son *figlio*

son-in-law *genero*

soon *subito, presto*

soul *anima (f.)*

soup *minestra (f.), zuppa (f.)*

south *sud*

space *spazio*

Spain *Spagna (f.)*

Spanish *spagnolo*

sparkling wine *spumante (m.)*

special *speciale*

spend, to *spendere (speso)*

spice *spezia (f.)*

spicy *piccante*

spider *ragno*

spirit *anima, spirito*

spiritual *spirituale*

splendid *splendido*

spoiled *guasto, rovinato*

sponge *spugna (f.)*

spoon *cucchiaio*

sport *sport (m.)*

sports ground *campo sportivo*

spouse *sposo/sposa (f.)*

spring *sorgente (f.), primavera (f.) (season)*

squid *calamari (m. pl.)*

stadium *stadio*

stage *palcoscenico*

stain *macchia (f.)*

stairs *scala (f.), le scale (f. pl.)*

stall *bancarella (f.)*

star *stella (f.)*

state *stato*

statement *affermazione (f.)*

station *stazione (f.)*

stationery store *cartoleria (f.)*

statue *statua (f.)*

steak *bistecca (f.)*

steal, to *rubare*

steel *acciaio*

step *passo*

stepfather *patrigno*

stepsister *sorellastra (f.)*

stewardess *hostess (f.)*

still (again) *ancora*

stingy *avaro, tirchio*

stitch *punto*

stockings *calze (f. pl.), i collant (m. pl.)*

stomach *stomaco, pancia*

stone *pietra (f.), sasso*

stop *fermata (f.)*

stop, to *fermare*

storm *tempesta (f.)*

story *storia (f.)*

stove *stufa (f.)*

straight *diritto*

strange *strano*

straw *cannuccia (f.), fieno* (hay)

strawberry *fragola (f.)*

stream *rio; ruscello*

street *strada (f.), via (f.)*

stress *stress*

stress, to *stressare*

strike *sciopero*

stroll, to *passeggiare*

strong *forte*

struggle *lotta (f.)*

student *studente (m.)/ studentessa (f.)*

study *studio*
study, to *studiare*
stuff *roba (f.)*
stuffed *ripieno*
stupendous *stupendo*
stupid *stupido*
subject *materia (f.), soggetto*
subscription *abbonamento*
substitute, to *sostituire*
subtitle *sottotitolo*
suburbs *periferia (f.)*
subway *metropolitana (f.)*
succeed, to *riuscire*
such *tale*
suffer, to *soffrire (sofferto)*
suffice, to *bastare*
sugar *zucchero*
suit *abito, vestito*
suitable *adatto*
summer *estate (f.)*
sun *sole (m.)*
Sunday *domenica*
sunrise *alba (f.)*
sunset *tramonto*
supermarket *supermercato*
sure *sicuro*
surgeon *chirurgo*
surgery *chirurgia (f.)*
surname *cognome (m.), nome di famiglia*
surprise *sorpresa (f.)*
surprise, to *sorprendere (sorpreso)*
surround, to *circondare*
swallow *rondine (f.)*
swallow, to *inghiottire*
swamp *palude (f.)*
swear, to *giurare*
sweater *maglia (f.); maglione (m.)*
Sweden *Svezia (f.)*
sweet *dolce*
swim, to *nuotare*
swimming pool *piscina (f.)*
Switzerland *Svizzera*

symbol *simbolo*
symphony *sinfonia (f.)*
symptom *sintomo*
synagogue *sinagoga (f.)*
synthetic *sintetico*
system *sistema (m.)*

T

table *tavolo (restaurant), tavola*
tablecloth *tovaglia (f.)*
tablet *compressa (f.)*
tag *etichetta (f.)*
tailor *sarto*
take, to *prendere (preso)*
tall *alto*
tan, to *abbronzarsi*
tape *adesivo, nastro*
task *compito, impegno*
taste *gusto, sapore (m.)*
taste, to *assaggiare*
tax *tassa (f.)*
taxi *tassì (m.)*
taxi meter *tassametro*
tea *tè (m.)*
teach, to *insegnare*
teacher *insegnante (m./f.)*
team *squadra (f.)*
telephone *telefono*
telephone, to *telefonare*
telephone call *telefonata (f.)*
telephone card *carta telefonica (f.)*
tell, to *dire (detto), raccontare*
temple *tempio*
ten *dieci*
tender *tenero*
tent *tenda (f.)*
tenth *decimo*
terrace *terrazzo*
thank, to *ringraziare*
thank you! *grazie!*
that *quello/quella*
that which *ciò, quel che*
theater *teatro*
theme *tema (m.)*

then *allora, poi*
there *ci, lì/là*
there is *c'è*
therefore *perciò, quindi*
thermometer *termometro*
they *loro*
thief *ladro*
thin *magro*
thing *cosa (f.)*
think, to *pensare*
third *terzo*
thirst *sete (f.)*
thirteen *tredici*
thirty *trenta*
this *questo*
this evening *stasera*
this morning *stamattina*
thought *pensiero*
thousand *mille (pl. mila)*
three *tre*
throw, to *buttare*
thunder *tuono*
Thursday *giovedì*
thus *dunque*
ticket *biglietto*
ticket counter *biglietteria (f.)*
tide *marea (f.)*
tie *cravatta (f.)*
tie, to *legare*
tight *stretto*
tile *piastrella (f.)*
time *ora (f.), tempo*
tip *mancia (f.)*
tire *pneumatico*
tired *stanco*
tissue *fazzoletto di carta*
to *a, in*
tobacco shop *tabaccheria (f.)*
today *oggi*
toe *dito (pl. le dita)*
together *insieme*
toilet *gabinetto, toilette (f.)*
toilet paper *carta igienica (f.)*
token *gettone (m.)*
tolerance *tolleranza (f.)*

toll   *pedaggio*
toll-free number   *numero verde*
tomato   *pomodoro*
tomorrow   *domani*
tongue   *lingua (f.)*
tonight   *stanotte*
too   *troppo*
tooth   *dente (m.)*
toothbrush   *spazzolino da denti*
toothpaste   *dentifricio*
topic   *argomento, soggetto*
total   *totale*
touch, to   *toccare*
tour   *giro*
tourism   *turismo*
tourist   *turista (m./f.)*
toward   *verso*
tower   *torre (f.)*
town square   *piazza (f.)*
toy   *giocattolo*
track   *binario*
tradition   *tradizione (f.)*
traffic   *traffico*
traffic light   *semaforo*
tragic   *tragico*
train   *treno*
transfer, to   *trasferirsi*
transform, to   *trasformare*
translate, to   *tradurre (tradotto)*
translation   *traduzione (f.)*
transport, to   *trasportare*
trash   *rifiuti (m. pl.)*
trash can   *bidone della spazzatura*
travel, to   *viaggiare*
tree   *albero*
tremendous   *tremendo*
trip   *viaggio*
tropical   *tropicale*
trouble   *guaio*
truck   *camion (m.)*
true   *vero*
trust   *fiducia (f.)*
trust, to   *fidarsi*
truth   *verità (f.)*
try, to   *provare*

tub   *vasca (f.)*
Tuesday   *martedì*
tulip   *tulipano*
tunnel   *galleria (f.), sotterraneo*
turn   *turno*
turn off, to   *spegnere (spento)*
twelve   *dodici*
twenty   *venti*
two   *due*
type, kind   *specie (f.), tipo*

U

ugly   *brutto*
umbrella   *ombrello*
uncle   *zio*
uncomfortable   *scomodo*
understanding   *comprensione (f.)*
understood!   *capito!*
underwear   *biancheria intima (f.)*
unemployed   *disoccupato*
unfortunately   *purtroppo*
unhealthy   *malato*
unified   *unificato*
unique   *unico*
united   *unito*
United States   *gli Stati Uniti (m. pl.)*
unmarried   *celibe (m.), nubile (f.)*
unpleasant   *antipatico, spiacevole*
until   *fino a*
unusual   *insolito*
urgent   *urgente*
usage   *uso*
use, to   *usare*
useless   *inutile*
usual   *solito*

V

vacation   *vacanza (f.)*
vaccination   *vaccinazione (f.)*
vacuum cleaner   *aspirapolvere (m.)*
validate, to   *convalidare*
validated   *convalidato*

validity   *validità*
valise   *valigia (f.)*
valley   *valle (f.)*
value   *valore (m.)*
variation   *variazione (f.)*
variety   *varietà (f.)*
various   *vario*
vase   *vaso*
VAT/sales tax   *I.V.A. (Imposta Valore Aggiunto)*
veal   *vitello*
vegetables   *verdura (f.)*
vegetarian   *vegetariano*
vehicle   *veicolo*
velocity   *velocità*
vengeance   *vendetta (f.)*
verb   *verbo*
very   *molto*
victim   *vittima (f.)*
view   *vista (f.)*
villa   *villa (f.)*
village   *villaggio*
vine   *vigna (f.)*
vinegar   *aceto*
violence   *violenza (f.)*
violet   *violetta (f.)*
visible   *visibile*
visit   *visita (f.)*
visit, to   *visitare*
vitamin   *vitamina (f.)*
vocabulary   *vocabolario*
voice   *voce (f.)*
volleyball   *pallavolo (f.)*
vote, to   *votare*
vowel   *vocale (f.)*

W

wagon   *vagone (m.)*
wait, to   *aspettare*
waiter   *cameriere*
waiting room   *sala d'attesa (f.)*
waitress   *cameriera (f.)*
walk, to   *camminare, passeggiare*
wall   *muro, parete (f.)*
wallet   *portafoglio*

walnut *noce (f.)*
want, to *volere*
war *guerra (f.)*
warm *caldo*
warm, to *riscaldare*
warn, to *avvertire*
warning *avviso*
wash, to *lavare*
wasp *vespa (f.)*
watch *orologio*
water *acqua (f.)*
wave *onda (f.)*
we *noi*
weak *debole*
wear, to *indossare, portare*
weather *tempo*
Wednesday *mercoledì*
week *settimana (f.)*
weekend *fine settimana (m.)*
weigh, to *pesare*
weight *peso*
welcome! greetings! *benvenuto!*
well *pozzo*
well (adv.) *bene*
west *ovest, Occidente*
wet *bagnato*
what *che, che cosa*
wheel *ruota (f.)*
when *quando*
where *dove*
wherever *ovunque*
which *quale*
while *mentre*
whistle, to *fischiare*
white *bianco*
who *chi*
wholesale *all'ingrosso*
why *perché*
wide *largo*
widespread *diffuso*
widow *vedova (f.)*
widower *vedovo*
wife *moglie (f.)*
wild *selvaggio, selvatico*
willing *disposto*

win, to *vincere (vinto)*
wind *vento*
window *finestra (f.), finestrino*
windshield *parabrezza (m.)*
wine *vino*
wine bar *enoteca (f.)*
winery *azienda vinicola (f.)*
winter *inverno*
wise *saggio*
wish *desiderio, voglia (f.)*
witch *strega (f.)*
with *con*
within *fra*
without *senza*
wolf *lupo*
woman *donna (f.), signora (f.)*
wood *legno*
woods *bosco, selva (f.)*
wool *lana (f.)*
work *lavoro*
work, to *lavorare*
worker *impiegato, operaio*
world *mondo*
worm *baco*
worried *preoccupato*
worry, to *preoccuparsi*
worse *peggio*
wrap, to *incartare*
write, to *scrivere (scritto)*
writer *scrittore*
wrong *torto*
wrong, to be *sbagliare; sbagliato (adj.)*

X–Y

x-ray *radiografia (f.)*
xylophone *xilofono*

yawn, to *sbadigliare*
year *anno*
yell, to *gridare*
yellow *giallo*
yes *sì*
yesterday *ieri*
yoga *yoga (m.)*

yogurt *yogurt (m.)*
you *Lei* (polite), *tu* (familiar), *voi pl.*
you are welcome! *prego!*
young *giovane*

Z

zero *zero*
zipper *cerniera (f.)*
zone *zona (f.)*
zoo *zoo*

Italian to English

A

a, ad at, in, to, by
a bordo on board
abbandonare to abandon
abbastanza enough
abbazia (f.) abbey
abbigliamento clothing
abbonamento subscription
abbracciare to hug
abbronzarsi to get tanned
abitante (m./f.) resident, inhabitant
abitare to live
abito outfit, suit
abitudine (f.) habit
abolire to abolish
accademia (f.) academy
accanto a beside, next to
accendere (acceso) to light, to turn on
accento accent
accesso access
accettare to accept
acciaio steel
accidenti! darn!
acciuga (f.) anchovy
accompagnare to accompany
accorciare to shorten
accordo agreement

aceto vinegar

acqua (f.) water

acqua non potabile do not drink water

acquario aquarium

acquistare to acquire

acustico acoustic

adatto suitable, appropriate

adempimento fulfillment

adesso now

adorabile adorable

adulto adult

aereo airplane

aeroporto airport

affare (m.) business, deal

affascinare to fascinate

affermare to affirm, to assert

affermazione (f.) statement

affetto affection

affettuoso affectionate

affittare to rent

affittasi for rent

affitto rent

affollato crowded

agente (m./f.) agent

agenzia (f.) agency

aggettivo adjective

aggiungere (aggiunto) to add

aggressivo aggressive

agile agile

aglio garlic

agnello lamb

agosto August

agricoltura (f.) agriculture

aiutare to help

aiuto! help!

al coperto indoor

al forno baked or roasted

al sangue rare (meat)

alba (f.) sunrise

albergo hotel

albero tree

albicocca (f.) apricot

alcol (m.) alchohol

alcolico alcoholic

alcuni/alcune some

alfabeto alphabet

alimentari (m. pl.) groceries

all'aperto outdoor, open air

allacciare to fasten, to buckle

allegria (f.) happiness

allegro happy

allenarsi to train (sports)

allergia (f.) allergy

allergico allergic

allievo pupil

alloggiare to lodge

allora then

almeno at least

altezza (f.) height

alto tall

altopiano plateau

altro other

alzare to raise, lift

alzarsi to get up

amare to love

amaro bitter

ambasciata (f.) embassy

ambiente (m.) environment

ambizione ambition

ambulanza (f.) ambulance

americano American

amicizia (f.) friendship

amico/amica (f.) friend

ammalato sick, ill

amministrazione (f.) management, administration

ammirare to admire

amore (m.) love

ampio ample

anatra (f.) duck

analisi (f.) analysis

anche also

ancora still, again, yet

andare to go

andata e ritorno round-trip (ticket)

anello ring

anfiteatro amphitheater

anima (f.) spirit

animale (m.) animal

animato animated, lively

annegare to drown

anno year

anno bisestile leap year

annoiarsi to get bored

annunciare to announce

antenato ancestor

antibiotici (m. pl.) antibiotics

antico ancient, antique

antipasto appetizer

antipatico unpleasant, disagreeable

antiquariato antiques

anzi and even, but rather

anziano elderly

aperitivo aperitif

aperto open; *(all'aperto)* outside

apparecchiare to set

appartamento apartment

appartenere to belong

applaudire to applaud

apposta on purpose, deliberately

apprezzare to appreciate

approvare to approve of

aprile April

aprire (aperto) to open

aquila (f.) eagle

arancia (f.) orange

archeologia (f.) archaeology

architettura (f.) architecture

area (f.) area

argento silver

argomento topic, subject

aria (f.) aria, air, appearance

aria condizionata (f.) air conditioning

aristocratico aristocratic

aroma (m.) aroma

arrabbiarsi to get angry

arrabbiato angry

arredamento furnishings

arretrato backward

arrivare to arrive

arrivederci! See you later!

arrivo arrival

arrosto roasted

arte (f.) art

articolo article

artista (m./f.) artist

artrite (f.) arthritis

ascensore (m.) elevator

asciutto dry

ascoltare to listen to

asilo kindergarten, day care center

aspettare to wait for

aspirapolvere (m.) vacuum cleaner

aspirina (f.) aspirin

assaggiare to taste

assaltare to assault

assegno check

assicurare to ensure, insure

assicurazione (f.) insurance

assistenza (medica) (f.) assistance, insurance (health)

associazione (f.) association

assolutamente absolutely

assumere (assunto) to hire, to assume

Assunzione (f.) Feast of the Assumption

astrologia (f.) astrology

astronauta (m./f.) astronaut

atleta (m./f.) athlete

atletica athletics

atrio (m.) atrium

attaccare to attach, to attack

attacco (m.) attack

atteggiamento attitude

attendere prego! please hold!

attento careful, attentive

attenzione! attention! warning!

atterraggio landing

attimo moment

attirare to attract

attività (f.) activity

attivo active

atto document, record

attore (m.) actor

attraversare to cross

attraverso across

attrezzato equipped

attribuire to attribute

attrice (f.) actress

attuale actual, current

attualità (f.) current event

auguri! best wishes!

aumentare to increase

australiano Australian

austriaco Austrian

autobus (m.) bus

automatico automatic

automobile (f.) (abb. auto) car

autonoleggio car rental

autore author

autoritario authoritarian

autostop (m.) hitchhiking

autostrada (f.) highway

autunno (m.) autumn

avanti forward

avaro stingy

avere to have

avvenimento (m.) event

avvenire to happen

avventura (f.) adventure

avverbio (m.) adverb

avvertire to warn

avvicinarsi to approach, to get near

avvocato lawyer

azienda (f.) firm, company

azione (f.) action

azzurro light blue

B

babbo dad

baccano ruckus

baciare to kiss

bacio kiss

baco worm

bagnato wet

bagno bath

baia (f.) bay

balcone (m.) balcony

ballo dance

bambino baby, child

banca (f.) bank

bancarella (f.) stall, booth

banco counter

Bancomat (m.) ATM

bar (m.) bar, café

barba (f.) beard

barbiere (m.) barber

barca (f.) boat

barca a vela (f.) sailboat

barista (m./f.) bartender

barocco Baroque

barzelletta (f.) joke

base (f.) base

basso short, low

bastare to be enough, to suffice

battere to beat

batteria (f.) battery; drum

Befana (f.) Epiphany (January 6)

bellezza (f.) beauty

benché although

bene well

benvenuto! welcome! greetings!

benzina (f.) gasoline

bere (bevuto) to drink

berretto (m.) cap

bestia (f.) beast

bevanda (f.) refreshment

biancheria intima (f.) underwear

bianco white

Bibbia (f.) Bible

biberon (m.) baby bottle

bibita (f.) refreshment, beverage

bicchiere (m.) glass

biglietteria (f.) ticket counter

biglietto (m.) ticket

binario (m.) track, platform

biodegradabile biodegradable

biologia (f.) biology

biondo blond

birra (f.) beer

biscotto   cookie
bisogno   need
bistecca (f.)   steak
blu   blue
bocca (f.)   mouth
boccone (m.)   morsel, nibble
bollettino (m.)   bulletin, news
bollire   to boil
bordo, a   aboard
borsa (f.)   bag, purse
borsetta (f.)   purse, handbag
bosco (m.)   woods
bottega (f.)   shop
bottiglia (f.)   bottle
bottone (m.)   button
braccialetto (m.)   bracelet
braccio (m.), braccia (f. pl.)   arm
braciola (f.)   chop
bravo   good, able
breve   brief, short
brioche (f.)   brioche, croissant
britannico   British
brodo (m.)   broth
bronchite (f.)   bronchitis
bronzo   bronze
bruciare   to burn
bruno   brown-haired
brutto   ugly
bucato (m.)   laundry
buffo   funny
buffone (m.)   buffoon, clown, fool
buio (m.)   darkness
Buon Anno!   Happy New Year!
Buon compleanno!   Happy birthday!
Buongiorno!   Good day, hello!
Buon Natale!   Merry Christmas!
Buona feste!   Happy holidays!
Buona Pasqua!   Happy Easter!
buono   good
burro (m.)   butter
burrone (m.)   canyon
bussare   to knock
busta (f.)   envelope

bustina (f.)   bag
buttare   to throw

C

c'è   there is
cabina (f.)   cabin
cacciavite (m.)   screwdriver
cadere   to fall
caffè (m.)   coffee, café
calamari (m. pl.)   squid
calciatore (m.)   soccer player
calcio (m.)   soccer, kick
caldo   heat, hot (adj.)
calmare   to calm
calze (f. pl.)   stockings
calzini (m. pl.)   socks
calzolaio (m.)   shoe repair
calzoleria (f.)   shoe store; shoe maker
calzoncini (m. pl.)   shorts
cambiare   to change, to exchange
cambio (m.)   exchange
camera (f.)   room
cameriera (f.)   waitress, maid
cameriere (m.)/cameriera (f.)   waiter/waitress
camicetta (f.)   blouse
camicia (f.)   shirt
caminetto (m.)   fireplace
camino (m.)   chimney
camion (m.)   truck
camminare   to walk
campagna (f.)   country, countryside
campana (f.)   bell
campanello   doorbell
campanile (m.)   bell tower
campeggio (m.)   camping
campionato (m.)   match, championship
campo (m.)   field
campo sportivo (m.)   sports ground
canadese   Canadian

canale (m.)   channel
cancello (m.)   gate
cancro (m.)   cancer
candela (f.)   candle
candidato (m.)   candidate
cane (m.)   dog
cannuccia (f.)   drinking straw
canottaggio (m.)   canoeing
cantante (m./f.)   singer
cantare   to sing
cantina (f.)   basement, cellar
caotico   chaotic
capace   capable
capelli (m. pl.)   hair (on head)
capitare   to happen
capito!   understood!
cappella (f.)   chapel
cappello (m.)   hat
cappotto (m.)   overcoat
capra (f.)   goat
carabiniere (m.)   police officer
caramella (f.)   candy
carattere (m.)   character
caratteristico   characteristic, typical
carcere (m.)   jail, prison
carciofo   artichoke
caricare   to load
carino   cute, pretty
carne (f.)   meat
caro   dear, expensive
carota (f.)   carrot
carriera (f.)   career
carta (f.)   paper
carta di credito (f.)   credit card
carta d'identità (f.)   identification card
carta igienica (f.)   toilet paper
carta stradale (f.)   map
carta telefonica (f.)   telephone card
cartello (m.)   sign
cartoleria (f.)   stationery store
cartolina (f.)   postcard
casa (f.)   house, home

casalinga (f.) housewife
casco (m.) helmet
cassa (f.) cash register
casseruola (f.) saucepan
cassetta postale (f.) mailbox
castano brown
castello (m.) castle
catalogo (m.) catalogue
categoria (f.) category
catena (f.) chain
cattedrale (f.) cathedral
cattivo bad, evil, naughty
cattolico Catholic
cavallo (m.) horse
cavatappi (m.) corkscrew
cavo (m.) cable
celebrare to celebrate
celibe (m.) unmarried man, single
cena (f.) dinner
cenare to dine
cento one hundred
centrale central
centro center, downtown
ceramica (f.) ceramic
cercare to search, look for
cerniera (f.) zipper
certificato certificate
certo certain, sure, of course!
cervello brain
che what? which? that
che cosa what?
chi who? whom? the one who
chiacchiera (f.) chat
chiacchierare to chat
chiamare to call
chiamarsi to call oneself (to be named)
chiaro clear, light
chiave (f.) key
chiedere (chiesto) to ask
chiesa (f.) church
chilogrammo kilogram
chilometro kilometer
chirurgia (f.) surgery
chirurgo surgeon

chitarra (f.) guitar
chiudere (chiuso) to close
chiuso closed
chiusura festiva (f.) closed for the holidays
ci there
ciao hello, hi, bye
ciascuno each, each one
cibo food
ciclismo cycling
cieco blind
cielo sky, heaven
ciliegia (f.) cherry
cimitero cemetery
Cina China
cinema (m.) cinema
cinese Chinese
cinquanta fifty
cinque five
cintura (f.) belt
cintura di sicurezza (f.) seat belt
ciò that which
cioccolata (f.) chocolate
cipolla (f.) onion
circa about, approximately
circo circus
circolo circle
circondare to surround
citare to quote
citazione (f.) quote
città city
cittadinanza (f.) citizenship
cittadino/cittadina (f.) citizen
civico civic
civile civil
classe (f.) class
classico classical
classificazione (f.) classification
cliente (m./f.) client, customer
clima (m.) climate
cognata (f.) sister-in-law
cognato brother-in-law
cognome (m.) surname
coincidenza (f.) connection, coincidence
colazione (f.) breakfast, lunch

collaborare to collaborate
collana (f.) necklace
collant (m. pl.) stockings
collega (m./f.) colleague
collina (f.) hill
collo neck
colloquio interview
colonia (f.) colony
colore (m.) color
coltello knife
coltivare to cultivate
comandamento commandment
combattere to fight
come how, like, as
cominciare to begin, to start
commesso/commessa (f.) sales clerk
comodo convenient, comfortable
compiere to accomplish
compito homework, task, chore
compleanno birthday
complimento compliment
comporre (composto) to compose
comportamento behavior
comportarsi to behave
composizione (f.) composition
comprare to buy
comprensione (f.) understanding
compressa (f.) tablet, pill
comune (m.) municipality, common (adj.)
comunicare to communicate
comunismo communism
comunità community
comunque however, no matter how
con with
concentrazione (f.) concentration
concerto concert
concetto concept
concezione (f.) conception
conchiglia (f.) seashell
concludere (concluso) to conclude
concorso contest, exam
condividere (condiviso) to share

condizionale (m.) conditional (verb mood)

condizione (f.) condition

condominio condominium

condurre (condotto) to lead, to carry out

conferenza (f.) conference, lecture

confessare to confess

conflitto conflict

conforto comfort, convenience

congratulazioni! congratulations!

congresso meeting, conference

coniglio rabbit

coniugare to conjugate

coniugazione (f.) conjugation

conoscenza (f.) knowledge, acquaintance

conoscere (conosciuto) to know someone

conquistare to conquest

consecutivo consecutive

conseguenza (f.) consequence

conservanti (m. pl.) preservatives

considerare to consider

consigliare to advise, to recommend

consolare to console

consonante (f.) consonant

consumo consumption, waste

contadino/contadina farmer, peasant

contanti (m. pl.) cash

contare to count

contattare to contact

contatto contact

conte count

contemporaneo contemporary

contenere to contain

contento glad, satisfied

contessa (f.) countess

contestare to challenge, dispute

continente (m.) continent

continuare to continue

conto check, bill, account

contorno side dish

contraccettivo contraceptive

contrario opposite

contrasto contrast

contro against

controllare to check

controllo check, control

contusione (f.) bruise

convalidare to validate

convalidato validated

convento convent

conversazione (f.) conversation

convincere (convinto) to convince

coperta (f.) blanket, cover

coperto cover charge

copia (f.) copy

coppa (f.) cup

coppia (f.) couple

coraggio courage

corda (f.) rope

coro chorus, choir

corpo body

correggere (corretto) to correct

correre (corso) to run

corretto correct

corriera (f.) bus

corriere messenger, courier

corrispondere (corrisposto) to correspond

corsa (f.) race

corsia (f.) lane

corso course

corte (f.) court

cortese courteous

cosa thing, what

cosa c'è? what is it?

così so, thus

così così so-so

cosmetici (m. pl.) cosmetics

costa (f.) coast

costare to cost

costiera (f.) cliff

costituzione (f.) constitution

costo cost, price

costola (f.) rib (anatomy)

costoletta (f.) rib (culinary)

costoso costly, expensive

costruire to build, construct

costume (m.) costume

cotone (m.) cotton

cotto cooked

cravatta (f.) tie

creare to create

creazione (f.) creation

credere to believe

credito credit

crema (f.) cream

crescere (cresciuto) to grow

cric (m.) jack (car)

crisi (f.) crisis

cristiano Christian

croccante crunchy

croce (f.) cross

crociera (f.) cruise

cronaca (f.) report

crostata (f.) pie

crudo raw, uncooked

cubano Cuban

cubo cube

cuccetta (f.) berth

cucchiaio spoon

cucinare to cook

cugino/cugina (f.) cousin

cui whom, that, which

culla (f.) crib

cultura (f.) culture

culturale cultural

cuocere (cotto) to cook

cuoio leather

cuore (m.) heart

cupola (f.) dome

cura (f.) care

curare to care for, to look after

curiosità (f.) curiosity

curioso curious, strange

curva (f.) curve

cuscino pillow

D

da from, by
Danimarca Denmark
dannato damned
danneggiato damaged
danza (f.) dance
dappertutto everywhere
dare to give
data (f.) date
davanti a in front of
davvero really
dea (f.) goddess
debole weak
decidere (deciso) to decide
decimo tenth
decisione (f.) decision
dedicare to dedicate
definire to define
definizione (f.) definition
delfino dolphin
delizioso delicious
della casa homemade
democratico democratic
democrazia (f.) democracy
denaro money
densità (f.) density
dente (m.) tooth
dentifricio toothpaste
dentista (m./f.) dentist
dentro inside
desiderio wish, desire
destinazione (f.) destination
destino destiny
destro right
detersivo detergent
deviazione (f.) detour
di of, about, from
di solito usually
di stagione in season
diabete (m.) diabetes
dialogo dialogue
diamante (m.) diamond
diapositiva (f.) slide
diarrea (f.) diarrhea

dicembre December
dichiarare to declare
diciannove nineteen
diciassette seventeen
diciotto eighteen
didattica (f.) pedagogy, teaching
dieta (f.) diet
dietro a behind
difendere (difeso) to defend
difetto defect
differenza (f.) difference
difficile difficult
diffuso widespread, diffuse
diga (f.) dam
digerire to digest
dimagrire to lose weight
diminuire to decrease
dimostrare to demonstrate
dimostrazione (f.) demonstration
dinamico energetic
dio god
dipartimento department
dipendere (dipeso) to depend
dipingere (dipinto) to paint
dire (detto) to say, to tell
diretto direct
direttore/direttrice (f.) director
direzione (f.) direction
dirigere (diretto) to manage, to direct
Diritto law
diritto straight (adv.)
disco record
discorso speech, discussion
discoteca (f.) discothèque
discussione (f.) discussion
discutere (discusso) to discuss
disegnare to draw
disegno drawing, design
disgrazia (f.) accident, misfortune
disoccupato unemployed
dispiacere (dispiaciuto) to be sorry
disponibile available
disposto willing

distanza (f.) distance
distinguere (distinto) to distinguish
distratto distracted, absent-minded
distributore di benzina gas pump
distruggere (distrutto) to destroy
dito (pl. le dita) finger, toe
ditta (f.) firm, business
dittatura (f.) dictatorship
divano sofa
diverso different
divertirsi to enjoy oneself
dividere (diviso) to divide
divieto prohibition
divieto di sosta no parking
divisione (f.) division
divorziare to get divorced
divorziato divorced
dizionario dictionary
dizione (f.) diction
doccia (f.) shower
documento document
dodici twelve
dogana (f.) customs
dolce sweet
dolce dessert
dollaro dollar
dolore (m.) pain
domandare to question
domani tomorrow
domenica Sunday
domestica (f.) maid
domicilio residence
donna (f.) woman
dopo after (prep.), afterward (adv.)
doppiare to dub
doppio double
dormire to sleep
dottore/dottoressa (f.) doctor
dove where
dovere to have to, to must
dozzina (f.) dozen
droga (f.) drug

drogheria (f.) drugstore; corner store
duca (m.) duke
duchessa (f.) duchess
due two
dunque thus, then
duomo cathedral, dome
durante during
durare to last
duro hard, tough

E

e, ed and
è is
ebbene well then, so
ebreo Hebrew, Jewish
eccellente excellent
eccetera et cetera
eccetto except
ecco here is, there is
economia (f.) economy
economico inexpensive
edera (f.) ivy
edicola (f.) newsstand
edificio building
effetto effect
efficiente efficient
Egitto Egypt
elegante elegant
elementare elementary
elemosina (f.) alms
elenco list, directory
elettricità (f.) electricity
elezione (f.) election
elicottero helicopter
eliminare to eliminate
emergenza (f.) emergency
emicrania (f.) migraine
emigrare to emigrate
enorme enormous
enoteca (f.) wine bar
entrambi both
entrare to enter
entrata (f.) entrance

Epifania (f.) Epiphany (January 6)
equitazione (f.) horse riding
ernia (f.) hernia
errore (m.) error
esagerare to exaggerate
esame (m.) exam
esaminare to examine
esattamente exactly
esatto exact
esaurito sold out
escludere (escluso) to exclude
escursione (f.) excursion
esistere (esistito) to exist
esotico exotic
esperienza (f.) experience
esplodere (esploso) to explode
esportare to export
espressione (f.) expression
espresso express
esprimere (espresso) to express
essenza (f.) essence
essenziale essential
essere (stato) to be
est east
estate (f.) summer
estero abroad
età (f.) age
etichetta (f.) tag, label
etto hectogram
Europa (f.) Europe
evento event
evitare to avoid
evocare to evoke

F

fa ago
fabbrica (f.) factory
fabbricare to manufacture
faccenda (f.) thing, matter, chore
faccia (f.) face
facile easy
facoltà (f.) school
fagiolo bean

falegname (m.) carpenter
fame (f.) hunger
famiglia (f.) family
famoso famous
fantascienza (f.) science fiction
fantasia (f.) fantasy
fantasma (m.) ghost, phantom
fare (fatto) to do, to make
farina (f.) flour
farmacia (f.) pharmacy
faro headlight, lighthouse
fascismo fascism
fase (f.) phase
fastidio bother, annoyance
fatica (f.) effort
fatto fact
fattoria (f.) farm
favola (f.) fable
fazzoletto di carta tissue
febbraio February
febbre (f.) fever
fede (f.) faith
fegato liver
felice happy
feltro felt
femmina (f.) female
ferita (f.) wound
fermare to stop
fermata (f.) stop
fermo still
Ferragosto Assumption Day (August 15)
ferro iron
ferrovia (f.) railroad
festa (f.) holiday
festeggiare to celebrate
fiaba (f.) fable, tale
fiammiferi (m. pl.) matches
fianco side
fidanzata (f.) fiancée
fidanzato fiancé
fidarsi to trust
fiducia (f.) trust
fiera (f.) fair
fiero proud

figlia (f.) daughter
figlio son
fila (f.) line, row
filetto filet
filosofia (f.) philosophy
filtro filter
finalmente finally
finanza (f.) finance
finanziare to finance
fine (f.) end
fine settimana weekend
finestra (f.) window
finire to finish
fino a until, as far as
fioraio florist
fiore (m.) flower
Firenze Florence
firma (f.) signature
fiscale fiscal
fischiare to whistle
fisica (f.) physics
fissare to set up
fisso set (adj.), fixed (adj.)
fiume (m.) river
foglia (f.) leaf
foglio sheet of paper
fon (m.) hair dryer
fondato founded
fondo bottom
fonetica (f.) phonetics
fontana (f.) fountain
football soccer, football
forbici (f. pl.) scissors
forchetta (f.) fork
foresta (f.) forest
forma (f.) form
formaggio cheese
formale formal
formulare to formulate, to compose
fornaio baker
forno oven
forse maybe
forte strong
fortezza (f.) fortress

fortuna (f.) fortune
fotocopia (f.) photocopy
fotografia (f.) photograph
fra within, in, between, among
fragile fragile
fragola (f.) strawberry
francese French
Francia (f.) France
francobollo postage stamp
frase (f.) phrase, sentence
frate (m.) friar
fratello brother
freddo cold
frequentare to frequent
fresco fresh
fretta (f.) haste, hurry
frigorifero refrigerator
fritto fried
frontiera (f.) border
frutta (f.) fruit
fruttivendolo green-grocer
fumare to smoke
fumetto comic strip
funerale (m.) funeral
fungo mushroom
funivia (f.) cable car, gondola
funzionare to function, to work
fuoco fire
fuori outside
furbo clever, sly (slang)
futuro future

G

gabinetto toilet
galleria (f.) tunnel, gallery
gallina (f.) hen
gamba (f.) leg
gambero shrimp
gara (f.) contest
garage (m.) garage
garantire to guarantee
garofano carnation
gatto cat
gattopardo leopard
gelateria (f.) ice-cream parlor

gelato ice cream
genere (m.) genre, type
genero son-in-law
generoso generous
genesi (f.) genesis
genitori (m. pl.) parents
gennaio January
gente (f.) people
gentile kind, polite
gentilezza (f.) kindness
geografia (f.) geography
Germania (f.) Germany
gerundio gerund
Gesù Jesus
gettone (m.) token
ghiaccio ice
già already
giacca (f.) jacket
giallo yellow
Giappone (m.) Japan
giapponese Japanese
giardino garden
ginecologo/ginecologa (f.) gynecologist
ginnastica (f.) gymnastics, exercise
giocare to play
giocattolo toy
gioco game
gioia (f.) joy
gioielleria (f.) jewelry store
giornalaio newspaper vendor
giornale (m.) newspaper
giornalista (m./f.) journalist
giornata (f.) day
giorno day
giovane young
giovedì Thursday
girare to spin, to shoot (a film)
giro tour
gita (f.) excursion
giù down
giubbotto coat
giudicare to judge
giugno June

giurare to swear

giurisprudenza (f.) law

giusto just, right, correct

gonna (f.) skirt

gotico gothic

governo government

grammatica (f.) grammar

grammo gram

grande big, large

grappa (f.) grappa

grasso fat

gratis free of charge

grave serious, grave

gravità (f.) gravity

grazia (f.) grace

grazie! thank you!

Grecia Greece

greco Greek

greggio raw, crude

gridare to yell, to shout

grigio gray

griglia (f.) grill

grosso large

grotta (f.) cave

gruccia (f.) hanger

gruppo group

guadagnare to earn

guaio trouble

guancia (f.) cheek

guanti (m. pl.) gloves

guardare to look at, to watch

guardaroba (m.) cloakroom

guasto spoiled, rotten

guasto breakdown

guerra (f.) war

guida (f.) guide

guidare to drive

gustare to taste

gusto taste

H

hobby (m.) hobby

hockey (m.) hockey

hostess (f.) stewardess

hotel (m.) hotel

I

I.V.A. (Imposta Valore Aggiunto) VAT/sales tax

idea (f.) idea

ideale (m.) ideal

identificare to identify

identità (f.) identity

idioma (m.) idiom

idolo idol

ieri yesterday

ignorante ignorant

ignorare to ignore

illustrare to illustrate

illustrazione (f.) illustration

imbarco boarding

imitazione (f.) imitation

immacolato immaculate

immaginare to imagine

immaginazione (f.) imagination

immagine (f.) image

immenso immense

immigrazione (f.) immigration

imparare to learn

impegno commitment, task

imperativo imperative

imperfetto imperfect

impermeabile (m.) raincoat

impero empire

impiegato worker, employee, official

importante important

importare to import, to matter

impossibile impossible

imprenditore entrepreneur

impressione (f.) impression

in in, to, at

in fretta in a hurry

incartare to wrap

incidente (m.) accident

incinta pregnant

inciso engraved

includere (incluso) to include

incominciare to begin, to start

incontrare to meet

incredibile incredible

incrocio crossing

incubo nightmare

indefinito indefinite

indiano Indian

indicare to indicate

indicazione (f.) direction, indication

indice (m.) index, forefinger

indietro back, behind

indigestione (f.) indigestion

indipendenza (f.) independence

indiretto indirect

indirizzo address

indispensabile indispensable

indossare to wear

indovinare to guess

indovinello riddle

industria (f.) industry

infarto heart attack

infatti in fact

inferiore inferior, lower

infermiera (f.) nurse

inferno hell

infezione (f.) infection

infiammazione (f.) inflammation

infinito infinitive

inflazione (f.) inflation

influenza (f.) flu

informare to inform

informazione (f.) information

ingegnere engineer

Inghilterra (f.) England

inghiottire to swallow

inglese English

ingrassare to get fat

ingrediente (m.) ingredient

ingresso entrance

ingrosso wholesale

iniezione (f.) injection

iniziare to begin

inizio beginning

innamorarsi to fall in love with

inno hymn

inoltre also

inquinamento pollution

inquinato polluted
insalata (f.) salad
insegnante (m./f.) teacher
insegnare to teach
inserire to insert
insetto insect
insicuro insecure
insieme together
insistere (insisto) to insist
insolito unusual
insulina (f.) insulin
intelligente intelligent
intendere (inteso) to mean
intenzione (f.) intention
interessante interesting
intermezzo intermission
internazionale international
interno internal, inside
interpretare to interpret
interprete interpreter
interrogativo interrogative
interrompere (interrotto) to interrupt
interurbana (f.) long-distance call
intervallo interval
intervista (f.) interview
intorno a around
introdurre (introdotto) to introduce
inutile useless
invece instead
inverno winter
inviare to mail, to send
invitare to invite
invito invitation
io I
Irlanda Ireland
irlandese Irish
irregolare irregular
iscritto student, member
isola (f.) island
ispirazione (f.) inspiration
istituto institute
istruzione (f.) instruction

Italia (f.) Italy
italiano Italian
itinerario itinerary

J–K–L

jeans jeans

ketchup ketchup
kosher kosher

là there
labbro lip
ladro thief
lamentare to mourn, to grieve
lamentarsi to complain
lago lake
lampada (f.) light
lampadina (f.) lightbulb
lampo lightning flash
lampone (m.) raspberry
lana (f.) wool
largo wide
lasciare to let, to leave behind
latino Latin
lato side
latte (m.) milk
latteria (f.) dairy store
lattuga (f.) lettuce
laurea (f.) degree
lavanderia (f.) laundry service
lavanderia a secco dry cleaner
lavandino sink
lavare to wash
lavorare to work
lavoro work
leccare to lick
legare to tie
legge (f.) law
leggere (letto) to read
leggero light
legno wood
lei she, her
Lei (polite) you
lenzuolo sheet

lettera (f.) letter
letteratura (f.) literature
letto bed
lezione (f.) lesson
lì there
libero free
libertà (f.) liberty
libreria (f.) bookstore
libretto libretto, little book
libro book
licenziare to fire someone
licenziarsi to resign
limonata (f.) lemonade
limone (m.) lemon
linea (f.) line
lingua (f.) language, tongue
linguistica (f.) linguistics
lino linen
liquore (m.) liquor
lista (f.) list, menu
litigare to argue, to fight
litro liter
livello level
locale local
locale (m.) place
lodare to praise
logistica (f.) logistics
lontano far
loro they, them
lotta (f.) struggle
lozione (f.) lotion
luce (f.) light
luglio July
lui he, him
luna (f.) moon
luna di miele (f.) honeymoon
lunedì Monday
lunedì dell'Angelo Easter Monday
lunghezza (f.) length
lungo long
luogo place
lupo wolf
lusso luxury

M

ma but

macchia (f.) stain

macchina (f.) automobile, car, machine

macchina fotografica (f.) camera

macellaio butcher

macelleria (f.) butcher shop

madre (f.) mother

madrelingua (f.) native speaker

magazzino department store

maggio May

maggioranza (f.) majority

magia (f.) magic

maglia (f.) sweater, pullover

magnifico magnificent

magro thin

mai never, ever

maiale (m.) pork, pig

mais (m.) corn

malato unhealthy, sick

malattia (f.) illness

male evil; *fa male* (it hurts)

mamma (f.) mom, mother

mancia (f.) tip

mancare to lack, to be missing

mandare to send

mangiare to eat

mania (f.) obsession

maniera (f.) manner, way

maniglia (f.) handle

mano (f.) (pl. le mani) hand

mantello cape

mantenere to maintain

manzo beef

marca (f.) brand, type

marciapiede (m.) sidewalk

mare (m.) sea

marea (f.) tide

marina (f.) marina

marito husband

marmellata (f.) jam

marmo marble

marrone brown

martedì Tuesday

marzo March

maschile masculine

massimo maximum

matematica (f.) mathematics

materia (f.) subject

matita (f.) pencil

matrimonio matrimony, marriage

mattina (f.) morning

matto crazy

maturo ripe, mature

meccanico mechanic

medicina (f.) medicine

medico doctor

Medioevo Middle Ages

meglio better

mela (f.) apple

melanzana (f.) eggplant

melone (m.) melon, cantaloupe

meno less

mensa (f.) cafeteria

mensile monthly

menta (f.) mint

mentalità (f.) mentality

mente (f.) mind

mento chin

mentre while

menù (m.) menu

meraviglioso marvelous

mercante (m./f.) merchant

mercato market

merce (f.) merchandise

mercoledì Wednesday

meritare to deserve

merletto lace

mese (m.) month

messa (f.) Mass

messaggio message

Messico (m.) Mexico

metà half

metallo metal

metodo method

metropolitana (f.) subway

mettere (messo) to put, to place

mezzanotte (f.) midnight

mezzo half; mode (of transportation)

mezzogiorno noon

mi me, to me

miele (m.) honey

miglio (pl. le miglia) mile

migliorare to improve

migliore the best

mille (pl. mila) thousand

minestra (f.) soup

ministro minister

minoranza (f.) minority

minore smaller, less

minuto minute

miope near-sighted

mischiare to mix

miseria (f.) poverty

misto mixed

misura (f.) measure, size

mito myth

mittente (m./f.) sender

mobile (m.) piece of furniture

modello model

moderno modern

modesto modest

modo manner, method, way

modulo form

moglie (f.) wife

molo dock

molto a lot, much, very

momento moment

monastero monastery

mondo world

moneta (f.) coin

monolocale (m.) single room, studio

montagna (f.) mountain

monumento monument

morbido soft, smooth

morire (morto) to die

morte (f.) death

mosaico mosaic

mosca (f.) fly (insect)

mostra (f.) show (art)

motivo motive

motocicletta (f.) motorcycle

motore (m.) motor

motorino scooter

mucca (f.) cow

multa (f.) fine, ticket

muro wall

muscolo muscle

museo museum

musica (f.) music

musicista (m./f.) musician

mussulmano Muslim

muto mute

mutuo loan

N

narrativa (f.) narrative, story, fiction

nascere (nato) to be born

nascita (f.) birth

nascondere (nascosto) to hide

naso nose

nastro tape

Natale, Buon Christmas, Merry

natura (f.) nature

naturale natural

nausea (f.) nausea

nave (f.) ship

nazionalità (f.) nationality

nazione (f.) nation

ne some of, about it

né ... né neither ... nor

neanche not even

nebbia (f.) fog

necessario necessary

necessità (f.) need, necessity

negativo negative

negozio shop

nemico enemy

nemmeno not even

neppure neither, not even

nero black

nervoso nervous

nessuno no one, nobody

neve (f.) snow

nido nest

niente nothing

nipote grandson, granddaughter, nephew, niece

nocciola (f.) hazelnut

nocciolina (f.) peanut

noce (f.) walnut

noi we, us

noioso boring

noleggiare to rent

nome (m.) noun, name

nome da nubile maiden name

nome del coniuge name of spouse

non not

nonna (f.) grandmother

nonno grandfather

nono ninth

nonostante notwithstanding

nord north

normale normal

Norvegia Norway

notizia (f.) news

notte (f.) night

notturno nocturne

novanta ninety

nove nine

novembre November

novità (f.) news

nubile unmarried woman, single

nulla nothing

numero number

numero verde toll-free number

nuora (f.) daughter-in-law

nuotare to swim

nuovo new

nuvola (f.) cloud

O

o or

obbligare to oblige

obbligo obligation

occasione (f.) occasion, bargain

occhiali (m. pl.) eyeglasses

occhiata (f.) glance

occhio eye

Occidente West

occupare to occupy

occupato busy, occupied

oceano ocean

odiare to hate

odorare to smell

odore (m.) aroma, odor

offerta (f.) offer

oggetti smarriti (m. pl.) lost property

oggetto object

oggi today

ogni each, every

Ognissanti All Saint's Day (November 1)

ognuno everybody

Olanda (f.) Holland

olio oil

oliva (f.) olive

oltre more than, in addition to

ombra (f.) shadow

ombrello umbrella

onda (f.) wave

onesto honest

onore (m.) honor

opera (f.) opera, work

operaio worker

operazione (f.) operation

opinione (f.) opinion

opposto opposite

oppure or

ora (f.) hour, now

ora di punta (f.) rush hour

orario schedule

ordinale ordinal

ordinare to order

ordine (m.) order

orecchini (m. pl.) earrings

orecchio ear

oreficeria (f.) jeweler, goldsmith

orgoglioso proud

Oriente East, Orient

origano oregano

originale original

origine (f.) origin

oro gold
orologio watch, clock
oroscopo horoscope
orso bear
orto garden
oscuro dark, obscure
ospedale (m.) hospital
ospite (m./f.) guest
osso (pl. le ossa) bone
ostello hostel
ottanta eighty
ottavo eighth
ottenere to obtain
ottico optician
ottimo excellent, best
otto eight
ottobre October
ottone brass
ovest west
ovunque wherever
ovvio obvious

P

pacco package, parcel
pace (f.) peace
padella (f.) frying pan
padre (m.) father
padrino godfather
padrone/padrona (f.) boss, landlord, owner
paese (m.) country, town
pagamento payment
pagare to pay
pagina (f.) page
pagnotta (f.) loaf
paio (pl. le paia) pair
palazzo building, palace
palco box (theater)
palcoscenico stage
palestra (f.) gym
palla (f.) ball
pallacanestro (f.) basketball
pallavolo (f.) volleyball
palude (f.) swamp, marsh
pancetta (f.) bacon

panchina (f.) bench
pane (m.) bread
panetteria (f.) bakery
panino sandwich
panna (f.) cream
pannolino diaper
panorama (m.) panorama, view
pantaloni (m. pl.) pants
papa (m.) pope
papà (m.) daddy, pop
parabrezza (m.) windshield
paradiso paradise
paragone (m.) comparison
parcheggio parking lot
parco park
parente (m./f.) relative
parere (parso) to seem, to appear; opinion *(m.)*
parete (f.) inside wall
parte (f.) part
partecipare to participate
partenza (f.) departure
partire to depart, to leave
partita (f.) game, match
partito political party
Pasqua Easter
passaporto passport
passare to pass
passatempo hobby
passato past
passeggiare to stroll
passeggiata (f.) stroll, walk
passione (f.) passion
passo step
pasta (f.) pasta, pastry
pasticceria (f.) pastry shop
pasto meal
patata (f.) potato
patente (f.) driver's license
patria (f.) homeland
patrigno stepfather
patto agreement, pact
paura (f.) fear
pavimento floor
pazzo crazy

peccato! what a shame!
pedaggio toll
peggio worse
pelo hair
pelle (f.) skin, leather
pelletteria (f.) leather goods shop
pelliccia (f.) fur
pellicola (f.) film
pena (f.) penalty
penisola (f.) peninsula
penna (f.) pen, feather
pensare to think
pensiero thought, idea
pensione (f.) inn
pepe (m.) pepper
peperone (m.) bell pepper
per for, in order to
per favore please
per piacere please
pera (f.) pear
percento percentage
percezione (f.) perception
perché why, because
perciò therefore
percorso route
perdere (perso) to lose
perdonare to pardon
pericolo danger
pericoloso dangerous
periferia (f.) suburbs
periodo period
permesso! excuse me!
permettere (permesso) to permit
però but, however
persino even
persona (f.) person
personaggio character, type (of person)
pesante heavy
pesare to weigh
pesca (f.) peach
pesce (m.) fish
pescheria (f.) fish store
peso weight

pettinare to comb
petto chest
pezzo piece
piacere (m.) pleasure
piacersi (piaciuto) to be pleasing, to like
piacevole pleasant
pianeta (m.) planet
piangere (pianto) to cry
piano floor, softly (adv.)
pianta (f.) plant
pianterreno ground floor
pianura (f.) plain
piastrella (f.) ceramic tile
piatto plate
piazza (f.) town square
piccante spicy
picco peak
piccolo small
piede (m.) foot
pieno full
pietra (f.) stone
pigro lazy
pila (f.) battery
pillola (f.) pill
pioggia (f.) rain
piovere to rain
piramide (f.) pyramid
piscina (f.) swimming pool
pisello pea
pista (f.) track, trail, slope
pistola (f.) pistol
pittura (f.) painting
più more
piuma (f.) feather
piuttosto rather
plastica (f.) plastic
plurale (m.) plural
pneumatico tire
un po' a little
poco not very much
poesia (f.) poem, poetry
poi then, afterward
poiché since
polenta (f.) cornmeal

politica (f.) politics
polizia (f.) police
poliziotto police officer
pollame (m.) poultry
polmone (m.) lung
polpetta (f.) meatball
polvere (f.) dust
pomeriggio afternoon
pomodoro tomato
pompelmo grapefruit
pompiere (m.) fire fighter
ponte (m.) bridge
popolazione (f.) population
porco pig, pork
porta (f.) door
portabagagli (m.) porter
portacenere (m.) ashtray
portafoglio wallet
portare to bring, to carry
porto harbor, port
Portogallo Portugal
porzione (f.) portion
posizione (f.) position
possibile possible
possibilità (f.) possibility
posta (f.) mail, post office
postino postal carrier
posto seat, place
potere to be able to, can
povero poor
pozzo well
pranzare to dine, to eat lunch
pranzo lunch, supper
pratica (f.) practice
pratico convenient, practical
prato field
preciso precise
preferenza (f.) preference
preferire to prefer
prefisso area code
pregare to pray, to beg, to ask
preghiera (f.) prayer
prego! you are welcome!
prendere (preso) to take
prenotare to make a reservation

prenotazione (f.) reservation
preoccuparsi to worry
preoccupato worried
preparare to prepare
presbite far-sighted
presentare to present
presente (m.) present
presidente president
presso in care of (c/o)
prestare to lend
presto quickly, early
prete (m.) priest
prezzemolo parsley
prezzo price
prezzo d'entrata admission charge
prigione (f.) prison
prima before
primavera (f.) spring
primo first, before
principale principal, main
principe prince
principessa (f.) princess
problema (m.) problem
prodotto product
produrre (prodotto) to produce
produzione (f.) production
professione (f.) profession
professore/professoressa (f.) professor
profilattico condom
profumeria (f.) cosmetics shop
profumo perfume
progetto project
programma (m.) plan, program
progressivo progressive
progresso progress
promettere (promesso) to promise
pronome (m.) pronoun
pronto ready, hello (telephone)
pronto soccorso emergency room; first aid
pronuncia (f.) pronunciation
pronunciare to pronounce
proporre (proposto) to propose

proposizione (f.) clause
proprietà privata (f.) private property
proprietario owner
proprio just, really
prosciutto ham
prossimo next
proteggere (protetto) to protect
protestante Protestant
provare to try, to experience
proverbio proverb
psicologia (f.) psychology
pubblicità (f.) publicity
pubblico public
pugno fist
pulce (f.) flea
pulire to clean
pullman (m.) bus
punto period, point, stitch
puntuale punctual
puntura (f.) injection, insect bite
purché provided that
pure also
puro pure
purtroppo unfortunately

Q

qua here
quaderno notebook
quadro painting, picture
qualche some
qualche volta sometimes
qualcosa something
qualcuno someone
quale which
qualità (f.) quality
qualsiasi any
qualunque any
quando when
quantità (f.) quantity
quanto? how much?
quaranta forty
quartiere (m.) neighborhood
quarto fourth, quarter

quasi almost
quattordici fourteen
quattro four
quello/quella that
questione (f.) matter
questo this one
questura (f.) police headquarters
qui here
quindi therefore
quindici fifteen
quinto fifth
quotidiano daily (adj.)
quotidiano daily paper

R

rabbino rabbi
racchetta (f.) racket
raccontare to tell (a story)
radersi to shave
radiatore (m.) radiator
radice (f.) root
radio (f.) radio
radiografia (f.) x-ray
raffreddore (m.) cold
ragazza (f.) girl
ragazzo boy
ragno spider
rallentare slow down
rame (m.) copper
rana (f.) frog
rapido express train
rapina (f.) robbery
rapporto relationship
rappresentare to represent
raramente rarely, seldom
raro rare, scarce
rasoio razor
razza (f.) breed, race
re king
realizzare to achieve
recente recent
recitare to recite
regalare to give a present
regalo gift, present

reggiseno bra
regina (f.) queen
regione (f.) region
regista (m./f.) movie director
registratore tape recorder
religione (f.) religion
rendere (reso) to render, to give back
repubblica (f.) republic
residenza (f.) residence
resistenza (f.) resistance
respiro breath
responsabile responsible
restare to remain, to stay
resto rest, change
rettile (m.) reptile
reumatismo rheumatism
revisione (f.) revision
ricamare to embroider
riccio curl; hedgehog; urchin (*riccio di mare*)
ricco rich
ricetta (f.) recipe, prescription
ricevere to receive
ricevimento reception
ricevuta (f.) receipt
richiesta (f.) request
ricordare to remember
ridere (riso) to laugh
riempire to fill
rifiuti (m. pl.) trash
riflessivo reflexive
riflettere (riflesso) to reflect
rifugio refuge
rilasciato issued
rilassante relaxing
rimanere (rimasto) to remain
rimborso refund
Rinascimento the Renaissance
ringraziare to thank
rio stream
riparare to repair
ripetere to repeat
ripieno stuffed, filled
riscaldamento heat

riscaldare to warm, to heat
riserva d'acqua (f.) reservoir
riserva naturale (f.) nature preserve
riservato reserved
riso rice
risolvere (risolto) to resolve
rispettare to respect
rispondere (risposto) to respond
risposta (f.) answer, response
ristorante (m.) restaurant
risultato result
ritardo delay
ritmo rhythm
ritornare to return
ritratto portrait
riuscire to succeed
rivista (f.) magazine
roba (f.) stuff, things
rocca (f.) fortress
roccia (f.) rock
romantico romantic
romanzo novel, fiction, romance
rompere (rotto) to break
rondine (f.) swallow (bird)
rosa pink
rosa (f.) rose
rosso red
rotto broken
rovine (f. pl.) ruins
rubare to steal
rubinetto faucet
rullino roll of film
rumoroso noisy
ruota (f.) wheel
rupe (f.) cliff
ruscello stream
russo Russian

S

sabato Saturday
sabbia (f.) sand
sacchetto small bag
sacco a pelo sleeping bag

saggio wise
saggio essay
sala (f.) room, hall
sala d'attesa (f.) waiting room
sala da pranzo (f.) dining room
salagiochi (f.) game room
salario salary
saldo sale, discount
sale (m.) salt
salire to climb, to mount
salmone (m.) salmon
salotto living room, lounge
salsa (f.) sauce
salsiccia (f.) sausage
salumi (m. pl.) cold cuts, meats
salutare to greet
salute (f.) health
salvietta (f.) wipe
sangue (m.) blood
santo/santa (f.) saint
sapere to know something
sapone (m.) soap
sapore (m.) taste
sarto tailor
sbadigliare to yawn
sbagliare to be mistaken; to make a mistake
sbarcare to land, to disembark
scacchi (m. pl.) chess
scadenza (f.) expiration
scala (f.) stairs
scambiare to exchange
scambio exchange
scapolo bachelor
scappare to escape, to run away
scarpa (f.) shoe
scatola (f.) box
scavare to excavate
scegliere (scelto) to choose
scemo silly, idiotic
scena (f.) scene
scendere to descend, to get off
scherzare to joke
schiuma (f.) foam
schizzo sketch

sci (m.) skiing; skiis (m. pl.)
sci di fondo cross-country skiing
sciare to ski
sciarpa (f.) scarf
scienza (f.) science
sciopero strike
scocciare to bother, to annoy
scommettere (scommesso) to bet
scomodo uncomfortable
sconto discount
scontrino receipt
scoprire (scoperto) to discover
scorso last, past
scotto overdone
Scozia (f.) Scotland
scrittore writer
scrivania (f.) desk
scrivere (scritto) to write
scultura (f.) sculpture
scuola (f.) school
scuro dark
scusare to excuse
scusarsi to apologize
sdraiarsi to lie down
se if
sé oneself (himself, herself, …)
sebbene although
secco dry
secolo century
secondo second
sedativo sedative
sedersi to sit down
sedia (f.) chair
sedici sixteen
segnale (m.) signal, sign
segnare to mark, to note
segno sign
segretaria (f.) secretary
seguente following
seguire to follow
selva (f.) woods, forest
selvaggio wild, savage
selvatico wild, untamed
semaforo traffic light
sembrare to seem

semestre (m.) semester

semplice simple

sempre always

senape (f.) mustard

Senato Senate

sensazione (f.) sensation, feeling

senso unico one-way street

sentiero path, track

sentimento feeling, sentiment

sentire to hear, to smell, to taste

sentirsi to feel

senza without

separare to separate

separato separated

sera (f.) evening

serbatoio gas tank

serenata (f.) serenade

sereno calm, good weather

serio serious

serpente (m.) snake

servizio service

sessanta sixty

sesso sex, gender

sessualità (f.) sexuality

seta (f.) silk

sete (f.) thirst

settanta seventy

sette seven

settembre September

settimana (f.) week

settimo seventh

severo severe, strict

sfidare to challenge

sfortuna (f.) misfortune, bad luck

sforzo effort

si oneself, each other, one

sì yes

Sicilia (f.) Sicily

siciliano Sicilian

sicuro safe, sure

sigaretta (f.) cigarette

sigaro cigar

significare to signify

significato meaning

signora (f.) Mrs., Ms., woman

signore (m.) Mr., Sir, man

signorina (f.) miss, young lady

silenzio silence

simbolo symbol

simpatico nice, kind

sinagoga (f.) synagogue

sincero sincere

sindaco mayor

sinfonia (f.) symphony

singolare singular

singolo single

sinistro left

sintetico synthetic

sintomo symptom

sipario curtain (theater)

sistema (m.) system

situazione (f.) situation

slip (m. pl.) briefs

slittino sled

smettere (smesso) to quit

snello slender

snob snob

società (f.) company

soffice soft

soffitto ceiling

soffrire (sofferto) to suffer

soggetto subject

sognare to dream

solamente only

soldato soldier

soldi (m. pl.) money

sole (m.) sun

solito usual

solo alone

sonnifero sleeping pill

sonno sleep

sono I am, they are

sopra above, on

soprabito overcoat

soprattutto above all

sordo deaf

sorella (f.) sister

sorellastra (f.) stepsister, half-sister

sorgente (f.) spring

sorpasso passing

sorprendere (sorpreso) to surprise

sorpresa (f.) surprise

sorridere (sorriso) to smile

sosta (f.) stop, pause

sostituire to substitute

sotterraneo tunnel

sotto beneath

sottotitolo subtitle

Spagna (f.) Spain

spaventare to scare, to frighten

spazio space

spazzatura (f.) trash can

spazzola (f.) brush

spazzolino da denti toothbrush

specchio mirror

speciale special

specie (f.) type, kind

spedire to send

spegnere (spento) to turn off

spendere (speso) to spend

speranza (f.) hope

sperare to hope

spesa (f.) expense, shopping

spesso often

spettacolo show

spezia (f.) spice

spiaggia (f.) beach

spiegare to explain

spilla (f.) brooch, pin

spingere (spinto) to push

spirito spirit

spirituale spiritual

splendido splendid

sporco dirty

sport (m.) sport

sportello counter, window

sposare to marry

sposato married

sposo/sposa (f.) spouse

spugna (f.) sponge

spumante (m.) sparkling wine

spuntino snack

squadra (f.) team

stabilire to establish
stadio stadium
stagione (f.) season
stagno swamp
stamattina this morning
stampa (f.) print, press
stanco tired
stanotte tonight
stanza (f.) room
stare (stato) to be, to remain, to stay
stasera this evening
Stati Uniti (m. pl.) United States
stato state, government, condition
statua (f.) statue
stazione (f.) station
stella (f.) star
stesso same
stivale (m.) boot
stoffa (f.) fabric, cloth
stomaco stomach
storia (f.) history, story
strada (f.) street
straniero foreigner, foreign (adj.)
strano strange
strega (f.) witch
stressare to stress
stretto tight
studente/studentessa (f.) student
studiare to study
studio study
stufa (f.) stove
stupendo stupendous
su on top of, on, up
subito soon, immediately
succedere (successo) to happen
succo juice
sud south
suocera (f.) mother-in-law
suocero father-in-law
suonare to sound, to play
superare to overcome, to accomplish

supermercato supermarket
sveglia (f.) alarm clock
svegliarsi to wake up
svendita (f.) sale
Svezia (f.) Sweden
sviluppare to develop
Svizzera (f.) Switzerland

T

tabaccheria (f.) tobacco shop
tabella (f.) schedule, timetable
taglia (f.) size
tagliare to cut
tale such, like, similar
talvolta sometimes
tamburo drum
tanto so much, so many, a lot
tappo cork
tardi late
targa (f.) license plate
tariffa (f.) fare, charge
tasca (f.) pocket
tassa (f.) tax
tassametro taxi meter
tassì (m.) taxi
tavola (f.) dinner table
tavolo table (restaurant)
tazza (f.) cup
te you
tè (m.) tea
teatro theater
tedesco German
tegame (m.) saucepan
tegola (f.) shingle
telefonare to telephone
telefonata (f.) telephone call
telefono telephone
telegiornale (m.) news program
tema (m.) theme
tempesta (f.) storm
tempio temple
tempo weather, time
tenda (f.) tent
tenere to hold, to keep
tenero tender, affectionate

termometro thermometer
terra (f.) earth, dirt
terracotta (f.) terracotta; ceramic
terrazzo terrace
terzo third
tessera (f.) card, ticket
testa (f.) head
tetto roof
timido shy
tipo type, kind
tipografia (f.) printing
tirare to pull
tirchio stingy
toccare to touch
toilette (f.) toilet
tolleranza (f.) tolerance
topo mouse
tornare to return
torre (f.) tower
torta (f.) cake
torto wrong, fault
tosse (f.) cough
totale total
tovaglia (f.) tablecloth
tovagliolo napkin
tra between
tradizione (f.) tradition
tradurre (tradotto) to translate
traduzione (f.) translation
traffico traffic
traghetto ferry
tragico tragic
tramonto sunset
trasferirsi to transfer, to move
trasformare to transform
trasmettere (trasmesso) to broadcast
trasportare to transport
trattare to treat
tre three
tredici thirteen
tremendo tremendous
treno train
trenta thirty

triste   sad
tropicale   tropical
troppo   too
trovare   to find
tu   you (familiar)
tuffo   dive
tulipano   tulip
tuono   thunder
turismo   tourism
turista (m./f.)   tourist
turno   turn
tutt'e due   both
tuttavia   however, yet
tutti   everyone
tutto   everything, all

U

ubriacarsi   to get drunk
uccello   bird
uccidere (ucciso)   to kill
udire   to hear
ufficio   office
ufficio cambio   money exchange office
ufficio informazioni   information office
ufficio oggetti smarriti   lost and found
ufficio postale   post office
ultimo   last
umano   human
umidità (f.)   humidity
umile   humble
umore   humor, mood
un   a, an
una   a, an
undici   eleven
unico   unique, only
unificato   unified
unito   united
uno   one, a, an
uomo   man
uovo (pl. le uova)   egg
urbano   city, local
urgente   urgent

urlare   to shout
usare   to use
uscire   to exit
uscita (f.)   exit
uso   usage
uva (f.)   grapes

V

vacanza (f.)   vacation
vaccinazione (f.)   vaccination
vaglia postale (m.)   money order
vagone (m.)   wagon; carriage
valanga (f.)   avalanche
validità (f.)   validity
valigia (f.)   bag, valise, suitcase
valle (f.)   valley
valore (m.)   value
valuta (f.)   currency, money
vantaggio   advantage
variazione (f.)   variation
varietà (f.)   variety
vario   various
vasca (f.)   tub
vaso   vase
vecchio   old
vedere (visto)   to see
vedova (f.)   widow
vedovo   widower
veicolo   vehicle
vegetariano   vegetarian
veleno   poison
velocità (f.)   velocity
vendere   to sell
vendetta (f.)   vengeance
vendita (f.)   sale
venerdì   Friday
venire   to come
venti   twenty
vento   wind
veramente   really
verbo   verb
verde   green
verdura (f.)   vegetables
vergogna (f.)   shame

verità (f.)   truth
vernice (f.)   paint
vero   true, genuine
verso   toward, near, about
vescovo   bishop
vespa (f.)   wasp
vestire   to dress
vestito   dress, suit
vetrina (f.)   shop window
vetro   glass
vettura (f.)   carriage, railroad car
vi   there (adv.), to you
via (f.)   street, way
via   away
viaggiare   to travel
viaggio   trip
viale (m.)   boulevard, avenue
vicino   neighbor, near (adj.)
vicolo   alley, lane
vietato   prohibited
vietato l'ingresso   no entrance
vigile   traffic police officer
vigile del fuoco   firefighter
vigna (f.)   vine
villa (f.)   villa
villaggio   village
vincere (vinto)   to win
vino   wine
viola   purple
violenza (f.)   violence
violetta (f.)   violet (flower)
violenza (f.)   violence
visibile   visible
visita (f.)   visit
visitare   to visit
viso   face
vista (f.)   view
vita (f.)   life
vitamina (f.)   vitamin
vitello   veal
vittima (f.)   victim
vivace   lively
vivere (vissuto)   to live
vivo   alive

vocabolario   vocabulary
vocale (f.)   vowel
voce (f.)   voice
voglia (f.)   wish, desire
voi   you (plural)
volare   to fly
volentieri!   gladly!
volere   to want
volo   flight
volpe (f.)   fox
volta (f.)   time, occurrence
votare   to vote
voto   grade; vote
vuoto   empty

X–Y–Z

xilofono   xylophone

yoga (m.)   yoga
yogurt (m.)   yogurt

zaino   backpack
zampa (f.)   paw, leg
zanzara (f.)   mosquito
zero   zero
zia (f.)   aunt
zio   uncle
zona (f.)   zone, section
zoo   zoo
zucchero   sugar
zuppa (f.)   soup

Verb Tables

Think of your verb tables as the scales on a piano. The more you practice, the less you have to think about what you're doing. If nothing else, verb tables can also serve as an effective sleeping aid during *le ore piccole*. *Buona Notte!*

Reflexive Verbs (*I Verbi Reflessivi*)

All reflexive verbs use *essere* in compound tenses such as the *passato prossimo* (present perfect). Reflexive verbs are conjugated according to regular rules and include the following reflexive pronouns:

mi (myself)   *ci* (ourselves)

ti (yourself)   *vi* (yourselves)

si (himself, herself, yourself)   *si* (themselves)

The following table includes some commonly used reflexive verbs.

English	Italiano	English	Italiano
to be bored	*annoiarsi*	to graduate	*laurearsi*
to call	*chiamarsi*	to know each other	*conoscersi*
to comb one's hair	*pettinarsi*	to put on makeup	*truccarsi*
to get dressed	*vestirsi*	to notice	*accorgersi*
to enjoy	*divertirsi*	to obtain a diploma	*diplomarsi*
to fall asleep	*addormentarsi*	to put on	*mettersi*
to feel	*sentirsi*	to realize	*rendersi conto*
to get angry	*arrabbiarsi*	to remember/to remind	*ricordarsi*
to get married	*sposarsi*	to stop	*fermarsi*
to get up	*alzarsi*	to wake up	*svegliarsi*
		to wash oneself	*lavarsi*

Regular Verbs (*I Verbi Regolari*)

After you've mastered the following verbs, you'll be ready to use all the tenses. (Consult Barron's *501 Italian Verbs* for a more comprehensive list.) The following tables chart out the most important verb conjugations. Remember that the imperative is only used in the second person *tu*, and the third person *Lei* (You polite). Also in the *voi* form (you plural).

Infinito (Infinitive)	Presente (Present)	Passato Prossimo (Present Perfect)	Imperativo (Imperative)	Imperfetto (Imperfect)	Futuro (Future)	Condizionale (Conditional)	Congiuntivo (Subjunctive)	Passato Remoto (Past Definite/Absolute)
parlare (to speak)	parlo	ho parlato	*	parlavo	parlerò	parlerei	parli	parlai
	parli	hai parlato	parla, non parlare	parlavi	parlerai	parleresti	parli	parlasti
	parla	ha parlato	parli (Lei)	parlava	parlerà	parlerebbe	parli	parlò
	parliamo	abbiamo parlato	parliamo	parlavamo	parleremo	parleremmo	parliamo	parlammo
	parlate	avete parlato	parlate	parlavate	parlerete	parlereste	parliate	parlaste
	parlano	hanno parlato	*	parlavano	parleranno	parlerebbero	parlino	parlarono
scrivere (to write)	scrivo	ho scritto	*	scrivevo	scriverò	scriverei	scriva	scrissi
	scrivi	hai scritto	scrivi, non scrivere	scrivevi	scriverai	scriveresti	scriva	scrivesti
	scrive	ha scritto	scriva (Lei)	scriveva	scriverà	scriverebbe	scriva	scrisse
	scriviamo	abbiamo scritto	scriviamo	scrivevamo	scriveremo	scriveremmo	scriviamo	scrivemmo
	scrivete	avete scritto	scrivete	scrivevate	scriverete	scrivereste	scriviate	scriveste
	scrivono	hanno scritto	*	scrivevano	scriveranno	scriverebbero	scrivano	scrissero
partire (to depart)	parto	sono partito/a	*	partivo	partirò	partirei	parta	partii
	parti	sei partito/a	parti, non partire	partivi	partirai	partiresti	parta	partisti
	parte	è partito/a	parta (Lei)	partiva	partirà	partirebbe	parta	partì
	partiamo	siamo partiti/e	partiamo	partivamo	partiremo	partiremmo	partiamo	partimmo
	partite	siete partiti/e	partite	partivate	partirete	partireste	partiate	partiste
	partono	sono partiti/e	*	partivano	partiranno	partirebbero	partano	partirono

continues

Infinito (Infinitive)	Presente (Present)	Passato Prossimo (Present Perfect)	Imperativo (Imperative)	Imperfetto (Imperfect)	Futuro (Future)	Condizionale (Conditional)	Congiuntivo (Subjunctive)	Passato Remoto (Past Definite/Absolute)
capire (to understand)	capisco	ho capito	*	capivo	capirò	capirei	capisca	capii
	capisci	hai capito	capisci, non capire	capivi	capirai	capiresti	capisca	capisti
	capisce	ha capito	capisca (Lei)	capiva	capirà	capirebbe	capisca	capì
	capiamo	abbiamo capito	capiamo	capivamo	capiremo	capiremmo	capiamo	capimmo
	capite	avete capito	capite	capivate	capirete	capireste	capiate	capiste
	capiscono	hanno capito	*	capivano	capiranno	capirebbero	capiscano	capirono

Essere (to Be), Avere (to Have)

As usual, the verbs *essere* and *avere* stand in a class all on their own. They are used as *verbi ausiliari* (auxiliary verbs) in compound tenses.

Infinito (Infinitive)	Presente (Present)	Passato Prossimo (Present Perfect)	Imperativo (Imperative)	Imperfetto (Imperfect)	Futuro (Future)	Condizionale (Conditional)	Congiuntivo (Subjunctive)	Passato Remoto (Past Definite/Absolute)
essere (to be)	sono	sono stato/a	*	ero	sarò	sarei	sia	fui
	sei	sei stato/a	sii, non essere	eri	sarai	saresti	sia	fosti
	è	è stato/a	sia(Lei)	era	sarà	sarebbe	sia	fu
	siamo	siamo stati/e	siamo	eravamo	saremo	saremmo	siamo	fummo
	siete	siete stati/e	siate	eravate	sarete	sareste	siate	foste
	sono	sono stati/e	*	erano	saranno	sarebbero	siano	furono
avere (to have)	ho	ho avuto	*	avevo	avrò	avrei	abbia	ebbi
	hai	hai avuto	abbi, non avere	avevi	avrai	avresti	abbia	avesti
	ha	ha avuto	abbia (Lei)	aveva	avrà	avrebbe	abbia	ebbe
	abbiamo	abbiamo avuto	abbiamo	avevamo	avremo	avremmo	abbiamo	avemmo
	avete	avete avuto	abbiate	avevate	avrete	avreste	abbiate	aveste
	hanno	hanno avuto	*	avevano	avranno	avrebbero	abbiano	ebbero

Irregular Verbs (*I Verbi Irregolari*)

The more you read through the myriad irregularities that make *la bella lingua* so special, the sooner you'll begin to recognize these forms.

Infinito (Infinitive)	Presente (Present)	Passato Prossimo (Present Perfect)	Imperativo (Imperative)	Imperfetto (Imperfect)	Futuro (Future)	Condizionale (Conditional)	Congiuntivo (Subjunctive)	Passato Remoto (Past Definite/Absolute)
andare (to go)	vado	sono andato/a	*	andavo	andrò	andrei	vada	andai
	vai	sei andato/a	vai, non andare	andavi	andrai	andresti	vada	andasti
	va	è andato/a	vada (Lei)	andava	andrà	andrebbe	vada	andò
	andiamo	siamo andati/e	andiamo	andavamo	andremo	andremmo	andiamo	andammo
	andate	siete andati/e	andate	andavate	andrete	andreste	andiate	andaste
	vanno	sono andati/e	*	andavano	andranno	andrebbero	vadano	andarono
dire (to say)	dico	ho detto	*	dicevo	dirò	direi	dica	dissi
	dici	hai detto	di', non dire	dicevi	dirai	diresti	dica	dicesti
	dice	ha detto	dica (Lei)	diceva	dirà	direbbe	dica	disse
	diciamo	abbiamo detto	diciamo	dicevamo	diremo	diremmo	diciamo	dicemmo
	dite	avete detto	dite	dicevate	direte	direste	diciate	diceste
	dicono	hanno detto	*	dicevano	diranno	direbbero	dicano	dissero
dovere (to have to)	devo	ho dovuto	*	dovevo	dovrò	dovrei	debba (deva)	dovei/dovetti
	devi	hai dovuto	*	dovevi	dovrai	dovresti	debba (deva)	dovesti
	deve	ha dovuto	*	doveva	dovrà	dovrebbe	debba (deva)	dové/dovette
	dobbiamo	abbiamo dovuto	*	dovevamo	dovremo	dovremmo	dobbiamo	dovemmo
	dovete	avete dovuto	*	dovevate	dovrete	dovreste	dobbiate	doveste
	devono	hanno dovuto	*	dovevano	dovranno	dovrebbero	debbano	doverono/
							(devano)	dovettero

continues

Infinito (Infinitive)	Presente (Present)	Passato Prossimo (Present Perfect)	Imperativo (Imperative)	Imperfetto (Imperfect)	Futuro (Future)	Condizionale (Conditional)	Congiuntivo (Subjunctive)	Passato Remoto (Past Definite/Absolute)
fare (to do/make)	faccio	ho fatto	*	facevo	farò	farei	faccia	feci
	fai	hai fatto	fa', fai, non fare	facevi	farai	faresti	faccia	facesti
	fa	ha fatto	faccia (Lei)	faceva	farà	farebbe	faccia	fece
	facciamo	abbiamo fatto	facciamo	facciamo	faremo	faremmo	facciamo	facemmo
	fate	avete fatto	fate	facevate	farete	fareste	facciate	faceste
	fanno	hanno fatto	*	facevano	faranno	farebbero	facciano	fecero
morire (to die)	muoio	sono morto/a	*	morivo	morirò	morirei	muoia	morii
	muori	sei morto/a	muori, non morire	morivi	morirai	moriresti	muoia	moristi
	muore	è morto/a	muoia (Lei)	moriva	morirà	morirebbe	muoia	morì
	moriamo	siamo morti/e	moriamo	moriamo	moriremo	moriremmo	moriamo	morimmo
	morite	siete morti/e	morite	morivate	morirete	morireste	moriate	moriste
	muoiono	sono morti/e	*	morivano	moriranno	morirebbero	muoiano	morirono
nascere (to be born)	nasco	sono nato/a	*	nascevo	nascerò	nascerei	nasca	nacqui
	nasci	sei nato/a	nasci, non nascere	nascevi	nascerai	nasceresti	nasca	nascesti
	nasce	è nato/a	nasca (Lei)	nasceva	nascerà	nascerebbe	nasca	nacque
	nasciamo	siamo nati/e	nasciamo	nascevamo	nasceremo	nasceremmo	nasciamo	nascemmo
	nascete	siete nati/e	nascete	nascevate	nascerete	nascereste	nasciate	nasceste
	nascono	sono nati/e	*	nascevano	nasceranno	nascerebbero	nascano	nacquero
potere (to be able)	posso	ho potuto	*	potevo	potrò	potrei	possa	potei
	puoi	hai potuto	*	potevi	potrai	potresti	possa	potesti
	può	ha potuto	*	poteva	potrà	potrebbe	possa	poté
	possiamo	abbiamo potuto	*	potevamo	potremo	potremmo	possiamo	potemmo
	potete	avete potuto	*	potevate	potrete	potreste	possiate	poteste
	possono	hanno potuto	*	potevano	potranno	potrebbero	possano	poterono

Infinito (Infinitive)	Presente (Present)	Passato Prossimo (Present Perfect)	Imperativo (Imperative)	Imperfetto (Imperfect)	Futuro (Future)	Condizionale (Conditional)	Congiuntivo (Subjunctive)	Passato Remoto (Past Definite/Absolute)
rimanere (to remain)	rimango	sono rimasto/a	*	rimanevo	rimarrò	rimarrei	rimanga	rimasi
	rimani	sei rimasto/a	rimani, non rimanere	rimanevi	rimarrai	rimarresti	rimanga	rimanesti
	rimane	è rimasto/a	rimanga (Lei)	rimaneva	rimarrà	rimarrebbe	rimanga	rimase
	rimaniamo	siamo rimasti/e	rimaniamo	rimanevamo	rimarremo	rimarremmo	rimaniamo	rimanemmo
	rimanete	siete rimasti/e	rimanete	rimanevate	rimarrete	rimarreste	rimaniate	rimaneste
	rimangono	sono rimasti/e	*	rimanevano	rimarranno	rimarrebbero	rimangano	rimasero
salire (to go up)	salgo	sono salito/a	*	salivo	salirò	salirei	salga	salii
	sali	sei salito/a	sali, non salire	salivi	salirai	saliresti	salga	salisti
	sale	è salito/a	salga (Lei)	saliva	salirà	salirebbe	salga	salì
	saliamo	siamo saliti/e	saliamo	salivamo	saliremo	saliremmo	saliamo	salimmo
	salite	siete saliti/e	salite	salivate	salirete	salireste	saliate	saliste
	salgono	sono saliti/e	*	salivano	saliranno	salirebbero	salgano	salirono
sapere (to know)	so	ho saputo	*	sapevo	saprò	saprei	sappia	seppi
	sai	hai saputo	sappi, non sapere	sapevi	saprai	sapresti	sappia	sapesti
	sa	ha saputo	sappia (Lei)	sapeva	saprà	saprebbe	sappia	seppe
	sappiamo	abbiamo saputo	sappiamo	sapevamo	sapremo	sapremmo	sappiamo	sapemmo
	sapete	avete saputo	sappiate	sapevate	saprete	sapreste	sappiate	sapeste
	sanno	hanno saputo	*	sapevano	sapranno	saprebbero	sappiano	seppero

continues

Infinito (Infinitive)	Presente (Present)	Passato Prossimo (Present Perfect)	Imperativo (Imperative)	Imperfetto (Imperfect)	Futuro (Future)	Condizionale (Conditional)	Congiuntivo (Subjunctive)	Passato Remoto (Past Definite/Absolute)
venire (to come)	vengo	sono venuto/a	*	venivo	verrò	verrei	venga	venni
	vieni	sei venuto/a	vieni, non venire	venivi	verrai	verresti	venga	venisti
	viene	è venuto/a	venga (Lei)	veniva	verrà	verrebbe	venga	venne
	veniamo	siamo venuti/e	veniamo	venivamo	verremo	verremmo	veniamo	venimmo
	venite	siete venuti/e	venite	venivate	verrete	verreste	veniate	veniste
	vengono	sono venuti/e	*	venivano	verranno	verrebbero	vengano	vennero
volere (to want)	voglio	ho voluto	*	volevo	vorrò	vorrei	voglia	volli
	vuoi	hai voluto	vuoi, non volere	volevi	vorrai	vorresti	voglia	volesti
	vuole	ha voluto	voglia (Lei)	voleva	vorrà	vorrebbe	voglia	volle
	vogliamo	abbiamo voluto	vogliamo	volevamo	vorremo	vorremmo	vogliamo	volemmo
	volete	avete voluto	vogliate	volevate	vorrete	vorreste	vogliate	voleste
	vogliono	hanno voluto	*	volevano	vorranno	vorrebbero	vogliano	vollero

Forming Past Participles for Compound Tenses

The *participio* (participle) is essential to forming compound tenses, including the present perfect, called the *passato prossimo* in Italian. It's used to indicate "I have … studied/wondered/achieved …," and it's formed by using one of the two *verbi ausiliari* (auxiliary verbs), *avere* (to have) and *essere* (to be).

So how do you determine which helping verb to use? As a rule, *verbi transitivi* (transitive verbs) take *avere* and answer the question *what?* In other words, a *trans*itive verb *transports* you to a direct object the way you eat (verb) an apple (direct object). You study. What do you study? Italian. Use little linguistic tricks to help you remember.

Intransitive verbs, called *verbi intransitivi*, take *essere*. An intransitive verb like *nascere* (to be born) takes you somewhere but cannot take an object. You're born. That's it. No object. Similarly, motion verbs such as *andare* (to go), *tornare* (to return), *uscire* (to go out), and *venire* (to come) utilize *essere* as their helping verb.

To form a participle for regular verbs:

Verbs ending in *-are: parlare* (to speak) becomes *parlato* (spoken).

Verbs ending in *-ere: credere* (to believe) becomes *creduto* (believed).

Verbs ending in *-ire: finire* (to finish) becomes *finito* (finished).

The following table maps out more than 50 irregular past participles used in compound tenses such as the *passato prossimo*. As a reminder, I've added (*a*) to indicate that the verb requires *essere* as its helping verb, and therefore the participle must change to reflect gender and number. All reflexive verbs ending in *-si*, such as *alzarsi* (to get up), also take *essere* as their helping verb. It may seem like a lot at first, but if you start making connections (and keep those synapses charged) with words you already know, you'll recognize patterns. The key is the *recognizing part*, that moment when you rediscover what's been there all along.

Infinitive	Past Participle	Infinitive	Past Participle
accludere (to enclose)	*accluso*	*muovere* (to move)	*mosso*
apparire (to appear)	*apparso(a)*	*nascere* (to be born)	*nato(a)*
aprire (to open)	*aperto*	*offendere* (to offend)	*offeso*
assumere (to hire)	*assunto*	*offrire* (to offer)	*offerto*
chiedere (to ask)	*chiesto*	*parere* (to seem)	*parso(a)*
chiudere (to close)	*chiuso*	*piacere* (to please)	*piaciuto(a)*
congiungere (to join)	*congiunto*	*piangere* (to cry)	*pianto*
convincere (to convince)	*convinto*	*prendere* (to take)	*preso*
correre (to run)	*corso*	*rendere* (to render)	*reso*
crescere (to grow)	*cresciuto(a)*	*restare* (to remain/stay)	*restato(a)*
cuocere (to cook)	*cotto*	*ridere* (to laugh)	*riso*
decidere (to decide)	*deciso*	*rimanere* (to remain)	*rimasto(a)*
dipendere (to depend)	*dipeso(a)*	*rispondere* (to respond)	*risposto*
dipingere (to paint)	*dipinto*	*rompere* (to break)	*rotto*
dire (to say)	*detto*	*scegliere* (to choose)	*scelto*
discutere (to discuss)	*discusso*	*scendere* (to descend)*	*sceso(a)*
distinguere (to distinguish)	*distinto*	*scomparire* (to disappear)	*scomparso(a)*
divenire (to become)	*divenuto(a)*	*scoprire* (to discover)	*scoperto*
dividere (to divide)	*diviso*	*sorgere* (to rise)	*sorto(a)*
emergere (to emerge)	*emerso(a)*	*succedere* (to happen/succeed)	*successo(a)*
esistere (to exist)	*esistito(a)*	*tradurre* (to translate)	*tradotto*
esprimere (to express)	*espresso*	*sopravvivere* (to survive)*	*sopravvissuto(a)*
essere (to be)	*stato(a)*	*uccidere* (to kill)	*ucciso*
fare (to do/make)	*fatto*	*vedere* (to see)	*visto/veduto*
giungere (to add)	*giunto(a)*	*venire* (to come)	*venuto(a)*
leggere (to read)	*letto*	*vincere* (to win)	*vinto*
mettere (to put)	*messo*	*vivere* (to live)*	*vissuto(a)*
morire (to die)	*morto(a)*		

Some verbs can take both avere *and* essere *as a helping verb in compound tenses.*

Idiomatic Expressions

More *espressioni idiomatiche* exist than I could ever offer here, but I've provided a few of my favorites along with the more commonly used.

Common Idioms

The following two tables provide a sample of the most commonly used Italian idioms.

The Italian verb *andare* is used in a number of expressions, including *andare matto* (to go crazy)!

Va Bene: Idioms with *Andare* (to Go)

English	Italiano
Get out of here! You're kidding!	*Ma va!*
How's it going?	*Come va?*
It's going well/badly.	*Va bene/male.*
to go around; to take a spin	*andare in giro*
to go crazy	*andare matto*
to go to pieces	*andare in pezzi*
to go to the other world	*andare all'altro mondo*
to let something go	*lasciare andare*

In Italian, you use the verb *fare* (to do or make) most often when you would use the English verb *to take*. You *take* a shower in English, but you *do* a shower (*fare la doccia*) in Italian.

Fa Freddo: Idioms with *Fare* (to Do/to Make)

English	Italiano
Mind your business!	*Fatti gli affari tuoi!*
to be clever; sly	*fare il furbo*
to be dog cold	*fare un freddo cane*
to be spirited (to be a wiseguy)	*fare lo spiritoso*
to do homework	*fare i compiti*
to do the wee hours (to burn the midnight oil)	*fare le ore piccole*
to go Roman (to go Dutch)	*fare alla romana*
to live like a dog	*fare una vita da cani*
to make love	*fare l'amore*
to pretend (to fake)	*fare finta*
to take a picture	*fare una foto*
to take a shower	*fare la doccia*

Idioms Expressing Your Opinion

The following table summarizes the idioms you can use to express yourself and your opinion.

Secondo Me (in My Opinion)

English	Italiano
Agreed.	*D'accordo.*
Amen, you said it.	*Parole d'oro.*
Among other things …	*Fra l'altro …*
anyhow	*comunque*
anyway; or "at any cost"	*in ogni modo*
Certainly; right	*senz'altro*
Easy to say!	*È facile a dirsi!*
Forget it!	*Lascia perdere! Lascia stare!*
Holy heaven! Good heavens!	*Santo cielo!*
How boring!	*Che barba! Che noia!*
How disgusting!	*Che schifo!*

English	Italiano
I believe so/not.	*Credo di sì/no.*
I think so/not.	*Penso di sì/no.*
in my opinion	*secondo me*
It doesn't matter.	*Non importa.*
It is better this way.	*Meglio così.*
It's worth it.	*Vale la pena.*
Luckily!	*Meno male!*
My goodness!	*Santa pace!*
naturally	*naturalmente*
No way! God forbid!	*Per carità!*
now then, well	*allora, dunque*
on the contrary	*al contrario; tutt'altro*
Really?	*Davvero? Sul serio?*
so much the better/worse	*tanto meglio/peggio*
That's crazy!	*Roba da matti!*
That's enough!	*Basta!*
to tell the truth	*per dire la verità*
What a mess!	*Che macello!*
What a shame!	*Che peccato!*
What cabbage!	*Che cavolata!*
What rubbish!	*Che roba!*
without a doubt	*senza dubbio*
You are wrong. (fam.)	*Hai torto.*

Idioms Involving Time

The following table lists time-related idioms.

Un'ora Buona (a Solid Hour)

English	Italiano
a full hour	*un'ora buona*
about an hour	*un'oretta*
at any time	*a qualunque ora*
daylight saving time	*ora legale*
early	*di buon'ora*
for the time being	*per il momento*

continues

English	*Italiano*
in no time	*in un batter d'occhio*
in the early hours	*nelle prime ore*
It was about time!	*Alla buon'ora!*
rush hour	*l'ora di punta*
the wee hours	*le ore piccole*
Time is money.	*Il tempo è denaro.*
to be on time	*essere in orario*

Italian Colloquialisms

Whether lonely dogs, hungry wolves, or depressed potatoes, Italian possesses thousands of idiomatic expressions and colloquialisms.

In Bocca al Lupo! (Break a Leg!)

English	*Italiano*
at any cost—no matter what	*a tutti i costi*
It's a deal.	*Affare fatto.*
Of course! You can bet your life!	*Altro che!*
Amen	*Amen*
Very nice! (ironic)	*Bella roba!*
That's really good! (ironic)	*Bell'affare!*
Lucky you!	*Buon per te!*
no matter what	*caschi il mondo*
There are ways and ways!	*C'è modo e modo!*
What's the matter with you?	*Che ti passa per la testa?*
Those that sleep won't catch fish. The early bird gets the worm.	*Chi dorme non piglia pesci.*
God forbid!	*Ci mancherebbe altro!*
It takes much more than that!	*Ci vuole altro!*
like mamma made him (naked as a jay bird)	*come mamma l'ha fatto*
Excuse my French.	*Con rispetto parlando.*
It is out of this world.	*Cose dell'altro mondo.*
to cost an eye from your head; to cost an arm and a leg	*costare un occhio della testa*
a lot	*da morire*
on the other hand	*d'altro canto*
to give a hand	*dare una mano*
Of mothers, there is only one.	*Di mamma ce n'è una sola.*

English	Italiano
Let's hope for the best!	*Che Dio ce la mandi buona!*
to be in seventh heaven	*essere al settimo cielo*
to be in trouble; to have problems	*essere nei guai*
to be in the clouds	*essere nelle nuvole*
to be alone as a dog	*essere solo come un cane*
to be a fish out of water	*essere un pesce fuor d'acqua*
out of fashion	*fuori moda*
I smell a rat.	*Gatta ci cova.*
to spin one's head	*girare la testa*
Leave me alone.	*Lasciami stare.*
Lies have short legs.	*Le bugie hanno le gambe corte.*
southpaw (a leftie)	*mancino ("little hand")*
In your dreams!	*Manco per sogno!*
to eat like a beast	*mangiare come una bestia*
better than nothing	*meglio di nulla*
Not even in your dreams!	*Nemmeno per sogno!*
That's all.	*Non c'è altro.*
I can't stand it anymore.	*Non ne posso più.*
nude and crude (the plain truth)	*nudo e crudo*
As you like! All right then!	*Padronissimo!*
to tease or joke	*prendere in giro (to take around)*
to fade into nothing (to go up in smoke)	*sfumare nel nulla*
Sweet dreams!	*Sogni d'oro!*
They're like two drops of water. (two peas in a pod; one and the same)	*Sono come due gocce d'acqua.*
dead tired	*stanco da morire*
to touch iron (to knock on wood)	*toccare ferro*
to want the bottle full and the wife drunk	*volere la botte piena e la moglie ubriaca*

Tongue Twisters

33

I couldn't resist and had to include a few of these Italian tongue twisters. Get your mouth around a *sciog<ilingua* (literally, tongue melter) and see how well you do. Listen to Michele on the audio as he goes through these tongue twisters.

- *A quest'ora il questore in questura non c'è!*
- *Al pozzo dei pazzi una pazza lavava le pezze. Andò un pazzo e buttò la pazza con tutte le pezze nel pozzo dei pazzi.*

- *Andavo a Lione cogliendo cotone, tornavo correndo cotone cogliendo.*
- *Apelle figlio d'Apollo fece una palla di pelle di pollo tutti i pesci vennero a galla per vedere la palla di pelle di pollo fatta d'Apelle figlio d'Apollo.*
- *Caro conte chi ti canta tanto canta che t'incanta.*
- *Chi ama chiama chi ama, chiamami tu che chi ami chiami. Chi amo chiameró se tu non chiami.*
- *Figlia, sfoglia la foglia sfoglia la foglia, figlia.*
- *Sopra la panca la capra campa sotto la panca la capra crepa.*

Italian *Grammatica* at a Glance

If I could give you an intravenous transfer of knowledge, I would. Since I can't, I've provided you with a quick summary of some of the more important elements related to Italian grammar you need to know.

Basic Grammar

In this mini-grammar guide, you'll find all the most important basics outlined and defined, including tables highlighting the Italian articles, adjectives, adverbs, prepositions, and possessives.

The Definite Articles

	Singular	Plural	Examples
Masculine	*il*	*i*	*il libro* (the book) → *i libri* (the books)
	lo	*gli*	*lo scienziato* (the scientist) → *gli scienziati* (the scientists)
	l'	*gli*	*l'albero* (the tree) → *gli alberi* (the trees)
Feminine	*la*	*le*	*la casa* (the house) → *le case* (the houses)
	l'	*le*	*l'italiana* (the Italian woman) → *le italiane* (the Italian women)

Noun and Adjective Endings

	Singular		Plural
Masculine	*-o*	→	*-i*
Feminine	*-a*	→	*-e*
M/F	*-e*	→	*-i*

Commonly Used Prepositions

English	*Italiano*	English	*Italiano*
at, in, to	*a*	at, in, to	*in*
with	*con*	for	*per*
from	*da*	between, among	*tra/fra*
of, from	*di*		

Contractions

Preposition	Masculine				Feminine			
	Singular		Plural		Singular		Plural	
	il	*lo*	*l'*	*i*	*gli*	*la*	*l'*	*le*
a	*al*	*allo*	*all'*	*ai*	*agli*	*alla*	*all'*	*alle*
da	*dal*	*dallo*	*dall'*	*dai*	*dagli*	*dalla*	*dall'*	*dalle*
di	*del*	*dello*	*dell'*	*dei*	*degli*	*della*	*dell'*	*delle*
in	*nel*	*nello*	*nell'*	*nei*	*negli*	*nella*	*nell'*	*nelle*
su	*sul*	*sullo*	*sull'*	*sui*	*sugli*	*sulla*	*sull'*	*sulle*

Additional Useful Prepositions

English	*Italiano*	English	*Italiano*
through, across	*attraverso*	far	*lontano*
inside	*dentro*	above	*sopra*
until	*fino a*	below	*sotto*
outside	*fuori*	toward	*verso*
together	*insieme*	close	*vicino*

Commonly Used Adjectives

English	*Italiano*	English	*Italiano*
beautiful	*bello*	small	*piccolo*
big	*grande*	difficult	*difficile*
easy	*facile*	bad	*cattivo*
good	*buono*	stupid	*stupido*
intelligent	*intelligente*	short	*basso*
tall	*alto*	small	*piccolo*
young	*giovane*		

Possessive Adjectives

Possessive	Singular		Plural	
	Masculine	**Feminine**	**Masculine**	**Feminine**
my	*il mio*	*la mia*	*i miei*	*le mie*
your (informal)	*il tuo*	*la tua*	*i tuoi*	*le tue*
his/her	*il suo*	*la sua*	*i suoi*	*le sue*
Your (polite)	*il Suo*	*la Sua*	*i suoi*	*le Sue*
our	*il nostro*	*la nostra*	*i nostri*	*le nostre*
your	*il vostro*	*la vostra*	*i vostri*	*le vostre*
their	*il loro*	*la loro*	*i loro*	*le loro*

Commonly Used Adverbs

You can form many adverbs by adding *-mente* to the feminine singular adjective. Adjectives ending in *-e* (*dolce, intelligente, verde,* and so on) remain the same:

> *allegra* (happy) → *allegramente* (happily)
>
> *dolce* (sweet) → *dolcemente* (sweetly)
>
> *sincera* (sincere) → *sinceramente* (sincerely)

Adverbs work with adjectives and nouns. The words *no* and *yes* are also adverbs.

Commonly Used Irregular Adverbs

English	*Italiano*
after	*dopo*
always	*sempre*
badly	*male*
before	*prima*
enough	*abbastanza*
immediately	*subito*
later	*più tardi*
never	*mai*
never, ever	*mai*
now	*adesso*
often	*spesso*
so	*tanto*

continues

English	*Italiano*
too much	*troppo*
very	*assai*
very, a lot	*molto*
well	*bene*

Asking Questions

English	*Italiano*
how much?	*quanto/a/i/e?*
how?	*come?*
what?	*che cosa?*
when?	*quando?*
where?	*dove?*
which?	*quale/i?*
who?	*chi?*
whose?	*di chi?*
why?	*perché?*

Index

W–X–Y–Z